DATE DUE

Patent Law
Essentials

Patent Law Essentials

A Concise Guide

FOURTH EDITION

Alan L. Durham

 **PRAEGER**

AN IMPRINT OF ABC-CLIO, LLC
Santa Barbara, California • Denver, Colorado • Oxford, England

Library of Congress Cataloging-in-Publication Data

Durham, Alan L., 1963–
    Patent law essentials : a concise guide / Alan L. Durham. – Fourth edition.
      pages cm
    Includes bibliographical references and index.
    ISBN 978–1–4408–2878–2 (cloth) – ISBN 978–1–4408–2879–9 (ebook) 1. Patent
laws and legislation–United States. I. Title.
  KF3114.85.D87   2013
  346.7304'86–dc23   2012040633

ISBN: 978–1–4408–2878–2
EISBN: 978–1–4408–2879–9

17 16 15   2 3 4 5

This book is also available on the World Wide Web as an eBook.
Visit www.abc-clio.com for details.

Praeger
An Imprint of ABC-CLIO, LLC

ABC-CLIO, LLC
130 Cremona Drive, P.O. Box 1911
Santa Barbara, California 93116-1911

This book is printed on acid-free paper ∞

Manufactured in the United States of America

For my wife, Laura

Contents

Introduction   xi

1   OVERVIEW   1
    1.1   Origins   1
    1.2   Summary and Roadmap   3
    1.3   Sources of Law   7

2   PATENTS DISTINGUISHED FROM OTHER RIGHTS   9
    2.1   Copyrights   9
    2.2   Trademarks   11
    2.3   Trade Secrets   12
    2.4   Patents   14

3   READING A PATENT   17
    3.1   General Information   18
    3.2   Drawings   20
    3.3   Specification   20
    3.4   Claims   22

4   PATENTABLE SUBJECT MATTER   25
    4.1   Laws and Phenomena of Nature   26
    4.2   Living Organisms   28

	4.3	Abstract Ideas	29
	4.4	Business Methods	30
	4.5	Mental Processes	32
	4.6	Computer Programs	32
	4.7	Printed Matter	35
5		**PATENT PROSECUTION**	**37**
	5.1	Examination	37
	5.2	Continuations and Continuations-in-Part	40
	5.3	Divisional Applications	42
	5.4	Interferences and Derivation Proceedings	43
	5.5	Reissue	44
	5.6	Reexamination and Review	46
6		**OWNERSHIP AND OTHER RIGHTS**	**51**
	6.1	Inventorship	51
	6.2	Assignments	54
	6.3	Licenses	55
7		**INTERPRETING PATENT CLAIMS**	**63**
	7.1	"Ordinary Meaning"	66
	7.2	The Specification	68
	7.3	The Prosecution History	73
	7.4	Other Claims	74
	7.5	Validity	75
	7.6	Preambles	76
	7.7	Special Claim Formats	79
8		**CONDITIONS OF PATENTABILITY**	**85**
	8.1	Examination and Litigation	85
	8.2	Presumption of Validity	86
	8.3	Assignor Estoppel	88
	8.4	Utility	88
	8.5	Definiteness	92
	8.6	Enablement	97
	8.7	Best Mode	103

8.8	Written Description Requirement	105
8.9	Novelty and Obviousness	110
8.10	Double Patenting	157

9	ENFORCEABILITY DEFENSES	161
9.1	Inequitable Conduct	161
9.2	Misuse	166

10	INFRINGEMENT	171
10.1	Patent Term	171
10.2	Geographic Limitations	173
10.3	State of Mind	175
10.4	Direct and Indirect Infringement	175
10.5	Literal Infringement	179
10.6	The Doctrine of Equivalents	182
10.7	Equivalence in the Context of Means-Plus-Function Claims	203
10.8	The Reverse Doctrine of Equivalents	206
10.9	The Experimental Use Defense	207
10.10	The Prior Commercial Use Defense	209

11	PATENT LITIGATION	211
11.1	Jurisdiction and Venue	213
11.2	Declaratory Judgment	215
11.3	Burden of Proof	217
11.4	The Role of Judge and Jury	217
11.5	Bifurcation	220
11.6	Preliminary Injunctions	220
11.7	Summary Judgment	222
11.8	Remedies	223
11.9	The International Trade Commission	237
11.10	Judgments of Invalidity	237

12	SPECIAL TOPICS	239
12.1	Design Patents	239
12.2	Plant Patents	242

Note on Sources　　　　　　　　　　　　　　　　245

Appendix A: Sample Utility Patents　　　　　　247

Appendix B: Sample Design Patents　　　　　　265

Index　　　　　　　　　　　　　　　　　　　273

Introduction

This book began with an expert witness. A preeminent authority in a specialized field of engineering, he had been hired to testify on the defendant's behalf in a high-stakes patent infringement case. Like many people who find themselves confronting the arcane system of patent law for the first time, he wanted know the "rules of the game." At the time there were expansive resources for lawyers, generally in many volumes, and study aids directed at law students, but no books I could recommend offering the right mixture of sophistication and simplicity. If there were such a book, I thought, I could use it myself. As an attorney in the field, I knew the standard rules of patent law, but I did not always have at my fingertips recent authorities to support them. Those authorities had to be sought out in the multivolume treatises or the indexed case reporters—a time-consuming chore simply because they included so much material. I determined to write for myself a concise book on patent law that could serve either purpose. It would be accessible enough, I hoped, to introduce non-lawyers to the rules of the game while being sophisticated enough to provide attorneys a useful desk reference—a starting place, at least, for further research. This is the result of that ambition, now in its fourth edition. I have been pleased to learn that not only attorneys and engineers have found it useful but also business people, judges, patent examiners, professors, and law students—some of whom have contacted me with encouraging feedback. I thank them all.

As this edition goes to press, patent law is changing. The America Invents Act, signed into law on September 16, 2011, accounts for the most significant shift in the rules of patent law since the 1952 Patent Act. In determining priority between competing inventors or deciding whether a patented invention was actually new, the law in the United States has always emphasized the date of the invention. For patents and patent applications filed before March 16, 2013, that will remain the case. But for patents and patent applications filed after March 16, 2013, the dates that matter are the filing date of the patent application and the date of the inventor's public disclosure. Now the inventor who first imagines the better mousetrap may lose out to the inventor who first tries to patent it. Although in some respects the new rules are simpler, so long as some of the older patents remain in force (which they will for another 20 years or so), a familiarity with patent law requires knowledge of *two* sets of rules—one for the older patents and one for the new.

Meanwhile, the courts continue to struggle with one of the most fundamental questions in patent law—what sort of invention can be patented? Many significant technological advancements are occurring today in the fields of biotechnology and computer science. Yet patentable inventions in biotechnology cannot embrace laws of nature, and inventions in computer science cannot be reduced to abstract ideas. The dividing line between what is patentable and unpatentable has become very difficult to discern. Is a computer-implemented business method patentable subject matter? Is a method of treating a disease? Attempts to provide bright lines and easy answers have failed. At present there is much uncertainty and too many cases where "it depends" is all one can say. Yet the stakes could not be higher, as intellectual property becomes one of the most valuable assets a business can own—often deciding the balance of power in both the marketplace and the courtroom. The years to come, without a doubt, will be interesting times for patent law.

As before, I wish to thank my friends, colleagues, and students at the University of Alabama School of Law for their inspiration and encouragement. Dean Kenneth Randall and the Law School Foundation have supplied critical and much-appreciated support for my research. I also thank my former colleagues at Morrison & Foerster and Brown & Bain, whose understanding and flexibility made the first edition of this book a reality. Finally, I thank inventor Bill Oviatt, whose ingenious Teeter Pong mousetrap I have used as example in this book and in many a Patent Law class.

CHAPTER 1

Overview

1.1 ORIGINS

The historical antecedents of the United States patent system are often traced to seventeenth-century England. Until then, a "patent" might refer to nothing more than a legally sanctioned monopoly, granted to reward a loyal subject or sold to raise funds for the government. A merchant guild, for example, might purchase a patent for the exclusive right to sell playing cards. Freedom from competition allowed the patent owner to sell in larger volumes and at a higher price. Undoubtedly popular with the government and with the patent owners, these "odious monopolies" were a source of resentment to consumers and potential competitors. In 1624, the Crown relented and the Statute of Monopolies, abolishing the general power of the monarch to grant exclusive rights, became law. Importantly, the statute ending the general practice of monopolies specifically exempted patents allowing inventors the exclusive right to their inventions.

The tradition of granting patents to inventors continued in colonial America and, in spite of some skepticism by influential thinkers such as Thomas Jefferson, it was incorporated in the laws of the United States. The framers of the Constitution provided to Congress, in Article I, Section 8, the power to "promote the Progress of Science and [the] useful Arts, by securing for limited Times to Authors and Inventors the exclusive Right to their respective Writings and Discoveries." This brief language is the source of both patent law and copyright law in the United States.[1] The specifics were left to Congress and to the Patent and Trademark Office (also known as the Patent Office, or PTO), a division of the Department of Commerce created in 1836. The federal courts also have played a significant role in interpreting, supplementing, and perhaps, on some occasions, rewriting the rules set down by Congress.

Although patent law has evolved in some ways, the theories behind it are much the same today as they were in the beginning. One theory, which still has an eighteenth-century flavor, is that inventors possess a natural right to their inventions that must be recognized by law. Creations are naturally the property of those who labored to create. The more common theory, and the one most clearly reflected in the Constitution, is that patents provide the encouragement necessary for industrial advancement. If a budding Edison feared that the rewards of his inventive efforts would be reaped by copyists—copyists who did not even bear the costs of original research—he might abandon the laboratory for other pursuits. Society would then be denied the benefit of useful inventions. If an inventor can obtain a patent ensuring that only he will profit from his invention, he is more likely to invest the time, effort, skill, and resources necessary to discover new technologies.[2]

Patents also benefit society by making available precise descriptions of new inventions. A patent is a public document published by the United States government. One requirement of a patent is that it describe the invention, in both words and drawings, in such detail that other persons in the field can understand the invention and practice it themselves. During the term of the patent, when only the patent owner and licensees have the legal right to practice the invention, this information may be of limited interest. But when the patent expires, the invention enters the public domain. The millions of patents that have already expired are a resource that may be freely exploited by anyone, and even an unexpired patent can

---

[1] When the Constitution was drafted, "science" was used in a broader sense than it is today and was generally synonymous with "knowledge." "Arts" also held a different meaning, and the term "useful arts" probably referred to what we would now call "technology." Although counterintuitive, the prevailing view of legal historians is that patent law promotes the "arts," while copyright law promotes "science."

[2] Another theory, popular with some legal scholars, is that patents make the exploitation of resources more efficient by putting in charge a single entity—the owner of the patent. If multiple parties, without legal restriction, could race to exploit a newly discovered and valuable invention, much wasteful duplication of effort would occur. The costs of such waste are born, ultimately, by society. Other scholars argue that the stimulating effects of competition counterbalance the waste of duplication.

provide inspiration for new and different approaches to technological problems.

The view that a patent is a kind of bargain between the inventor and the public, by which the inventor receives a limited monopoly in exchange for disclosing the invention to the public, is of more than theoretical interest. Together with the overall constitutional goal of promoting the "useful arts," the bargain model of patents helps to shape the specific rules that determine whether a patent is valid or invalid. In particular, this model will resurface as we examine the principle of enablement in Section 8.6.

1.2 SUMMARY AND ROADMAP

A book about patent law is difficult to organize because an understanding of one principle is so often dependent on an understanding of other principles, ad infinitum. As a *New Yorker* article once observed, patent law is "apt to plunge all but the stoutest minds into dizzying swirls of logic."[3] What follows is a sort of roadmap to this book that may keep the reader better oriented as we wind our way through the maze.

Chapter 1 (this chapter) introduces the reader to some of the history and theory underpinning patent law and concludes with a brief discussion of the laws, judicial opinions, and other authorities that are cited throughout this book.

Chapter 2 distinguishes patents from other forms of intellectual property rights with which patents are often confused. Specifically, Chapter 2 briefly discusses copyrights, which protect works of authorship such as books, musical compositions, and motion pictures; trademarks, which protect brand names and logos; and trade secrets, which are a form of confidential business information protected by law.

Chapter 3 leads the reader through a close examination of an actual United States patent found in Appendix A. This includes the patent drawings; the specification, which is a detailed prose description of the inventor's work; and the claims. The claims are the last portion of a patent, and they describe in careful terms exactly what the patent covers.

Chapter 4 discusses the kinds of discoveries that can or cannot be patented, with sections devoted to the laws and phenomena of nature, living organisms, abstract ideas, business methods, mental processes, computer programs, and printed matter. Patentable subject matter is a challenging area and one that has seen important developments in recent court decisions.

---

[3] John Seabrook, *The Flash of Genius*, THE NEW YORKER, Jan. 11, 1993, at 40.

Chapter 5 explains the process one goes through to obtain a patent from the United States Patent Office—a process known as patent prosecution. Some of the complexities discussed include patent applications that spawn offspring, known as continuations, continuations-in-part, or divisional applications; interferences and derivation proceedings, which determine rights between rival claimants; and various forms of postgrant Patent Office review, including supplemental examination, reissue, and reexamination.

Chapter 6 examines the issue of inventorship—that is, who should or should not be credited as an inventor—and how an inventor can convey rights to a patented invention, either by assignment or by license. Chapter 6 also discusses how rights to a patented invention can be conveyed, intentionally or unintentionally, by an implied license.

Chapter 7 deals with the issue of interpreting patent claims. This is a difficult but extremely important issue because deciding what a patent claim *means* is the starting point for determining if the patent is valid or infringed. Chapter 7 reviews some of the tools used to interpret patent claims, including the patent specification and the prosecution history. Chapter 7 also discusses problems associated with certain specialized claim formats. Among these are product-by-process claims, which describe the invention in terms of the way it is made, and means-plus-function claims, which describe claim elements in terms of the functions they perform.

Chapter 8 is one of the longer chapters because it deals with the various conditions of patentability. If a patent application fails to meet any one of these conditions, it should be rejected by the Patent Office. If the application nevertheless slips through the Patent Office, the patent can be held invalid by a court. In fact, in most cases where a charge of infringement results in a lawsuit, the accused infringer argues that the patent is invalid.

Chapter 8 begins with a general discussion of the conditions of patentability, including the presumption that any patent is valid until proven otherwise. The specific topics covered in Chapter 8 include the utility requirement, which means that the patented invention must perform some useful function; the definiteness requirement, which means that the claims must be reasonably precise in identifying the patented invention; the enablement requirement, which means that the patent must include enough information so that others can practice the claimed invention without undue experimentation; and the written description requirement, which means that the patent specification, as filed, must demonstrate possession of the invention ultimately claimed.

Chapter 8 then looks at the novelty requirement, which in many respects is the key to patentability. The claimed invention must be *new* and *nonobvious* in comparison to the prior art. Recent legislation known as the America Invents Act has significantly changed the kinds of prior art that can invalidate a patent or prevent its issue. The new standard emphasizes the date of the patent application, and in certain cases the date of the inventor's public disclosure, rather than the date on which the invention occurred. These changes apply to patents and patent applications filed after March 16, 2013; patents filed before that date remain subject to the older rules. Chapter 8 therefore discusses both sets of rules in some detail.

Chapter 8 also discusses anticipation, which invalidates a claim covering an invention found in the prior art, and obviousness, which invalidates a claim covering subject matter that would have been obvious to a person of ordinary skill. If an invention is obvious, perhaps as an elaboration or a combination of prior inventions, it is not considered worthy of a patent. Obviousness is a difficult and subjective inquiry, invariably conducted in hindsight. Chapter 8 examines some of the "secondary considerations," such as commercial success, that are intended as more objective measures of whether an invention was obvious.

Chapter 8 concludes with an examination of double patenting. Double patenting is a ground for invalidating a patent if the same inventor had already patented the invention. This prevents an inventor from obtaining multiple patents on the same thing, thereby extending the period of the patent monopoly beyond the intended span.

Chapter 9 examines two defenses to a charge of infringement that can lead to a holding that a patent is unenforceable. If a patent is unenforceable, a court will not use its powers to prevent that patent from being infringed. The first such defense discussed in Chapter 9 is inequitable conduct. Inequitable conduct occurs if an applicant intentionally deceives the Patent Office during prosecution. The other unenforceability defense discussed in Chapter 9 is misuse. Misuse refers to attempts to leverage the patent monopoly beyond its intended scope—for example, by requiring that anyone practicing the patented invention purchase an *unpatented* product from the patent owner. This kind of "tying" and other forms of misuse may violate the federal antitrust laws in addition to rendering a patent unenforceable.

Chapter 10 is another lengthy chapter because it deals with the subject of infringement. After a preliminary discussion covering the temporal and geographical limitations of a patent, Chapter 10 discusses direct and indirect infringement. Direct infringement includes making, using, selling, offering to sell, or importing into the United States something that falls within the scope of a patent claim. Indirect infringement means inducing or contributing to infringement by someone else—for example, by supplying a part that can only be used in a patented combination. An indirect infringer is liable in the same way that a direct infringer is liable.

Chapter 10 then discusses literal infringement, which occurs if the infringing product or process includes each and every element required by a patent claim exactly as described. Next is a discussion of the doctrine of equivalents, a doctrine holding that a product or process can still infringe a claim even though it is *different* from what the claim literally requires as long as the differences are insubstantial. This is a difficult concept, even for experts and judges, so it is covered in some detail. Chapter 10 discusses how the doctrine of equivalents has evolved, and it examines some of the tests used to determine if a product or process is or is not equivalent to a claimed invention. Chapter 10 also discusses limitations on the scope of equivalency imposed by the prosecution history, the patent disclosure, and the prior art. Chapter 10 further considers equivalency in the related context of means-plus-function claims, as well as the reverse doctrine of equivalents, which holds that a product does not infringe, even though it is literally described by the patent claims, if it is sufficiently "changed in principle" from what the applicant actually invented. Chapter 10 discusses a little-used experimental-use exception to infringement and concludes with an examination of a prior-use defense recently introduced in the America Invents Act.

Chapter 11 explores the subject of patent litigation. Specific topics discussed include jurisdiction and venue, which determine the court where a suit for infringement can be filed; actions for declaratory judgment, which permit an accused infringer to sue a patent owner instead of waiting to be sued; burdens of proof, which determine who must prove what and how compelling the evidence must be; and the roles of judge and jury in deciding the various issues presented in a typical case. Chapter 11 also examines the kinds of relief that can be won in a suit for patent infringement. These include preliminary injunctions, which bar the continuance of the allegedly infringing activity during the pendency of the lawsuit; permanent injunctions, which permanently bar infringing activity if the patent owner prevails; and money damages, which compensate the patent owner for past infringement. The last-named relief can be in the form of lost profits or a reasonable royalty, and they can be increased as much as threefold if the infringement is found to have been willful. Chapter 11 also discusses defenses that can limit the recovery of damages, including the six-year statute of limitations, the patent owner's failure to properly mark products that it has sold, laches, and equitable estoppel. "Laches" refers to unreasonable delay in filing suit that somehow prejudices the accused infringer. "Equitable estoppel" refers to conduct by the patent owner that leads the accused infringer to believe that the patent owner will not pursue a claim.

Chapter 12 concludes the work with a discussion of specialized patents for ornamental designs and plant species.

Appendices A and B provide, respectively, samples of actual utility and design patents issued by the United States Patent Office.

1.3 SOURCES OF LAW

Several important sources of patent law are referenced throughout this book. One is the Patent Act, found at Title 35 of the United States Code. The Patent Act contains most of the legislation enacted by Congress that relates to patents. References to particular sections of the Act will generally be in the format "35 U.S.C. § ____." Other important authorities are the Code of Federal Regulations (37 C.F.R.) and the Manual of Patent Examining Procedure (MPEP), which set forth detailed rules and regulations for obtaining a patent.

In addition to the statutes, rules, and regulations, one can find countless reported court decisions interpreting the patent laws. As in any other field of federal law, the controlling precedents are those of the United States Supreme Court. However, the Supreme Court only rarely accepts appeals in patent cases, leaving most of the decision making to the lower courts. The most significant of these lower courts, at present, is the Federal Circuit Court of Appeals. Established in 1982, the Federal Circuit, based in Washington, D.C., hears all appeals of patent-related cases regardless of the place where the suit was initially filed. Except on those occasions when the Supreme Court intervenes, the Federal Circuit is the ultimate authority on what patent laws mean, and all inferior courts, as well as the Patent Office, are bound by its interpretations.

Cases referred to in this book are accompanied by citations, generally in the footnotes. The standard citation format includes the name of the case, followed by the volume of the official reporter in which it appears, the abbreviated name of the official reporter, the relevant page numbers, and in parentheses an identification of the court and the date of the decision. For example, *Absolute Software, Inc. v. Stealth Signal, Inc.*, 659 F.3d 1121, 1139–40 (Fed. Cir. 2011) refers to a case of that name reported in volume 659 of the *Federal Reporter* (Third Series) beginning at page 1121. The pages of particular interest are pages 1139–40, and the decision was rendered by the Federal Circuit Court of Appeals in 2011. These citations are provided in case the reader needs additional information or authority to support a particular proposition.

CHAPTER 2

Patents Distinguished from Other Rights

People sometimes confuse patents with copyrights or trademarks, saying, for example, that George Lucas has a "patent" on the name "Star Wars." Patents, copyrights, trademarks, and trade secrets are all legal means of protecting "intellectual property"–a term referring to the intangible creations of the human mind in which the law recognizes some form of ownership. However, patents, copyrights, trademarks, and trade secrets are each governed by a unique body of rules and requirements, and, in spite of some overlap, they are generally designed to protect different sorts of intellectual creations. Therefore, a good starting point for explaining what a patent *is* may be to explain what it is *not.*

2.1 COPYRIGHTS

Copyrights protect "works of authorship," broadly defined by statute to include writings in the conventional sense and, among other things, dramatic works, musical compositions, choreography, paintings, sculptures, photographs, motion pictures, audio recordings, and architecture. To some degree, any work of authorship has an aspect of creative expression. Copyright protects this expression, not the underlying ideas. Although idea and expression can be difficult to sort out, one could, for example, borrow the information published in this book without violating its copyright. No matter what labor was expended to compile the information, it can be freely used.[1] On the other hand, duplicating a book's language or organization could tread on areas of expression—creative choices unique to the author and protected by copyright.

Copyrights do not apply to technological innovations or to the useful features of products. A new and more efficient spark plug design could not be copyrighted. Some useful products do have an aesthetic aspect that can protected by copyright, but the artistic component of the design must be distinguishable from the utilitarian component. For example, a belt buckle might be copyrighted as a sculpture,[2] but the copyright cannot prevent the borrowing of some mechanical aspect of the design, such as an improved latching mechanism. In this respect a copyright is the antithesis of a patent, which is specifically intended to protect technological advancements. If one had both a copyright and a patent on the same belt buckle, the copyright would protect only the aesthetic appearance of the belt buckle, and the patent would protect only the mechanism by which it worked.[3]

As we will see in Section 8.9.4, an invention is patentable only if it is sufficiently new and different when compared to prior inventions that persons skilled in the field would not have considered it obvious. In contrast, copyright law has no requirement of novelty. As long as the work of authorship is an original product of the author's imagination, a copyright cannot be denied simply because the work is similar to others that have gone before. This may be the case because of the difficulty of judging novelty or obviousness in relation to the kinds of creative works that are traditionally protected by copyright. Who can say whether the latest mystery novel is an obvious variation of the thousands that have gone before? By the same token, independent creation is a complete defense to infringement of copyright, regardless of the similarity of two works. If two songs are nearly identical to one another, but it can be shown that the second composer never had access to the first composition, the second composer committed no act of infringement.[4] Patent law is very different. One who innocently infringes a patent, perhaps not even knowing that the patent or the patented product exists, can still be held accountable in the courts.

One area in which patent and copyright converge is in the protection of computer software. Software blurs the boundaries between a work of

---

[1] *See* Feist Publications, Inc. v. Rural Telephone Service Co., 499 U.S. 340, 347 (1991) (facts are not copyrightable because they "do not owe their origin to an act of authorship").

[2] *See* Kieselstein-Cord v. Accessories By Pearl, Inc., 632 F.2d 989 (2d Cir. 1980).

[3] Unless the patent were a "design patent," a special category of patent discussed in Section 12.1.

[4] Although the similarity of the two works could be considered evidence that the second composer did not, in fact, work independently.

authorship and a machine. From the perspective of a programmer, a computer program is a kind of writing. It is expressed in a language, which resembles in some respects ordinary human languages, and the process of authorship involves some of the aesthetic choices and personal style associated with other forms of writing. Copyright, rather than patent, would seem the proper vehicle for protecting this expression. On the other hand, a program is akin to a machine part as soon as it is executed by a computer. The program controls the operation of the computer much as cogs and wheels may have controlled a machine of an earlier era. From this perspective, a computer program seems outside of the subject matter protected by copyright and more suitable for protection by patent.

Courts and scholars have struggled for decades to determine the proper application of copyright and patent law to computer software. At present, both forms of protection are available, though each has its limitations. A computer program can be copyrighted, but this may not prevent someone else from extracting the functional aspects of the program to incorporate in a new program. The functional aspects of computer software can be patented as long as they meet the various requirements of patentability (such as novelty and nonobviousness) and as long as the patent steers clear of monopolizing an abstract idea, mathematical algorithm, or principle of nature. These special concerns are discussed in some detail in Chapter 4.

2.2 TRADEMARKS

Trademarks are governed by federal statutes, by state laws, and by common law. A trademark is a device, such as a word, phrase, or symbol, that is used to represent the brand origin of a product. A consumer who finds the word "Nike" on a shoe box, or the familiar Nike "swoosh" symbol, is entitled to conclude that the shoe sold in the box is the genuine article. The overriding purpose of trademark law is the protection of consumers, and disputes in this area are usually resolved by determining whether consumers would be confused by the use of a mark that is similar to the mark of another business. If another shoe manufacturer adopted the name "Nikke" for its line of products, the original Nike would doubtless challenge such use as unfair and confusing. Patents are granted only on inventions—not on labels, logos, or brand names. Trademarks, on the other hand, do not secure exclusive rights to the functional aspects of a product.[5]

---

[5] Traffix Devices, Inc. v. Marketing Displays, Inc., 532 U.S. 23, 29 (2001).

2.3 TRADE SECRETS

Patents are not the only way that inventors can prevent others from taking advantage of their labors. Another option is to keep the invention a secret. An inventor cannot do both. As soon as a patent issues, the invention becomes public knowledge. This is a part of the bargain that the inventor strikes with the government in order to obtain the patent monopoly. However, the process of applying for a patent can be kept confidential. If an inventor applies for a patent but the application is rejected, the inventor can abandon the attempt and still retain some protection by keeping the invention a secret.

Whether an inventor is better advised to patent an invention or simply keep it under wraps may depend on the nature of the invention. If it is something that will be revealed as soon as products incorporating the invention are placed on the market, the notion of keeping the invention secret may be self-defeating. On the other hand, certain inventions can be exploited without making them public. For example, an ordinary product, indistinguishable from any other, might be manufactured less expensively because of an innovative process. The process might be better protected through secrecy than through a patent, which would only last for a limited term.

If secret information is of the kind that gives one an advantage in business, it may be protectable under trade secret law. Trade secrets are largely governed by state laws rather than federal law, so there is some geographic variation. However, nearly all states have adopted, in some form, a model statute known as the Uniform Trade Secrets Act. The definition of "trade secret" under the Uniform Act extends to various forms of information, including "a formula, pattern, compilation, program, device, method, technique or process."[6] Although such things as formulas, devices, and processes are also within the area of potentially patentable inventions,[7] trade secret law imposes a different set of requirements. In order to qualify as a protectable trade secret under the Uniform Act, the information must "derive independent economic value, actual or potential, from not being generally known to, and not being readily ascertainable by proper means by, other persons who can obtain economic value from its disclosure or

---

[6] Uniform Trade Secrets Act §1(4).

[7] Trade secret law can also be used to protect certain kinds of business information that would not be patentable—for example, customer lists and marketing plans. As long as information is secret and valuable to a business, it can be protected as a trade secret, even though it is not an invention in the usual sense.

use."[8] In other words, not only must the information be secret, it must also be *valuable*. In addition, the information must be "the subject of efforts that are reasonable under the circumstances to maintain its secrecy."[9] A company that is lax about security may be unable to resort to trade secret law to protect its information from use or disclosure. Patent law, in contrast, requires neither that an invention be economically valuable nor (under most circumstances) that it have been kept secret.[10]

While patent law speaks of "infringement," trade secret law forbids "misappropriation." Misappropriation includes unauthorized disclosure or use of trade secret information by someone who has a duty to keep the information secret or limit its use.[11] Employees, for example, are generally duty-bound to refrain from using or disclosing the trade secret information of their employers. So is anyone who has signed a contract or confidentiality agreement promising to protect the information. An employee of a soda company who published his or her employer's secret formula on the Internet, or who used the formula to devise a rival soda, would likely be held liable for trade secret misappropriation.

Misappropriation also includes the use of information known to be derived from someone under a duty to keep it confidential and acquisition of the secret information by "improper means."[12] A person who bribed a soda company employee in order to obtain the secret formula would likely be guilty of misappropriation. Finally, misappropriation can occur, under the Uniform Act, if trade secret information is used by persons who know that the information has come into their possession only because of a mistake. If a soda manufacturer received an email from a competitor setting out a secret formula, and it was evident that the email had actually been intended for someone else, the rival would probably not be permitted to use the formula.

Trade secret law differs from patent law in requiring either some connection with a duty, contractual or otherwise, to protect the confidential information, the use of improper means to acquire the information, or an evident mistake. If the information was acquired under other circumstances, it can be freely used. For example, the Uniform Act allows the acquisition of information by "reverse engineering." Reverse engineering

---

[8] Uniform Trade Secrets Act §1(4)(i).

[9] Uniform Trade Secrets Act §1(4)(ii).

[10] An exception arises if the inventor disclosed the invention publicly more than one year before filing a patent application. See Section 8.9.1.7.

[11] Uniform Trade Secrets Act §1(2)(ii).

[12] *Id.*

means beginning with the finished product and analyzing it to determine the process by which it was developed or the principle of its operation. As long as the finished product was acquired legitimately–by purchasing it on the open market, for example–it is not a violation of trade secret law to reverse engineer the product and use the resulting information in a competing product. Hence, if a rival soda manufacturer could analyze a beverage and determine the formula by which it was manufactured, trade secret law would not prevent the rival from discovering and using that information. Patent law, in contrast, does not distinguish between information acquired legitimately or illegitimately. A product can still infringe a patent even though it was the result of reverse engineering or independent development.

Trade secret law might seem at odds with patent law, which requires the public disclosure of information in exchange for exclusive rights. The Supreme Court, however, has ruled that the two bodies of law are not incompatible, and federal patent law does not preempt state trade secret laws.[13] One complements the other, and inventors have a choice of means to protect their inventions, the most appropriate of which will be determined by the circumstances.

2.4 PATENTS

Patents cover practical inventions in the "useful arts." Any technological advance, from a new microchip to an improved formula for bubble gum, can be the subject of a patent. A special form of patent known as a "design patent" can protect some forms of artistic expression (see Section 12.1), but the usual kind of patent–the "utility patent"–applies only to technological inventions. As a result, a patent cannot be granted for a painting, a novel, a song, a product name, or a company logo.

In order to obtain a patent, an inventor must file an application with the United States Patent and Trademark Office, and the application must describe the invention in such a way that persons skilled in the field could practice the invention. The application must conclude with numbered "claims" that describe in precise terms exactly what the patent is intended to cover. A patent can be granted, or if granted can be held valid in the courts, only if the claims describe an invention that is both *new* and *nonobvious*. Patent law thus includes a requirement of novelty that is absent from copyright and trademark law.

---

[13] Kewanee Oil Co. v. Bicron Corp., 416 U.S. 470 (1974).

Once an application issues as a patent, the patent generally remains in force until 20 years after the date the application was filed. During that time, no one without the permission of the patent owner can (within the geographical limits of the United States) make, use, sell, offer to sell, or import the invention described by the patent claims. To do so is an infringement of the patent, regardless of whether the infringer copied the inventor's ideas or discovered them independently. In contrast to trademark law, which requires that the protected mark be *used* in business, a patent owner can choose to practice the claimed invention, license it to others, or prevent its practice altogether.[14]

---

[14] Until recently, a patent owner had unquestioned power to prevent anyone from practicing the claimed invention. However, since the Supreme Court's decision in *eBay Inc. v. MercExchange L.L.C.*, 547 U.S. 388 (2006), courts no longer issue injunctions automatically, even after a patent has been found valid and infringed. Particularly where the patent owner does not practice the claimed invention itself, a court may determine that the balance of hardships and the interests of the public counsel against entering a permanent injunction. Without an injunction, the patent owner is essentially forced to accept a compulsory license arrangement, where infringement cannot be stopped but the patent owner collects an ongoing royalty. See Section 11.8.

CHAPTER 3

Reading a Patent

Anyone interested in patent law should take the time to study an actual patent. Copies of three United States patents can be found in Appendix A of this book. The examples have been chosen for the sake of simplicity and brevity and to show that inventors are still searching for a "better mousetrap."

The first patent claims a device for trapping a mouse with the help of a ping-pong ball. The mouse enters a tube, the tube tips forward as the mouse heads for the "smelly bait," and a ping-pong ball rolls down to block the mouse's escape. In the second patent, bait lures the mouse onto a bridge. Although the bridge appears to be secure, the weight of the mouse causes the bridge to spin sideways, sending the mouse plunging headlong into a bucket. The third patent claims a trap made from a soda can.

Although none of these inventions is complex, each patent includes the basic components found in patents awarded to the most sophisticated advancements. The first patent will be used as an example for most of the following discussion, but the reader should examine all three in order to get a feel for the way patents are organized.

3.1 GENERAL INFORMATION

Patents are officially known by their serial numbers, printed at the top right-hand corner of the patent.[1] For the sake of convenience, patents are often referred to by the last name of the first listed inventor or by the last three digits of the patent's serial number. The first patent in Appendix A would be referred to as the Oviatt patent or as the '918 patent. The date on which the patent issued appears directly below the serial number.

The title of the Oviatt patent appears at the top of the left-hand column: "Mousetrap for Catching Mice Live." The title of a patent has little official significance and can sometimes be misleading.[2] The description of the "Mousetrap for Catching Mice Live" suggests that the trap can be immersed in water and the rodent drowned. The name of the inventor, or inventors, appears directly below the title, together with the inventor's place of origin. Beneath the inventor's name is the name of any person or company to whom the inventor assigned rights in the patent prior to the date of issue.[3] Because the Oviatt patent shows no assignee, ownership of the patent evidently was retained by the inventor. Patent rights can be assigned after the patent issues. When this is the case, the transfer of ownership will not be evident from the patent itself, but it may be recorded in the Patent Office's prosecution history file.

Moving down the left-hand column of the Oviatt patent, the next item to appear is the number of the original patent application.[4] The Patent Office assigns each patent application a serial number. It is not the same serial number ultimately assigned to the patent itself. Although this can result in some confusion, it allows reference to applications that never issued as patents. The Oviatt patent is the result of a single application, numbered 347,890. Often the situation is more complicated. The applicant may have filed one application, which was rejected and abandoned in favor of a

---

[1] Serial numbers on recent patents are followed by a "kind code" indicating the type of document one is looking at. These codes are typically either B2 (indicating an issued patent published before as an application) or B1 (indicating a patent not published as an application).

[2] *See* Pitney Bowes, Inc. v. Hewlett-Packard Co., 182 F.3d 1298, 1312 (Fed. Cir. 1999) ("[T]he purpose of the title is not to demarcate the precise boundaries of the claimed invention but rather to provide a useful reference tool for future classification purposes. . . . [W]e certainly will not read limitations into the claims from the patent title.").

[3] See Section 6.2.

[4] The next item on more recent patents is an indication of whether the patent term has been extended to account for delays during prosecution. See Section 10.1.

"continuation" or a "continuation-in-part" application.[5] Sometimes this happens several times, resulting in a chain of applications preceding the patent ultimately issued. In such cases, the patent provides the "family history" as well as the serial number of the original application.

The Patent Office assigns each application to subject matter categories, which are sometimes narrowed to very particular fields. This is done so that the Patent Office (or anyone else) can conveniently search a given area and determine what has been patented so far. On the Oviatt patent, this classification information appears next to the bracketed numbers [51] and [52], the first part relating to international classification and the second to U.S. classification. Oviatt's mousetrap has been assigned to U.S. subject matter Class 43: "Fishing, Trapping and Vermin Destroying." It can be found specifically under subclasses 60 ("Traps:Imprisoning"), 61 ("Traps: Imprisoning: Swinging or Sliding Closure"), and 66 ("Traps:Self and Ever Set:Nonreturn Entrance: Victim Opened").

As discussed in Section 5.1, part of the Patent Office's duty on receiving an application is to search its collection of prior patents to determine whether the application claims something new. The Field of Search area shows the categories that were reviewed by the Patent Office in its search for earlier patents. In the case of the Oviatt patent, the Patent Office searched the same subclasses noted above, with the addition of subclasses 58 ("Traps"), 67 ("Traps:Self and Ever Set:Nonreturn Entrance:Victim Opened"), and 75 ("Traps:Self-Reset:Smiting"). The search categories established by the Patent Office provide a brief catalog of modern technology. Class 43 is a testament to man's continuing war with the mouse, including subcategories for "impaling," "explosive," "choking or squeezing" and "electrocuting" traps, in addition to those that "smite."

Moving downwards, the next section of the patent is a list of prior art references cited by the Patent Office during prosecution of the application. Prior art, discussed in Section 8.9, includes earlier patents and publications disclosing inventions similar to the one claimed by the patent applicant. The cited references are those that the Patent Office considered closest to the patented invention, though not so close as to prevent the patent from issuing. Looking once again to the Oviatt patent, the Patent Office cited three patents as prior art, two of them more than 75 years old: the Turnbo patent, issued in 1909; the Cushing patent, issued in 1917; and the Sackett patent, issued in 1988. All disclose some form of trap with a tilting mechanism to prevent the victim's escape.

---

[5] See Sections 5.2 and 5.3.

Next to appear are the name of the patent examiner, or examiners, who reviewed the application for the Patent Office and the name of the counsel or patent agent who represented the inventor during this process.

The paragraph entitled "Abstract" provides a summary of the invention.[6] This is the place to look for the gist of the invention before tackling the detailed description that follows the drawings. The abstract typically includes a brief description of how the invention works and why it is useful.

3.2 DRAWINGS

After the abstract appear the patent drawings. These are often far more helpful in understanding the invention than a written description alone would be. Although drawings are not required for every patent, nearly all include some form of illustration. The Oviatt patent, like most patents, shows the invention from a variety of views so that all details are readily visible. Figures 3 and 8 show the invention before the mouse has sprung the trap. Figure 9 shows the movement of the ping-pong ball and the appearance of the trap after it has tipped forward on its pivot. Figure 2 is a "mouse eye view." Patents sometimes include exploded views, cross sections, or views of individual components when those views are helpful to understand the invention. Some patents include graphs or flow charts.

Patent drawings are generally surrounded by numbers and arrows, as are the drawings in the Oviatt patent. These are reference numbers corresponding to the written description of the invention found in the body of the patent. For example, the Oviatt patent identifies sphere 9 as the ping-pong ball, lump 10 as the bait, and rodent M as the mouse.[7] Patent drawings sometimes depict different embodiments of the invention. Figure 1 of the Oviatt patent shows the trap set up on a stand made of wire, whereas Figure 5 shows the trap resting on the edge of a plastic ring. The inclusion of alternative embodiments shows that the inventor's ideas were not limited to a particular implementation of the invention.

3.3 SPECIFICATION

After the drawings comes the section of the patent referred to as the "specification." The specification describes the invention, or technology

---

[6] I use the term "invention" here to refer loosely to the technological advancement described in the patent disclosure. In a specific sense, the "invention" is defined by the patent claims. See Section 3.4.

[7] Note that the numbers used in labeling a patent drawing need not be consecutive. The Oviatt patent uses numbers 90 and 100, but there is no 89 or 99.

related to the invention, in words rather than pictures. Often the specification begins with a "Background of the Invention" section discussing the technology as it existed before the patented invention was made. This allows the inventor to point out the shortcomings of what has gone before and highlight the advantages of the patented invention. The Oviatt patent begins in typical fashion by describing the health menace posed by mice and the disadvantages of typical traps that kill the mouse, where it is left to decompose, smell, and endanger children and pets. Oviatt then explains that his own invention avoids these problems by trapping the mouse alive.

Many specifications include a "Summary of the Invention" section, which is used to list the objectives of the patented invention. Oviatt states that the "main object" of his invention is to "trap a mouse alive." Other, subsidiary objectives are to provide an inexpensive trap, a trap that can be immersed in water to drown the mouse, and a trap that is reusable.

The next section of the Oviatt patent is, again in typical fashion, a "Brief Description of the Drawings." This portion of the patent explains in the most general way what is depicted in the drawings: Figure 1 is a top view, Figure 3 is a cross section, and Figure 5 is an alternative embodiment.

The next section of the Oviatt patent is entitled "Description of the Preferred Embodiment." Almost any patent has a similar section where the inventor describes the "preferred embodiment" in great detail, identifying in the process all of the components visible in the drawings. The preferred embodiment is the inventor's favored implementation of the invention. Inventions are usually general concepts that, at a detailed level, could be implemented in any number of ways. In the Oviatt patent, the tilting tube and the rolling ball are general concepts that characterize the invention. Oviatt might be entitled to claim any mousetrap that shares those features. But in the specification, we learn of the inventor's preference for a ping-pong ball and we are given two possible designs for the fulcrum on which the trap teeters—one a stand preferably made of wire, and the other a plastic ring with one flat edge.

Disclosure at this level of detail satisfies two requirements of the patent laws: that inventors provide in the specification sufficient information to allow persons skilled in the field to practice the invention, and that inventors disclose the *best* way they know of to practice the invention. These requirements, known respectively as the "enablement" and "best mode" requirements, are discussed in Sections 8.6 and 8.7.[8] The details discussed

---

[8] Although the America Invents Act eliminated concealment of the best mode as an invalidity defense, the statutory language still calls for its disclosure.

in the specification *do not,* under most circumstances, limit what the patent covers. Even though the specification describes a ping-pong ball, the patent might still cover a similar mousetrap that used a rubber ball.

In fact, the Oviatt specification includes warnings to that effect. Before the numbered claims, we find the following caveat: "Although the present invention has been described with reference to preferred embodiments, numerous modifications and variations can be made and still the result will come within the scope of the invention."

3.4 CLAIMS

The last and most important section of a patent consists of the numbered "claims." The claims, not the drawings or the specification, define what the patent covers and what will infringe. In the Oviatt patent we find eight claims.

Claims come in two forms—independent claims and dependent claims. An independent claim stands by itself, whereas a dependent claim explicitly refers to another claim and incorporates its terms by reference.[9] Claim 1 of the Oviatt patent is an independent claim. Claim 2 is a dependent claim because it refers to "The mousetrap of claim 1 wherein...." Claim 2 is read as though it incorporates all of the language of Claim 1 plus the additional language of Claim 2. Claim 3 is another dependent claim, which this time refers to Claim 2 ("The mousetrap of claim 2 wherein..."). Because Claim 2 depends from Claim 1, the effect of Claim 3 is to incorporate *all* of the language of Claims 1, 2, and 3.

Claims generally begin with a "preamble" that establishes the context of the invention. As discussed in Section 7.6, the preamble is sometimes treated as a claim limitation and sometimes as introductory language that has no legal effect. This can have important consequences. Claim 1 of the Oviatt patent begins with the preamble "A mousetrap comprising...." If this were the last reference in the claim to a mouse, the effect given to the preamble would determine whether the claim covered an otherwise identical squirrel trap. The preamble usually ends with the term "consisting of" or "comprising."[10]

---

[9] *See* Monsanto Co. v. Syngenta Seeds, Inc., 503 F.3d 1352, 1357 (Fed. Cir. 2007). One cannot infringe a dependent claim without also infringing the independent claim to which it refers. *Id.* at 1359. A dependent claim is invalid if, through some error of drafting, it somehow fails to incorporate all of the elements of the independent claim. Pfizer, Inc. v. Ranbaxy Labs. Ltd., 457 F.3d 1284, 1291–92 (Fed. Cir. 2006).

[10] See Section 7.6.

The indented paragraphs following the preamble are the claim "elements" or claim "limitations." Almost all patent claims cover a combination of elements or limitations. Looking at Claim 1 of the Oviatt patent, we find the following combination set forth:

1. A mousetrap comprising:

   a main tube having a central fulcrum means, a bait end, and a ball end;

   a base stand having a means to support the main tube at the fulcrum;

   said bait end further comprising mouse bait and a main tube closure;

   said ball end further comprising a ball and a main tube closure;

   an entrance tube depending down from the main tube at the central fulcrum means, and angled toward the ball end;

   said entrance tube having a mouse entrance adjacent a supporting surface for the base stand; and

   said main tube having a horizontal load position where said ball rests at the ball end, wherein a mouse enters the mouse entrance, walks toward the base up the entrance tube, and passes the fulcrum means, thereby causing the main tube to teeter down at the bait end, and cause the ball to roll down the main tube and then down the entrance tube, functioning to block an egress of the mouse out the mouse entrance.

Claim 1 of the Oviatt patent would cover any mousetrap that included each of the elements described. If a mousetrap did not incorporate one or more of the described elements, it would fall outside the scope of the claim. Hence if a mousetrap did not tip like the Oviatt mousetrap but instead relied on a spring-loaded mechanism to shoot a ping-pong ball down the tube to trap the mouse, that trap would lack the "fulcrum means" required by Claim 1, and it would fall outside the literal scope of the claim.[11]

The language used in patent claims is generally more formal and technical, and sometimes more obscure, than everyday language. Claim 1 of the Oviatt patent is not a particularly bad example, but it does include terms such as "fulcrum means," "supporting surface," "horizontal load position" and "egress," which might seem more grandiose than the invention requires. Claim drafters, whether inventors or attorneys, resort to such technical or pseudotechnical language because of the importance of the

---

[11] *See* Section 10.5. As discussed in Section 10.6, a product that differs from what the claim literally requires may still infringe, under the "doctrine of equivalents," if the differences are insubstantial.

words to the legal effect of the patent. Insofar as possible, the claim language must describe exactly what the patent covers. Claim drafters therefore must be precise in their description of the invention but must not limit themselves by the choice of language to something narrower than the inventor intends to claim.

The Oviatt patent has three independent claims–Claims 1, 6, and 8–and five dependent claims. A patent generally can have as many claims as the inventor desires, although more claims can mean paying the Patent Office an additional fee. Each claim can be treated in some respects as if it were a separate patent. Although people often speak of a patent being infringed, it is really a claim, or a series of claims, that is infringed. A device may infringe one claim of a patent but not another, perhaps because of a minor variation in language. An inventor who describes the invention through more than one claim decreases the chance that a potentially infringing product will escape because of some small difference. Using more than one claim is also a hedge against the possibility that a claim will be held invalid by the courts. One claim may be held invalid, while another, with slightly different language, survives.[12]

Note how the Oviatt patent describes the same concept in slightly different terms in Claims 1, 6, and 8. Claim 1 speaks of a pair of tubes–a "main tube" and an "entrance tube." Claim 8, on the other hand, speaks of a " 'Y' shaped tube." The Oviatt patent also illustrates how dependent claims are often used to include details described in the specification but omitted from the broader claims. For example, Claim 4 specifically limits the "ball" of Claim 1 to a "ping-pong ball." If it proved to be the case that a mousetrap had been invented prior to Oviatt's that used a rubber ball, the broader claim might be held invalid while the narrow claim might not.

---

[12] *See* 35 U.S.C. § 282 ("Each claim of a patent . . . shall be presumed valid independently of the validity of other claims. . . .").

CHAPTER 4

Patentable Subject Matter

The subject matter of patents, it has been said, includes "anything under the sun that is made by man."[1] Advancements in chemistry, biotechnology, electronics, aeronautics, communications, computer science, manufacturing, and a host of other disciplines have been, and continue to be, patented. From paper clips to rocket engines, patents cover the full spectrum of technology, or what the Constitution calls the "useful arts." Section 101 of the Patent Act, defining the boundaries of patent-eligible subject matter, encompasses "any new and useful process, machine, manufacture, or composition of matter."[2] Most inventions fall easily into one or more of those categories.

But some products of human ingenuity do not.[3] A new musical composition or a marketing theme would be difficult to characterize as a "process" or "manufacture." Other forms of intellectual property, like copyrights or trademarks, are a better fit. Even in technological disciplines where one would expect patentable advancements–disciplines like medicine and computer programming–not everything "new and useful" is patentable. In spite

---

[1] Diamond v. Chakrabarty, 447 U.S. 303, 309 (1980).

[2] "Manufacture" refers to an article produced by a manufacturing process. *In re* Nuitjen, 500 F.3d 1346, 1356 (Fed. Cir. 2007). "Composition of matter" is a broad term most often applied to chemical compounds and the like, but it could literally refer to any agglomeration of physical substances. *See Chakrabarty*, 447 U.S. at 308.

[3] For example, the Federal Circuit denied claims to a "signal" because it did not constitute a process, machine, manufacture, or composition of matter. *In re* Nuitjen, 500 F.3d 1346, 1353 (Fed. Cir. 2007).

of the broad language of § 101, patents cannot be granted to laws of nature, natural phenomena, or abstract ideas.[4] Although the trend for many years had been for the subject matter of patents to expand into areas previously thought off-limits, these long-recognized categories of *un*patentable subject matter have featured prominently in recent decisions of the Supreme Court.

4.1 LAWS AND PHENOMENA OF NATURE

The courts have long held that the truths of nature cannot be patented, even by the people who discover those truths.[5] The clearest examples can be found in the formulas of mathematics or the physical sciences. Pythagoras may have been the first to appreciate that the sums of the squares of the two sides of a right triangle are equal to the square of the hypotenuse, but such insights do not qualify as patentable inventions.[6] Similarly, Einstein could not have patented the relationship of mass to energy in the form of the equation $E = mc^2$.[7] On the other hand, one could patent a novel apparatus, method, or composition of matter that puts a principle of nature to practical application: for example, a new surveying instrument that makes use of the Pythagorean theorem or a nuclear reactor based on Einstein's discovery.[8] Because the formulas of science and mathematics are generalized descriptions of the universe, any invention, at some level, can be described by those formulas.[9] As long as the invention is not the formula itself but a useful application or embodiment of the formula, it is potentially patentable.[10]

The rule against patenting nature applies to discovered materials as well as to abstract relationships and physical laws. The discovery of a new mineral in the earth or a plant in the forest does not entitle the discoverer

---

[4] Mayo Collaborative Services v. Prometheus Labs., Inc., 132 S.Ct. 1289, 1293 (2012).

[5] *See* Mayo Collaborative Services v. Prometheus Labs., Inc., 132 S.Ct. 1289, 1293 (2012) ("Such discoveries are 'manifestations of . . . nature, free to all men and reserved exclusively to none.' ").

[6] *See* Parker v. Flook, 437 U.S. 584, 590 (1978).

[7] *See* Diamond v. Chakrabarty, 447 U.S. 303, 309 (1980) ("Einstein could not patent his celebrated law").

[8] *See* Mackay Radio & Telegraph Co. v. RCA, 306 U.S. 86, 94 (1939) ("While a scientific truth, or the mathematical expression of it, is not a patentable invention, a novel and useful structure created with the aid of knowledge of scientific truth may be.").

[9] *See Mayo*, 132 S.Ct. at 1293 ("all inventions at some level embody, use, reflect, rest upon, or apply laws of nature, natural phenomena, or abstract ideas"); Dickey-John Corp. v. Int'l Tapetronics Corp., 710 F.2d 329, 348 n.9 (7th Cir. 1983) ("all inventions that work can be explained in terms of basic truths").

[10] *See Mayo*, 132 S.Ct. at 1293–94.

to patent it.[11] On the other hand, someone who discovers a specific *use* for a natural material, can patent that method of use, so long as it is new and nonobvious.[12] Some problems can be avoided through careful claim drafting. The Patent Office denied one inventor a patent on a shrimp that was beheaded and cleaned but still protected by its shell.[13] Although the shrimp was no longer whole, that which remained was still a "product of nature" and in its original state. Had the inventor instead claimed a *method* of preparing a shrimp, the method would more likely have been held patentable subject matter.

It might be argued that the investigation of nature is a pursuit just as valuable as the development of technology and that awarding patents to significant discoveries would encourage such investigation. Why, then, are patents unobtainable? Nature, it is said, supplies researchers with the "basic tools of scientific and technological work."[14] Patents on discoveries in nature could encompass a vast and unknowable spectrum of practical applications, denying researchers access to the tools necessary for technological advancement. Moreover, the principles and phenomena of nature exist even before they are discovered, so the public may, in some sense, have used them already. For example, one researcher discovered that omitting antioxidants from vitamin supplements improved the effectiveness of other ingredients. The Federal Circuit found no patentable invention in that discovery because antioxidant-free vitamin supplements had already been available to the public, even if their unique benefits had not been appreciated.[15]

The most difficult cases are those where a patent claims an application of a natural law or phenomena but in a manner that adds little to the natural law or phenomena itself. In *Mayo Collaborative Services v. Prometheus Labs., Inc.*, the patentee claimed a method of treating gastrointestinal disorders by administering a drug and determining, by examining changes in the patient's blood, whether the dosage is too much or too little.[16] The treatment method was a "process," as required by § 101, but the physical effects of the drug were a product of nature. The Supreme Court held that the claimed method did not add enough to the natural correlation to render it a patentable invention.

---

[11] *Chakrabarty*, 447 U.S. at 309.

[12] Similarly, a new use for an existing artificial compound can be patented, though the discoverer of the new use is not entitled to a patent on the compound itself. *See In re Schoenwald*, 964 F.2d 1122, 1124 (Fed. Cir. 1992).

[13] Ex Parte Grayson, 51 U.S.P.Q. 413 (Pat. Off. Bd. App. 1941).

[14] *Mayo*, 132 S.Ct. at 1293.

[15] Upsher-Smith Lab., Inc. v. Pamlan, L.L.C., 412 F.2d 1319, 1323 (Fed. Cir. 2005).

[16] *See Mayo*, 132 S.Ct. at 1295.

Administering drugs and monitoring patients were already routine activities, adding nothing significant to the whole.[17] In essence, the patent claimed the correlation between the drug and its physical effects—a natural phenomenon that the patentee did not invent and could not patent.[18]

4.2 LIVING ORGANISMS

Because of advances in biotechnology, living organisms that have been genetically modified may constitute patentable inventions. The landmark case in this area is *Diamond v. Chakrabarty*,[19] which considered whether a genetically engineered bacteria, so devised that it could break down crude oil, could be patented. The bacteria was useful because it could be used to treat oil spills, and it was new. No naturally occurring bacteria possessed the same abilities. The Supreme Court held that living organisms can be patented so long as they meet all of the criteria set forth in the patent statute. Although the bacteria were living creatures, they were also, literally speaking, "manufactures"—products of the laboratory, not products of nature. They were "made by man" and eligible for patenting.[20]

The principles of *Chakrabarty* were later extended to multicellular organisms. In 1988, Harvard University obtained a celebrated patent on a genetically engineered mouse useful in laboratory studies because it is particularly susceptible to cancer. Plants can also be patentable inventions—a prominent example being food crops genetically modified to withstand the application of herbicides.[21] On the other hand, patent law has so far drawn the line at a genetically modified improved human being. Longstanding PTO policy,[22] and a provision of the recent America Invents Act,[23] deny a patent to any claim encompassing a human organism.

---

[17] *See id.* at 1298.
[18] *Id.*; *see also* Laboratory Corp. v. Metabolite Labs., Inc., 548 U.S. 124 (2006) (concerning a method of diagnosing a vitamin deficiency by observing the level of a certain amino acid in a patient's blood).
[19] 447 U.S. 303 (1980).
[20] *Id.* at 310.
[21] *See* Monsanto Co. v. Bowman, 657 F.3d 1341 (Fed. Cir. 2011). Although a special kind of patent, discussed in Section 12.2, is available for plant life, the Supreme Court has held a new plant can be the subject of a utility patent. J.E.M. AG Supply, Inc. v. Pioneer Hi-Bred Int'l, Inc., 534 U.S. 124 (2001).
[22] *See* M.P.E.P. § 2105.
[23] America Invents Act § 33(a).

Although living things can be patented, the rule forbidding the patenting of natural phenomena is still an important limitation. *Chakrabarty* notwithstanding, one cannot patent a newly discovered but naturally occurring bacterium. The same limitation applies to biological substances like DNA–the complex molecule that encodes genetic traits. DNA is useful in a number of ways when extracted from its natural surroundings, and researchers have patented DNA sequences by claiming them in their isolated state. Whether isolated DNA counts as a patentable human-made manufacture or an unpatentable natural phenomenon is currently the subject of debate. The Federal Circuit addressed the issue in *Association for Molecular Pathology v. USPTO,*[24] where a divided court held that the chemical differences between isolated DNA and DNA in its natural surroundings were enough for it to qualify as a human-made invention.[25] Although the Supreme Court has yet to weigh in substantively, it vacated the Federal Circuit's decision for further consideration in light of *Mayo.*[26] Genetic research is so important and so lucrative that future developments in this area must be closely watched.

4.3 ABSTRACT IDEAS

The most general category of unpatentable subject matter, and the hardest to define, is the category of "abstract ideas." All patentable inventions are ideas, and all patent claims are, in important respects, abstract. The claims of the Oviatt patent[27] do not describe a particular mousetrap; they describe a *class* of mousetraps that share the enumerated characteristics. But to condemn the Oviatt invention as an "abstract idea" would be to condemn all patented inventions. On the other hand, a claim can be so removed from any specific, concrete application that a court will not allow it to be patented. A claim to a method of analyzing a complex system–*any* complex system–and diagnosing its problems through logical deductions is the kind of disembodied invention likely to be dismissed as an abstract idea, even if, in form, it constitutes a process.[28] Although some cases may be easy, the inherently abstract nature of patent claims, and their application to processes as well as machines, makes the line between abstract and nonabstract a difficult one to draw.

---

[24] 653 F.3d 1329 (Fed. Cir. 2011).

[25] *Id.* at 1351–53 (relying on the "markedly different chemical structure" of isolated DNA).

[26] See Section 4.1.

[27] *See* Section 3.4 and Appendix A.

[28] *See In re* Grams, 888 F.2d 835, 837 (Fed. Cir. 1989) (characterizing the claimed invention as a "mathematical algorithm"); *In re* Meyer, 688 F.2d 789, 796 (C.C.P.A. 1982).

Part of the problem lies in the intangible nature of the advancements that often drive our information economy. A new investment strategy or a data-mining approach can be as valuable today as a new machine tool or a manu-facturing technique. Are innovations in these less corporeal fields still pat-entable inventions, or are they abstract ideas? In *Bilski v. Kappos,*[29] the Federal Circuit drew a bright line, using what it called the "machine or transformation test." In order for a process to be patentable, it had to trans-form a physical substance or it had to be tied to a particular machine.[30] The invention in question was a method of hedging risks in commodities trans-actions. It transformed nothing physical and it required no specific machi-nery, so the Federal Circuit held it ineligible for patenting. On appeal, the Supreme Court rejected the "machine or transformation test" as too rigid, but it too characterized the claimed invention as nothing more than an "abstract idea."[31] Hedging, it found, is a "fundamental economic practice" that should not be preempted.[32] The conclusion is accompanied by scant analysis, leaving many questions for the future. Whether an invention trans-forms something physically or requires a particular machine is still an important "clue,"[33] but it is not the decisive indicator of an abstract idea. Recently, the Federal Circuit has said that abstractness is a "coarse filter," to be applied only where the challenged claims are "manifestly abstract."[34]

4.4 BUSINESS METHODS

Business methods were long thought to be unpatentable, perhaps because they exceed the scope of the technology-oriented "useful arts." Accounting techniques and the like are far removed from the disciplines of science and engineering that are most suitable for the patent system.[35] However, the Federal Circuit bucked tradition in 1998 when, in *State*

---

[29] 545 F.3d 943 (Fed. Cir. 2008) (en banc).

[30] *Id.* at 954–55.

[31] Bilksi v. Kappos, 130 S.Ct. 3218, 3226–31 (2010).

[32] *Id.* at 3231.

[33] *Id.* at 3226–27.

[34] Research Corp. Technologies, Inc. v. Microsoft Corp., 627 F.3d 859, 869 (Fed. Cir. 2010).

[35] *See* Ex Parte Murray, 9 U.S.P.Q.2d 1819 (PTO Bd. Pat. App. & Int. 1988) (holding unpat-entable an accounting method allowing users to enter, categorize, and total expenditures and to display the results in an expense analysis report). On the other hand, an apparatus used in business—like a cash register—would normally be considered patentable subject matter. An apparatus is a technological means to an end.

Street Bank & Trust Co. v. Signature Financial Gp.,[36] it rejected the business-method exception to patentability as "ill-conceived" and thinly supported. Business methods, the court held, are subject to the same standards of patentability as any other method. The patented invention in *State Street* involved a system for organizing a group of mutual funds under the common ownership of a partnership–an arrangement that produced economies of scale and tax advantages. The claims described a system and method for performing the necessary accounting, but in such broad terms that anyone creating such a fund and using a computer would necessarily infringe. The court found that the claims were not unpatentably abstract because the computerized manipulation of data representing money is a "useful, concrete and tangible result."[37]

Since then, the phrase "useful, concrete and tangible result" has fallen into disfavor. In *Bilski*, the Federal Circuit held the *State Street* language "inadequate,"[38] and the Supreme Court, hearing the appeal, did not revive it.[39] On the other hand, the Supreme Court declined an opportunity in *Bilski* to hold that all business methods are unpatentable.[40] We are left with the possibility that many patented business methods are, like Bilski's hedging scheme, abstract ideas, but it will take further developments in the law to identify with any confidence which business methods those are.[41] The Federal Circuit has, at times, embraced a "technological arts" criterion that would exclude many business methods.[42] The court recently abandoned that approach as unworkable,[43] but perhaps in the wake of *Bilski* it will reconsider.

---

[36] 149 F.3d 1368 (Fed. Cir. 1998).

[37] *Id.* at 1373.

[38] Bilski v. Kappos, 545 F.3d 943, 960 (Fed. Cir. 2008) (en banc).

[39] *See* Bilski v. Kappos, 130 S.Ct. 3218, 3232 n.1 (2010) (Stevens, J, concurring) ("it would be a grave mistake to assume that anything with a 'useful, concrete and tangible result' . . . may be patented"). In an earlier opinion, Justice Breyer, dissenting from a dismissal of certiorari, wrote that the Supreme Court had never embraced the "useful, concrete and tangible result" standard of patentability, and that, "if taken literally," it would contradict prior decisions of the Supreme Court. Laboratory Corp. v. Metabolite Labs., 548 U.S. 124, 136 (2006).

[40] *Bilski*, 130 S.Ct. at 3228–29.

[41] *See id.* at 3231 (inviting the Federal Circuit to devise limiting criteria applicable to business methods).

[42] *See In re* Comiskey, 499 F.3d 1365, 1374 (Fed. Cir. 2007) (patentable subject matter must be limited to advancements in the "useful arts").

[43] *Bilski*, 545 F.3d at 960 ("the contours of such a test . . . would be unclear because the meanings of the terms 'technological arts' and 'technology' are both ambiguous and ever-changing").

4.5 MENTAL PROCESSES

The Supreme Court has included "mental processes" among the inventions that are not patentable subject matter.[44] In a case involving a patent application for a system of legal arbitration, the Federal Circuit held that "mental processes–or processes of human thinking–standing alone are not patentable even if they have practical application."[45] A process that can be carried out in the human mind or by a machine–like a process of calculation–is likely to be held unpatentable, unless it is accompanied by significant physical steps.[46] On the other hand, processes that *include* mental steps have been held patentable subject matter.[47] For example, a manufacturing process that requires some exercise of human judgment can still be a patentable invention. The treatment of mental processes may be refined in the aftermath of the Supreme Court's recent *Bilski* and *Mayo* decisions. A process that occurs entirely in the human mind is a likely candidate for an "abstract idea." On the other hand, if the process includes further steps–like concrete actions taken after reasoning one's way to a conclusion–then *Mayo* may be relevant to whether the extra steps are enough to make the process patent eligible.[48]

4.6 COMPUTER PROGRAMS

Computer programming is a technological endeavor, and the software industry is a significant component of the United States economy. Yet courts have often struggled with the issue of whether innovations in programming should be patentable. The problem is that programming is close to mathematics. Even the most sophisticated computer programs simply

---

[44] *See, e.g.*, Mayo Collaborative Services v. Prometheus Labs., Inc., 132 S.Ct. 1289, 1293 (2012); Bilski v. Kappos, 130 S.Ct. 3218, 3255 (2010); Gottschalk v. Benson, 409 U.S. 63, 67 (1972).

[45] *In re* Comiskey, 499 F.3d 1365, 1377(Fed. Cir. 2007); *see also* CyberSource Corp. v. Retail Decisions, Inc., 654 F.3d 1366, 1371 (Fed. Cir. 2011) ("Following the Supreme Court, we have similarly held that mental processes are not patent-eligible subject matter because the 'application of [only] human intelligence to the solution of practical problems is no more than a claim to a fundamental principle.' ").

[46] *See* Parker v. Flook, 437 U.S. 584, 586 (1978) (calculations that could be made with "pencil and paper," and that were unaccompanied by significant postsolution activity, were ineligible for patenting); Gottschalk v. Benson, 409 U.S. 63, 67 (1972) (mathematical algorithm could be performed "without a computer"); *CyberSource*, 654 F.3d at 1372.

[47] *See* Classen Immunotherapies, Inc. v. Biogen Idec, 659 F.3d 1057, 1065–66 (Fed. Cir. 2011).

[48] See Section 4.1.

manipulate data and execute mathematical operations, although they do it with great speed. Mathematics is one of those "universal truths," or "abstract ideas," that belong to everyone.

The Supreme Court has addressed the patentability of computer programs on three occasions. The first case, *Gottschalk v. Benson*,[49] involved a method of converting binary-coded numbers from one format to another. The method did not rely on a new kind of computer. It could be performed with any computer, then existing or yet to be invented, and it could be used in an unlimited variety of applications. The court held the applicant's claims unpatentable, finding that the method embodied an abstract idea or a mathematical truth rather than the application of an idea to a specific technological end. The court denied that it intended to bar the patentability of computer programs altogether. Instead, it focused on the preemptive effect of allowing an inventor to patent a method that is "not limited to any particular art or technology, to any particular apparatus or machinery, or to any particular end use."[50]

In *Parker v. Flook*,[51] the invention involved the use of a computer to update an "alarm limit." An alarm limit is a number used to indicate an abnormal, possibly dangerous condition arising during the catalytic conversion of hydrocarbons. During certain stages of the operation, the alarm limit needs to be adjusted or updated. As in *Benson*, the court found the software algorithm unpatentable. Even though Flook claimed the algorithm only in connection with a catalytic conversion process, and even though a certain amount of specific "post-solution activity" followed the calculation (namely, the adjustment of the alarm limit), the court still found that patenting the process would be tantamount to patenting an abstract idea or phenomenon of nature. The postsolution activity was insignificant–the kind of token addition that any competent draftsman might devise.[52]

The last case of the "Supreme Court trilogy" was *Diamond v. Diehr*.[53] while the facts in *Diehr* are curiously similar to those in *Flook*, the result was very different. Diehr's invention involved a process for curing rubber inside a molding press. In order to determine the proper time to open the press and remove the finished article, Diehr's method called for constant measurement of the temperature inside the press. A computer used this data and the well-known Arrhenius equation to periodically recalculate

[49] 409 U.S. 64 (1972).
[50] *Id.* at 64.
[51] 437 U.S. 584 (1978).
[52] *Id.* at 590.
[53] 450 U.S. 175 (1981).

the time necessary for the rubber to cure. When the calculated optimum and the actual curing time were the same, the computer opened the press automatically. This time, the court found the invention to be patentable subject matter.

The majority in *Diehr* viewed the invention not as a mathematical algorithm per se but as a method of curing rubber that happened to make use of a mathematical algorithm. Viewed in this light, Diehr's method was an industrial process for "transforming ... an article ... into a different state or thing"–the kind of process that has always been considered patentable.[54] The use of an equation and a programmed computer did not make the process as a whole unpatentable. Although *Flook* had seemingly dismissed "field of use" limitations as the key to patentability, the *Diehr* court distinguished *Flook* as a case in which the claimed method did nothing more than calculate a number, hardly mentioning the physical process steps associated with that calculation. If the claims in *Flook* had been drafted with additional references to the catalytic conversion process, perhaps they too would have been patentable.

The Federal Circuit's treatment of software inventions has been less than consistent. At times, the court has suggested that a computer programmed with new software is patentable subject matter so long as it produces a "useful, concrete and tangible result"–a concept so expansive that it includes the management of a mutual fund.[55] Later, it announced that no process can be patented, including a computer-implemented process, unless it is tied to a particular machine or, like Diehr's rubber-curing method, it transforms a physical substance into a different state or thing.[56] After the Supreme Court's decision in *Bilski v. Kappos*,[57] both propositions have been repudiated. Instead, the future of software patentability seems to lie in refining the concept of an "abstract idea." When programming innovations are, like Diehr's, closely tied to specific, technological ends, they are likely to pass the "coarse filter" of patentable subject matter.[58] When

---

[54] *Id.* at 184.

[55] State Street Bank & Trust Co. v. Signature Financial Gp., 149 F.3d 1368, 1373 (Fed. Cir. 1998); *see also In re* Alappat, 33 F.3d 1526, 1545 (Fed. Cir. 1994) (en banc) ("[new] programming creates a new machine, because a general purpose computer in effect becomes a special purpose computer once it is programmed to perform particular functions").

[56] Bilski v. Kappos, 545 F.3d 943, 954–55 (Fed. Cir. 2008) (en banc).

[57] 130 S.Ct. 3218 (2010).

[58] *See* Research Corp. Technologies, Inc. v. Microsoft Corp., 627 F.3d 859, 868 (Fed. Cir. 2010) (holding patentable a computer-implemented process for rendering a halftone image–an invention having "functional and palpable applications in the field of computer technology").

they embody more generalized and fundamental concepts, like Benson's invention, they are likely to be rejected.

4.7 PRINTED MATTER

Another exception to patentability concerns "printed matter." Generally speaking, a manufactured article or composition of matter is not patentable if the only thing that distinguishes it from prior inventions is the presence of pictures or writing. One could not, for example, obtain a utility patent for a baseball cap merely because it bears a new team logo, even though the cap is new and useful, and caps, as such, are articles of manufacture.

On the other hand, an invention that involves printed matter may be patentable as long as the invention as a whole calls for a new structure or the printed matter bears a novel functional relationship to the "substrate"–that is, the physical object on which the matter is printed. In one instance, an inventor applied for a patent on a scheme for deliberately mislabeling a measuring cup to solve the problem of measuring when making less than a full recipe. A cook who wishes to prepare, for example, one-third of the amount specified in a recipe may be left with the difficult task of measuring quantities such as 1/3 of 2/3 of a cup. The inventor conceived of a measuring cup for fractional portions. The cook who wishes to make a 1/3 recipe simply selects the 1/3 recipe cup, and when he fills the cup to the 2/3 cup mark, he actually has the desired 2/9 cup. Although the markings were the only difference between the inventor's measuring cups and other measuring cups, the useful relationship between the markings and the cups was enough to place the invention within the scope of patentable subject matter.[59]

A similar issue can arise in the case of computer storage media, which function to store information, though not in printed form. Is a computer disk patentable merely because it contains new information? Some applicants have successfully patented "Beauregard claims,"[60] which claim a computer-readable medium, such as a disk or storage device, that includes program instructions for executing some form of computer-implemented process.[61] Although the storage medium is a tangible, man-made object, the Federal Circuit has held that this does not resolve the question of

---

[59] Application of Miller, 418 F.2d 1392 (C.C.P.A. 1969).

[60] Named after *In re Beauregard*, 53 F.3d 1583 (Fed. Cir. 1995).

[61] *See* CyberSource Corp. v. Retail Decisions, Inc., 654 F.3d 1366, 1373 (Fed. Cir. 2011).

patentable subject matter. If the instructions amount to an abstract idea or a mental process, a claim to the medium on which they are stored still does not qualify as patentable subject matter.[62] By the same reasoning, it is likely that a computer disk containing a new literary work or a new work of art would not qualify as patentable.

---

[62] *See id.* at 1374–76.

CHAPTER 5

Patent Prosecution

5.1 EXAMINATION

The process of applying for a patent, also known as patent "prosecution," begins when the inventor, on his or her own or through an agent or attorney, files an application with the Patent Office for "examination." The application includes essentially the same things that a patent would include–a specification describing the invention in detail, drawings, and claims.[1] The Patent Office assigns the application to a "patent examiner" who has expert knowledge in the field of the invention. Because the Patent Office requires a filing fee, an issue fee, and various other fees, obtaining a patent can easily cost several thousand dollars, exclusive of any fees paid to a patent attorney or agent.[2]

The patent examiner searches for "prior art" patents already granted on similar inventions in order to determine if the invention claimed in the application is new and nonobvious.[3] The examiner also reviews the application to determine if it meets the other requirements of a valid patent,

---

[1] As discussed below, a "provisional application" may omit the claims.

[2] Reduced fees are available to individuals and "small entities" (see MPEP § 509.02), but the costs are still considerable. The America Invents Act creates the new category of "micro entity" eligible for steeper discounts. The status of micro entity can be claimed by employees of institutions of higher education and by low-income individuals. *See* 35 U.S.C. § 123. A current fee schedule can be obtained by visiting the PTO website at http://www.uspto.gov.

[3] *See* Sections 8.9.3 through 8.9.4.

such as having claims that are sufficiently definite.[4] After reviewing the application and searching for prior art, the examiner prepares a written "office action" to tell the applicant which claims are "allowed" or rejected and to explain any problems with the application. In many cases the examiner will reject the claims as originally filed on grounds that the invention is already disclosed in, or obvious in light of, prior patents.

Following such a rejection, the applicant is permitted to file a written response. Sometimes the response is to argue the point with the examiner and attempt to explain, on legal or technical grounds, why the claims should be allowed after all. Often the response is to amend the claims in an effort to distinguish the invention from what has gone before. It is also possible to cancel claims or add new claims. When claims are amended or new claims added, the applicant should explain why the changes overcome the problems found by the examiner.[5]

After a response from the applicant, the examiner prepares another office action, which may allow the claims or reject them once again. This process continues until the claims are allowed or until the examiner announces that the rejection is "final," which generally occurs after the second rejection.[6] A final rejection can be appealed to the Patent Trial and Appeal Board,[7] and from there to the Federal Circuit Court of Appeals.[8] If the situation appears hopeless, the application can be abandoned.

Although patent prosecution resembles a court proceeding in some respects—applicants are typically represented by attorneys who present legal arguments to the examiner "judge"—the situation differs in a very significant respect. In a typical court proceeding, the judge hears argument and evidence presented by adversaries having opposing points of view. Patent prosecution is "ex parte," meaning that there is no adversary present. It is the job of the examiner to represent the interests of the public

---

[4] *See* Section 8.5.

[5] Although the claims can be amended, the specification cannot be changed to add "new matter." 37 C.F.R. § 1.118. "New matter" can be added only by filing a "continuation-in-part." See Section 5.2.

[6] Applicants who pay a fee can request extended examination without the need to resort a continuation of the kind discussed in Section 5.2. 35 U.S.C. § 132(b). This is called a request for continued examination (RCE).

[7] Before March 16, 2013, the Patent Trial and Appeal Board was known as the Board of Patent Appeals and Interferences.

[8] *See* 35 U.S.C. § 141. Alternatively, an applicant disappointed with the decision of the Board may file a civil action in the U.S. District Court for the Eastern District of Virginia, from which any further appeal would be, again, to the Federal Circuit. *See* 35 U.S.C. § 145.

and ensure that no patent issues unless it meets all of the legal requirements. Yet the opportunity to present unrebutted arguments provides applicants with a great advantage, and that advantage is magnified in litigation by the presumption that all issued patents are valid.[9]

Because patent prosecution is ex parte, the individuals involved are held to a higher standard of candor and fair dealing than is typical of court proceedings. If, for example, the applicant is aware of a prior art reference that renders obvious some of the applicant's claims, the applicant must bring that to the attention of the examiner. If the applicant, or the applicant's attorney, fails in that duty of candor, the patent may later be held unenforceable by a court.[10]

The United States long conducted patent examinations in secret. Today, applications are, by default, published 18 months after filing, or sooner if the applicant requests.[11] Applicants may prefer swift publication because of the opportunity to obtain "provisional rights" before the patent issues.[12] On the other hand, an applicant can avoid publication by certifying that the invention has not and will not be the subject of an application in another country that *already* requires publication 18 months after filing.[13]

Although publication of patent applications is now common, the law still allows few opportunities for interested parties to intervene. If an application is published, § 122(c) of the Patent Act forbids, without the consent of the applicant, any form of third-party opposition or protest following the publication of the pending application.[14] The America Invents Act creates one exception. Section 122(e) of the Patent Act, effective September 16, 2012, allows a third party to submit for consideration and inclusion in the record a prior patent, patent application, or printed publication, together with a concise description of its relevance.[15] This should give potential infringers some opportunity to influence the examination.

"Provisional applications" are also a recent addition to the Patent Act.[16] A provisional application includes a specification and drawings, but it need

---

[9] See Section 8.2.

[10] See Section 9.1.

[11] 35 U.S.C. § 122(b). This applies to utility patents, not design patents. See 35 U.S.C. § 122 (b)(2)(A)(iv). Design patents are discussed in Section 12.1.

[12] *See* Section 10.1.

[13] 35 U.S.C. § 122(b)(2)(B)(i).

[14] 35 U.S.C. § 122(c).

[15] *See* 35 U.S.C. § 122(e).

[16] *See* 35 U.S.C. § 111(b).

not include any claim.[17] Within 12 months, the applicant must file an ordinary application or the provisional application will be deemed abandoned.[18] The advantage of a provisional application is that it allows an inventor to file an application, and obtain a priority date, before the applicant is ready to formulate a claim.[19] In addition, while the applicant enjoys the benefits of the provisional application's early filing date, the resulting patent does not expire until 20 years after the filing date of the ordinary application.[20] Nevertheless, applicants should approach this with caution. The benefit of the earlier filing date can be obtained only if the disclosures of the provisional application satisfy the requirements of § 112 of the Patent Act, including the enablement[21] and written description[22] requirements. Because satisfaction of those requirements ultimately depends on what is claimed, preparing one's disclosure before one is ready to formulate a claim may be a hazardous affair.[23]

Prosecution is a slow process and may take years. All of the documents filed by the applicant or by the examiner become part of the "prosecution history" of the patent. The prosecution history (also known as the "file history" or "file wrapper") becomes available to the public if the patent issues, and it is an important resource for interpreting what the claims mean. If in response to a rejection the applicant argues in favor of a narrow claim interpretation, that same interpretation is likely to be adopted by a court in any subsequent litigation.[24]

5.2 CONTINUATIONS AND CONTINUATIONS-IN-PART

In some instances, an applicant may choose to start over, in a sense, by filing a "continuation." A continuation is an application that has the same disclosure as the prior application (i.e., the same specification) but new

---

[17] 35 U.S.C. § 111(b)(2).

[18] 35 U.S.C. § 111(b)(5).

[19] *See* 35 U.S.C. § 119(e)(1).

[20] *See* Section 10.1.

[21] *See* Section 8.6.

[22] *See* Section 8.8.

[23] *See* New Railhead Mfg, L.L.C. v. Vermeer Mfg. Co., 298 F.3d 1290, 1297 (Fed. Cir. 2002) (because the disclosure of a provisional application did not adequately describe the later-claimed invention, the patentee could not obtain the early filing date necessary to avoid invalidation).

[24] *See* Section 7.3.

claims.[25] As long as the continuation is filed before the original application is abandoned, and as long as the continuation includes an explicit reference to the original application, the continuation, and any patent claims that issue from it, will be treated as though filed on the date that the original application was filed.[26] As in the case of reliance on a provisional application,[27] the earlier filing date may be important in determining the priority of the invention as compared to other inventions or references. The original application may be abandoned after the continuation is filed, or prosecution of the two applications may continue in parallel.

The second application may lead to another, and a chain of applications can be created in this way. The application that comes last on the chain receives the benefit of the first application's filing date, as long as each link in the chain meets the requirements of continuity—that is, each application includes the same disclosure as the one preceding it, and it was filed before the preceding application was abandoned. Related applications are often referred to using a family tree analogy, in which case an earlier application may be referred to as the "parent" or "grandparent" of a later application.

On other occasions, an applicant may choose to file a "continuation-in-part." A continuation-in-part is like a continuation, but it includes *additional disclosure* in the specification.[28] A continuation-in-part might be filed if the applicant discovers an improvement on the basic invention disclosed in the original application and desires a patent claim to match. The important difference between a continuation and a continuation-in-part is that the latter is entitled to the filing date of the original application *only* as to claims supported by the disclosure of the original application.[29] Any claim supported by newly added material (referred to as "new matter") is entitled only to the filing date of the continuation-in-part application.[30]

---

[25] *See* Transco Prods. Inc. v. Performance Contracting, Inc., 38 F.3d 551, 555 (Fed. Cir. 1994); M.P.E.P. § 201.07. One reason to file a continuation is to permit the amendment of claims that have already been subject to a "final" rejection. *See Transco,* 38 F.3d at 559. Hence the availability of extended examination (35 U.S.C. § 132(b)) reduces the need for continuations.

[26] *See* Mendenhall v. Cedarapids, Inc., 5 F.3d 1557, 1565 (Fed. Cir. 1993); 35 U.S.C. § 120; M.P.E.P. § 201.11. If the original application names more than one joint inventor, the continuation must name the same inventors or a subset of them. 35 U.S.C. § 120; *In re* Chu, 66 F.3d 292, 297 (Fed. Cir. 1995).

[27] *See* Section 5.1.

[28] *See Transco,* 38 F.3d at 555; M.P.E.P. § 201.08.

[29] The support must be adequate to satisfy the written description requirement of 35 U.S.C. § 112. *See* Section 8.8.

[30] *See* Augustine Medical, Inc. v. Gaymar Indus., Inc., 181 F.3d 1291, 1302 (Fed. Cir. 1999); Waldemar Link GmbH v. Osteonics Corp., 32 F.3d 556, 558 (Fed. Cir. 1994).

Suppose, for example, that an inventor filed an application for a basic mousetrap on January 1, 2010. The application disclosed and claimed the combination of a spring, a latch, and a trigger to release the spring when disturbed by a mouse. Later that month, the inventor discovered a new kind of trigger less likely to release the spring prematurely. Because the original application was still in prosecution, the inventor filed, on February 1, 2010, a continuation-in-part disclosing both the basic mouse-trap design of the first application and the improved trigger. If the second application includes a claim having nothing to do with the new trigger, and the claim is fully supported by the disclosure of the original applica-tion, that claim will receive the benefit of the January 1 filing date. However, a claim that does refer to the new trigger is entitled only to the February 1 filing date. If another inventor filed an application on a mouse-trap trigger on January 15, 2010, the difference would be significant in determining priority.

An exception to the rules just described arises if the matter newly added to the continuation-in-part application is *inherent* in the original applica-tion, even though not explicitly disclosed. Suppose that the inventor of the mousetrap realized that the design disclosed in the original application was more compact than most, so that the trap could be slipped into a smaller space. The inventor might decide to file a second application, styled as a continuation-in-part, explicitly pointing out this newly discov-ered advantage, and a claim might be drafted that referred explicitly to the trap's dimensions. As long as this characteristic had been inherent in the design originally disclosed, though not discussed, the claim would be entitled to the filing date of the original application.[31]

5.3 DIVISIONAL APPLICATIONS

Another complication in a patent family tree arises when, in the view of the examiner, the application claims more than one distinct invention. For example, the same application might claim both a new mousetrap design and a new "synthetic cheese" to be used as bait, either of which could be used without the other. The examiner might determine that each was a sep-arate invention that should be claimed in its own application subject to its own fees and prior art search. When this occurs, the examiner issues a "restriction requirement" compelling the applicant to choose which of the

---

[31] *See* Therma-Tru Corp. v. Peachtree Doors Inc., 44 F.3d 988, 992–93 (Fed. Cir. 1995); Kennecott Corp. v. Kyocera Int'l, Inc., 835 F.2d 1419, 1421–23 (Fed. Cir. 1987).

two inventions to pursue. The other invention can be made the subject of a "divisional" application. The divisional application includes the pertinent part of the original disclosure, and it is entitled to the same filing date.[32]

5.4 INTERFERENCES AND DERIVATION PROCEEDINGS

Because it is not uncommon for the same invention to occur to more than one inventor, it is not uncommon for two patent applications to claim essentially the same subject matter. Until recently, competing claims were resolved by determining, in "interference" proceedings, which of the rival inventors invented first.[33] Interferences were trial-like proceedings conducted by the Board of Patent Appeals and Interferences (now known as the Patent Trial and Appeal Board), using "counts" (essentially, claims) that describe the invention at issue. The first party to file an application, known as the "senior party," was presumed to be the first inventor unless the "junior party" could prove otherwise.[34] Interference proceedings were complex, expensive, and time consuming and could delay issuance of a patent for years.

The America Invents Act will make interferences obsolete. With respect to applications filed after March 16, 2013, it will no longer matter who invented first. Where there are rival inventors, the important question will be who *filed* first, and that can be determined without difficulty. The only question that may remain is whether the first applicant to file actually derived the invention from the other applicant rather than coming up with it independently. In those cases, the first applicant to file is not an inventor at all and is not entitled to a patent. Going forward, "derivation proceedings" to explore that more limited issue will take the place of interferences. The America Invents Act also provides for civil proceedings by the owner of one patent against the owner of an earlier-filed patent claiming the same invention to resolve issues of derivation.[35] An action of this sort must be filed within one year of the issuance of the earlier-filed patent.[36]

---

[32] *See* 35 U.S.C. § 121; M.P.E.P. § 201.06; Transco Prods. Inc. v. Performance Contracting, Inc., 38 F.3d 551, 555 (Fed. Cir. 1994).

[33] *See* Case v. CPC Int'l, Inc., 730 F.2d 745, 748 (Fed. Cir. 1984). The rules of priority are those discussed in Section 8.9.1.4. Two applications claim the same invention if each invention is obvious in light of the other. *See* Medichem, S.A. v. Rolabo, S.L., 437 F.3d 1157, 1161 (Fed. Cir. 2006) ("two-way" test requiring that invention A would anticipate or render obvious invention B if it came first, and vice-versa).

[34] *See* Brown v. Barbacid, 276 F.3d 1327, 1332–33 (Fed. Cir. 2002).

[35] 35 U.S.C. § 291.

[36] *See* 35 U.S.C. § 291(b).

5.5 REISSUE

"Reissue" is a procedure for correcting errors in a patent. The error may be a defect in the specification or drawings, or the applicant's claims may have been too broad or too narrow in comparison to what the applicant could rightfully claim.[37] If the claims are too narrow, they may fail to protect the full measure of the invention; if too broad, they may run afoul of the prior art.

The reissue application cannot add "new matter" to the original application,[38] and the patentee can wait no more than two years to seek claims through reissue that would broaden the scope of the original claims.[39] If the PTO allows the reissue, the applicant must "surrender" the original patent in favor of the revised version.[40] The latter is enforced from its own

---

[37] *See* 35 U.S.C. § 251; AIA Eng'g Ltd. v. Magotteaux Int'l S/A, 657 F.3d 1264, 1272 (Fed. Cir. 2011); *In re* Mostafazadeh, 643 F.3d 1353, 1358 (Fed. Cir. 2011). Failing to include a narrow dependent claim as a hedge against invalidity is an error than can be corrected through reissue. *In re* Tanaka, 640 F.3d 1246, 1251–52 (Fed. Cir. 2011). The reissue provision is " 'remedial in nature, based on fundamental principles of equity and fairness, and should be construed liberally.' " MBO Labs., Inc. v. Becton, Dickinson & Co., 602 F.3d 1306, 1313 (Fed. Cir. 2010). Minor errors of a clerical or typographical nature can be rectified without further examination by a "certificate of correction." *See* 35 U.S.C. §§ 254–55; Central Admixture Pharmacy Services, Inc. v. Advanced Cardiac Solutions, P.C., 482 F.3d 1347, 1353 (Fed. Cir. 2007). If correcting the error would mean broadening the claim, the error (and how to correct it) must be clearly evident to persons examining the original document. *See Central Admixture*, 482 F.3d at 1353; Arthrocare Corp. v. Smith & Nephew, Inc., 406 F.3d 1365, 1374–75 (Fed. Cir. 2005). The PTO examines *all* claims of a patent during reissue proceedings, including those that are unchanged from the original patent. A patentee who initiates a reissue proceeding therefore runs some risk that a claim already issued will be held invalid when looked at again. *See* Hewlett-Packard Co. v. Bausch & Lomb Inc., 882 F.2d 1556, 1563 (Fed. Cir. 1989).

[38] *See* Section 5.2. Furthermore, the reissued patent must claim the same invention disclosed, if not adequately claimed, in the original patent. *See* Hester Indus., Inc. v. Stein, Inc., 142 F.3d 1472, 1484 (Fed. Cir. 1998). This is similar to the "written description" requirement, discussed in Section 8.8.

[39] 35 U.S.C. § 251; *AIA*, 657 F.3d at 1272. If there is any conceivable device or method that would infringe the new claims but would not have infringed the original claims, the new claims are "broader" and cannot be obtained more than two years after the patent issued. *See* Predicate Logic, Inc. v. Distributive Software, Inc., 544 F.3d 1298, 1303 (Fed. Cir. 2008); Tillotson, Ltd. v. Walbro Corp., 831 F.2d 1033, 1037 n.2 (Fed. Cir. 1987). On the other hand, an original claim and a reissue claim may be identical in scope, even if they do not use precisely the same words (e.g., one could refer to "12 inches" where the other refers to "one foot"). *See* Anderson v. International Eng'g & Mfg., Inc., 160 F.3d 1345, 1349 (Fed. Cir. 1998).

[40] 35 U.S.C. §§ 251–52.

date of issue, and it expires when the original patent would have expired.[41] Any claims carried forward in substantially identical form are enforceable as though they had been in effect from the issue date of the original patent. In other words, a court can assess damages for infringement after and *before* the reissue, even though the patentee "surrendered" the original claims.[42]

What constitutes a correctible error can be a difficult issue. An applicant's deliberate choice to cancel a broad claim in favor of a narrow one in order to avoid prior art is not an error that can be corrected by reissue, even if the applicant has second thoughts.[43] On the other hand, a patent attorney's "failure to appreciate the full scope of the invention" is enough to justify a reissue with broadened claims.[44]

Although patent claims can be broadened by reissue, Congress foresaw the potential unfairness to anyone who steered clear of the original narrow claims but not the new broader ones. To protect such persons, the law recognizes "intervening rights."[45] If, prior to the reissue, a person or corporation made, used, purchased, imported, or offered to sell a product that did not infringe the original narrow claims, that person or corporation may continue to use that product, or may sell it to someone else or offer it for sale, even if doing so would infringe the broadened claims.[46] If, for example, a business had in its inventory items manufactured before the reissue that

---

[41] 35 U.S.C. § 251. Reissued patents have serial number beginning with "Re" or ending the letter "E."

[42] *See* 35 U.S.C. § 252; Laitram Corp. v. NEC Corp., 952 F.2d 1357, 1360–61 (Fed. Cir. 1991).

[43] *In re* Serenkin, 479 F.3d 1359, 1362 (Fed. Cir. 2007) ("the deliberate action of an inventor or attorney during prosecution generally fails to qualify as a correctable error"); Medtronic, Inc. v. Guidant Corp., 465 F.3d 1360, 1372–73 (Fed. Cir. 2006); Mentor Corp. v. Coloplast, Inc., 998 F.2d 992, 994–95 (Fed. Cir. 1993); Hewlett-Packard, 882 F.2d at 1565 ("error" must involve "inadvertence, accident, or mistake"). The "recapture rule," in particular, prevents a patentee from regaining subject matter deliberately surrendered during prosecution of the original claims. *See AIA*, 657 F.3d at 1272; *Mostafazadeh*, 643 F.3d at 1358; *MBO*, 602 F.3d at 1313. The recapture rule applies where the claims have been broadened, the broadening relates to the subject matter surrendered, and the result is that " 'the surrendered subject matter has crept into the reissued claim.' " *Mostafazadeh*, 643 F.3d at 1358. A claim that violates the recapture rule is invalid. *See AIA*, 657 F.3d at 1272; *MBO*, 602 F.3d at 1313.

[44] *See Medtronic*, 465 F.3d at 1372; *Hester*, 142 F.3d at 1479–80. The error need not have been unavoidable or undiscoverable. *Medtronic*, 465 F.3d at 1372.

[45] *See* 35 U.S.C. § 252.

[46] *See id.*; Shockley v. Arcan, Inc., 248 F.3d 1349, 1360 (Fed. Cir. 2001). These absolute rights apply only to items that existed before the reissue, not to additional items of the same type. *Id.*

would infringe only the modified claims, that business would have the right to sell those products after the reissue without incurring liability.[47] Moreover, a court may allow additional items of the same nature to be made, used, or sold after the date of the reissue if "substantial preparation" to do so occurred before the reissue, and the court deems such measures equitable in light of the investments made and businesses commenced.[48] A business that had invested in a factory to manufacture the newly infringing item would likely be allowed to continue producing and selling the item even after the reissue. Naturally, these rights do not extend to anyone who made no investments in an infringing activity until after the date of reissue.

5.6 REEXAMINATION AND REVIEW

A variety of procedures, some of them introduced by the America Invents Act, allow issued patents to be reconsidered by the Patent Office when newly discovered prior art threatens the validity of the claims. These include supplemental examination, reexamination, post-grant review, and inter partes review.

5.6.1 Supplemental Examination

"Supplemental examination" is an opportunity for the Patent Office "to consider, reconsider, or correct information believed to be relevant to the patent," at the request of the patentee.[49] At the conclusion of the proceeding, the PTO issues a certificate indicating whether the information presented "raises a substantial new question of patentability."[50] If the answer is affirmative, the patent is reexamined, as discussed in Section 5.6.2.[51] Supplemental examination offers a shield against allegations that the patentee engaged in inequitable conduct by failing to disclose material information during prosecution of the patent.[52] A patent cannot be held unenforceable for inequitable conduct if the patentee discloses in supplemental examination information originally withheld.[53] If, however, the

---

[47] Marine Polymer Technologies, Inc. v. Hemcon, Inc., 659 F.3d 1084, 1091 (Fed. Cir. 2011) (discussing "absolute intervening rights" for products made before the date of reissue or reexamination).

[48] *See* 35 U.S.C. § 252; *Shockley*, 248 F.3d at 1360–61.

[49] 35 U.S.C. § 257(a).

[50] *Id.*

[51] 35 U.S.C. § 257(b). Here the reexamination need not be limited, as is ordinarily the case, to questions involving prior patents and printed publications. *Id.*

[52] See Section 9.1.

[53] 35 U.S.C. § 257(c).

PTO learns that fraud may have been committed in the course of the original examination, the available remedies include referring the matter to the Attorney General for further proceedings.[54] Supplemental examination is a new option that should lead to fewer claims of inequitable conduct, to the relief of the courts that have repeatedly complained of their proliferation.[55]

5.6.2 Reexamination

The traditional vehicle for reconsidering the validity of an issued patent is "reexamination."[56] Reexamination allows the Patent Office to reevaluate claims in light of newly discovered prior art patents or printed publications.[57] Reexamination may be requested by "[a]ny person at any time."[58] It may be requested by a potential infringer, who hopes that the challenged claims will be cancelled. Or it may be requested by the patentee, who hopes that the patent will emerge from reexamination stronger than ever, any doubts raised by the new prior art overcome. Unless it follows supplemental examination,[59] reexamination is limited to questions of patentability raised by newly discovered patents or printed publications. A patent cannot be reexamined due to potential invalidity on some other ground.

The party requesting reexamination must submit to the Patent Office a list of prior art and a statement explaining why it is pertinent.[60] The Patent Office forwards a copy of the request to the patent owner. Within three months, the Patent Office must decide whether the request raises "a substantial new question of patentability."[61] If the answer is no, the decision is final. If the answer is yes, the Patent Office orders a reexamination. At that point the patent owner may file a statement, including any

---

[54] 35 U.S.C. § 257(e). For the protection to apply, the request for supplemental examination must have predated the claim of inequitable conduct. 35 U.S.C. § 271(c)(2)(A).

[55] *See, e.g.,* Therasense, Inc. v. Becton, Dickinson & Co., 649 F.3d 1276, 1289 (Fed. Cir. 2011) (en banc) ("the inequitable conduct doctrine has plagued not only the courts but also the entire patent system").

[56] *See* 35 U.S.C. § 302.

[57] "Congress intended reexaminations to provide an important 'quality check' on patents that would allow the government to remove defective and erroneously granted patents." *In re* Swanson, 540 F.3d 1368, 1375 (Fed. Cir. 2008).

[58] 35 U.S.C. § 302.

[59] *See* Section 5.6.1.

[60] *See* 35 U.S.C. § 302.

[61] 35 U.S.C. § 303; *Swanson,* 540 F.3d at 1375 (the "requirement prevents potential harassment of patentees"). The "new question" may be based on prior art already considered by the Patent Office. 35 U.S.C. § 303(a); *Swanson,* 540 F.3d at 1375–76.

proposed changes to the claims, and the party requesting the re-examination may file a reply.[62]

If necessary, claims can be narrowed during reexamination so that they avoid the newly discovered prior art.[63] The opportunity to do so is one reason that a patentee might seek reexamination. The patentee is not allowed to enlarge the scope of the claims.[64] When the reexamination is concluded, the examiner issues a certificate canceling any claims held invalid, confirming any claims held patentable, and incorporating into the patent any new or revised claims.[65]

5.6.3 Post-Grant Review

A new alternative to reexamination is "post-grant review."[66] A petition for post-grant review can be filed by any person who is not the owner of the patent,[67] and it can be based on any theory of invalidity.[68] The petition must be submitted within nine months of the date on which the patent was granted.[69] Subsequently, the challenger must look to the alternative procedures of reexamination or inter partes review. The patent owner may file a preliminary response to the petition explaining why post-grant review is unwarranted.[70] If the Patent Office finds it is more likely than not that at least one of the challenged claims is unpatentable,[71] the post-grant review begins.

The petitioner takes part in the proceedings and bears the burden of demonstrating that a claim is unpatentable by a preponderance of the evidence—a lighter burden than the clear-and-convincing standard that

---

[62] 35 U.S.C. § 304. If the request for reexamination is made by someone other than the patentee, the patentee has no opportunity to make its views known until *after* the Patent Office has decided whether there is a "substantial new question of patentability." *See* 37 C.F.R. § 1.530(a); Platlex Corp. v. Mossinghoff, 771 F.2d 480, 483–84 (Fed. Cir. 1985).

[63] However, "[u]nless a claim granted or conferred upon reexamination is identical to an original claim, the patent cannot be enforced against infringing activity that occurred before issuance of the reexamination certificate. 'Identical' does not mean verbatim, but means at most without substantive change." Bloom Eng'g Co. v. North American Mfg. Co., 129 F.3d 1247, 1250 (Fed. Cir. 1997); *see also* Predicate Logic, Inc. v. Distributive Software, Inc., 544 F.3d 1298, 1305 (Fed. Cir. 2008).

[64] 35 U.S.C. § 305; *see also Predicate*, 544 F.3d at 1303.

[65] 35 U.S.C. § 307.

[66] *See* 35 U.S.C. §§ 321–29.

[67] 35 U.S.C. § 321(a).

[68] 35 U.S.C. § 321(b).

[69] 35 U.S.C. § 321(c).

[70] 35 U.S.C. § 323.

[71] 35 U.S.C. § 324(a).

applies to validity challenges in court.[72] The downside for the petitioner is that it cannot challenge the patent later on any ground that was raised, or that reasonably *could* have been raised, during post-grant review.[73] In other words, the petitioner must be well prepared and hold nothing back; it is a case of "now or never." Claims will be cancelled if they are found to be invalid.[74] The patentee may propose substitute claims,[75] but claims cannot be broadened, nor can they introduce "new matter."[76]

5.6.4 Inter Partes Review

"Inter partes review" closely resembles post-grant review.[77] The differences are, first, that a petition for inter partes review must be filed at least nine months *after* a patent is granted.[78] In other words, as soon as the window for post-grant review closes, the window for inter partes review opens. Second, the scope of inter partes review is more limited. As in the case of a traditional ex parte reexamination, the challenge can be based only on prior patents or printed publications.[79] If the petitioner chooses ex parte review rather than traditional reexamination, it has the advantage of full participation. On the other hand, the petitioner will not be permitted to later raise arguments in court that were raised, or that reasonably could have been raised, in the ex parte review.[80] As in the case of post-grant review, the petitioner must be prepared to present its best arguments.

The procedures available today for post-grant evaluations by the PTO are more complex than before and offer more opportunities for third-party participation. If they work as intended, fewer "bad patents" will survive long enough to be raised in litigation.

---

[72] 35 U.S.C. § 326(e).

[73] *See* 35 U.S.C. § 325(e).

[74] 35 U.S.C. § 328(b).

[75] 35 U.S.C. § 326(d).

[76] 35 U.S.C. § 326(d)(3).

[77] *See* 35 U.S.C. § 311–19.

[78] 35 U.S.C. § 311(c). If post-grant review proceedings are then ongoing, the petition for inter partes review must wait for them to conclude. *Id.*

[79] 35 U.S.C. § 311(b).

[80] 35 U.S.C. § 315(e); *see also* Bettcher Indus., Inc. v. Bunzl USA, Inc., 661 F.3d 629, 643 (Fed. Cir. 2011).

CHAPTER 6

Ownership and Other Rights

6.1 INVENTORSHIP

When a patent application is filed, it is important to designate the proper inventor of the subject matter claimed.[1] A patent can name a single inventor, or it can name two or more joint inventors.[2] It is often in the latter case that questions arise regarding who should or should not receive credit.

---

[1] *See* 35 U.S.C. §§ 111, 115–16; Beech Aircraft Corp. v. EDO Corp., 990 F.2d 1237, 1248 (Fed. Cir. 1993). The inventors named on the patent are presumed to be correctly named. *See* Bard Peripheral Vascular, Inc. v. W.L. Gore & Assoc., Inc., 670 F.3d 1171, 1179 (Fed. Cir. 2012); Falana v. Kent State University, 669 F.3d 1349, 1356 (Fed. Cir. 2012); Nartron Corp. v. Schukra U.S.A., Inc., 558 F.3d 1352, 1356 (Fed. Cir. 2009); Cook Biotech Inc. v. Acell, Inc., 460 F.3d 1365, 1381 (Fed. Cir. 2006). That presumption can be overcome only by "clear and convincing evidence." *Bard*, 670 F.3d at 1179; *Falana*, 669 F.3d at 1356; *Nartron*, 558 F.3d at 1356.

[2] *See Falana*, 669 F.3d at 1357 ("'A joint invention is the product of a collaboration between two or more persons working together to solve the problem addressed.'"). Each joint inventor named on an application need not have contributed to every claim. 35 U.S.C. § 116; *Falana*, 669 F.3d at 1357 ("'A contribution to one claim is enough.'"); Stern v. Trustees of Columbia University, 434 F.3d 1375, 1378 (Fed. Cir. 2006). If an application names A, B, and C as joint inventors, some claims may represent the work of A and B alone, or B and C alone, or A alone, or B alone, and so forth. Absent an agreement to the contrary, each inventor owns "a pro rata undivided interest in the entire patent, no matter what their respective contributions." Ethicon, Inc. v United States Surgical Corp., 135 F.3d 1456, 1465 (Fed. Cir. 1998). This is true even if an inventor contributed to the subject matter of only one claim in a patent having many claims. *Id.* at 1466.

An inventor is anyone who participated in the mental act of *conceiving* the invention.[3] If two people work together on a project and both contribute to a patentable idea, both can be named on the application as joint inventors. This is true whether the specific contribution of each is difficult to identify, as may be the case when an idea arises from collaborative "brainstorming,"[4] or whether the contribution of each inventor is a discrete component of the whole.

Not all contributions rise to the level of invention. Someone who had supervisory responsibility for a project but added nothing to the conception of the invention would not properly be considered an inventor. Similarly, someone who built or tested the completed invention but did not contribute to its conception could not be considered an inventor, no matter how important that person's contribution to the project as a whole.[5] Even someone who identifies a problem is not considered a co-inventor of the solution even though identifying the problem is often a significant step. As one court observed, "[i]t is one thing to suggest that a better mousetrap ought to be built; it is another thing to build it."[6]

---

[3] *See Bard,* 670 F.3d at 1179; *Stern,* 434 F.3d at 1378 (conception is the " 'touchstone of inventorship' "); Board of Ed. v. American Bioscience, Inc., 333 F.3d 1330, 1337 (Fed. Cir. 2003). The contribution should be to the *claimed* invention, not to peripheral matters that may have been discussed in the patent specification. *See* Caterpillar Inc. v. Sturman Indus., Inc., 387 F.3d 1358, 1378 (Fed. Cir. 2004).

[4] *See* Canon Computer Sys., Inc. v. Nu-Kote Int'l, Inc., 134 F.3d 1085, 1088 (Fed. Cir. 1998) ("As any member of a large discussion group well knows, it is often difficult to remember who first said what.").

[5] *See Board of Ed.,* 333 F.3d at 1338 ("One does not qualify as a joint inventor merely by assisting the actual inventor."); *Ethicon,* 135 F.3d at 1460 ("[O]ne of ordinary skill in the art who simply reduced the inventor's idea to practice is not necessarily a joint inventor, even if the specification discloses that embodiment to satisfy the best mode requirement."); Sewell v. Walters, 21 F.3d 411, 416–17 (Fed. Cir. 1994). On the other hand, if making a patented compound required more than ordinary skill, the person who devises a method of making the compound can be considered a joint inventor of the compound itself. *Falana,* 669 F.3d at 1358 ("the discovery of that method is as much a contribution to the compound as the discovery of the compound itself"). Although attorneys often assist inventors in preparing a patent application, they generally should not be considered joint inventors. *See* Solomon v. Kimberly-Clark Corp., 216 F.3d 1372, 1382 (Fed. Cir. 2000) ("An attorney performing that role should not be a competitor of the client, asserting inventorship as a result of representing his client.").

[6] Buildex Inc. v. Kason Indus. Inc., 4 U.S.P.Q.2d 1803, 1805–6 (E.D.N.Y. 1987); *see also Nartron,* 558 F.3d at 1359 (" '[o]ne who merely suggests an idea of a result to be accomplished, rather than a means of accomplishing it, is not a joint inventor' ").

Deciding who should be credited as an inventor can be a difficult task, as illustrated by the case of *Hess v. Advanced Cardiovascular Sys., Inc.*[7] The invention was a balloon angioplasty catheter–a device that can be threaded through a narrowed artery and then inflated in order to reduce the blockage. The doctors responsible for the invention had tried various materials without success, when they were referred to Mr. Hess, an engineer with Raychem who was familiar with that company's line of heat-shrinkable plastics. Hess identified specific materials that would provide the doctors with what they needed. The materials worked, the doctors obtained a patent, and the invention was a commercial success.

Eventually, Hess claimed that he should have been named on the patent as a co-inventor because the invention would not have succeeded without his contribution. The Federal Circuit disagreed. The court compared Hess's contribution to that of a scientific treatise or a product catalog; he merely provided information regarding existing technology. "The principles [Hess] explained to [the doctors] were well known and found in textbooks. Mr. Hess did no more than a skilled salesman would do in explaining how his employer's product could be used to meet a customer's requirements."[8] Still, one can understand why Hess felt that identifying the right materials for the new application added more to the inventive idea than the passive contributions of a textbook author.

For two or more persons to be named as joint inventors, they must have *collaborated* in some way.[9] Two inventors who were unaware of each other's work could not be considered joint inventors even if their efforts overlapped and even if the two inventors were employed by the same company.[10] Similarly, if inventor B simply builds on the published work of inventor A, the result is the sole invention of inventor B, not the joint invention of A and B. On the other hand, joint inventors need not have physically worked together at the same time, nor is it necessary that the contribution of each be equivalent in type or amount.[11] If inventor A partially completed an invention, then passed it along to inventor B with the

---

[7] 106 F.3d 976 (Fed. Cir. 1997).

[8] *Id.* at 981; *see also Board of Ed.*, 333 F.3d at 1342 ("teaching skills or general methods that somehow facilitate a later invention, without more, does not render one a coinventor").

[9] *Bard,* 670 F.3d at 1179 (joint inventorship requires " 'collaboration or concerted effort' "); *Falana,* 669 F.3d at 1358; Credle v. Bond, 25 F.3d 1566, 1574 (Fed. Cir. 1994). Accordingly, co-inventors should have had an "open line of communication" during the relevant period. *Bard,* 670 F.3d at 1179–80; *Falana,* 669 F.3d at 1358; *Cook Biotech,* 460 F.3d at 1373.

[10] Kimberly-Clark Corp. v. Procter & Gamble Dist. Co., 973 F.2d 911, 916 (Fed. Cir. 1992).

[11] 35 U.S.C. § 116; *Falana,* 669 F.3d at 1357.

intention that inventor B continue, A and B could be considered joint inventors of the finished invention. There are no distinctions drawn between co-inventors based on the significance, ingenuity, or timing of their contributions.[12]

If an application names the wrong inventors (as can easily happen given the ambiguities in defining the role of "inventor"), the application, or issued patent, can be corrected to name the proper inventors without affecting the validity of the patent.[13] The incorrect naming of the inventors cannot, however, have been deliberate.[14]

6.2 ASSIGNMENTS

Although the right to apply for a patent generally belongs to the inventor, often someone other than the inventor *owns* the patent. A transfer of rights of ownership is known as an "assignment." An assignment might include all rights in the patent or a more limited interest such as the exclusive right to a geographical area.[15] The assignee may file a document with

---

[12] The contribution of an inventor cannot, however, be so minor as to be "insignificant." *See Bard,* 670 F.3d at 1180; *Falana,* 669 F.3d at 1357 ("Each joint inventor . . . 'must contribute in some significant manner to the conception of the invention.' "); *Nartron,* 558 F.3d at 1356–57 (suggesting a lumbar support extender for an automobile seat was not a significant contribution but merely "the basic exercise of ordinary skill in the art"); Acromed Corp. v. Sofamor Danek Gp., Inc., 253 F.3d 1371, 1379 (Fed. Cir. 2001) ("a purported inventor must show that he made 'a contribution to the claimed invention that is not insignificant in quality, when that contribution is measured against the dimension of the full invention, and [did] more than merely explain to the real inventors well-known concepts and/or the current state of the art.' "). The contribution of a joint inventor must have been more than a mere exercise of ordinary skill in the art, which includes explaining to the true inventors concepts already well known. *See Bard,* 670 F.3d at 1183; *Nartron,* 558 F.3d at 1357.

[13] *See* 35 U.S.C. §§ 116(c) (correction of inventorship for a pending application), 256 (correction of inventorship for an issued patent). If the inventors are incorrectly named and the patent is not saved by correction, the patent can be considered invalid. *See Solomon,* 216 F.3d at 1381; Pannu v. Iolab Corp., 155 F.3d 1344, 1349–50 (Fed. Cir. 1998). If the problem *is* corrected, the validity of the patent is restored even for the period before the correction. Vikase Corp. v. American National Can Co., 261 F.3d 1316, 1329 (Fed. Cir. 2001).

[14] *See* 35 U.S.C. §§ 116(c), 256 (each referring to correction in cases of "error").

[15] 35 U.S.C. § 261. Courts usually characterize assignments of less than an entire interest as "licenses" rather than assignments. The Federal Circuit has called the borderline between assignments and licenses "impressionistic," urging that one focus less on labels than on the characteristics of the transferred rights—which, as we will see, can affect the transferee's ability to file suit. International Gamco, Inc. v. Multimedia Games, Inc., 504 F.3d 1273, 1279 (Fed. Cir. 2007).

the Patent Office recording the fact of the assignment.[16] An assignee who receives all rights to the patent by assignment is, henceforth, the party with the power to sue for infringement.[17]

A common element of an employment contract, particularly in the case of engineers and scientists, is that any patentable inventions made by the employee in the course of employment must be assigned to the employer. Even if the employment contract is silent, an obligation to assign will likely be implied if invention falls within the natural scope of the employee's duties.[18] Thus, while patents bear the name of individual inventors (hence the "Smith patent" or the "Jones patent"), often a corporate assignee owns the rights. In fact, a corporate assignee can prosecute a patent in the name of the inventor and ultimately obtain rights to the invention, even if the inventor refuses to cooperate.[19]

6.3 LICENSES

A patent license is a more limited transfer of rights than an assignment. A licensor retains ownership of the patent but grants the licensee the right to practice the claimed invention, usually in exchange for some sort of royalty. A license can be exclusive or nonexclusive. If it is exclusive, there is only one licensee, and only that licensee has the right to practice the claimed invention. Sometimes, but not always, a licensee obtains the right to "sublicense" others.

---

[16] 35 U.S.C. § 261. Failing to record the transfer may cause problems if another party, without notice of the assignment, subsequently purchased an overlapping interest. *See id.* (assignment void against a subsequent purchaser without notice, unless recorded before that purchase or within three months of the date of the patent).

[17] *See* Asymmetrx, Inc. v. Biocare Medical, LLC, 582 F.3d 1314, 1318 (Fed. Cir. 2009) (an action for infringement may be brought by the "patentee," meaning "the party to whom the patent was issued and the successors in title to the patent"); Rite-Hite Corp. v. Kelley Co., 56 F.3d 1538, 1551 (Fed. Cir. 1995).

[18] *See* Teets v. Chromalloy Gas Turbine Corp., 83 F.3d 403, 407 (Fed. Cir. 1996). Even if no agreement to assign is express or implied, if the inventor used company time or materials, or if the employee introduced the practice of the invention into the employer's business, a court is likely to recognize a "shop right" benefiting the employer. A shop right is a nonexclusive, nontransferable right allowing the employer to practice the invention, royalty free, even if the employee is allowed to patent the invention as an individual. *See* McElmurry v. Arkansas Power & Light Co., 995 F.2d 1576, 1580–82 (Fed. Cir. 1993).

[19] *See* 35 U.S.C. § 115(d) (providing for "substitute statements" in lieu of the inventor's oath, when the inventor is under an obligation to assign the invention but has refused to cooperate in the application).

An exclusive licensee may file suit against an infringer in order to preserve its exclusivity. Whether the owner of the patent must join in that suit, and be bound by the result, depends on the nature of the license. The issue turns on whether the license divides rights to the patent in such a way that a potential infringer might be subject to multiple claims. If the licensee owns "all substantial rights" to the patent–making the transfer an assignment in all but name–the licensee may sue on its own behalf.[20] The same is true if the licensee received an exclusive license to practice the patent in a geographical area.[21] On the other hand, an exclusive "field of use" license does not give the licensee standing to sue on its own. In *International Gamco*, the licensee received exclusive New York rights to use a computerized gaming system in the field of "lottery games." Because one could debate the meaning of "lottery games," a potential infringer in New York might have been subject to competing claims for royalties. Consequently, the licensee could not sue in its own name but had to involve the patent owner as co-plaintiff.[22] A *non*exclusive licensee cannot sue at all and must rely on the patent owner to protect its interests.[23]

Some patent owners practice the claimed invention themselves, while others profit by licensing others to do so.[24] Patent owners have no obligation to license.[25] Although this might give the patent owner the power to reap monopoly profits, such is the reward for discovering patentable innovations.[26] On the other hand, injunctions barring future infringement may

---

[20] *See* Alfred E. Mann Foundation for Scientific Research v. Cochlear Corporation, 604 F.3d 1354, 1359 (Fed. Cir. 2010); International Gamco, Inc. v. Multimedia Games, Inc., 504 F.3d 1273, 1276 (Fed. Cir. 2007).

[21] *International Gamco*, 504 F.3d at 1276.

[22] *Id.* at 1277–80. If a patentee refuses to cooperate as co-plaintiff, an exclusive licensee may join the patentee as a defendant. *See* Rite-Hite Corp. v. Kelley Co., 56 F.3d 1538, 1552 (Fed. Cir. 1995).

[23] *See Alfred E. Mann*, 604 F.3d at 1360; *Rite-Hite*, 56 F.3d at 1552.

[24] On occasion patent owners "cross-license" their patents, each patent owner granting to the other the right to practice some or all of the inventions in its patent portfolio. Where two or more companies hold basic patents in the same field of technology, this can be an expedient way to ensure that mutually destructive litigation does not take the place of competition in the marketplace.

[25] *See* 35 U.S.C. § 271(d)(4).

[26] Whether a patent really confers that kind of power depends on the availability of alternatives that easily substitute for the patented invention. If one has patented a mousetrap, but other mousetraps work just as well, there is no leverage for demanding more than a competitive profit. In the end, consumer demand in the marketplace decides the financial reward for any patentable advancement.

be refused even after an infringer has been successfully sued.[27] If the court finds that the adequacy of monetary relief and other factors counsel against entering a permanent injunction, the result is, in effect, a compulsory license to the infringer with royalties determined by the court.[28]

6.3.1 Implied Licenses

Sometimes patent licenses are not express but implied.[29] An implied license is a reflection of the shared expectations of parties who have had dealings with one another, even if those expectations were not made explicit.[30] An implied license, like an express license, is a defense to a claim of infringement.[31]

6.3.1.1 "First Sale"

Because a patent owner has, among other rights, the exclusive right to use the patented invention, a patent owner might sell a patented article, only to forbid its use by the purchaser. Needless to say, most purchasers expect to use the things they buy. In order to fulfill this expectation and similar ones, whenever a patented article is purchased from the patent owner without any express restriction or reservation of rights, the law recognizes an implied license allowing the purchaser to use the article, repair it,[32] or sell it to someone else. As stated in one Federal Circuit opinion, "an authorized sale of a patented product places that product beyond the reach of the patent. . . . The patent owner's rights with respect to the product end with its sale."[33] A patent owner who intends otherwise must make those intentions explicit.[34]

---

[27] eBay Inc. v. MercExchange, L.L.C., 547 U.S. 388, 391–94 (2006).

[28] *See* Paice LLC v. Toyota Motor Corp., 504 F.3d 1293, 1314–15 (Fed. Cir. 2007).

[29] Carborundum Co. v. Molten Metal Equipment Innovations, Inc., 72 F.3d 872, 878 (Fed. Cir. 1995).

[30] *See id.*; McCoy v. Mitsuboshi Cutlery, Inc., 67 F.3d 917, 920 (Fed. Cir. 1995) (implied license arises from "entire course of conduct" between the parties).

[31] *Carborundum,* 72 F.3d at 878.

[32] Unless the repairs are so extensive that they are really a "reconstruction" of the patented invention. See Section 10.4.

[33] Intel Corp. v. ULSI Sys. Technology, Inc., 995 F.2d 1566, 1568 (Fed. Cir. 1993); *see also* Hewlett-Packard Co. v. Repeat-O-Type Stencil Mfg. Corp., 123 F.3d 1445, 1451 (Fed. Cir. 1997).

[34] Explicit restrictions *are* possible. For example, one could sell a patented item with the requirement that it be used only once. Reuse of that item by the purchaser would constitute patent infringement. *See* Mallinckrodt, Inc. v. Medipart, Inc., 976 F.2d 700 (Fed. Cir. 1992).

The "first sale" of a patented article, without restrictions, is said to "exhaust" the rights of the patent owner.[35] In other words, whatever compensation the patent owner receives from the first sale is all the patent owner can expect, even if the article is sold and resold, used and reused, many times.[36] The same result follows a first sale by a licensee of the patent owner; the licensee may owe royalties to the patent owner, but the article sold is afterwards "free of the patent."[37]

A similar rule applies where a patent claims a method and the patent owner sells an apparatus used in that method.[38] For example, a patent might claim a "method of catching mice," and the apparatus sold might be a kind of mousetrap. Anyone who purchases a mousetrap expects to use it for catching mice, and if the only method of using the mousetrap is the same one claimed in the patent, the purchaser reasonably expects to use that method. Such expectations lead to the following rule: an unrestricted sale of an apparatus by the patent owner confers an implied license to use that apparatus to practice a patented method if the apparatus has no noninfringing uses.[39] On the other hand, if the apparatus does have other uses, one cannot imply a license to use the patented method.[40]

The purchase of a patented article does not give the buyer an implied license to create a new one using the purchased article as a template. One

---

[35] *See* Quanta Computer Inc. v. LG Electronics Inc., 128 S.Ct. 2109, 2115 (2008); Monsanto Co. v. Scruggs, 459 F.3d 1328, 1335–36 (Fed. Cir. 2006); Anton/Bauer Inc. v. PAG Ltd., 329 F.3d 1343, 1349 (Fed. Cir. 2003).

[36] The first sale must be an authorized sale by the patent owner or a licensee of the patent owner. If the product originated with an infringer, downstream purchasers can be held to infringe by using or reselling the product. *See Intel*, 995 F.2d at 1572–73 (Plager, J., dissenting). However, if the infringer was sued and compelled to pay money damages to the patentee, that payment amounts to a first sale and the infringing goods are subsequently beyond the reach of the patent. *See* King Instrument Corp. v. Otari Corp., 814 F.2d 1560, 1564 (Fed. Cir. 1987).

[37] *See* Unidisco, Inc. v. Schattner, 824 F.2d 965, 968 (Fed Cir. 1987). The sale by a licensee is still an "authorized sale" even if the licensee has failed to make promised payments to the patentee. Tessera, Inc. v. Int'l Trade Comm'n, 646 F.3d 1357, 1369–70 (Fed. Cir. 2011).

[38] *See Quanta*, 128 S.Ct. at 2117 ("methods . . . may be 'embodied' in a product, the sale of which exhausts the patent rights").

[39] *See id.* at 2119; Met-Coil Sys. Corp. v. Korners Unlimited, Inc., 803 F.2d 684, 686 (Fed. Cir. 1986). There is no ongoing right to practice the method after the apparatus is worn out. *See* Carborundum Co. v. Molten Metal Equipment Innovations, Inc., 72 F.3d 872, 878 (Fed. Cir. 1995).

[40] *See* Bandag, Inc. v. Al Bolser's Tire Stores, Inc., 750 F.2d 903, 924 (Fed. Cir. 1984). The alternative use need not be optimal, but it should be "reasonable." *See* Glass Equipment Development, Inc. v. Besten, Inc., 174 F.3d 1337, 1343 (Fed. Cir. 1999).

who buys a patented mousetrap is not authorized to make more mouse-traps.[41] This principle applies even to self-replicating articles, like seeds. In *Monsanto Co. v. Bowman*,[42] Monsanto sold seeds that had been geneti-cally modified to tolerate its own Roundup herbicide, a trait they passed on to subsequent generations. Buyers of Monsanto's seeds were authorized to plant them and to sell second-generation seeds for consumption only. Farmers who *planted* second-generation seeds were liable for infringing Monsanto's patent. Exhaustion did not apply because in selling the first-generation seeds Monsanto had never relinquished the right to control future generations.[43]

Issues of implied license and exhaustion often arise in the context of replacing worn or broken parts in a patented device. One who obtains a patented device from a legitimate source is permitted to repair that device, or replace a broken or exhausted part, without further obligation to the pat-ent owner.[44] On the other hand, one cannot "reconstruct" the patented device to such an extent that one is, in effect, "making" a new and infring-ing device.[45] If the substitution of a part effects a reconstruction rather than a repair of the patented device, that reconstruction can constitute an infringement, and whoever supplied the part may be found liable as a con-tributory infringer.[46]

---

[41] *See* Jazz Photo Corp. v. Int'l Trade Comm'n, 264 F.3d 1094, 1102 (Fed. Cir. 2001) ("the right to make the article remains with the patentee").

[42] 657 F.3d 1341 (Fed. Cir. 2011).

[43] *See id.* at 1348 ("once a grower . . . plants the commodity seeds containing Monsanto's . . . technology and the next generation of seed develops, the grower has created a newly infringing article").

[44] *See* Fuji Photo Film Co. v. Int'l Trade Comm'n, 474 F.3d 1281, 1296 (Fed. Cir. 2007) ("the replacement of a spent part [is] a fundamental example of a permissible repair"); Husky Injection Molding Sys. Ltd. v. R&D Tool & Eng. Co., 291 F.3d 780, 785–86 (Fed. Cir. 2002); Surfco Hawaii v. Fin Control Sys., Ltd., 264 F.3d 1062, 1065 (Fed. Cir. 2001). This is true whether or not the replaced part is one "essential" to the combination and whether or not the replaced part is the thing that distinguished the invention from the prior art. *See Fuji*, 474 F.3d at 1297; *Husky*, 291 F.3d at 786–87; Porter v. Farmers Supply Service, Inc., 790 F.2d 882, 885–86 (Fed. Cir. 1986). Parts can also be exchanged to *modify* the patented combination for reasons other than extending its useful life. *See Husky*, 291 F.3d at 786, 788 (modifications that are "kin to repair," involving a substitution for an easily replaceable part, are permitted); *Surfco*, 264 F.3d at 1065–66 (owner may replace the fins on a surfboard, even though the fins are not worn out, in order to make the surfboard safer).

[45] *See* Aro Mfg. Co. v. Convertible Top Replacement Co., 365 U.S. 336, 346 (1961).

[46] *See* FMC Corp. v. Up-Right, Inc., 21 F.3d 1073, 1076 (Fed. Cir. 1994). Contributory infringement is discussed in Section 10.4.

The line between "repair" and "reconstruction" is a difficult one to draw,[47] but courts generally have taken a broad view of what it is permissible to repair or replace.[48] If it is simply a matter of replacing a spent and easily replaceable component, the replacement will probably not be considered an infringement as long as the component is not the subject of a patent in its own right.[49] For example, the Federal Circuit held that supplying replacement liners for a biohazard disposal system was not an infringement of the related patent because the liners, only a component of the patented combination, were meant to be replaced after a single use.[50] In fact, though it defies logic, one may be allowed to replace an entire device over a period of time, by the successive replacement of worn-out or spent parts, as long as in no single instance are the replacements so extensive that they amount to reconstruction.[51] On the other hand, if the entire product is spent, as a patented torpedo would be spent following its explosion,[52] construction of a new item from what remains would not be permitted. Also, courts have

---

[47] *See Husky*, 291 F.3d at 784–85 (the courts "have struggled for years to appropriately distinguish between repair of a patented machine and reconstruction"). One court, in a passage cited with approval by the Federal Circuit, declined to adopt any bright-line test to distinguish between repair and reconstruction, placing its reliance instead on " 'the exercise of sound common sense and an intelligent judgment.' " *FMC*, 21 F.3d at 1079 (quoting Goodyear Shoe Machinery Co. v. Jackson, 112 F. 146, 150 (1st Cir. 1901)); *see also* Bottom Line Management, Inc. v. Pan Man, Inc., 228 F.3d 1352, 1355 (Fed. Cir. 2000) (no "bright line test"). The Federal Circuit has suggested a "concept of proportionality inherent in the distinction between repair and reconstruction." *Husky*, 291 F.3d at 786–87; *see also Fuji*, 474 F.3d at 1296 (no contention that refurbishment was "disproportionate to the overall value of the parts that were not replaced"). Such "proportionality" would lead one to distinguish between replacing the spark plugs on a vehicle (a permissible repair) and replacing the rest of the vehicle at a single stroke, retaining *only* the spark plugs (an impermissible reconstruction). Of course, few cases will be so easy to categorize.

[48] Sage Prods., Inc. v. Devon Indus., Inc., 45 F.3d 1575, 1578 (Fed. Cir. 1995).

[49] Although the distinction between replacement and repair is difficult to draw, the Federal Circuit has implied that the substitution of a new part for one that is "readily replaceable" is conduct within a "safe harbor." *See Husky*, 291 F.3d at 787. Consequently, the difficult cases involve parts that are *not* easily replaced. *See, e.g., Fuji*, 474 F.3d at 1296 (reloading film in a single-use camera was not impermissible reconstruction, even though the back of the camera had to be broken and replaced); *Bottom Line*, 228 F.3d at 1356 (refurbishing cooking surfaces with worn Teflon coatings was not impermissible reconstruction, even though it meant breaking welds).

[50] *Sage Prods.*, 45 F.3d 1575 (Fed. Cir. 1995).

[51] *See Husky*, 291 F.3d at 786; *FMC*, 21 F.3d at 1077.

[52] *See Husky*, 291 F.3d at 785.

sometimes balked at the replacement of a component clearly not meant to be, nor customarily considered to be, replaceable.[53]

6.3.1.2 Legal Estoppel

Another situation in which a patent license can be implied falls under the heading of "legal estoppel." Simply put, legal estoppel is a doctrine that prevents a patent owner from licensing one patent, only to make that license worthless by enforcing another.[54] Suppose that an inventor obtained two patents—one a broad patent covering a new mousetrap design, and the other a narrow patent covering a particular variation of that design. A mousetrap within the scope of the narrower patent would necessarily fall within the scope of the broader patent as well. Anyone who received an express license to the second patent would likely receive an implied license to the first under the principle of legal estoppel. Otherwise the patent owner could prevent the licensee from taking any benefit from the license it obtained.

6.3.1.3 Industry Standards

The preceding examples are merely common examples of implied licenses. Any conduct by a patentee that could lead one to infer a waiver or an abandonment of the patentee's rights may have similar effects.[55] An increasingly common example involves the adoption of a patented technology as an "industry standard." Many industries, such as the computer and telecommunications industries, depend on such standards to ensure that equipment from different manufacturers can work together. Once such a standard is adopted, companies in the industry are virtually

---

[53] In Sandvik Aktiebolag v. E.J. Co., 121 F.3d 669 (Fed. Cir. 1997), the Federal Circuit held that replacement of a carbide drill tip constituted reconstruction of the patented drill, rather than repair, even though the tip was only a component of the claimed combination. A number of factors influenced the court, including the elaborate procedures necessary to replace the tip, the long useful life of the tip compared to other components of the drill, the lack of any substantial industry in replacement tips, and the lack of any evidence that the patentee intended for the drill tip to be replaced. *Id.* at 673.

[54] *See* Transcore, LP v. Electronic Transaction Consultants Corp., 563 F.3d 1271, 1279 (Fed. Cir. 2009); Spindelfabrik Suessen-Schurr Stahlecker & Grill GmbH v. Schubert & Salzer Maschinenfabrik Atiengesellschaft, 829 F.2d 1075, 1080 (Fed. Cir. 1987). "The rationale . . . is to estop the grantor from taking back that for which he received consideration." *Spindelfabrik,* 829 F.2d at 1080.

[55] *See* Wang Labs., Inc. v. Mitsubishi Electronics America, Inc., 103 F.3d 1571, 1580 (Fed. Cir. 1997).

compelled to conform. If the industry standard is covered by a patent, should all companies in the industry be forced to pay a royalty? In some cases the answer is yes, but if the patent owner promoted the adoption of the technology as a standard and gave the impression that the standard could be practiced free of obligations, the circumstances could establish an implied license.[56] Otherwise an industry could be lured into adopting a standard, only later to be faced with claims of infringement.

---

[56] *See* Hynix Semiconductor Inc. v. Rambus Inc., 645 F.3d 1336, 1348 (Fed. Cir. 2011) (patentee's actions in a standards-setting context may be " 'so inconsistent with an intent to enforce its rights as to induce a reasonable belief that such right has been relinquished' "); *Wang,* 103 F.2d at 1575, 1581–82.

CHAPTER 7

Interpreting Patent Claims

The claims are the most important part of any patent. They define what the patented invention is.[1] Hence, the first step in determining whether a patent is valid or infringed is to analyze the claims and determine precisely what they mean.[2] This analysis is known as "claim construction" or "claim interpretation."[3]

---

[1] *See* Ariad Pharmaceuticals, Inc. v. Eli Lilly & Co., 598 F.3d 1336, 1347 (Fed. Cir. 2010) (en banc) ("Claims define the subject matter that, after examination, has been found to meet the statutory requirements for a patent. . . . Their principal function, therefore, is to provide notice of the boundaries of the right to exclude and to define limits. . . ."); Computer Docking Station Corp. v. Dell, Inc., 519 F.3d 1366, 1373 (Fed. Cir. 2008) ("The words of the claims define the scope of the patented invention."); Phillips v. AWH Corp., 415 F.3d 1303, 1312 (Fed. Cir. 2005) (en banc).

[2] In the rare instance that the parties do not dispute the meaning of the claims, a formal step of claim construction may be unnecessary. *See* Hakim v. Cannon Avent Gp., PLC, 479 F.3d 1313, 1318 (Fed. Cir. 2007).

[3] The Patent Office during prosecution will give claims their "broadest reasonable construction consistent with the specification." *In re* Suitco Surface, Inc., 603 F.3d 1255, 1259 (Fed. Cir. 2010); *see also In re* Bigio, 381 F.3d 1320, 1324 (Fed. Cir. 2004). This helps to ensure that newly issued claims do not encroach on the prior art. If the applicant did not intend the broader interpretation, the applicant can amend the claim language to make that clear. *See In re* Skvorecz, 580 F.3d 1262, 1267 (Fed. Cir. 2009) (broadest reasonable construction approach "is to facilitate exploring the metes and bounds to which the applicant may be entitled, and thus to aid in sharpening and clarifying the claims during the application stage, when claims are readily changed"). Once the patent has issued, courts no longer apply the broadest reasonable construction if the evidence better supports a narrow interpretation. *See* Atlantic Thermoplastics Co. v. Faytex Corp., 970 F.2d 834, 846 (Fed. Cir. 1992). In most other respects, the claim interpretation rules applied by the courts and the Patent Office are the same.

Claims are written in the English language, but they often employ an obscure technical vocabulary. The following is an example of patent claim language:

1. An aqueous cosmetic emulsion comprising:
    i) an isoparaffin;
    ii) a C8-C22 alkyl phosphate salt;
    wherein the isoparaffin and alkyl phosphate salt are present in a respective weight ratio of from about 40:1 to about 1:1, and said emulsion having a viscosity ranging from about 35 to about 90 Brookfield units as measured with a Brookfield Viscometer Model LTV using a #4 spindle rotating at 60 rpm at 25° C.[4]

The claim is for a hand lotion.

The opacity of claim language can be traced to two sources. First, because patents are awarded to technological advancements, a technical vocabulary is often best suited to describe what the invention is. The language of the preceding example would be meaningful to the chemist who invented the lotion and to other chemists who are likely to be reading the patent. Second, because of its legal significance, claim language must describe the invention precisely. If a claim employs a narrow term instead of a more accurate broader term, the patent may exclude a product legitimately within the scope of the applicant's invention. If the preceding example had used the term "hand lotion" instead of "cosmetic emulsion," the claim might have been too narrow to cover a face cream that consisted of the same combination of materials. On the other hand, if claim language is too broad, the patent may be anticipated by a prior art reference and made invalid.[5] The specific measure of viscosity in the preceding example may have been all that distinguished the invention from other lotions. Everyday language that would serve as a casual description of an invention will not do for a patent claim. Finding the right words to describe an invention, from both a technical and legal viewpoint, is one of the most important tasks faced by a patent attorney.

Patent claims should be interpreted from the perspective of their intended audience—persons skilled in the field of the invention at the time the patent application was filed.[6] When deciding what

---

[4] Conopco, Inc. v. May Dept. Stores Co., 46 F.3d 1556, 1560 (Fed. Cir. 1994).

[5] *See* Section 8.9.5.

[6] *See* Trading Technologies Int'l, Inc. v. Espeed, Inc., 595 F.3d 1340, 1351 (Fed. Cir. 2010); *Computer Docking Station*, 519 F.3d at 1373; *Phillips*, 415 F.3d at 1312–13; Dayco Products, Inc. v. Total Containment, Inc., 258 F.3d 1317, 1324 (Fed. Cir. 2001) ("If an argument offered in support of a particular claim construction is so convoluted and artificial that it would not be apparent to a skilled artisan reading the patent and the prosecution history, the argument is simply unhelpful to the performance of our task.").

a patent claim means, guidance can be found in the following sources:

- The "ordinary meaning" of a word
- The specification
- The prosecution history
- Other claims

Although patentees sometimes testify as to what they *intended* a claim to mean, such subjective, post hoc testimony carries little weight.[7] Indeed, even if what the claim says is clearly *not* what the applicant intended, a court may refuse to overlook unambiguous claim language. In *Chef America, Inc. v. Lamb-Weston, Inc.*,[8] the claim required that pizza dough be heated in an oven to a temperature of 400 to 800 degrees Fahrenheit, a temperature that would give pizza the consistency of a charcoal briquette. The patentee meant that the *oven* should be that hot, not the dough itself. The court refused to ignore the language of the claim, in spite of the absurd result: "we construe the claim as written, not as the patentees wish they had written it."[9]

Sometimes it is difficult to reconcile conflicting evidence on how claim language should be interpreted. For example, in *Vitronics Corp. v. Conceptronic, Inc*,[10] the critical term "solder reflow temperature" could have meant the temperature at which solder begins to melt or the higher temperature at which it flows freely. The standard literature in the field supported the former meaning, but the examples discussed in the patent only seemed consistent with the latter. The court had to choose because infringement depended on the proper definition.

On various occasions, the Federal Circuit has discussed procedures for weighing conflicting evidence. In *Vitronics*, the court emphasized "intrinsic" evidence—evidence, that is, found in the patent itself or in the

---

[7] *See* Solomon v. Kimberly-Clark Corp., 216 F.3d 1372, 1379 (Fed. Cir. 2000); Senmed, Inc. v. Richard-Allan Medical Indus., Inc., 888 F.2d 815, 819 (Fed. Cir. 1989).

[8] 358 F.3d 1371 (Fed. Cir. 2004).

[9] *Id.* at 1374; *see also* Rembrandt Data Technologies, LP v. AOL, LLC, 641 F.3d 1331, 1339 (Fed. Cir. 2011). Courts will sometimes correct an error in a patent claim if it is so obvious that "the correction is not subject to reasonable debate." *See* CBT Flint Partners, LLC v. Return Path, Inc., 654 F.3d 1353, 1358 (Fed. Cir. 2011). In one case, the court corrected the omission of a comma from a mathematical formula—a mistake that any person skilled in the art would have recognized. Ultimax Cement Mfg. Corp. v. CTS Cement Mfg. Corp., 587 F.3d 1339, 1353 (Fed. Cir. 2009). More serious mistakes can be corrected in the Patent Office through procedures like reissue. See Section 5.5.

[10] 90 F.3d 1576 (Fed. Cir. 1996).

prosecution history.[11] It approved resort to "extrinsic" evidence, like ech-nical dictionaries, only in the rare case that the intrinsic evidence was ambiguous.[12] On the other hand, some later cases–most notably *Texas Digital Systems, Inc. v. Telegenix, Inc.*[13]–emphasized the "plain meaning" of claim language, best exemplified by neutral sources like dictionaries.[14] Following *Texas Digital,* one might begin the process of claim interpretation with just the kind of extrinsic evidence dismissed in *Vitronics.*

In 2005, the Federal Circuit in *Phillips v. AWH Corp.*[15] addressed these contradictions through a hearing en banc. While the court found the recent emphasis on dictionaries overdone, it refrained from introducing a rigid hierarchy excluding extrinsic evidence in all but the rarest of cases. It admitted that there is "no magic formula or catechism" for construing claim language and no particular sequence of steps that a court must invar-iably apply. Rather, one must interpret claim language as it would be understood by persons in the field of the invention, which includes proper regard for what the patent itself has to say. Extrinsic evidence can be illumi-nating, but if the patent is perfectly clear one cannot contradict its meaning by resort to other sources of information.[16] In that respect, the court reaf-firmed *Vitronics* at the expense of *Texas Digital.* With that general guidance in mind, one can still usefully apply the rules discussed in the remainder of this chapter to the challenging task of claim interpretation.

7.1 "ORDINARY MEANING"

A natural place to begin one's claim interpretation is with the "ordinary meaning" of the terms from the perspective of a person skilled in the art at

---

[11] *Id.* at 1583.

[12] *See id.* ("In most situations, an analysis of the intrinsic evidence alone will resolve any ambiguity in a disputed claim term. In such circumstances, it is improper to rely on extrinsic evidence."). The emphasis on intrinsic evidence reflects the idea that patents must provide fair warning to the public. *See id.* ("The claims, specification, and file history, rather than extrinsic evidence, constitute the public record of the patentee's claim, a record on which the public is entitled to rely.").

[13] 308 F.3d 1193 (Fed. Cir. 2002).

[14] *See id.* at 1202–3 ("Dictionaries, encyclopedias and treatises, publicly available at the time the patent is issued, . . . are unbiased reflections of common understanding."); Interactive Gift Express, Inc. v. CompuServe Inc., 231 F.3d 859, 866 (Fed. Cir. 2000) ("Dictionaries, which are a form of extrinsic evidence, hold a special place. . . .").

[15] F.3d 1303 (Fed. Cir. 2005) (en banc).

[16] *See id.* at 1324.

the time of the invention.[17] Many cases speak of a "heavy presumption" that claim terminology should be given its ordinary or customary meaning.[18] On occasion, the ordinary meaning of a term may be apparent even to a layman.[19] Or if the term is not a technical one, its ordinary meaning may be found in a general-purpose dictionary.[20] Often the terms used in patent claims are technical terms with specialized meaning to persons skilled in the art of the invention.[21] On those occasions, a court may also look to technical dictionaries and similar references for assistance.[22] Of course, the claims are not to be read with a dictionary alone, as though one were translating a Russian novel word by word; instead, one must read

---

[17] *See* MySpace, Inc. v. Graphon Corp., 672 F.3d 1250, 1255 (Fed. Cir. 2012); Thorner v. Sony Computer Entertainment America LLC, 669 F.3d 1362, 1365 (Fed. Cir. 2012); American Piledriving Equip., Inc. v. Geoquip, Inc., 637 F.3d 1324, 1332 (Fed. Cir. 2011) ("ordinary and customary meaning" refers to " 'the meaning that the [language] would have to a person of ordinary skill in the art at the time of the invention' "); Lazare Kaplan Int'l, Inc. v. Photoscribe Technologies, Inc., 628 F.3d 1359, 1368 (Fed. Cir. 2010); Phillips v. AWH Corp., 415 F.3d 1303, 1312 (Fed. Cir. 2005) (en banc) ("We have frequently stated that the words of a claim 'are generally given their ordinary and customary meaning.' ").

[18] *See* Elbex Video, Ltd. v. Sensormatic Electronics Corp., 508 F.3d 1366, 1371 (Fed. Cir. 2007); Leibel-Flarsheim Co. v. Medrad Inc., 358 F.3d 898, 913 (Fed. Cir. 2004); CCS Fitness, Inc. v. Brunswick Corp., 288 F.3d 1359, 1366 (Fed. Cir. 2002).

[19] *See Phillips*, 415 F.3d at 1314; C.R. Bard, Inc. v. U.S. Surgical Corp., 388 F.3d 858, 863 (Fed. Cir. 2004) (questioning the need to consult references when the terms were as commonplace as "conformable" and "pliable").

[20] *See Phillips*, 415 F.3d. at 1314 (for nontechnical vocabulary "general purpose dictionaries may be helpful"); Greenberg v. Ethicon Endo-Surgery, Inc., 91 F.3d 1580, 1583 (Fed. Cir. 1996).

[21] Even terms that have nontechnical meanings may have to be placed in an appropriate technological context. *See* TAP Pharmaceutical Prods., Inc. v. Owl Pharmaceuticals, L.L.C., 419 F.3d 1346, 1354 (Fed. Cir. 2005). If the patentee uses a term that means *nothing* in the field of the invention, a court must look entirely to intrinsic evidence to construe it. *See* Network Commerce, Inc. v. Microsoft Corp., 422 F.3d 1353, 1359–60 (Fed. Cir. 2005) (the term "download component" had no "commonly understood meaning reflected in general dictionaries" nor any "specialized meaning in the relevant art"); Irdeto Access, Inc. v. Echostar Satellite Corp., 383 F.3d 1295, 1300 (Fed. Cir. 2004).

[22] *See* MIT v. Abacus Software, 462 F.3d 1344, 1351 (Fed. Cir. 2006) (where the specification provided no definition, explicit or implicit, of the term "scanner," the court could look to definitions from technical and general-purpose dictionaries); *Phillips*, 415 F.3d at 1314 ("Because dictionaries, and especially technical dictionaries, attempt to collect accepted meanings of terms used in various fields of science and technology . . . [they] can assist the court in determining the meaning of particular terminology to those of skill in the art of the invention").

the claims, as a person skilled in the art would, in the context of the entire patent document.[23]

Even expert testimony may be admitted "to clarify the patented technology and to explain its meaning through the eyes of experience."[24] On the other hand, courts are well aware that the opinions of experts maybe colored by hindsight and the interests of the litigants who employ them. Hence courts treat expert testimony with appropriate skepticism; unsupported assertions may be ignored, and expert testimony discounted if it is "at odds with the claim construction mandated by . . . the written record of the patent."[25]

7.2 THE SPECIFICATION

If a word has an "ordinary" or "plain meaning," one might suppose that its interpretation would be uncontroversial, yet words as simple as "on" and "a" have been the subject of intense debate in the context of infringement litigation.[26] One reason is that a patent applicant can be "his own lexicographer"–which is to say, an applicant can devise his own vocabulary to describe the invention.[27] Words can be used in ways that differ from

---

[23] *See* Atofina v. Great Lakes Chemical Corp., 441 F.3d 991, 996 (Fed. Cir. 2006) (court can choose from dictionary definitions as directed by intrinsic evidence); Free Motion Fitness, Inc. v. Cybex Int'l, Inc., 423 F.3d 1343, 1349 (Fed. Cir. 2005); *Phillips,* 415 at 1313.

[24] Aqua-Aerobic Sys., Inc v. Aerators Inc., 211 F.3d 1241, 1245 (Fed. Cir. 2000); *see also* Serio-US Indus., Inc. v. Plastic Recovery Technologies Corp., 459 F.3d 1311, 1319 (Fed. Cir. 2006); *Philips,* 415 F.3d at 1318 (expert testimony may be admitted "to provide background on the technology at issue, to explain how an invention works, to ensure that the court's understanding of the technical aspects of the patent is consistent with that of a person of skill in the art, or to establish that a particular term in the patent or the prior art has a particular meaning in the pertinent field.").

[25] *Network Commerce,* 422 F.3d at 1361; *Phillips,* 415 F.3d at 1318.

[26] Senmed, Inc. v. Richard-Allan Medical Indus., Inc., 888 F.2d 815, 819 (Fed. Cir. 1989); North American Vaccine, Inc. v. American Cyanamid Co., 7 F.3d 1571, 1575–76 (Fed. Cir. 1993).

[27] *See* Thorner v. Sony Computer Entertainment America LLC, 669 F.3d 1362, 1365 (Fed. Cir. 2012); Sinorgchem Co. v. Int'l Trade Comm'n, 511 F.3d 1132, 1136 (Fed. Cir. 2007); Honeywell Int'l, Inc. v. Universal Avionics Sys. Corp., 493 F.3d 1358, 1361 (Fed. Cir. 2007) ("When a patentee defines a claim term, the patentee's definition governs, even if it is contrary to the conventional meaning of the term."); Phillips v. AWH Corp., 415 F.3d 1303, 1316 (Fed. Cir. 2005) (en banc).

their ordinary sense, or new words can be invented. Applicants can dis-claim broader meanings that the ordinary sense of claim language would otherwise support.[28] Nevertheless, if the applicant uses words in a special-ized or unusual sense, that sense must be made clear in the patent specification.[29]

The patent specification is a place for the applicant to elaborate on the invention, and it serves as a "dictionary" to define, expressly or by implication, any specialized meaning to be given terms used in the claims. Accordingly, the specification is "the single best guide to the meaning of a disputed term."[30] In all cases it is highly relevant, and in many it is dispositive.[31] If the specification clearly shows that the appli-cant did not use a term in its ordinary sense, the specification takes precedence.[32]

Although the specification is an indispensable tool for claim interpreta-tion, there is always a danger that it will be used not to *define* a term used in a claim but to *add limitations* that do not appear in the claim at all. A specification must describe specific examples, or "preferred embodi-ments," that fall within the scope of the patent claims but are not

---

[28] *See Thorner*, 669 F.3d at 1366 (" 'The patentee may demonstrate intent to deviate from the ordinary and accustomed meaning of a claim term by including in the specification expressions of manifest exclusion or restriction, representing a clear disavowal of claim scope.' "); Abbott Labs. v. Sandoz, Inc., 566 F.3d 1282, 1288 (Fed. Cir. 2009) (en banc) ("inventors and applicants may intentionally disclaim, or disavow, subject matter that would otherwise fall within the scope of the claim").

[29] *See Thorner*, 669 F.3d at 1365 ("To act as its own lexicographer, a patentee must 'clearly set forth a definition of the disputed claim term' other than its plain and ordinary meaning."); Merck & Co. v. Teva Pharmaceuticals USA, Inc., 395 F.3d 1364, 1370 (Fed. Cir. 2005); Bell Atlantic Network Services, Inc. v. Covad Communications Gp., Inc., 262 F.2d 1258, 1268 (Fed. Cir. 2001). The specification "must clearly redefine a claim term 'so as to put a reasonable competitor or one reasonably skilled in the art on notice that the pat-entee intended to so redefine that claim term.' " Elekta Instrument S.A. v. O.U.R. Scientific Int'l. Inc., 214 F.3d 1302, 1307 (Fed. Cir. 2000).

[30] American Piledriving Equip., Inc. v. Geoquip, Inc., 637 F.3d 1324, 1333 (Fed. Cir. 2011); Kim v. Conagra Foods, Inc., 465 F.3d 1312, 1318 (Fed. Cir. 2006); *Phillips*, 415 F.3d at 1321; Vitronics Corp. v. Conceptronic, Inc., 90 F.3d 1576, 1582 (Fed. Cir. 1996).

[31] Eon-Net LP v. Flagstar Bancorp, 653 F.3d 1314, 1320–21 (Fed. Cir. 2011); *American Piledriving*, 637 F.3d at 1333; Lazare Kaplan Int'l, Inc. v. Photoscribe Technologies, Inc., 628 F.3d 1359, 1368 (Fed. Cir. 2010); *Phillips*, 415 F.3d at 1315.

[32] *Phillips*, 415 F.3d at 1316.

co-extensive with them.[33] The details of these preferred embodiments do not limit the scope of the claims.[34]

Consider, for example, the claims in *In re Paulsen*,[35] which described a "portable computer" with a hinged case allowing the display screen to be latched in an upright position during use. The patentee argued that the term "portable computer" did not include a calculator. If the claims did cover a calculator, they would be found invalid because of a prior Japanese patent. The patentee pointed out that the specific "portable computer" disclosed in the specification incorporated a sophisticated display, advanced data-processing capability, communications ports, and other attributes that are characteristic of a laptop personal computer rather than a calculator. Nevertheless, the court found that none of these things were required by the claims. Because the claims merely said "portable computer," and the court found that a calculator was a kind of "portable

---

[33] See Section 3.3. It is seldom correct to interpret claim language to exclude the patentee's own preferred embodiments. *See In re* Katz Interactive Call Processing Patent Litigation, 639 F.3d 1303, 1324 (Fed. Cir. 2011) ("there is a strong presumption against a claim construction that excludes a disclosed embodiment"); Oatey Co. v. IPS Corp., 514 F.3d 1271, 1277 (Fed. Cir. 2008); *Vitronics*, 90 F.3d at 1583 ("[s]uch an interpretation is rarely, if ever, correct and would require highly persuasive evidentiary support"). But on occasion no other reading of the claim language is possible. *See Elekta*, 214 F.3d at 1308 ("in light of the prosecution history and the unambiguous language of the amended claim, we conclude that this is the rare case in which such an interpretation is compelled"). Often certain claims were intended to cover only a subset of the preferred embodiments disclosed. *See* Helmsderfer v. Bobrick Washroom Equip., Inc. 527 F.3d 1379, 1383 (Fed. Cir. 2008).

[34] *See* MySpace, Inc. v. Graphon Corp., 672 F.3d 1250, 1255 (Fed. Cir. 2012); Thorner v. Sony Computer Entertainment America LLC, 669 F.3d 1362, 1366 (Fed. Cir. 2012) ("We do not read limitations from the specification into claims; we do not redefine words. Only the patentee can do that."); *Abbott Labs.*, 566 F.3d at 1288 ("When consulting the specification to clarify the meaning of claim terms, courts must take care not to import limitations into the claims from the specification."); *Phillips*, 415 F.3d at 1323 ("although the specification often describes very specific embodiments of the invention, we have repeatedly warned against confining the claims to those embodiments"). Even if the specification describes only one embodiment, the claims will not be limited to that embodiment without " 'words or expressions of manifest exclusion or restriction.' " Arlington Indus., Inc. v. Bridgeport Fittings, Inc., 632 F.3d 1246, 1254 (Fed. Cir. 2011); Trading Technologies Int'l, Inc. v. Espeed, Inc., 595 F.3d 1340, 1352 (Fed. Cir. 2010); *Abbott Labs.*, 566 F.3d at 1288. There is one clear exception to the rule that limitations found only in the specification cannot be read into the claims. This exception applies to claims drafted in the "means-plus-function" format provided for in 35 U.S.C. § 112(f). Claims of this type are discussed in Section 7.7.4.

[35] 30 F.3d 1475 (Fed. Cir. 1994).

computer" as that term is generally understood, the claims were broad enough to include a calculator.[36]

Sometimes, as in *Paulsen*, the patentee tries to "read into" the claims limitations found in the specification in order to narrow the claims sufficiently to avoid the prior art. In other cases, it is the accused infringer who seeks to read in those limitations in order to narrow the claim and avoid infringement. In neither case is the practice allowed.

There is often a fine line between "reading in" a limitation absent from the claims and using the specification to *interpret* the claims in a particular fashion.[37] The patentee in *Paulsen*, for example, might have argued that "computer" is a term with various meanings and that reading the claim language *in light of* the specification would suggest the narrower meaning. Resolving the tension between interpreting claim language in light of the specification and reading into the claim limitations found *only* in the specification depends upon how the specification characterizes the invention.[38] The specification may "refer[] to a limitation only as a part of less than all possible embodiments," or it may "suggest[] that the very character of the invention requires [that] the limitation be a part of every embodiment."[39] Consistent references to a particular embodiment as "this invention" or "the present invention" may lead a court to interpret claim language in a more limited way than would otherwise be the case.[40]

So long as the specification is only used to interpret what the claim language means, courts preserve the principle that it is the claims, not the disclosed embodiments, that measure the scope of the invention. Some recent cases, however, suggest using the specification to determine what it was the

---

[36] *Id.* at 1479–80.

[37] *See Abbott Labs.*, 566 F.3d at 1288 ("This court has recognized a 'fine line between' the encouraged and the prohibited use of the specification."); *Phillips*, 415 F.3d at 1323; Liebel-Flarsheim Co. v. Medrad Inc., 358 F.3d 898, 904 (Fed. Cir. 2004).

[38] Alloc, Inc. v. International Trade Comm'n, 342 F.3d 1361, 1370 (Fed. Cir. 2003).

[39] *Id.*

[40] *See* Absolute Software, Inc. v. Stealth Signal, Inc., 659 F.3d 1121, 1136 (Fed. Cir. 2011); Trading Technologies Int'l, Inc. v. Espeed, Inc., 595 F.3d 1340, 1353 (Fed. Cir. 2010); Edward Lifesciences LLC v. Cook Inc., 582 F.2d 1322, 1330 (Fed. Cir. 2009). The court may "suppl[y] a definition by implication" where "the specification manifests a clear intention to limit the term by using it in a manner consistent with only a single meaning." *Arlington*, 632 F.3d at 1254. If the specification strongly discourages a particular approach, the claims may be interpreted to exclude that approach. *See* Honeywell Int'l, Inc. v. ITT Indus., Inc., 452 F.3d 1312, 1320 (Fed. Cir. 2006) ("Repeated derogatory statements concerning one type of material" served as a disavowal of the subject matter: "If the written description could talk, it would say, 'Do not use carbon fibers.' ").

patentee "actually invented" and limiting the patentee to that "actual invention." For example, in *Retractable Technologies, Inc. v. Becton, Dickinson & Co.*,[41] the patentee claimed a retractable syringe, one element of which was "a hollow syringe body." The issue in dispute was whether the "body" had to be a one-piece structure or whether it could be built from multiple pieces. Although the claims did not refer to a "one-piece body," every example of the "body" discussed in the specification was made from a single piece, and the patentee distinguished prior art designs that failed to recognize the possibility of one-piece construction. The court concluded that "body" should be limited to a one-piece structure in order to "tether the claims to what the specifications indicate the inventor actually invented."[42]

This approach suggests that the scope of the patent is governed by the claim language and by the "actual invention," as revealed in the patent specification. Each is a "limiting factor."[43] If this means that the specification is both a tool for interpreting claim language *and* an independent basis for determining the scope of the patentee's right to exclude, it is a departure from what the Federal Circuit has previously called a "bedrock principle" of patent law–that the claims alone define what the patent covers.[44] It remains to be seen whether the Federal Circuit will apply this two-pronged analysis consistently.

---

[41] 653 F.3d 1296 (Fed. Cir. 2011).

[42] *Id.* at 1305. The opinion in *Retractable Technologies* was written by Judge Lourie, who had dissented in *Arlington*, a previous case involving a patented cable connector. The claims in *Arlington* required a circular "spring metal adapter." In every instance, the patent specification illustrated the "spring metal adapter" as a ring with a gap in it to provide flexibility. However, the court determined that the *claims* did not require such a gap; "spring metal" referred only to the type of metal from which the adapter must be constructed. Judge Lourie disagreed. It was clear to him that the patentee had contemplated a split ring adapter as a part of the invention and that the claims should be limited accordingly. "The bottom line of claim construction," he wrote, is "that the claims should not mean more that what the specification indicates, in one way or another, the inventors invented." *Arlington*, 632 F.3d at 1258 (Lourie, J., concurring in part and dissenting in part).

[43] *See MySpace*, 672 F.3d at 1256 ("An inventor is entitled to claim in a patent what he has invented, but no more. He can, however, claim less, to avoid prior art or for any other reason. Therefore, in construing a claim there are two limiting factors–what was invented, and what exactly was claimed."). Although it is true that a patentee cannot claim more than he or she has invented, the conventional way to deal with that issue is through the enablement and written description requirements discussed in Sections 8.6 and 8.8.

[44] *Arlington*, 632 F.3d at 1253 (" 'It is a "bedrock principle" of patent law that "the claims of a patent define the invention to which the patentee is entitled the right to exclude." ' "); *see also* Falana v. Kent State University, 669 F.3d 1314, 1355 (Fed. Cir. 2012) (" '[I]t is the *claims*, not the written description, which define the scope of the patent right.' ").

7.3 THE PROSECUTION HISTORY

Another resource for interpreting claim language is the prosecution history. The prosecution history is a complete record of the proceedings before the Patent Office, including the prior art cited during examination and any representations that may have been made by the applicant concerning the proper interpretation of the claims.[45] The prosecution history may be more ambiguous than the specification because it documents an ongoing discussion between the patent applicant and the examiner.[46] Nevertheless, the prosecution history can "demonstrat[e] how the inventor understood the invention and whether the inventor limited the invention ... making the claim scope narrower than it would otherwise be."[47]

Claims must be interpreted in the same way in litigation as they were in the Patent Office. Otherwise applicants could treat their claims as a "nose of wax" to be twisted one direction in prosecution (perhaps to avoid a close prior art reference), then another direction in litigation (perhaps to encompass an accused product similar to that reference).[48] Such inconsistency in interpretation would pervert the process of examination, and it would hinder potential competitors who should be entitled to rely on the public record in judging the scope of the patentee's claims.[49]

During prosecution, an applicant may disavow a claim interpretation that would otherwise have been plausible based on the ordinary meaning

---

[45] *See* Phillips v. AWH Corp., 415 F.3d 1303, 1318 (Fed. Cir. 2005) (en banc) ("the prosecution history can often inform the meaning of the claim language by demonstrating how the inventor understood the invention"); Trading Technologies Int'l, Inc. v. Espeed, Inc., 595 F.3d 1340, 1352 (Fed. Cir. 2010).

[46] *See Trading Technologies*, 595 F.3d at 1352.

[47] *Id.*; *Phillips*, 415 F.3d at 1318; Seachange Int'l, Inc. v. C-Core, Inc., 413 F.3d 1361, 1372 (Fed. Cir. 2005).

[48] *See* Vitronics Corp. v. Conceptronic, Inc., 90 F.3d 1576, 1583 (Fed. Cir. 1996); Southwall Technologies, Inc. v. Cardinal IG Co., 54 F.3d 1570, 1578 (Fed. Cir. 1995).

[49] *See* Springs Window Fashions LP v. Novo Indus., L.P., 323 F.3d 989, 995 (Fed. Cir. 2003) ("The public notice function of a patent and its prosecution history requires that a patentee be held to what he declares during the prosecution of his patent. A patentee may not state during prosecution that the claims do not cover a particular device and then change position and later sue a party who makes that same device for infringement.").

of the term.[50] The surrender must be "clear and unmistakable" from the perspective of a person of ordinary skill reviewing the prosecution history.[51] Occasionally, a court will overlook what was obviously a *mistaken* characterization of the invention by the applicant during prosecution.[52] This is appropriate, however, only when the error is so apparent that a reasonable person would not be misled.[53]

7.4 OTHER CLAIMS

Comparing different claims can assist in determining their meaning.[54] This particularly occurs in the context of the "doctrine of claim differentiation," which holds that each claim should be presumed to differ in

[50] *See* American Piledriving Equip., Inc. v. Geoquip, Inc., 637 F.3d 1324, 1336 (Fed. Cir. 2011) (the patentee, by arguing during prosecution that "integral" meant "one-piece," disavowed a broader construction); ERBE Elektromedizin GmbH v. Canady Technology LLC, 629 F.3d 1278, 1286–87 (Fed. Cir. 2010); Elbex Video, Ltd. v. Sensormatic Electronics Corp., 508 F.3d 1366, 1371 (Fed. Cir. 2007); Omega Eng'g, Inc. v. Raytek Corp., 334 F.3d 1314, 1324 (Fed. Cir. 2003) ("[W]here the patentee has unequivocally disavowed a certain meaning to obtain his patent, the doctrine of prosecution disclaimer attaches and narrows the ordinary meaning of the claim congruent with the scope of the surrender."). A disclaimer may occur "where an applicant argues that a claim possesses a feature that the prior art does not possess in order to overcome a prior art rejection." *Seachange*, 413 F.3d at 1372–73.

[51] Lazare Kaplan Int'l, Inc. v. Photoscribe Technologies, Inc., 628 F.3d 1359, 1370 (Fed. Cir. 2010); *Elbex*, 508 F.3d at 1371; *Seachange*, 413 F.3d at 1373 ("A disclaimer must be clear and unambiguous.").

[52] *See, e.g.*, Intervet America, Inc. v. Kee-Vet Labs., Inc., 887 F.2d 1050, 1053–54 (Fed. Cir. 1989).

[53] *See* Biotec Biologische Naturverpackungen GmbH v. Biocorp, Inc., 249 F.3d 1341, 1348 (Fed. Cir. 2001) ("An error in the prosecution record must be viewed as errors are in documents in general; that is, would it have been apparent to the interested reader that an error was made, such that it would be unfair to enforce the error."); Hockerson-Halberstadt, Inc. v. Avia Gp. Int'l, Inc., 222 F.3d 951, 957 (Fed. Cir. 2000) (distinguishing *Intervet* and denying the patentee the requested "mulligan that would erase from the prosecution history the inventor's disavowal of a particular aspect of a claim term's meaning").

[54] *See* American Piledriving Equip., Inc. v. Geoquip, Inc., 637 F.3d 1324, 1333 (Fed. Cir. 2011); Phillips v. AWH Corp., 415 F.3d 1303, 1314 (Fed. Cir. 2005) (en banc) ("Because claim terms are normally used consistently throughout the patent, the usage of a term in one claim can often illuminate the meaning of the same term in other claims."). A term is "presumed to have the same meaning throughout all the claims in the absence of any reason to believe otherwise." Digital-Vending Services Int'l, LLC v. University of Phoenix, Inc., 672 F.3d 1270, 1275 (Fed. Cir. 2012).

scope from every other claim.[55] If, for example, a dependent claim adds a limitation to an independent claim, one should presume that the same limitation is not present, implicitly, in both claims.[56] The assumption is that an applicant would not intentionally draft two claims that covered, in different words, precisely the same subject matter. The doctrine of claim differentiation is not absolute, however.[57] Sometimes the only reasonable interpretation of a claim is one that makes it redundant.

7.5 VALIDITY

Another basic principle of claim interpretation is that claims should, if possible, be read in a manner that preserves their validity.[58] Perhaps the underlying assumption is that the interpretation supporting validity must be what the Patent Office had in mind when it approved the application. Like the doctrine of claim differentiation, this principle does not

---

[55] *See* Bradford Co. v. Conteyor North America, Inc., 603 F.3d 1262, 1271 (Fed. Cir. 2010); Curtiss-Wright Flow Control Corp. v. Velan, Inc., 438 F.3d 1374, 1380 (Fed. Cir. 2006); Kraft Foods, Inc. v. International Trading Co., 203 F.3d 1362, 1366 (Fed. Cir. 2000) ("two claims of a patent are presumptively of different scope"). Usually, claim language should not be read in a manner that renders terms superfluous. *See Digital-Vending*, 672 F.3d at 1275; Beachcombers, Int'l, Inc. v. Wildwood Creative Prods., Inc., 31 F.3d 1154, 1162 (Fed. Cir. 1994) (an interpretation that renders a claim superfluous is "presumptively unreasonable").

[56] *See* Aspex Eyewear, Inc. v. Marchon Eyewear, Inc., 672 F.3d 1335, 1348 (Fed. Cir. 2012); *Curtiss-Wright*, 438 F.3d at 1380; *Phillips*, 415 F.3d at 1315; SunRace Roots Enterprise Co. v. SRAM Corp., 336 F.3d 1298, 1303 (Fed. Cir. 2003) (the "presumption is especially strong when the limitation in dispute is the only meaningful difference between an independent and dependent claim").

[57] *See* Regents of the University of California v. Dakocytomation California, Inc., 517 F.3d 1364, 1375 (Fed. Cir. 2008); *Curtiss-Wright*, 438 F.3d at 1380–81; *Kraft Foods*, 203 F.3d at 1368 (claim differentiation "is 'not a hard and fast rule' ").

[58] Liebel-Flarsheim Co. v. Medrad Inc., 358 F.3d 898, 911 (Fed. Cir. 2004); Tate Access Floors, Inc. v. Interface Architectural Resources, Inc., 279 F.3d 1357, 1367 (Fed. Cir. 2002); Apple Computer, Inc. v. Articulate Sys., Inc., 234 F.3d 14, 24 (Fed. Cir. 2000) ("'claims should be read in a way that avoids ensnaring the prior art if it is possible to do so' "). The rule applies, however, only if the meaning of the claim remains ambiguous in spite of the normal procedures of claim interpretation. *Liebel-Flarsheim*, 358 F.3d at 911.

justify a claim interpretation that is unreasonable or unsupported by the evidence.[59]

In any case, a claim must be interpreted in the same way when the issue is infringement as it is when the issue is validity.[60] If a claim is interpreted in a narrow fashion to avoid a potentially invalidating prior art reference, that same narrow interpretation must be applied when comparing the claim to the accused product. The meaning of a claim cannot change to suit the convenience of the patent owner.[61]

7.6 PREAMBLES

A peculiar rule of claim interpretation involves the "preamble"–the first paragraph of a patent claim, typically ending with the word "comprising." In the claim set out at the beginning of this chapter, the preamble language is "An aqueous cosmetic emulsion comprising. ..." The preamble often characterizes the category of invention or its intended use–for instance, a mousetrap or a "cosmetic emulsion"–but it does not in itself recite the checklist of claim elements that defines the patented invention. In such cases the preamble is not considered a claim limitation,[62] and this can have

---

[59] *See* Rembrandt Data Technologies, LP v. AOL, LLC, 641 F.3d 1331, 1339 (Fed. Cir. 2011) (courts will not " 'redraft claims, whether to make them operable or sustain their validity' "); Lucent Technologies, Inc. v. Gateway, Inc., 525 F.3d 1200, 1215 (Fed. Cir. 2008); Nazomi Communications, Inc. v. ARM Holdings, PLC, 403 F.3d 1364, 1368 (Fed. Cir. 2005) (interpretation preserving validity adopted only "if practicable"); Quantum Corp. v. Rodime, PLC, 65 F.3d 1577, 1584 (Fed. Cir. 1995) ("Although [courts] construe claims, if possible, so as to sustain their validity . . . it is well settled that no matter how great the temptations of fairness or policy making, courts do not redraft claims."). Claim construction should not *begin* with preserving the validity of the claim; when it does, "the construing court has put the validity cart before the claim construction horse." *Nazomi*, 403 F.3d at 1369.

[60] Kim v. Conagra Foods, Inc., 465 F.3d 1312, 1324 (Fed. Cir. 2006); Amgen, Inc. v. Hoechst Marion Roussel, Inc., 314 F.3d 1313, 1330 (Fed. Cir. 2003); Amazon.com, Inc. v. Barnesandnoble.com, Inc., 239 F.3d 1343, 1351 (Fed. Cir. 2001).

[61] A disadvantage borne by patent owners in litigation is that they must find a single claim interpretation that supports a finding of *both* validity and infringement. An accused infringer, on the other hand, can be satisfied with an interpretation that renders the claim invalid *or* a different interpretation that renders the claim not infringed. Which interpretation the court chooses may be a matter of indifference to the accused infringer.

[62] *See* American Medical Sys., Inc. v. Biolitec, Inc., 618 F.3d 1354, 1358 (Fed. Cir. 2010) (" 'Generally . . . the preamble does not limit the claims.' "); Symantec Corp. v. Computer Assoc. Int'l, Inc., 522 F.3d 1279, 1288 (Fed. Cir. 2008). "[I]t is assumed that the preamble language is duplicative of the language found in the body of the claims or merely provides context for the claims, absent any indication to the contrary in the claims, the specification or the prosecution history." *Symantec*, 522 F.3d at 1289.

important consequences. Imagine a product identical to the "cosmetic emulsion" described in the example but used as an industrial lubricant. If the preamble were disregarded, the lubricant would infringe the claim.[63]

Courts treat a preamble as a claim limitation only if it " 'recites essential structure or steps, or if it is necessary to give life, meaning, and vitality to the claim.' "[64] This is a nebulous distinction. On occasion the preamble must be counted because the "body" of the claim that follows includes references to language found there. The body of the claim used as an example refers to "said emulsion," so it is likely that a court would consider the "aqueous cosmetic emulsion" language a claim limitation.[65] On other occasions, preamble language is "essential" because the applicant relied upon it to distinguish the invention from the prior art.[66] On the other hand, if the preamble states an intended use or environment for the invention,

---

[63] In some cases, the patentee prefers the preamble to be treated as a claim limitation, so that the patent is not anticipated by the prior art. *See, e.g.*, Marrin v. Griffin, 599 F.3d 1290, 1292–93 (Fed. Cir. 2010) (claim to scratch-off labels allowing party guests to mark their beverage containers for identification, but mentioning the writing function that distinguished the invention only in the claim preamble).

[64] *American Medical*, 618 F.3d at 1358; *see also Symantec*, 522 F.3d at 1288; NTP, Inc. v. Research in Motion, Ltd., 418 F.3d 1282, 1305 (Fed. Cir. 2005); Bicon, Inc. v. Straumann Co., 441 F.3d 945, 952 (Fed. Cir. 2006). There is no "litmus test" for deciding if a preamble should be considered a claim limitation. *Bicon*, 441 F.3d at 952; *see also American Medical*, 618 F.3d at 1358 ("there is no simple test"). "To say that a preamble is a limitation if it gives 'meaning to the claim' may merely state the problem rather than lead one to the answer." Corning Glass Works v. Sumitomo Electric U.S.A., Inc., 868 F.2d 1251, 1257 (Fed. Cir. 1989). The decision must be made in the context of the entire patent, which may establish " 'what the inventors actually invented and intended to encompass by the claim.' " Catalina Mktg. Int'l, Inc. v. Coolsavings.com, Inc., 289 F.3d 801, 808 (Fed. Cir. 2002). Specifically, structures or steps recited in the preamble and "underscored as important by the specification" are more likely to be considered claim limitations. *Id.* A preamble is not limiting if it is " 'simply an introduction to the general field of the claim.' " Hearing Components, Inc. v. Shure, Inc., 600 F.3d 1357, 1366 (Fed. Cir. 2010).

[65] *See Bicon*, 441 F.3d at 952 ("when the limitations in the body of the claim 'rely upon and derive antecedent basis from the preamble, then the preamble may act as a necessary component of the claimed invention' "); *NTP*, 418 F.3d at 1306.

[66] *See Marrin*, 599 F.3d at 1294 ("[c]lear reliance on a preamble during prosecution can distinguish a claimed invention from the prior art and render the preamble a claim limitation"); *Hearing Components*, 600 F.3d at 1366 ("such reliance demonstrates that the feature disclosed in the preamble is necessary to the patentability of the claim"); *Symantec*, 522 F.3d at 1288.

but the remainder of the claim by itself describes what the invention *is*, then the preamble will not be treated as a part of the claim.[67]

If the claim read without the preamble leaves one guessing what the invention is, then the preamble cannot be ignored. In *Diversitech Corp. v. Century Steps, Inc.*,[68] the claim referred to an equipment-supporting base comprising a foam core and a cementitious coating. Without the preamble, the claim would have referred to the core and the coating, but one would have no idea what the invention really was. In *Diversitech* the court found the preamble necessary to define the invention. In contrast, in *STX LLC v. Brine, Inc.*,[69] the preamble boasted that the patented lacrosse stick would provide "improved handling and playing characteristics." Because the remainder of the claim stood alone as a structurally complete description of the stick, the court did not find that the preamble language limited the claim.[70]

On the subject of preambles, it is important to note the difference between "comprising" and "consisting of," the two phrases that typically conclude a claim preamble. "Comprising" is a term of art, meaning that the invention consists of the following combination of claim elements, by themselves or in combination with additional elements.[71] In *Gillette Co. v. Energizer Holdings, Inc.*,[72] the court found that claims to a razor "comprising" three blades could be applied to four-blade razors too. A four-blade

---

[67] "A preamble is not regarded as limiting ... 'when the claim body describes a structurally complete invention such that deletion of the preamble phrase does not affect the structure or steps of the claimed invention.'" *American Medical,* 618 F.3d at 1358; *see also Marrin,* 599. F.3d at 1294; *Symantec,* 522 F.3d at 1288; *Catalina,* 289 F.3d at 808 (preamble is not limiting where the patentee uses it "'only to state a purpose or intended use for the invention.'"). "[P]reamble language merely extolling benefits or features of the claimed invention does not limit the claim scope without clear reliance on those benefits or features as patentably significant." *Catalina,* 289 F.3d at 809. Moreover, a preamble is not limiting if it can be construed as "merely duplicative of the limitations in the body of the claim." *American Medical,* 618 F.3d at 1359. Similar rules apply to "whereby clauses." If a method claim describes a step "whereby" the invention accomplishes some task, the clause will be overlooked if it does no more than recite the intended result. On the other hand, if the whereby clause "states a condition that is material to patentability, it cannot be ignored in order to change the substance of the invention." Hoffer v. Microsoft Corp., 405 F.3d 1326, 1329 (Fed. Cir. 2005).

[68] 850 F.2d 675, 677–78 (Fed. Cir. 1988).

[69] 211 F.3d 588 (Fed. Cir. 2000).

[70] *Id.* at 591.

[71] *See* Carl Zeiss Stiftung v. Renishaw PLC, 945 F.2d 1173, 1178 (Fed. Cir. 1991); Water Technologies Corp. v. Calco, Ltd., 850 F.2d 660, 666 (Fed. Cir. 1988).

[72] 405 F.3d 1367 (Fed. Cir. 2005).

razor has three blades–plus one more. "Consisting of," on the other hand, means "the following elements *and no others*."[73] "Comprising" is the broader and generally more useful term. If the preamble ends with "consisting essentially of," the claim allows additional unrecited ingredients, but only if they do not change the basic characteristics of the combination.[74]

7.7 SPECIAL CLAIM FORMATS

Several specialized claim formats are available to inventors who wish to use them.

7.7.1 Jepson Claims

One specialized claim format is known as a "Jepson claim."[75] A Jepson claim covers an improvement to an existing product. The Jepson format includes a recitation of the pre-existing components in the preamble and the improvement in the body of the claim.[76] For example:

> In an instrument marker pen body including an ink reservoir and means for receiving a writing tip, *the improvement comprising* a pen arm holding means consisting of an integrally molded hinged member adapted to fold against a surface of the pen body and to be locked against said surface by engageable locking means and to receive and secure in place against said surface a pen arm when said hinged member is in its folded and locked position.[77]

The words "In a [pre-existing device], the improvement comprising" are typical of a Jepson claim. The significance of a Jepson claim is that the elements recited in the preamble are claim limitations, and the patent applicant, by implication, admits that those elements exist in the prior art.[78]

---

[73] *See* CIAS, Inc. v. Alliance Gaming Corp., 504 F.3d 1356, 1361 (Fed. Cir. 2007).

[74] *See Water Technologies*, 850 F.2d at 666.

[75] Named after Ex parte Jepson, 243 O.G. 525 (Ass't Comm'r Pat. 1917), the case that first approved the format.

[76] *See* Ethicon Endo-Surgery, Inc. v. U.S. Surgical Corp., 93 F.3d 1572, 1577 (Fed. Cir. 1996).

[77] Pentec, Inc. v. Graphic Controls Corp., 776 F.2d 309, 312 (Fed. Cir. 1985) (emphasis added).

[78] *Id.* at 315.

7.7.2 Markush Claims

Another specialized claim format is the "Markush claim," generally used to describe chemical and biological inventions. A Markush claim includes a claim element selected from a group of possibilities—for example, "a sugar selected from the group consisting of sucrose, fructose, and lactose."[79] "Markush groups" are used when there is no generic term that conveniently describes the desired claim element.[80]

7.7.3 Product-by-Process Claims

While most patent claims can be characterized as process, apparatus, or composition-of-matter claims, a "product-by-process" claim straddles the usual categories. A product-by-process claim, as the name suggests, describes a product made by a specific process. Traditionally, product-by-process claims have been used when the invention is best described in terms of how it is made rather than what it is.[81] Consider how an omelet could be described to someone who had never seen one. One might attempt to describe an omelet in physical or chemical terms, but a better approach would be to provide the recipe. At one time product-by-process claims were allowed only when the invention could not be described except through the "recipe"—for example, when the precise physical characteristics of the product could not be determined. Now they are allowed even if they are not strictly necessary.

Until recently, there was much confusion regarding the role to be given the process in interpreting a product-by-process claim. Some cases held that the process elements could be ignored when determining infringement, so that if the claim recited the product of process X, an identical product made by a different process would still infringe.[82] According to this way of thinking, the process recited in a product-by-process claim simply defines the product in a round-about manner. The subject matter of the claim is still the omelet, not the recipe. Other cases held the opposite, maintaining that only a product made by the recited process could infringe a

---

[79] For an example of a Markush claim, see *Merck & Co., Inc. v. Mylan Pharmaceuticals, Inc.*, 190 F.3d 1335, 1339 (Fed. Cir. 1999). A Markush claim can be anticipated if even one of the items in the listed group is found in the prior art. *See* Fresenius USA, Inc. v. Baxter Int'l, Inc., 582 F.3d 1288, 1298 (Fed. Cir. 2009).

[80] *See* Application of Weber, 580 F.2d 455, 457 n.4 (C.C.P.A. 1978).

[81] *See In re* Thorpe, 777 F.2d 695, 697 (Fed. Cir. 1985).

[82] *See, e.g.*, Scripps Clinic & Research Foundation v. Genentech, Inc., 927 F.2d 1565, 1583 (Fed. Cir. 1991) ("[T]he correct reading of product-by-process claims is that they are not limited to product[s] prepared by the process set forth in the claims.").

product-by-process claim.[83] After years of uncertainty, the Federal Circuit considered the issue en banc in *Abbott Labs. v. Sandoz, Inc.*[84] and decided that process terms in product-by-process claims limit the scope of the claim.[85] In other words, if a product-by-process claim describes a product made by process X, an identical product made by process Y does *not* infringe.[86] The court relied, in part, on the practical difficulty of determining that a product made by a different process is, in fact, identical, if the claims describe the patented product in terms of process alone.

7.7.4 Means-Plus-Function Claims

One form of specialized claim format that has become extremely common is the "means-plus-function" format authorized by 35 U.S.C. § 112(f).[87] At one time, courts held that a claim to an apparatus must describe the features of the apparatus in precise physical terms rather than in terms of the functions they perform. So, for example, a claim to a mouse-trap could properly refer to a "steel spring" but could not refer simply to a "means for snapping the trap shut." The latter claim would literally cover a mousetrap with a steel spring, a plastic spring, a rubber band, or any other mechanism that might close the trap. Such a claim would not adequately define the invention because it could cover many things that the patentee had not invented or disclosed.

Permitting a patentee to describe a feature of the invention in terms of its function does have certain advantages, however. In the prior example, the inventor might have in mind the steel spring, the plastic spring, the rubber band, and dozens of other means for snapping the trap shut, and the choice of which to use might have little to do with the essence of the invention. A person skilled in designing mousetraps who read the patent might also realize that various forms of springs and elastic bands could be used. In this situation, it would seem pointless to require the inventor to provide a long list of every variety of spring, rubber band, or similar device that the inventor could imagine. Moreover, it might be too easy for a competitor to avoid the patent simply by coming up with a closing mechanism that the patentee had neglected to list.

---

[83] *See, e.g.,* Atlantic Thermoplastics Co. v. Faytex Corp., 970 F.2d 834 (Fed. Cir. 1992).

[84] 566 F.3d 1282 (Fed. Cir. 2009).

[85] *Id.* at 1293.

[86] *See id.* at 1294 ("Because the inventor chose to claim the product in terms of its process . . . that definition also governs the enforcement of the bounds of the patent right. This court cannot simply ignore as verbiage the only definition supplied by the inventor.").

[87] Before the America Invents Act added subsection headings to § 112, the relevant language was referred to as § 112, Paragraph 6.

The result of this tension between convenience and the need for specificity in claim drafting was legislative compromise, embodied in § 112(f), which states:

> An element in a claim for a combination may be expressed as a means or step for performing a specified function without the recital of structure, material or acts in support thereof, and such claim shall be construed to cover the corresponding structure, material, or acts described in the specification and equivalents thereof.

Accordingly, an inventor can choose to describe an element of the invention as a physical structure (i.e., "steel spring") or as a "means" for performing a specified function (i.e., "means for snapping the trap shut"), leaving it to the specification to describe the physical structure that performs the function. If the inventor chooses the latter option, the claim will cover the specific structure disclosed in the specification and "equivalents" of that structure (i.e., a mousetrap with a steel spring or the equivalent of a steel spring).[88] Deciding what is "equivalent" is a matter discussed in Section 10.7.

Although any claim element including the word "means" is presumed to be a means-plus-function element construed in accordance with § 112(f),[89] that presumption can be rebutted if the claim element, contrary to the

---

[88] For an inventor to take advantage of § 112(f), the patent or prosecution history must provide a clear association between the means element and the corresponding structure in the specification. Default Proof Credit Card Sys., Inc. v. Home Depot U.S.A., Inc., 412 F.3d 1291, 1298 (Fed. Cir. 2005). If multiple structures described in the specification perform the specified function, the means element reads on each of them and their equivalents. *See* Linear Technology Corp. v. Impala Linear Corp., 379 F.3d 1311, 1322 (Fed. Cir. 2004); TI Gp. Automotive Sys., Inc. v. VDO North America, L.L.C., 375 F.3d 1126, 1137 (Fed. Cir. 2004). If *no* embodiment described in the specification provides structure to support the means-plus-function element, then the claim is invalid on grounds of indefiniteness. Blackboard, Inc. v. Desire2Learn, Inc., 574 F.3d 1371, 1382 (Fed. Cir. 2009); Biomedino, LLC v. Waters Technologies Corp., 490 F.3d 946, 950 (Fed. Cir. 2007); Intellectual Property Development Inc. v. UA-Columbia Cablevision of Westchester Inc., 336 F.3d 1308, 1319 (Fed. Cir. 2003). *See* Section 8.5.

[89] Inventio AG v. Thyssenkrupp Elevator Americas Corp., 649 F.3d 1350, 1356 (Fed. Cir. 2011); Rembrandt Data Technologies, LP v. AOL, LLC, 641 F.3d 1331, 1340 (Fed. Cir. 2011); Welker Bearing Co. v. PHD, Inc., 550 F.3d 1090, 1096 (Fed. Cir. 2008).

language of § 112(f), *does* recite structure.[90] For example, in *Envirco Corp. v. Clestra Cleanroom, Inc.*,[91] the Federal Circuit held that a claim element calling for a "second baffle means" was not a means-plus-function element because the claim recited structural information concerning the location and formation of the baffle.[92] The difference is significant; when a claim element is construed as a means-plus-function element, the patent owner is put to the additional burden of demonstrating that the structures of the accused product are identical or equivalent to the structures disclosed in the patent specification. Some patent applicants seem to overuse the "means" format, perhaps not appreciating the risks.[93]

Section 112(f) applies only to a "claim for a combination." A "single means claim" is invalid.[94] One cannot claim, for example, just "a means for catching a mouse" and leave it at that. The "means-plus-function" format can be used only when the claim breaks down the invention into specific components.

7.7.5 Step-Plus-Function Claims

The language of § 112(f) also provides for a "step-plus-function" claim—in other words, a process claim in which a step of the process is described solely in terms of the function performed by that step, without the recital of a specific act. Such a claim would cover the act described in the specification and its

---

[90] *See Rembrandt*, 641 F.3d at 1340 (" 'This presumption can be rebutted if the claim limitation itself recites sufficient structure to perform the claimed function in its entirety.' "); *Biomedino*, 490 F.3d at 950; *TI Gp.*, 375 F.3d at 1135; Micro Chemical, Inc. v. Great Plains Chemical Co., 194 F.3d 1250, 1257 (Fed. Cir. 1999). The presumption also fails if the claim element recites no function for the "means" to perform. *See* Allen Eng'g Corp. v. Bartell Indus., Inc., 299 F.3d 1336, 1347 (Fed. Cir. 2002). An element that does *not* use the word "means" is presumed *not* to be a "means-plus-function" element. *Inventio*, 649 F.3d at 1356 ("the presumption flowing from the absence of the word 'means' is a strong one that is not easily overcome"); Depuy Spine, Inc. v. Medtronic Sofamor Danek, Inc., 469 F.3d 1005, 1023 (Fed. Cir. 2006); MIT v. Abacus Software, 462 F.3d 1344, 1353 (Fed. Cir. 2006). However, the presumption will be rebutted and § 112(f) applied if, even in the absence of "means" vocabulary, the element employs functional language and omits an adequate disclosure of structure. *See Inventio*, 649 F.3d at 1356; *Welker*, 550 F.3d at 1096 ("mechanism for moving said finger" treated as a means-plus-function element because "mechanism," like "means," supplied no structural description); *MIT*, 462 F.3d at 1353-54; *but cf.* Lighting World, Inc. v. Birchwood Lighting, Inc., 382 F.3d 1354, 1358–61 (Fed. Cir. 2004) (although the term "connector" does not bring to mind any specific structure, it is still a structural term; it is not a nonce word like "widget" or "ram-a-fram").

[91] 209 F.3d 1360 (Fed. Cir. 2000).

[92] *Id.* at 1365.

[93] *See Allen Eng'g*, 299 F.3d at 1348 (patent applicant was "clearly enamored of the word 'means,' " using it repeatedly in conjunction with structural limitations).

[94] *See In re* Hyatt, 708 F.2d 712, 714 (Fed. Cir. 1983).

equivalents.[95] While it is comparatively easy to distinguish between a *function* and a *structure*, it is much more difficult to distinguish between a *function* and an *act*. Returning to the mousetrap example, a claim element that referred to a "means for snapping the trap shut" would clearly be a means-plus-function claim element because, other than the generic term "means," the language describes the physical structure solely in terms of the function it performs. Imagine, however, a mouse-trapping process claim, one element of which is "closing the trap to imprison the mouse." Is "closing the trap" (or for that matter "imprisoning the mouse") a "function" or an "act"? Does it describe the step itself or only the result of the step?

According to the Federal Circuit, a "function" refers to " '*what* a claim element ultimately accomplishes.' "[96] An "act" corresponds to " '*how* the function is accomplished.' "[97] This would suggest that "imprisoning the mouse" is a function and "closing the trap" is an act. However, it is difficult to maintain the supposed distinction. In *Masco Corp v. U.S.*, the court held that "transmitting a force" was an "act" because "transmitting" described *how* the force was conveyed through mechanical parts.[98] Yet "transmitting a force" could be understood as a necessary result, accomplished by the action of any number of mechanical contrivances—more of a *what* than a *how*.

The Federal Circuit seems reluctant to construe any claim as a step-plus-function claim—which is understandable given the difficulties. It has observed that "[i]f we were to construe every process claim containing steps described by an 'ing' verb, such as passing, heating, reacting, transferring, etc. into a step-plus-function limitation, we would be limiting process claims in a manner never intended by Congress."[99] Unless patentees find the step-plus-function option indispensable, which is unlikely considering how seldom courts hold it to apply, perhaps the best solution would be legislation removing the problematic language from § 112(f).

---

[95] The term "step for" suggests an intention to invoke § 112(f), though the term "steps of" does not. Masco Corp. v. U.S., 303 F.3d 1316, 1327 (Fed. Cir. 2002).

[96] *Id.* (emphasis in original).

[97] *Id.* (emphasis in original); *see also* Seal-Flex, Inc. v. Athletic Track and Court Construction, 172 F.3d 836, 849–50 (Fed. Cir. 1999) (Rader, J., concurring).

[98] *Masco*, 303 F.3d at 1328; *see also* O.I. Corp. v. Tamar Co., 115 F.3d 1576 (Fed. Cir. 1997) ("the step [] of . . . passing the [material] through a passage" construed as an "act" rather than a function).

[99] *O.I.*, 115 F.3d at 1583; *see also* Cardiac Pacemakers, Inc. v. St. Jude Medical, Inc., 381 F.3d 1371, 1382 (Fed. Cir. 2004) ("Method claims necessarily recite the steps of the method, and the preamble words that 'the method comprises the steps of' do not automatically convert each ensuing step into the form of [§ 112(f)]."). Claims that use the term "step for" are *not* presumed to be drafted with § 112(f) in mind; however, claims that *omit* the words "step for" are presumed to be ordinary method claims. *Id.* at 1382–83.

CHAPTER 8

Conditions of Patentability

8.1 EXAMINATION AND LITIGATION

Before a patent issues, the application must go through a process of "examination" by the Patent Office.[1] The purpose of the examination is to ensure that the application meets various requirements imposed by law. These requirements, which are explained in some detail in the pages that follow, include the following:

- The invention must have *utility*.
- The claims must be *definite*.
- The specification must *enable* the practice of the invention and must disclose the inventor's *best mode* of practicing the invention.[2]
- The claimed invention must be *novel*–that is, it must be *new* and *nonobvious* in comparison to the prior art.

In spite of the examination process, patents sometimes issue that fail to meet these fundamental requirements. This is not always the fault of the Patent Office. For example, the Patent Office cannot judge whether a claim is novel in comparison to an earlier product if, as not infrequently occurs, the Patent Office is not even aware of the earlier product. Moreover, patent

---

[1] *See* Section 5.1.
[2] Although the statute still requires disclosure of the inventor's best mode, because of the America Invents Act failure to disclose the best mode is no longer grounds to hold a patent invalid. *See* Section 8.7.

examination is not a practical forum for inquiring into certain questions, such as whether the invention works as the applicant claims it does. Questions like these can be explored effectively only in an adversarial proceeding. For all of these reasons, courts have the power to find an issued patent invalid,[3] and invalidity is a complete defense to infringement.[4]

The patentability requirements discussed in this chapter are relevant in the examination process, where they can be grounds for rejecting an application, and in the litigation context, where they can be grounds for holding an already issued patent invalid. There are some procedural differences in the way these requirements are enforced in the Patent Office and in the courts. For example, when judging whether a claim is novel, the Patent Office will give the claim its "broadest reasonable construction consistent with the specification"[5] A court will not.[6] Nevertheless, the rules and precedent that apply in one context generally apply in the other context as well.

8.2 PRESUMPTION OF VALIDITY

Although courts have the power to hold an issued patent invalid, they do not discount the work of the Patent Office entirely. All patents are presumed valid, and the burden of overcoming that presumption rests with the accused infringer.[7] The presumption of validity can only be overcome by "clear and convincing evidence."[8] This standard of proof is something less than the "beyond a reasonable doubt" standard of criminal law, but it

---

[3] *See* Pfizer, Inc. v. Apotex, Inc., 480 F.3d 1348, 1359 (Fed. Cir. 2007) ("a court is never bound by an examiner's finding in an ex parte patent application proceeding"); Quad Environmental Technologies Corp. v. Union Sanitary Dist., 946 F.2d 870, 876 (Fed. Cir. 1991) ("The courts are the final arbiter of patent validity and, although courts may take cognizance of, and benefit from, the proceedings before the patent examiner, the question is ultimately for the courts to decide, without deference to the rulings of the patent examiner.").

[4] Lough v. Brunswick Corp., 86 F.3d 1113, 1123 (Fed. Cir. 1996).

[5] *In re* Suitco Surface, Inc., 603 F.3d 1255, 1259 (Fed. Cir. 2010).

[6] *See* Atlantic Thermoplastics Co. v. Faytex Corp., 970 F.2d 834, 846 (Fed. Cir. 1992).

[7] 35 U.S.C. § 282 ("A patent shall be presumed valid. . . . The burden of establishing invalidity of a patent or any claim thereof shall rest on the party asserting such invalidity"); Microsoft Corp. v. i4i L.P., 131 S.Ct. 2238, 2243 (2011); Pfizer, Inc. v. Apotex, Inc., 480 F.3d 1348, 1359 (Fed. Cir. 2007). The presumption is "related to the presumption that the PTO does its job properly." Superior Fireplace Co. v. Majestic Prods. Co., 270 F.3d 1358, 1367 n.1 (Fed. Cir. 2001).

[8] *Microsoft*, 131 S.Ct. at 2245–46; Tokai Corp. v. Easton Enterprises, Inc., 632 F.3d 1358, 1367 (Fed. Cir. 2011); Uniloc USA Inc. v. Microsoft Corp., 632 F.3d 1292, 1321 (Fed. Cir. 2011); *Pfizer*, 480 F.3d at 1359.

requires more than just a preponderance of the evidence.[9] The presumption of validity applies only after a patent has issued; there is no presumption in the Patent Office in favor of the applicant.[10]

Some older cases found a weakened presumption of validity where the challenger relied on evidence that was not considered by the Patent Office.[11] The Federal Circuit, in contrast, has always maintained that the presumption of validity is ever-present and unchanging, no matter what grounds of invalidity may be asserted. [12] The Supreme Court confirmed that position recently.[13] Nevertheless, the challenger's burden of producing clear and convincing evidence is easier to meet if the argument is new because the court is not put in the position of contradicting the expertise of the Patent Office.[14]

The presumption of validity applies separately to each claim of a patent.[15] Even if Claim 1 has been proven invalid by clear and convincing evidence, Claim 2 is unaffected until a challenger proves that it, too, is invalid. Generally, a patentee's goal in litigation is to prove infringement of at least one valid claim.

---

[9] *Pfizer*, 480 F.3d at 1359 n.5 ("The 'clear and convincing' standard is an intermediate standard which lies somewhere in between the 'beyond a reasonable doubt' and the 'preponderance of the evidence' standards of proof."). Clear and convincing evidence must produce an "abiding conviction" that the facts are "highly probable." *Id.*

[10] *In re* Morris, 127 F.3d 1048, 1054 (Fed. Cir. 1997).

[11] *See Microsoft*, 131 S.Ct. at 2250–51.

[12] *Pfizer*, 480 F.3d at 1359–60; Hybritech Inc. v. Monoclonal Antibodies, Inc., 802 F.2d 1367, 1375 (Fed. Cir. 1986) ("the presumption remains intact and on the challenger throughout the litigation, and the clear and convincing evidence standard does not change").

[13] *Microsoft*, 131 S.Ct. at 2250.

[14] *Id.* at 2251 ("Simply put, if the PTO did not have all material facts before it, its considered judgment may lose significant force. . . . And, concomitantly, the challenger's burden to persuade the jury of its invalidity defense by clear and convincing evidence may be easier to sustain."); *Hybritech*, 802 F.2d at 1375 (new prior art "may facilitate the challenger's meeting [its] burden of proof"). A challenger relying on prior art already considered by the PTO " 'has the added burden of overcoming the deference that is due a qualified government agency presumed to have properly done its job.' " *Tokai*, 632 F.3d at 1367; *see also* Ultra-Tex Surfaces, Inc. v. Hill Bros. Chemical Co., 204 F.3d 1360, 1367 (Fed. Cir. 2000) (describing the "additional burden" faced by the challenger who relies on "the very same references that were before the examiner"). In such cases, the challenger's burden may be described as "enhanced." *Tokai*, 632 F.3d at 1367 ("although the standard of proof does not depart from that of clear and convincing evidence, a party challenging validity shoulders an enhanced burden if the invalidity argument relies on the same prior art considered during examination").

[15] 35 U.S.C. § 282 ("Each claim of a patent . . . shall be presumed valid independently of the validity of other claims; dependent or multiple dependent claims shall be presumed valid even though dependent upon an invalid claim.").

8.3 ASSIGNOR ESTOPPEL

Assignor estoppel is a doctrine that prevents one who assigns patent rights from arguing when convenient that the same patent is invalid. Consider the following scenario. An inventor obtains a patent on a new apparatus and assigns all rights to his employer.[16] The inventor receives valuable consideration for the assignment—perhaps a bonus—but afterward leaves his employer to form his own company. He then sells a product alleged by his former employer to be covered by the patent. The inventor can argue about the scope of the patent he assigned, but he cannot assert an invalidity defense like anticipation or obviousness.[17]

Anyone who assigns patent rights to another in exchange for valuable consideration[18] implicitly acknowledges the validity of the patent and gives up the right to challenge that validity later on. In fairness, "an assignor should not be permitted to sell something and later assert that what was sold is worthless, all to the detriment of the assignee."[19] The rule applies to the individual who assigned the patent, and it may apply to others with whom that individual is involved. For example, if the defendant company is not owned by the inventor/assignor but it employs him in a position of responsibility, the company may still be barred from contesting the validity of the patent.[20]

8.4 UTILITY

Section 101 of the Patent Act states that a patent may be granted to the discoverer of a "new and useful" invention. Article 1, Section 8 of the Constitution also speaks of promoting the "useful" arts. From these

---

[16] *See* Section 6.2.

[17] *See* Pandrol USA, LP v. Airboss Railway Prods., Inc., 424 F.3d 1161, 1166 (Fed. Cir. 2005); Mentor Graphics Corp. v. Quickturn Design Sys., Inc., 150 F.3d 1374, 1378 (Fed. Cir. 1998) ("Without exceptional circumstances (such as an express reservation by the assignor of the right to challenge the validity of the patent or an express waiver of the assignee of the right to assert assignor estoppel), one who assigns a patent surrenders with that assignment the right to later challenge the validity of the assigned patent.").

[18] The "valuable consideration" need not be a separate payment or bonus. Where the inventor/assignor is an employee of a corporation, that employee's regular salary is likely to be considered adequate consideration, at least if the invention was within the scope of the inventor/assignor's employment. *See* Diamond Scientific Co. v. Ambico, Inc., 848 F.2d 1220, 1225 (Fed. Cir. 1988).

[19] *Id.* at 1224; *see also Pandrol*, 424 F.3d at 1166–67 (assignor estoppel prevents "unfairness and injustice").

[20] *See* Shamrock Technologies, Inc. v. Medical Sterilization, Inc., 903 F.2d 789, 793 (Fed. Cir. 1990).

sources, courts have derived the rule, known as the utility requirement, that an invention must be useful before it can be patented.[21]

A patentable invention must have a "specific and substantial utility"– meaning a practical or real-world application.[22] Incremental achievements in basic research, important to researchers as *steps* toward practical advancements, still lack the immediate benefit needed to satisfy the utility requirement.[23] Similarly, the discovery of a new substance, or a process for making a substance, does not warrant a patent unless a use for that substance has been identified.[24] In these cases a patent might only impede the further research required to produce genuinely useful discoveries.[25] Accordingly, an application must describe the utility of the claimed invention in terms that are specific, not speculative or nebulous.[26] One cannot, for example, merely argue that the substance one has discovered holds promise as research tool.[27]

New pharmaceuticals present a special problem because years of testing may be required to demonstrate that they are safe and effective. In *In re Brana*,[28] the Federal Circuit held that animal studies could provide sufficient evidence of utility, even though FDA approval would require further

---

[21] *See* Stiftung v. Renishaw PLC, 945 F.2d 1173, 1180 (Fed. Cir. 1991). The utility requirement does not apply to design patents, discussed in Section 12.1.

[22] *In re* Fischer, 421 F.3d 1365, 1371 (Fed. Cir. 2005); *see also In re* '318 Patent Infringement Litigation, 583 F.3d 1317, 1324 (Fed. Cir. 2009) ("The utility requirement prevents mere ideas from being patented.").

[23] *See* '*318 Patent,* 583 F.3d at 1324 ("The utility requirement ... prevents the patenting of a mere research proposal or an invention that is simply an object of research."); *Fischer,* 421 F.3d at 1375.

[24] *See In re* Ziegler, 992 F.2d 1197, 1201–03 (Fed. Cir. 1993) (that a compound can produce a "film" is an inadequate statement of utility, if the usefulness of the film itself is unclear).

[25] *See* '*318 Patent,* 583 F.3d at 1324. Although the unavailability of patents for basic scientific research may discourage endeavors that would ultimately prove of great benefit, courts have concluded as a matter of policy that it is more important to leave scientific knowledge unencumbered until it reaches the stage of practical application. *See* Brenner v. Manson, 383 U.S 519, 534 (1966).

[26] *Fischer,* 421 F.3d at 1371. In one case, the patentee hypothesized that a compound tested for treatment of amnesia could be effective against Alzheimer's disease. Because there were insufficient reasons to expect the Alzheimer's application to be successful, the invention was too speculative to have the required real-world utility. '*318 Patent,* 538 F.3d at 1327. Patents, the court warned, are not granted in exchange for " 'vague intimations of general ideas that may or may not be workable.' " *Id.* at 1324.

[27] Because other countries have different requirements regarding such disclosures, *see Cross v. Iizuka,* 753 F.2d 1040 (Fed. Cir. 1985), these problems may arise when the applicant attempts to rely on a foreign application in order to establish priority.

[28] 51 F.3d 1560 (Fed. Cir. 1995).

testing.[29] The court explained that if full FDA approval were required before a patent could be granted, the costs would discourage some companies from patenting, and perhaps from developing, potentially important discoveries.

Inventions that serve a relatively trivial purpose still have utility. One can find many patents claiming toys, novelties, and the like. If they serve their purpose, they are useful enough to receive a patent.[30] The only kinds of practical invention categorically excluded from patentability on grounds of non-utility are those whose purpose is deemed illegal or immoral. Until 1977, this principle barred patents on gambling machines.[31] The exclusion still applies to any invention useful only in committing a crime or fraud–such as a method of counterfeiting currency.[32]

One of the more curious utility cases from the Federal Circuit is *Juicy Whip, Inc. v. Orange Bang, Inc.*,[33] where the invention was a beverage dispenser of the type one might see at the concession stand of a movie theater. The dispenser appeared to dispense the beverage from a supply in a glass bowl. In fact, the machine mixed the beverage elsewhere as it was dispensed–a more practical option, but somehow less tempting to purchasers.[34] Although the purpose of the invention was to mislead consumers,

[29] *Brana*, 51 F.3d at 1568 ("Usefulness in patent law, and in particular in the context of pharmaceutical inventions, necessarily includes the expectation of further research and development. The stage at which an invention in this field becomes useful is well before it is ready to be administered to humans."); *see also '318 Patent*, 583 F.3d at 1324–25 (animal tests and in vitro experiments may establish utility).

[30] "The threshold of utility is not high: An invention is 'useful' under section 101 if it is capable of providing some identifiable benefit." Juicy Whip, Inc. v. Orange Bang, Inc., 185 F.3d 1364, 1366 (Fed. Cir. 1999). One patent demonstrating the potential breadth of the concept of utility is U.S. patent No. 5,457,821, entitled "Hat Simulating a Fried Egg." According to the specification, "[t]he hat finds utility, for example, as an attention-getting item in connection with promotional activities at trade shows, conventions, and the like. Further the hat is useful in connection with egg sale promotions in the egg industry." Perhaps a design patent would have been more appropriate. *See* Section 12.1.

[31] *See* Tol-O-Matic, Inc. v. Proma Produkt-Und Marketing Gesellschaft M.b.H, 945 F.2d 1546, 1552 (Fed. Cir. 1991).

[32] " 'All that the law requires is that the invention should not be frivolous, or injurious to the well-being, good policy, or good morals of society. The word *useful* therefore is incorporated into the act in contradistinction to mischievous or immoral.' " *Id.* at 1553 (emphasis in original). Even the exception for inventions with immoral or illegal purposes "has not been applied broadly in recent years." *Juicy Whip*, 185 F.3d at 1366–67.

[33] 185 F.3d 1364 (Fed. Cir. 1999).

[34] "The display bowl is said to stimulate impulse buying by providing the consumer with a visual beverage display. A pre-mix display bowl, however, has a limited capacity and is subject to contamination by bacteria." *Id.* at 1365.

the court found that the invention had utility. As the court observed, "[i]t is not at all unusual for a product to be designed to appear to viewers to be something it is not," examples including imitation diamonds and simulated leather.[35] It is the task of other government agencies, not the Patent Office, to protect consumers from potential deception.[36]

It might be argued that an invention is useful only if it is an improvement over the prior art. However, an invention can still be patented even if it is inferior to, or no better than, existing devices or methods.[37] As the Federal Circuit has observed, "[a]n invention need not be the best or the only way to accomplish a certain result, and it need only be useful to some extent and in certain applications."[38] It would be difficult, and perhaps pointless, for the Patent Office to attempt to assess in every case whether the claimed invention is really an improvement. An invention inferior to its predecessors in some respects may be superior in others. In many cases, the advantages of a particular invention cannot be fully appreciated until long after it is patented. In the end, the Patent Office is not in the business of judging whether one invention is better than another. This is one reason why the popular conception of a patent as an award for technological achievement is misguided. In spite of the frequent attempts of advertising to imply that a product is "so good it's patented," patents reflect novelty, not merit.

Inventions must achieve a minimum level of operability because an invention that fails to work at all cannot be said to have utility.[39] In most cases, the Patent Office accepts the applicant's representation that the invention works.[40] The Patent Office is not equipped to perform experiments. But

---

[35] *Id.* at 1367. The comparison may be a bit unfair. Imitation goods may *substitute* for the real thing without necessarily *fooling* anyone. The purpose of the beverage dispenser seems to have been only to mislead.

[36] *Id.* at 1368.

[37] Demaco Corp. v. F. Von Langsdorff Licensing Ltd., 851 F.2d 1387, 1390 (Fed. Cir. 1988) ("The patent statute does not require that a patentable invention be superior to all prior devices.").

[38] *Stiftung,* 945 F.2d at 1180; *see also* Envirotech Corp. v. Al George, Inc., 730 F.2d 753, 762 (Fed. Cir. 1984) ("the fact that an invention has only limited utility and is only operable in certain applications is not grounds for finding lack of utility").

[39] Process Control Corp. v. Hydreclaim Corp., 190 F.3d 1350, 1358 (Fed. Cir. 1999); *Tol-O-Matic,* 945 F.2d at 1553 (referring to the "total incapacity" that could lead to a finding of nonutility). On the other hand, if a claimed invention achieves some of its objectives but not others, it will still be deemed to have utility. *Stiftung,* 945 F.2d at 1180 (" 'When a properly claimed invention meets at least one stated objective, utility under § 101 is clearly shown.' "). If a claimed invention is an impossibility, the patent fails on grounds of enablement (see Section 8.6) as well as utility. *Process Control,* 190 F.3d at 1358.

[40] *See* Rasmusson v. Smithkline Beecham Corp., 413 F.3d 1318, 1323 (Fed. Cir. 2005).

occasionally the nature of the invention raises suspicions, as when applicants, defying the most fundamental principles of physics, attempt to patent perpetual motion machines. On such occasions, the applicant may be required to come forward with experimental evidence demonstrating that the invention succeeds.[41] In one case where the claimed device purported to produce more energy than it consumed, the Patent Office arranged for tests to be conducted by the Bureau of Standards. Unfortunately, those tests were unsuccessful.[42]

While the Patent Office has limited means to challenge claims on grounds of inoperability or impossibility, this is not necessarily the case in litigation. A party charged with patent infringement may offer evidence demonstrating that whatever is required by the claim is either physically impossible or useless.[43] On the other hand, if a claim actually has been infringed, a court will be reluctant to find that the invention lacks utility. As one court observed, "People rarely, if ever, appropriate useless inventions."[44]

8.5 DEFINITENESS

The function of patent claims is to identify the subject matter covered by the patent. If patent infringement can be compared to trespassing, the claims serve as the boundary markers that define what is, or is not, an encroachment on the inventor's exclusive territory.[45] The law therefore requires that the claims have a definite meaning understandable to those skilled in the art.[46] This requirement is embodied in 35 U.S.C. § 112(b), which provides that

---

[41]One example of an invention met with skepticism is discussed in *Fregau v. Mossinghoff,* 776 F.2d 1034 (Fed. Cir. 1985). The claimed method was supposed to enhance the density and flavor of beverages by passing them through a magnetic field. The Patent Office did not consider the experimental evidence offered by the applicant convincing. Strangely, the Patent Office also found several examples of close, and equally unbelievable, prior art.

[42]*See* Newman v. Quigg, 877 F.2d 1575 (Fed. Cir. 1989). Inventions based on cold fusion are treated with great skepticism, but baldness cures have entered the realm of the believable. *See In re* Swartz, 232 F.3d 862 (Fed. Cir. 2000) (cold fusion); *In re* Cortright, 165 F.3d 1353 (Fed. Cir. 1999) (baldness cures).

[43]*See* Raytheon Co. v. Roper Corp., 724 F.2d 951, 956–57 (Fed. Cir. 1983).

[44]*Raytheon,* 724 F.2d at 959.

[45]*See* S3 Inc. v. Nvidia Corp., 259 F.3d 1364, 1369 (Fed. Cir. 2001) ("The purpose of claims is not to explain the technology or how it works, but to state the legal boundaries of the patent grant.").

[46]*See* Halliburton Energy Services, Inc. v. M-I LLC, 514 F.3d 1244, 1249 (Fed. Cir. 2008) ("Because claims delineate the patentee's right to exclude, the patent statute requires that the scope of the claims be sufficiently definite to inform the public of the bounds of the protected invention. . . . Otherwise, competitors cannot avoid infringement, defeating the public notice function of patent claims."); Young v. Lumenis, Inc., 492 F.3d 1336, 1346 (Fed. Cir. 2007); All Dental Prodx, LLC v. Advantage Dental Prods., Inc., 309 F.3d 774, 779–80 (Fed. Cir. 2002).

the "specification shall conclude with one or more claims particularly pointing out and distinctly claiming the subject matter which the inventor . . . regards as the invention."

The test for compliance is whether a person experienced in the field of the invention, reading the claims and the patent specification, would understand the scope of the subject matter covered by the claims.[47] If the claims are so vague or unclear that those in the industry cannot reasonably determine what does or does not infringe the patent, the claims may be held unpatentable or invalid. The Federal Circuit has described the indefiniteness threshold as "somewhat high" [48]–invalidating only claims that are "insolubly ambiguous" and impossible to narrow.[49] A claim is not indefinite merely because it is difficult to interpret.[50]

---

[47] *See* Spansion, Inc. v. International Trade Comm'n, 629 F.3d 1331, 1344 (Fed. Cir. 2010); Hearing Components, Inc. v. Shure Inc., 600 F.3d 1357, 1367 (Fed. Cir. 2010); Microprocessor Enhancement Corp. v. Texas Instruments Inc., 520 F.3d 1367, 1374 (Fed. Cir. 2008). Like enablement, discussed in Section 8.6, definiteness is determined from the perspective of one skilled in the art at the time the patent application was filed. W.L. Gore & Assoc, Inc. v. Garlock, Inc., 721 F.2d 1540, 1557 (Fed. Cir. 1983). A term that can be defined only in terms of a subjective point of view–like "aesthetically pleasing"–is indefinite. Datamize, LLC v. Plumtree Software, Inc., 417 F.3d 1342, 1350 (Fed. Cir. 2005) ("The scope of claim language cannot depend solely on the unconstrained, subjective opinion of a particular individual purportedly practicing the invention.").

[48] *See* Amgen, Inc. v. Hoechst Marion Roussel, Inc., 314 F.3d 1313, 1342 (Fed. Cir. 2003).

[49] *See* Star Scientific, Inc. v. R.J. Reynolds Tobacco Co., 655 F.3d 1364, 1373 (Fed. Cir. 2011) (an indefinite claim is one "not amenable to construction"); Honeywell Int'l , Inc. v. United States, 609 F.3d 1292, 1301 (Fed. Cir. 2010); *Hearing Components*, 600 F.3d at 1366. "Insolubly ambiguous" is the standard applied in the courts after a patent has issued. During prosecution, when the applicant still has a chance to substitute clearer terminology, a claim that is not "insolubly ambiguous" may be rejected for indefiniteness if it is open to more than one interpretation. Ex parte Miyazaki, 89 USPQ2d 1207, 1211 (Bd. Pat. App. & Int. 2008).

[50] *Star Scientific*, 655 F.3d at 1373 (claims are not indefinite even if the task of interpreting them is "formidable" and the conclusion "one over which reasonable persons will disagree"); *Honeywell*, 609 F.3d at 1301; Funai Electric Co. v. Daewoo Electronics Corp., 616 F.3d 1357, 1372 (Fed. Cir. 2010) ("An ungainly claim is not thereby indefinite, when its meaning can be understood by a person experienced in the field of the invention, on review of the patent documents."). A claim is not indefinite merely because it is difficult to determine whether one's own product infringes. The difficulty may lie in the inadequacy of testing procedures, not imprecision in the claim language. *See Spansion*, 629 F.3d at 1346; Invitrogen Corp. v. Biocrest Mfg., L.P., 424 F.3d 1374, 1384 (Fed. Cir. 2005). Nor is a claim indefinite simply because it is broad. Ultimax Cement Mfg. Corp. v. CTS Cement Mfg. Corp., 92 USPQ2d 1865, 1873 (Fed. Cir. 2009) ("Merely claiming broadly does not render a claim insolubly ambiguous, nor does it prevent the public from understanding the scope of the patent.").

Because language is inherently imprecise, the law requires only such precision in claim drafting as the subject matter permits.[51] In *Orthokinetics, Inc. v. Safety Travel Chairs, Inc.*,[52] the patent claimed a wheel chair with a part "so dimensioned" that it could be inserted in the space between the seats and door frame of an automobile. The claim did not state what those dimensions should be, nor could it have stated them precisely because they would vary depending on the model. However, the dimensions for any particular automobile could easily be obtained by one skilled in the art. The court held that the claim language was as precise as the subject matter permitted: "patent law does not require that all possible lengths corresponding to the spaces in hundreds of different automobiles be listed in the patent, let alone that they be listed in the claims."[53] On the other hand, in *Halliburton Energy Services, Inc. v. M-I LLC*, the court held indefinite claims describing a "fragile gel." The patent lacked any quantitative measure of fragility, and to say that the gel must be "adequate for the circumstances" did not resolve the ambiguity.[54]

The test for indefiniteness is whether the claim language is understandable when read in light of the specification. One function of the specification is to serve as a dictionary or glossary for any claim terms that might have a specialized meaning.[55] The specification may provide a specific definition for otherwise ambiguous claim language, or it may provide a test for measuring whether a product falls within the intended meaning of

---

[51] Hybritech Inc. v. Monoclonal Antibodies, Inc., 802 F.2d 1367, 1385 (Fed. Cir. 1986); *see also Star Scientific*, 655 F.3d at 1373 ("Absolute clarity is not required to find a claim term definite."); *Hearing Components*, 600 F.3d at 1367 (a patentee need not define the invention with " 'mathematical precision' "); *S3*, 259 F.3d at 1367 (" 'If the claims when read in light of the specification reasonably apprise those skilled in the art of the scope of the invention, § 112 demands no more.' "). It has been observed that a patent claim is " 'one of the most difficult legal instruments to draw with accuracy.' " Slimfold Mfg. Co. v. Kinkead Indus., Inc., 810 F.2d 1113, 1117 (Fed. Cir. 1987); *see also Funai*, 616 F.3d at 1372 ("the drafting of patent documents is the most challenging of tasks").

[52] 806 F.2d 1565 (Fed. Cir. 1986).

[53] *Id.* at 1576; *see also Star Scientific*, 655 F.3d at 1374 ("controlled environment" was not indefinite, although the patent provided no specific parameters, because persons skilled in the art would know how to adjust the conditions for curing tobacco to secure the desired results); *Young*, 492 F.3d at 1346 ("near" in the context of a procedure for declawing a cat was not indefinite because it was dependent on the physical characteristics of each cat).

[54] *Halliburton*, 514 F.3d at 1254–56.

[55] *See* Martek Biosciences Corp. v. Nutrinova, Inc., 579 F.3d 1363, 1380 (Fed. Cir. 2009) ("When a patentee explicitly defines a claim term in the patent specification, the patentee's definition controls."); Vitronics Corp. v. Conceptronic, Inc., 90 F.3d 1576, 1582 (Fed. Cir. 1996) (the specification "acts as a dictionary").

the claim.[56] Even if some experimentation is required to determine the boundaries of the claim, the claim will not be held indefinite if the language is as precise as the subject matter permits.[57] The prosecution history also may provide information to clarify the meaning of a disputed term.[58]

In spite of the requirement that claims use definite language, such "words of degree" as "generally," "approximately," and "substantially equal to" are commonly used.[59] While these terms are inherently inexact, they are often tolerated because they are as precise as the subject matter allows.[60] For example, in *Rosemount, Inc. v. Beckman Instruments, Inc.*,[61] the patent claims described a device having one component "in close proximity" to another. The court found that "close proximity" was a term used and understood in the industry. Had the inventor been forced to specify a precise dimension (e.g., "within 0.5 centimeters"), the claim would likely have been narrower than the true scope of the invention. Moreover, requiring a precise definition of "close proximity" in the patent specification would "turn the construction of a patent into a mere semantic quibble that serves no useful purpose."[62]

On the other hand, a court will treat words of degree with suspicion if, in litigation, the patentee argues that the term is broad enough to encompass the accused product but narrow enough to avoid the prior art, with no suggestion as to where the line in between should be drawn.[63] In *Amgen, Inc. v.*

---

[56] *See* Shatterproof Glass Corp. v. Libbey-Owens Ford Co., 758 F.2d 613, 624 (Fed. Cir. 1985); Seattle Box Co. v. Industrial Crating & Packing, Inc., 731 F.2d 818, 826 (Fed. Cir. 1984); W.L. Gore & Assoc., Inc. v. Garlock, Inc., 721 F.2d 1540, 1557–58 (Fed. Cir. 1983).

[57] Exxon Research & Eng'g Co. v. U.S., 265 F.3d 1371, 1379 (Fed. Cir. 2001).

[58] *See All Dental Prodx*, 309 F.3d at 780 ("The prosecution history can . . . be relied upon to clarify claim meaning and hence provide definiteness."); Texas Instruments Inc. v. U.S. Int'l Trade Comm'n, 871 F.2d 1054, 1063 (Fed. Cir. 1989) ("The public is entitled to know the scope of the claims but must look to both the patent specification and the prosecution history, especially where there is doubt concerning the scope of the claims.").

[59] *See* Andrew Corp. v. Gabriel Elec., Inc., 847 F.2d 819, 821 (Fed. Cir. 1988).

[60] *See Hearing Components*, 600 F.3d at 1367 ("Not all terms of degree are indefinite.").

[61] 727 F.2d 1540 (Fed. Cir. 1984).

[62] *Id.* at 1547. The Patent Office guidelines also require only a "reasonable degree of particularity and distinctness." M.P.E.P. § 2173.02. "Some latitude in the manner of expression and the aptness of terms should be permitted even though the claim language is not as precise as the examiner might desire." *Id.*

[63] *See Datamize*, 417 F.3d at 1347 (claims must " 'clearly distinguish what is claimed from what went before in the art and clearly circumscribe what is foreclosed from future enterprise' " (*quoting* United Carbon Co. v. Binney & Smith Co., 317 U.S. 228, 236 (1942)); *see also Spansion*, 629 F.3d at 1346 ("[w]hether a patent clearly differentiates itself from specific prior art" is an important factor when judging indefiniteness).

Chugai Pharmaceuticals Co.,[64] the patentee claimed a protein having a "specific activity" of "at least about 160,000 IU/AU." A prior art product exhibited a "specific activity" of 128,620 IU/AU. Because nothing in the claims, the specification, the prosecution history, or the prior art provided any hint as to whether, for example, a protein having a "specific activity" of 145,000 IU/AU would come within the scope of the claims, the court held that the term "about" was insufficiently definite in the context of that patent.

A claim element drafted in means-plus-function format[65](e.g., in a mousetrap claim, "a means for attracting a mouse") recites a function to be performed without specifying the structure to perform it. An infringing device must perform the recited function with structure that is identical or equivalent to the corresponding structure described in the patent specification (e.g., a morsel of mouse-attracting cheese). If the patent specification describes *no* structure to perform the recited function (e.g., no cheese or anything else to attract a mouse), then there is no basis for comparison and the claim is indefinite.[66] Failure to disclose adequate structure for means-plus-function elements has become a particular concern with computer-implemented inventions. For example, in *Ergo Licensing LLC v. Carefusion 303 Inc.*,[67] the patent concerned a system for infusing fluids into a patient, one element of the system being a "control means." The specification disclosed no structure to perform the "controlling" function other than to suggest that it would be done by a general-purpose computer. In such cases, the Federal Circuit requires that the disclosure of "structure" include a software algorithm–a series of steps to be performed by the computer in carrying out the recited

---

[64] 927 F.2d 1200 (Fed. Cir. 1991).

[65] *See* Section 7.7.4.

[66] Blackboard, Inc. v. Desire2Learn, Inc., 574 F.3d 1371, 1382 (Fed. Cir. 2009) ("If the specification does not include an adequate disclosure of the structure that corresponds to the claimed function, the patentee will have 'failed to particularly point out and distinctly claim the invention' "). The specification cannot simply disclose a "black box" that achieves a desired outcome. *Id.* at 1383. Nor is it enough that a person skilled in the art could *devise* some structure that would work; the patentee must describe the structure in the specification. *Id.* at 1385; Aristocrat Technologies Australia PTY Ltd. v. International Game Technology, 521 F.3d 1328, 1337 (Fed. Cir. 2008). Moreover, the patentee must clearly link the structure to the function so a person skilled in the art can identify the basis for comparison. Noah Sys. Inc. v. Intuit Inc., 675 F.3d 1302, 1311–12 (Fed. Cir. 2012). The requirement that specific structure be disclosed prevents a patentee from indulging in "pure functional claiming." *Blackboard,* 574 F.3d at 1385.

[67] 673 F.3d 1361 (Fed. Cir. 2012).

function.[68] Because the patentee in *Ergo Licensing* disclosed no such algorithm, the court held the claim indefinite.

A definite claim provides competitors of the patent owner with fair warning of what will or will not infringe the patent. If claim language is vague, competitors must proceed at their peril, and the uncertainty provides the patent owner with what is, in effect, a broader claim. Yet the laudable effects of the definiteness requirement are undermined to some extent by the "doctrine of equivalents."[69] According to that doctrine, even a product that is not literally described by the claim language may infringe if the differences are "insubstantial." The effect is to add an extra dimension of uncertainty to every patent claim. The tension between the definiteness requirement and the doctrine of equivalents is one of the reasons that the latter doctrine, though long established, is often criticized.[70]

8.6 ENABLEMENT

As discussed in Section 1.1, a patent can be regarded as a bargain between the inventor and the public. In exchange for a monopoly on the invention for a period of years, the inventor must disclose the invention in such clear terms that, when the patent has expired, the public at large can take advantage of the invention. This concept is behind the "enablement" and "best mode" requirements.[71] The enablement requirement comes from the following language of 35 U.S.C. §112(a):

The specification shall contain a written description of the invention, and of the manner and process of making and using it, in such full, clear, concise, and exact terms as to *enable* any person skilled in the

---

[68] *Id.* at 1364; *see also Noah Sys.*, 675 F.3d at 1312; Typhoon Touch Technologies Inc. v. Dell Inc., 659 F.3d 1376, 1384 (an algorithm is " 'a series of instructions for the computer to follow.' "). The algorithm may be described in any understandable form, including flow charts, prose descriptions, or mathematical formulas. *Noah Sys.*, 675 F.3d at 1312; *Typhoon*, 673 F.3d at 1385. If the function recited in the claim (e.g., storing data) could be performed by any general-purpose computer without special programming, then a simple reference to a computer may provide sufficient disclosure of structure. *Noah Sys.*, 675 F.3d at 1312 n.8; *In re Katz* Interactive Call Processing Patent Litigation, 639 F.3d 1303, 1316 (Fed. Cir. 2011). This is a "narrow exception" that did not apply in *Ergo Licensing* because performing the controlling function "require[d] more than merely plugging in a general-purpose computer." 673 F.3d at 1365.

[69] *See* Section 10.6.

[70] *See* Section 10.6.3.

[71] The enablement requirement also helps to fix the date of invention for purposes of determining priority. The inclusion of an enabling disclosure in a patent application demonstrates that the applicant had a completed invention no later than the filing date.

art to which it pertains, or with which it is most nearly connected, to make and use the same. . . .

To satisfy the enablement requirement, the patent must describe the invention in such clear and exact terms that persons skilled in the art can make and use the invention without "undue experimentation."[72] Because patents are intended to be read and used by those skilled in the art, the specification need not include information that such persons would already know.[73] A patent on an improved radio antenna need not disclose the entire theory and practice of how to build a radio, beginning with Marconi. Persons skilled in the radio art would know the basics already and would only have to be informed of the inventor's improvement.[74]

A patent can be enabling even though *some* experimentation is necessary, so long as the experimentation is not "undue."[75] The definition of "undue" varies depending on the nature of the invention and expectations in the industry.[76]

---

[72] Streck, Inc. v. Research & Diagnostic Sys., Inc., 665 F.3d 1269, 1288 (Fed. Cir. 2012); Transocean Offshore Deepwater Drilling, Inc. v. Maersk Contractors USA, Inc., 617 F.3d 1296, 1305 (Fed. Cir. 2010); Alza Corp. v. Andrx Pharmaceuticals, LLC, 603 F.3d 935, 940 (Fed. Cir. 2010); Martek Biosciences Corp. v. Nutrinova, Inc., 579 F.3d 1363, 1378 (Fed. Cir. 2009).

[73] *Streck,* 665 F.3d at 1288 ("a specification need not disclose what is well-known in the art"); Koito Mfg. Co. v. Turn-Key-Tech, LLC, 381 F.3d 1142, 1156 (Fed. Cir. 2004); Chiron Corp. v. Genentech, Inc., 363 F.3d 1247, 1254 (Fed. Cir. 2004); Hybritech Inc. v. Monoclonal Antibodies, Inc., 802 F.2d 1367, 1384 (Fed. Cir. 1986) ("[A] patent need not teach, and preferably omits, what is well known in the art."). On the other hand, the knowledge of those skilled in the art is meant to *supplement* the enabling disclosure, not to substitute for it. *Streck,* 665 F.3d at 1288; *Alza,* 603 F.3d at 940–41. The enabling disclosure cannot supply only " 'a starting point, a direction for further research.' " *Alza,* 603 F.3d at 941.

[74] *See* S3 Inc. v. Nvidia Corp., 259 F.3d 1364, 1371 (Fed. Cir. 2001) ("To hold otherwise would require every patent document to include a technical treatise for the unskilled reader. Although an accommodation to the 'common experience' of lay persons may be feasible, it is an unnecessary burden for inventors and has long been rejected as a requirement of patent disclosures.").

[75] *Alza,* 603 F.3d at 940 ("[e]nablement is not precluded where a 'reasonable' amount of routine experimentation is required to practice a claimed invention"); *Chiron,* 363 F.3d at 1253. A patent disclosure is not meant to be a "production specification." *Koito,* 381 F.3d at 1156.

[76] Factors to consider include the amount of experimentation required, the presence or absence of guidance in the patent disclosure, the skill of those practicing in the field, and the extent to which the art is "predictable." *See Streck,* 665 F.3d at 1288; *Alza,* 603 F.3d at 940; *Martek,* 579 F.3d at 1378. If the patentee cannot succeed in implementing its own invention, this suggests that the patent disclosure is nonenabling. Ormco Corp. v. Align Technology, Inc., 498 F.3d 1307, 1319 (Fed. Cir. 2007).

Even time-consuming experimentation may not be "undue" if the experiments are routine. In the biotechnology industry, for example, isolating cells that produce a desired antibody may require testing many cells and discarding all but a few. If the screening is routine and the patent specification tells the experimenter how to proceed, the disclosure is likely to suffice.[77]

Patentees risk violating the enablement requirement when they reserve as a trade secret some piece of information necessary to practice the claimed invention.[78] In one case a patentee claimed a machine-tool control system but did not disclose the proprietary software that made the system work.[79] Without better evidence that commercially available software could be substituted, the court found the patent nonenabling. To have constructed the necessary software from scratch would have required as much as two years of "undue" experimentation. On the other hand, another patent that failed to disclose software passed muster where supplying a substitute would have been a comparatively quick and straightforward task for an experienced programmer.[80]

In the case of inventions that depend on the use of living materials, such as microorganisms or cultured cells, words alone may be insufficient to enable one skilled in the art to make and use the invention. A sample of the biological materials may be necessary to begin. In such cases, inventors can satisfy the enablement requirement by depositing samples of the material in a certified depository where they are available to researchers in the field.[81] In other cases, it may be sufficient to direct researchers to commercial sources of supply or provide them with the directions necessary to produce the materials for themselves.

As far as the enablement requirement is concerned, the specification need disclose only some manner in which the invention can be practiced. It need not disclose every manner of practicing the invention, or even the best manner.[82]

---

[77] *See In re* Wands, 858 F.2d 731 (Fed. Cir. 1988).

[78] *See* Section 2.3.

[79] White Consolidated Indus. v. Vega Servo-Control, Inc., 713 F.2d 788 (Fed. Cir. 1983).

[80] Northern Telecom, Inc. v. Datapoint Corp., 908 F.2d 931 (Fed. Cir. 1990).

[81] *See* 37 C.F.R. § 1.802; M.P.E.P. § 2401 *et seq.*; Ajinomoto Co. v. Archer-Daniels-Midland Co., 228 F.3d 1338, 1345–46 (Fed. Cir. 2000).

[82] *See Transocean*, 617 F.3d at 1307 (a patent does not have to enable "the most optimized configuration, unless this is an explicit part of the claims"); Engel Indus., Inc. v. Lockformer Co., 946 F.2d 1528, 1533 (Fed. Cir. 1991). A patent claim that fails the utility requirement because it *cannot* work necessarily fails the enablement requirement also. *See In re* '318 Patent Infringement Litigation, 583 F.3d 1317, 1324 (Fed. Cir. 2009).

Moreover, the inventor need not understand or disclose the principles that make the invention work.[83]

Whether a specification is enabling is measured at the time the patent application was filed.[84] If the claimed invention cannot be practiced without technology developed after that date, the patent is invalid. On the other hand, applicants are not put to the impossible task of describing *additional* means of practicing the claimed invention that have not yet been invented,[85] even though in such cases one could question whether the claim was overbroad.[86]

8.6.1 Scope of Enablement

Enablement questions arise when the patent claims are substantially broader than the specific embodiments disclosed in the specification. Patent claims are often, in a certain sense, generic. A claim might (hypothetically) cover *every* mousetrap that included the combination of (1) a spring, (2) a latch, and (3) a trigger to unhook the latch and release the spring when disturbed by a mouse. The specification might disclose in detail only *one* example of such a trap—with a particular kind of spring, latch, and trigger. If the claim covers other versions of the trap that are

---

[83] *See* Process Control Corp. v. Hydreclaim Corp., 190 F.3d 1350, 1359 (Fed. Cir. 1999) ("an otherwise valid patent covering a meritorious invention should not be struck down simply because of the patentee's misconceptions about scientific principles concerning the invention"); *In re* Cortright, 165 F.3d 1353, 1359 (Fed. Cir. 1999) (" '[I]t is not a requirement of patentability that an inventor correctly set forth, or even know, how or why the invention works.' "); Newman v. Quigg, 877 F.2d 1575, 1581 (Fed. Cir. 1989).

[84] *Alza,* 603 F.3d at 940; *'318 Patent,* 583 F.3d at 1323; Plant Genetic Sys., N.V. v. DeKalb Genetics Corp., 315 F.3d 1335, 1339 (Fed. Cir. 2003).

[85] *See* Epistar Corp. v. Int'l Trade Comm'n, 566 F.3d 1321, 1336 (Fed. Cir. 2009) (patentees are " 'not required to describe in the specification every conceivable and possible future embodiment of [the] invention' "); Invitrogen Corp. v. Clontech Labs., Inc., 429 F.3d 1052, 1071 (Fed. Cir. 2005) ("Enablement does not require the inventor to foresee every means of implementing an invention at pains of losing his patent franchise. Were it otherwise, claimed inventions would not include improved modes of practicing those inventions. Such narrow patent rights would rapidly become worthless. . . ."); *Chiron,* 363 F.3d at 1254 ("The law does not expect an applicant to disclose knowledge invented or developed after the filing date. Such disclosure would be impossible.").

[86] *See* Section 8.6.1.

not discussed at all, is the specification adequate to enable one skilled in the art to practice the claimed invention?

It is said that the enabling disclosure in the specification must be "commensurate in scope" with the claims.[87] But until recently, at least in the case of "predictable arts," courts seemed to allow patent applicants considerable leeway to claim the invention broadly, even though the specification disclosed very few of the specific alternatives that one might employ.[88] If the specification disclosed a plastic spring for the mousetrap, persons skilled in the art would know how to substitute a steel spring without additional instruction. In "unpredictable arts," such as chemistry and biotechnology, the courts demanded a more extensive disclosure, apparently because one functioning example leads less reliably to other successful means of practicing the invention. Even a tiny change in the structure of a molecule, for example, may have large and unanticipated effects. One patentee claimed all possible sequences of DNA that would produce the protein EPO, which stimulates the production of red blood cells, or any analog of EPO that would have a similar effect.[89] The specification disclosed the information needed to prepare EPO and just a few of its analogs. The court found that the number of possible DNA sequences within the scope of the claim vastly outstripped the enabling disclosure: "There may be many other genetic sequences that code for EPO-type products. [The patentee] has told us how to make and use only a few of them and is therefore not entitled to claim all of them."[90]

---

[87] *See, e.g.,* Chiron Corp. v. Genentech, Inc., 363 F.3d 1247, 1253 (Fed. Cir. 2004); National Recovery Technologies, Inc. v. Magnetic Separation Sys., Inc., 166 F.3d 1190, 1195–96 (Fed. Cir. 1999); Amgen, Inc. v. Chugai Pharmaceutical Co., 927 F.2d 1200, 1213 (Fed. Cir. 1991). "Pioneering" inventions that establish an entirely new field of inquiry (*see* Section 10.6.7) may support broad claims, but they are subject to the same requirement that the claims "bear a reasonable correlation to the scope of enablement." *See* Plant Genetic Sys., N.V. v. DeKalb Genetics Corp., 315 F.3d 1335, 1339–40 (Fed. Cir. 2003).

[88] "If an invention pertains to an art where the results are predictable, e.g., the mechanical as opposed to the chemical arts, a broad claim can be enabled by disclosure of a single embodiment. . . ." Spectra-Physics, Inc. v. Coherent, Inc., 827 F.2d 1524, 1533 (Fed. Cir. 1987); *see also* Epistar Corp. v. Int'l Trade Comm'n, 566 F.3d 1321, 1336 (Fed. Cir. 2009).

[89] *Amgen,* 927 F.2d at 1212–14.

[90] *Id.* In contrast, in *Streck, Inc. v. Research & Diagnostic Sys., Inc.,* 665 F.3d 1269, 1289 (Fed. Cir. 2012), the court held an enabling disclosure adequate where the subject matter omitted from the specification "worked in exactly the same way" as the subject matter disclosed.

Now the courts are applying a stricter standard even where the invention falls within the mechanical or electronic arts. If the claim encompasses alternative manners of practicing the invention but the specification teaches only one of those alternatives, the claim may be held invalid for failing to enable the "full scope" of the claim.[91] For example, in *Sitrick v. Dreamworks, LLC,*[92] the patent claimed a system for integrating user-created images into existing movies or video games. Because the specification did not describe how to apply the technology to movies (as opposed to video games), and the teachings of one could not be applied to the other, the patent was invalid.[93] The court observed that enabling the full scope of the claim is a *quid quo pro* of the patent bargain, and a "patentee who chooses broad claim language must make sure the broad claims are fully enabled."[94] The Federal Circuit seems to have turned to the enablement requirement, as it earlier turned to the written description requirement,[95] to curb the natural tendency of patentees to claim as broadly as they can. Consequently, patentees are well-advised to have some claims, at least, that adhere closely to the disclosed embodiments, particularly where the broader claims include some distinctly implied but incompletely enabled alternatives.

---

[91] Sitrick v. Dreamworks, LLC, 516 F.3d 993, 999 (Fed. Cir. 2008); *see also* Automotive Technologies Int'l, Inc. v. BMW of North America, Inc., 501 F.3d 1274, 1285 (Fed. Cir. 2007) (because "claims must be enabled to correspond to their scope," a patent on a side-impact crash sensor claiming mechanical and electronic sensors, but enabling only the former, was invalid); Liebel-Flarsheim Co. v. Medrad, Inc., 481 F.3d 1371, 1380 (Fed. Cir. 2007) (claims encompassed injectors with and without pressure jackets, but the patent did not enable the jacketless alternative); AK Steel Corp. v. Sollac, 344 F.3d 1234, 1244 (Fed. Cir. 2003) ("[W]hen a range is claimed, there must be reasonable enablement of the scope of the range"). If the claim encompasses an alternative that the specification *discourages* as impractical, it is difficult to argue that the alternative could be implemented with reasonable experimentation. *See AK Steel,* 344 F.3d at 1244.

[92] 516 F.3d 993 (Fed. Cir. 2008).

[93] *Id.* at 1000–1.

[94] *Id.* at 999. That is not to say that the specification must describe explicitly every possible embodiment of the claimed invention; the " 'artisan's knowledge of the prior art and routine experimentation can often fill gaps, interpolate between embodiments, and perhaps even extrapolate beyond the disclosed embodiments, depending upon the predictability of the art.' " *AK Steel,* 344 F.3d at 1244; *see also Chiron,* 363 F.3d at 1253. Because persons skilled in the art have few other sources of useful information, "nascent" technologies require a more thorough disclosure. *Chiron,* 363 F.3d at 1254. In *Sitrick,* the alternative embodiment would have differed so much from the disclosed embodiment that it could not have been accomplished through extrapolation.

[95] *See* Section 8.8.

8.7 BEST MODE

The best mode requirement, like the enablement requirement, arises from the language of 35 U.S.C. § 112(a), which provides that a specification "shall set forth the best mode contemplated by the inventor ... of carrying out the invention." The "best mode" means the best manner of practicing the invention, or the best operative example, known to the inventor when the patent application was filed. If the inventor of a hypothetical mousetrap envisioned two variants of the claimed invention, one using an inferior plastic spring and the other a superior steel spring, the best mode requirement would demand that the better embodiment be disclosed in the patent, even though both came within the scope of the claim.[96]

Like the enablement requirement, the best mode requirement reflects the bargain model of patent law. If a patentee is to be awarded a monopoly on an invention for a period of years, the public is entitled to disclosure of the best that the patentee has to offer. If there were no best mode requirement, patentees might be tempted to disclose the least effective or most impractical embodiments of their inventions, perhaps reserving the better embodiments as trade secrets.[97]

Nevertheless, the best mode requirement lost most of its force on September 16, 2011, when the America Invents Act became law. Before that date, an accused infringer could challenge the validity of an issued patent for failure to disclose the best mode. The revised Patent Act has

---

[96] *See* High Concrete Structures, Inc. v. New Enterprise Stone & Lime Co., 377 F.3d 1379, 1383 (Fed. Cir. 2004) ("The best mode requirement precludes inventors 'from applying for patents while at the same time concealing from the public preferred embodiments of their inventions which they have in fact conceived.'").

[97] "[T]he best mode requirement ... ensure[s] that a patent applicant plays 'fair and square' with the patent system. It is a requirement that the *quid pro quo* of the patent grant be satisfied. One must not receive the right to exclude others unless at the time of filing he has provided an adequate disclosure of the best mode known to him of carrying out the invention." Amgen, Inc. v. Chugai Pharmaceutical Co., 927 F.2d 1200, 1209–10 (Fed. Cir. 1991); *see also* Wellman, Inc. v. Eastman Chemical Co., 642 F.3d 1355, 1360 (Fed. Cir. 2011) ("'The best mode requirement creates a statutory bargained-for-exchange by which a patentee obtains the right to exclude others from practicing the claimed invention for a certain time period, and the public receives knowledge of the preferred embodiments for practicing the claimed invention.'").

eliminated that defense.[98] Unlike much of the America Invents Act, the elimination of the best mode defense applies to all patents, not only those applied for after its effective date. Although § 112 still requires disclosure of the inventor's best mode, because best mode problems typically come to light in litigation, not during patent prosecution, the best mode requirement now seems a dead letter. The disclosure is required, but no penalty follows its omission.

If patent applicants take advantage of this by concealing the best implementations of their inventions, an important element of the patent bargain will be lost. On the other hand, there are several positive aspects to the elimination of the best mode defense. First, it conforms our own patent law to that found in other countries, so that inventors applying for patents both here and abroad no longer have to worry about a special pitfall applying to United States applications alone. Second, it eliminates from patent litigation a very difficult factual inquiry. The best mode defense depended on what the inventor *believed,* as of the filing date, to be the best mode of practicing the invention–a subjective question not easily resolved.[99] Third, it avoids the complex issue of identifying the choices that constitute a "mode of the invention" subject to the disclosure requirement. If the inventor of a mousetrap devised a new method of fabricating plastic parts for it, reasonable

---

[98] 35 U.S.C. § 282(b)(3)(A) ("the failure to disclose the best mode shall not be a basis on which any claim of a patent may be canceled or held invalid or otherwise unenforceable"). Failure to disclose the inventor's best mode could, formerly, be a basis for holding a patent unenforceable on grounds of inequitable conduct. *See* Section 9.1. The phrase "otherwise unenforceable" in the statute appears to eliminate this possibility as well.

[99] *See* Bayer A.G. v. Schein Pharmaceuticals, Inc., 301 F.3d 1306, 1314 (Fed. Cir. 2002) ("Unlike enablement, the existence of a best mode is a purely subjective matter depending upon what the inventor actually believed at the time the application was filed."). Sometimes the inventor's contemporaneous documents, discovered in litigation, could be used to prove that a superior manner of practicing the invention was known to the inventor but not disclosed. *See, e.g.,* Dana Corp. v. IPC Ltd. Partnership, 860 F.2d 415, 418–20 (Fed. Cir. 1988). Or the means adopted by the patentee for commercializing the invention could be revealing. *See, e.g.,* Northern Telecom v. Datapoint Corp., 908 F.2d 931, 940 (Fed. Cir. 1990). A further issue was whether the inventor's best mode was described in the patent in sufficient detail that persons skilled in the art could recognize it and practice it for themselves. *See* Go Medical Indus., Pty., Ltd. v. Inmed Corp., 471 F.3d 1264, 1271 (Fed. Cir. 2006); *Bayer,* 301 F.3d at 1320; Eli Lilly & Co. v. Barr Labs., Inc., 222 F.3d 973, 981 (Fed. Cir. 2000). The best mode requirement could be met even if "routine details" within the competence of persons skilled in the art were omitted, *see* Liquid Dynamics Corp. v. Vaughan Co., 449 F.3d 1209, 1223 (Fed. Cir. 2006), and even if "some experimentation" would be required, *see Eli Lilly,* 222 F.3d at 984.

minds could differ as to whether that method was a mode of practicing the claimed mousetrap invention or a different invention altogether.[100] Now such questions are moot. Perhaps, in the end, the efficiencies of eliminating the best mode defense will prove compensation enough for the potential weakening of patent disclosures.

8.8 WRITTEN DESCRIPTION REQUIREMENT

Another test of validity is the written description requirement, taken from the following language of 35 U.S.C. § 112(a):

The specification shall contain a *written description of the invention*, and of the manner and process of making and using it, in such full, clear, concise, and exact terms as to enable any person skilled in the art to which it pertains, or with which it is most nearly connected, to make and use the same. . . .

The written description requirement is one of the more nebulous concepts in patent law, in part because it is so easily confused with the definiteness and enablement requirements and in part because its function seems largely redundant of those other tests. It is, after all, the function of the

---

[100] *See Bayer*, 301 F.3d at 1315 ("only preferred ways of 'carrying out [the] invention' need be disclosed"). The statutory phrase "mode . . . of carrying out [the] invention" is " 'not definable with precision.' " *Id.* The focus must be on the nature of the invention as defined by the claims. *See* AllVoice Computing PLC v. Nuance Communications, Inc., 504 F.3d 1236, 1246 (Fed. Cir. 2007) ("the alleged best mode is not a way of practicing the claimed invention at all. . . . [o]nly the claimed invention is subject to the best mode requirement"); Cardiac Pacemakers, Inc. v. St. Jude Medical, Inc., 381 F.3d 1371, 1379 (Fed. Cir. 2004) (requiring disclosure of unclaimed subject matter would make " 'the disclosure . . . boundless, and the pitfalls endless'"); *Bayer*, 301 F.3d at 1314–15 (inventor's "every preference" need not be disclosed). On the other hand, the obligation to disclose the inventor's best mode is not limited to the "innovative aspects" of the claimed combination. Ajinomoto Co. v. Int'l Trade Comm'n, 597 F.3d 1267, 1274 (Fed. Cir. 2010). Patentees who manufactured a product covered by the patent at the time the application was filed were particularly vulnerable to allegations that important information was omitted from the disclosure. The accused infringer could simply question the patentee, in ever greater detail, about its own product until uncovering, inevitably, some choice the patentee considered "best" that had not been discussed in the patent. The Federal Circuit warned against this sort of "trap." *See* Wahl Instruments, Inc. v. Acvious, Inc., 950 F.2d 1575, 1581 (Fed. Cir. 1991).

claims to describe the invention in precise terms.[101] Why should the *specification* also be required to describe the invention? On the other hand, if "description" refers to an enabling disclosure, as the remainder of the sentence seems to imply, why not leave that to the enablement requirement?

The Federal Circuit made some attempt to sort out the confusion in *Vas-Cath Inc. v. Mahurkar.*[102] As the court explained, the written description requirement is in part an historical accident, traceable to the late eighteenth century when patents were not required to have claims. In those days, it was the function of the specification to enable the practice of the invention *and* to describe it to potential infringers. Today, the written description requirement plays an important role where the claim language has changed during prosecution of the patent application.

As discussed in Section 5.1, applicants commonly change or "amend" claims during patent prosecution. The patent examiner may object to the claims as filed for any number of reasons, including the applicant's failure to distinguish the invention from the prior art. The applicant may respond by substituting new language. Such changes are allowed as long as the specification *as filed* supports the modified claims. In most cases, the specification itself remains the same throughout prosecution.

Even when the United States still adhered to the first-to-invent system, the filing date of the patent application was often critical for establishing priority— for deciding, in other words, whether the applicant was entitled to a patent because the applicant was the first to invent, or whether the applicant was not entitled to a patent because someone else invented first.[103] If the application fully described the claimed invention, then the applicant's date of invention was, at the very latest, the applicant's filing date. But if the applicant amended the claims during prosecution, they might describe a new and different invention than that originally disclosed. Then the application date would have no bearing on the actual date of invention. As the United States transitions to a first-to-file system, the filing date bears even more directly on questions of priority between inventors. One function of the written description requirement is to preserve the integrity of the filing date on

---

[101] The specification must conclude with "one or more claims particularly pointing out and distinctly claiming the subject matter which the inventor . . . regards as the invention." 35 U.S.C. § 112(b). The definiteness requirement pertaining to claims is discussed in Section 8.5.

[102] 935 F.2d 1555, 1560–64 (Fed. Cir. 1991).

[103] A foreign patent application can be of similar importance if the applicant relies on that application for the patent's filing date.

questions of priority by requiring a *match* between the invention claimed and the invention described in the specification.[104]

In order to satisfy the written description requirement, the patent specification must " 'reasonably convey[] to those skilled in the art that the inventor had possession of the claimed subject matter as of the filing date.' "[105] Possession itself is not the issue, but the adequacy of the disclosure to *demonstrate* possession.[106] Hence, the description requirement cannot be satisfied by other evidence, such as sworn testimony, that the applicant did possess (though he did not adequately describe) the claimed subject matter.[107] The level of detail required depends on the scope of the invention and the state of knowledge in the field.[108]

---

[104] The description requirement " 'guards against the inventor's overreaching by insisting that he recount his invention in such detail that his future claims can be determined to be encompassed within his original creation.' " *Vas-Cath*, 935 F.2d at 1561; *see also In re* Wright, 866 F.2d 422, 424 (Fed. Cir. 1989) ("When the scope of a claim has been changed by amendment in such a way as to justify an assertion that it is directed to a *different invention* than was the original claim, it is proper to inquire whether the newly claimed subject matter was *described* in the patent application when filed as the invention of the applicant. That is the essence of the so-called 'description requirement.' " (emphasis in original)). If the patentee is attempting to rely on the filing date of a "parent" or "grandparent" application (*see* Section 5.2), and that application does not adequately describe the subsequent claim, the result may not be that the claim is invalid but only that it cannot rely on the earlier filing date. *See* Bradford Co. v. Conteyor North America, Inc., 603 F.3d 1262, 1269 (Fed. Cir. 2010); Reiffin v. Microsoft Corp., 214 F.3d 1342, 1346 (Fed. Cir. 2000).

[105] Boston Scientific Corp. v. Johnson & Johnson, 647 F.3d 1353, 1362 (Fed. Cir. 2011) (quoting Ariad Pharmaceuticals, Inc. v. Eli Lilly & Co., 598 F.3d 1336, 1351 (Fed. Cir. 2010) (en banc)); *see also* Centocor Ortho Biotech, Inc. v. Abbott Labs., 636 F.3d 1341, 1348 (Fed. Cir. 2011); ICU Medical, Inc. v. Alaris Medical Sys., Inc., 558 F.3d 1368, 1377 (Fed. Cir. 2009); Carnegie Mellon University v. Hoffman-La Roche Inc., 541 F.3d 1115, 1122 (Fed. Cir. 2008).

[106] *See Boston Scientific*, 647 F.3d at 1361 (" '[T]he hallmark of the written description requirement is disclosure.' ").

[107] *See* Enzo Biochem, Inc. v. Gen-Probe Inc., 296 F.3d 1316, 1330 (Fed. Cir. 2002). The applicant may "possess" the invention even though there has been no actual reduction to practice. Falkner v. Inglis, 448 F.3d 1357, 1366–67 (Fed. Cir. 2006). On the other hand, an applicant cannot possess technology that did not exist at all. Chiron Corp. v. Genentech, Inc., 363 F.3d 1247, 1255 (Fed. Cir. 2004).

[108] *See* Billups-Rothenberg, Inc. v. Associated Regional and University Pathologists, Inc., 642 F.3d 1031, 1036 (Fed. Cir. 2011); *Carnegie Mellon*, 541 F.3d at 1122; Capon v. Eshhar, 418 F.3d 1343, 1357 (Fed. Cir. 2005). A broad claim is more likely to be supported if results in the field are relatively predictable. *See Capon*, 418 F.3d at 1359–60; Bilstad v. Wakalopulos, 386 F.3d 1116, 1125 (Fed. Cir. 2004). If a written description is impossible, as may be the case with biological or chemical discoveries that are not entirely understood, deposit of a physical sample can suffice. *Capon*, 418 F.3d at 1357; *see also Enzo Biochem*, 296 F.3d at 1326.

A "mere wish or plan" to obtain the claimed invention does not demonstrate that the applicant "possessed" it.[109]

Problems can arise if the specification discloses only a single species of a claimed genus.[110] For example, in *In re Curtis*,[111] the application claimed dental floss made of PTFE (better known as "Teflon") improved with a friction-enhancing coating. Because of the nonstick properties for which PTFE is known, it is difficult to find a material that will adhere to it. The inventor, surprised to find *anything* that would work, discovered and disclosed one possibility—microcrystalline wax. This disclosure did not show that the inventor was "in possession" of a broad genus including any and all friction-enhancing coatings, particularly when the art was notoriously unpredictable.[112]

In order to demonstrate possession of a genus, the specification must disclose either "a representative number of species" within that genus, or structural features common to all.[113] The description should allow persons

---

[109] *Boston Scientific*, 647 F.3d at 1362; *Centocor*, 636 F.3d at 1348. "The written description requirement exists to ensure that inventors do not 'attempt to preempt the future before it has arrived.' " *Billups-Rothenberg*, 642 F.3d at 1036; *see also In re* Katz Interactive Call Processing Patent Litigation, 639 F.3d 1303, 1319 (Fed. Cir. 2011) (the written description requirement " 'is to ensure that the scope of the right to exclude, as set forth in the claims, does not overreach the scope of the inventor's contribution to the art as described in the patent specification.' "). The problem of "preempting the future" has been of particular concern with patents claiming varieties of DNA. A claim to all DNA that achieves a certain result is not permitted without an adequate description of the members of the genus. That requires more than a functional description and a potential method of isolating the DNA. It requires "a description of the DNA itself." *Billups-Rothenberg*, 642 F.3d at 1036; Fiers v. Revel, 984 F.2d 1164, 1170 (Fed. Cir. 1993).

[110] *See* Regents of the University of California v. Eli Lilly & Co., 119 F.3d 1559, 1567–68 (Fed. Cir. 1997); *Vas-Cath*, 935 F.2d at 1561–62.

[111] 354 F.3d 1347 (Fed. Cir. 2004).

[112] *Id.* at 1353. Similar problems occur if the disclosure is not too specific but too general. The disclosure of a large genus may lack any "blaze marks" leading persons skilled in the art to (and showing possession of) a particular species later singled out in a claim. *See* Purdue Pharma L.P. v. Faulding Inc., 230 F.3d 1320, 1326 (Fed. Cir. 2000). "[O]ne cannot disclose a forest in the original application, and then later pick a tree out of the forest and say here is my invention." *Id.*

[113] *Billups-Rothenberg*, 642 F.3d at 1037. The number of species that must be disclosed depends on the nature of the invention and progress in the field. *Boston Scientific*, 647 F.3d at 1363; *Ariad*, 598 F.3d at 1350. If the technology is predictable and well understood, disclosure of a smaller number of species may adequately demonstrate possession of the entire genus. *See Boston Scientific*, 647 F.3d at 1363. If the genus includes substantial variations and the art is unpredictable, only a larger number of species may be "representative." *See Carnegie Mellon*, 541 F.3d at 1124.

skilled in the art to "visualize or recognize" the genus the patentee claims.[114] A "generic statement of the invention's boundaries," particularly when presented in functional terms, does not demonstrate possession of the genus.[115]

It may appear that the enablement requirement, discussed in Section 8.6, would prevent an applicant from claiming more than the specification can support. If a claim really reflects a different invention than that described in the specification, it seems unlikely that the specification could enable one to practice the claimed invention. However, according to the Federal Circuit and its predecessor court, " 'it is possible for a specification to *enable* the practice of invention as broadly as it is claimed, and still not *describe* that invention.' "[116] An example of this distinction can be found in *Martin v. Mayer*,[117] where the invention concerned an electrical cable constructed of various layers, including a conductor, a dielectric, and a "high frequency absorption medium." One of the claims at issue required a "harness" composed of more than one such cable. The specification as filed disclosed only a single cable. A person skilled in the art might have been *enabled* by the description of the solitary cable to construct a harness of several cables (particularly if the later-filed claim suggested it), but the specification included no written description to demonstrate that the patentee had conceived of that invention when the application was filed.

A patent specification can demonstrate possession of the invention even if it does not employ precisely the same terms as the claims.[118] In *In re Wright*,[119] for example, the claim language "not permanently fixed," as applied to a microcapsule powder used in an imaging process, did not appear in the specification. Yet the specification included enough information, including a warning that the powder not be disturbed, to show that the invention as originally contemplated and disclosed included powder that was "not permanently fixed."

---

[114] *Boston Scientific*, 647 F.3d at 1363; *Ariad*, 598 F.3d at 1350.

[115] *Billups-Rothenberg*, 642 F.3d at 1037; *Ariad*, 598 F.3d at 1349. Functional language may suffice if there is an established correlation between structure and function, *Billups-Rothenberg*, 642 F.3d at 1037, but that correlation is often absent in the chemical and biochemical arts.

[116] *Vas-Cath*, 935 F.2d at 1561 (emphasis in original). In *Ariad*, 598 F.3d at 1343–45, the Federal Circuit en banc rejected a reading of § 112 that would have merged the written description and enablement language into a single statutory requirement.

[117] 823 F.2d 500 (Fed. Cir. 1987).

[118] *See* Lampi Corp. v. American Power Prods., Inc., 228 F.3d 1365, 1378 (Fed. Cir. 2000).

[119] 866 F.2d 422, 425 (Fed. Cir. 1989).

The written description requirement seems most useful, and most distinct from the other requirements of patentability, when claims have changed during prosecution. Until recently, some judges of the Federal Circuit believed that the description requirement should be invoked *only* as "a priority policeman."[120] But in the en banc case *Ariad Pharmaceuticals, Inc. v. Eli Lilly & Co.,*[121] the Federal Circuit held definitively that the written description requirement applies to all claims, not only those amended during prosecution. For example, an unmodified claim that encompasses a "vast genus of chemical compounds" may be invalid under the written description requirement if the specification does not show that the inventor actually "possessed" such an immense array when the application was filed.[122] Timing is not the issue here; the issue is whether the applicant's contribution to the art, as demonstrated in the patent disclosure, is enough to warrant broad claims. This general concern with overbroad claiming can also be addressed through the enablement requirement, which necessitates a disclosure "commensurate in scope" with the claims.[123]

8.9 NOVELTY AND OBVIOUSNESS

Because an invention can be patented only if it is *new*, an important part of patent prosecution and patent litigation is comparing the claimed invention to prior inventions to determine if the claimed invention is novel. Prior inventions, as well as patents, patent applications, and publications that disclose prior inventions, are known as "prior art references." If a claimed invention is identical to one or more prior art references, the claim is "anticipated."[124] If the claimed invention differs from the prior art, but the differences are of the sort that would occur to a person of ordinary skill, the claim is "obvious."[125] Either is sufficient grounds for holding a claim unpatentable or invalid.

The America Invents Act of 2011 significantly changed the kinds of prior art to which a patent or patent application must be compared in order to determine if the claimed invention is novel and nonobvious. These changes apply to patents and patent applications having an effective filing date after March 16, 2013. Earlier patents and patent applications are subject to the rules that were already in effect. Because it will be many years

---

[120] *See* Enzo Biochem, Inc. v. Gen-Probe Inc., 63 U.S.P.Q.2d 1618, 1624 (Fed. Cir. 2002) (nonprecedential opinion; Rader, J., dissenting).

[121] 598 F.3d 1336 (Fed. Cir. 2010) (en banc).

[122] *Id.* at 1349.

[123] *See* Section 8.6.1.

[124] *See* Section 8.9.5.

[125] *See* Section 8.9.6.

before all of the patents subject to the earlier rules expire, it is important to understand the traditional categories of prior art described in the materials that follow. The rules that apply to patents and patent applications filed after March 16, 2013, are discussed in Section 8.9.2.

8.9.1 Defining Prior Art (Patents Filed before March 16, 2013)

35 U.S.C. § 102 begins "A person shall be entitled to a patent unless . . ." and the following paragraphs list circumstances under which a patent *cannot* be granted. If a patent issues even though it violates one of these conditions, the patent can be held invalid in the course of infringement litigation. The version of § 102 discussed here is the one that governs patents and patent applications with an effective filing date before March 16, 2013.

8.9.1.1 *Prior Knowledge, Use, Patents, and Publications (§ 102(a))*

Section 102(a) reads as follows:

A person shall be entitled to a patent unless—
(a) the invention was known or used by others in this country, or patented or described in a printed publication in this or a foreign country, before the invention thereof by the applicant for patent. . . .

Section 102(a) identifies four kinds of prior art reference that might invalidate a patent if they occurred before the applicant's date of invention:[126]

1. Prior knowledge of the invention by others in *this* country.
2. Prior use of the invention by others in *this* country.
3. A prior patent on the invention in *any* country.
4. A prior "printed publication" of the invention in *any* country.[127]

Patents, printed publications, prior use, and prior knowledge are four common categories of prior art. One feature they share is that, to some degree, they all place the invention in the possession of the public.[128]

---

[126] The "date of invention" is discussed in Section 8.9.1.4.

[127] The earlier version of § 102(a) excludes prior use or knowledge of the invention in a foreign country, perhaps because in an earlier era such knowledge or use would have been difficult to verify. The revised version of § 102, discussed in Section 8.9.2, makes no such distinctions.

[128] *See* Ormco Corp. v. Align Technology, Inc., 463 F.3d 1299, 1305 (Fed. Cir. 2006) ("Art that is not accessible to the public is generally not recognized as prior art."); Carella v. Starlight Archery & Pro Line Co., 804 F.2d 135, 139 (Fed. Cir. 1986). A prior patent at least gives the public *knowledge* of the invention and the expectation of possessing it as soon as the patent has expired.

If an invention has already been the subject of a patent or printed publication, or if the invention is one that has already been known or used, granting a patent on the invention would not "promote the progress of . . . the useful arts."[129] On the contrary, it would take away an invention that the public had already enjoyed. In § 102, "[s]ociety, speaking through Congress and the courts, has said 'thou shalt not take it away.' "[130]

Although prior use, prior knowledge, prior patents, and prior publications are fairly straightforward concepts, they have been refined through judicial analysis, primarily to clarify the extent to which a reference must be publicly available. For example, while "known or used" could literally refer to secret knowledge or secret use, § 102(a) has been interpreted to require knowledge or use that is accessible to the public.[131] Similarly, the term "patented" means that the invention was *disclosed* in a patent, not merely that it was encompassed within the scope of a broad patent claim.[132] "Patented" can refer to the rights granted by foreign countries, even if they differ somewhat from U.S. patent rights,[133] but the foreign patent must be "available to the public."[134]

"[D]escribed in a printed publication" may be the language of § 102(a) that has received the most intense judicial scrutiny.[135] "Printed" is not to be taken literally. Information distributed through other forms of media–such as photographs, CD-ROMs, or microfilm–can qualify as printed publications.[136] The two critical characteristics of a printed publication are (1) that it is "accessible" to the public and (2) that it includes an "enabling disclosure."

---

[129] *See* Section 1.1.

[130] Kimberly-Clark Corp. v. Johnson & Johnson, 745 F.2d 1437, 1453–54 (Fed. Cir. 1984).

[131] *See* Astra Aktiebolag v. Andrx Pharmaceuticals, Inc., 483 F.3d 1364, 1380 (Fed. Cir. 2007) (secret information is not prior art); Minnesota Mining & Mfg. Co. v. Chemque, Inc., 303 F.3d 1294, 1301 (Fed. Cir. 2002); Woodland Trust v. Flowertree Nursery, Inc., 148 F.3d 1368, 1370 (Fed. Cir. 1998).

[132] *See In re* Benno, 768 F.2d 1340, 1346 (Fed. Cir. 1985).

[133] *See In re* Carlson, 983 F.2d 1032 (Fed. Cir. 1992).

[134] *See Carlson*, 983 F.2d at 1037. The standard of "availability" is rather low. *See id.* at 1037–38 (a German Geschmacksmuster can qualify as a publicly available patent under § 102, even though one must travel to a courthouse in a remote German city in order to see the design to which it applies).

[135] The same term also appears in 35 U.S.C. § 102(b). *See* Section 8.9.1.7.

[136] *See In re* Klopfenstein, 380 F.3d 1345, 1348 n.2 (Fed. Cir. 2004) (the meaning of "printed publication" has changed since it was first used; today it means "a perceptible description of the invention, in whatever form it may have been recorded"); *In re* Hall, 781 F.2d 897, 898 (Fed. Cir. 1986) ("The statutory phrase 'printed publication' has been interpreted to give effect to ongoing advances in the technologies of data storage, retrieval, and dissemination.").

"Accessible" means that "interested members of the public could obtain the information if they wanted to."[137] Most books, technical journals, and other materials normally thought of as publications are easily accessible to the public, but inventions are sometimes disclosed in classified documents or documents distributed only on a confidential basis (e.g., documents for the internal use of a corporation). Those do not qualify as "publications."[138] On the other hand, distribution of even a small number of copies without restriction can be considered sufficient.[139]

Some of the most difficult cases arise when a document has not been distributed but has been made available in a library or similar collection. In *In re Hall,*[140] for example, the potentially invalidating reference was a doctoral thesis. Although the thesis had not been published in the usual sense, it had been deposited in a university library in Germany where it was, theoretically, available for review. The court held that "a single catalogued thesis in one university" might "constitute sufficient accessibility to those interested in the art exercising reasonable diligence."[141] On the other hand, in *In re Cronyn,*[142]

---

[137] Constant v. Advanced Micro-Devices, Inc., 848 F.2d 1560, 1569 (Fed. Cir. 1988); *see also In re* NTP, Inc., 654 F.3d 1279, 1296 (Fed. Cir. 2011) (a reference is "publicly available" if it has been " 'disseminated or otherwise made available to the extent that persons interested and ordinarily skilled in the subject matter or art exercising reasonable diligence, can locate it' "); *In re* Lister, 583 F.3d 1307, 1311 (Fed. Cir. 2009); SRI Int'l, Inc. v. Internet Security Sys., Inc., 511 F.3d 1186, 1194 (Fed. Cir. 2008). Accessibility to the public " 'has been called the touchstone in determining whether a reference constitutes a "printed publication.' " *Lister,* 583 F.3d at 1311. If the publication is accessible, it is irrelevant whether anyone in particular *actually* reviewed it. *Id.* at 1314; *SRI,* 511 F.3d at 1197.

[138] *See* Northern Telecom, Inc. v. Datapoint Corp., 908 F.2d 931, 936–37 (Fed. Cir. 1990); Cordis Corp. v. Boston Scientific Corp., 561 F.3d 1319, 1333–34 (Fed. Cir. 2009) (binding legal obligations are not essential; "professional and behavioral norms" against distribution may disqualify a document subject to limited distribution as a "printed publication"); *but cf.* Cooper Cameron Corp. v. Kvaerner Oilfield Prods., Inc., 291 F.3d 1317, 1323–24 (Fed. Cir. 2002) (in spite of a "confidential" label, a report may have been sufficiently available to the public to qualify as prior art). Restricted publications might serve as evidence of a prior invention under § 102(g). *See* Section 8.9.1.3.

[139] *See* Massachusetts Institute of Technology v. A.B. Fortia, 774 F.2d 1104, 1109 (Fed. Cir. 1985) (paper that was discussed at a conference attended by 50 to 100 interested persons and that was distributed "on request" to at least six persons without restrictions, constituted a publication); *but cf.* Preemption Devices, Inc. v. Minnesota Mining & Mfg. Co., 732 F.2d 903, 906 (Fed. Cir. 1984) (six copies of an article sent to a "friend" were not a publication). Sometimes the "interested public" to whom the publication must be available is a relatively small group. *See Cooper Cameron,* 291 F.3d at 1324.

[140] 781 F.2d 897 (Fed. Cir. 1986).

[141] *Hall,* 781 F.2d at 900.

[142] 890 F.2d 1158 (Fed. Cir. 1989).

the court held that three undergraduate theses did not constitute "printed publications." The court held that, in this case, the documents "were not accessible
to the public because they had not been either cataloged or indexed in a meaningful way."[143] They could have been located only by sorting through a collection of index cards kept in a shoe box in the university's chemistry department.
These cases obviously draw fine, and somewhat arbitrary, distinctions.
Although the undergraduate theses in *Cronyn* would have been difficult to
track down, as a practical matter the thesis in *Hall* might have been equally
elusive.[144]

A *display* of information may also qualify as a "printed publication." In
In re Klopfenstein,[145] printed materials were affixed to poster boards and displayed at a professional conference for two and a half days. The materials
were seen by numerous persons skilled in the relevant art, who could have
copied the information at their leisure. Although the materials were neither
distributed nor indexed in a library, the court found that the display qualified as a printed publication because it was accessible to the interested
public.[146]

The other important requirement of a printed publication is that it
include an "enabling disclosure" of the invention.[147] An enabling disclosure is a description of the invention that would allow a person skilled in

---

[143] *Cronyn*, 890 F.2d at 1161.

[144] A case illustrating the low standard of accessibility is *Bruckelmyer v. Ground Heaters, Inc.*,
445 F.3d 1374 (Fed. Cir. 2006). The disputed reference was a Canadian patent application. Because the relevant illustrations related to cancelled claims, they were omitted
from the issued patent. Nevertheless, a person skilled in the art might have been led by
the patent to investigate the patent's file history, and upon doing so would have discovered the missing illustrations. The majority found the "roadmap" provided by the issued
patent sufficient to lead a diligent researcher to the original application, although it is difficult to imagine this actually occurring. *Id.* at 1379. In *Lister*, the court found that a manuscript on file with the Copyright Office was publicly accessible, in spite of the difficulty of
traveling to Washington, D.C. to view it, but only as of the date that the manuscript could
be located by searching an electronic database. *See Lister*, 583 F.3d at 1313–17.

[145] 380 F.3d 1345 (Fed. Cir. 2004).

[146] Factors relevant to the court's decision included "the length of time the display was
exhibited, the expertise of the target audience, the existence (or lack thereof) or reasonable expectations that the material displayed would not be copied, and the simplicity
or ease with which the material displayed could have been copied." *Id.* at 1350.

[147] *Bard Peripheral Vascular, Inc. v. W.L. Gore & Assoc., Inc.*, 670 F.3d 1171, 1184 (Fed.
Cir. 2012); *Orion IP, LLC v. Hyundai Motor America*, 605 F.3d 967, 975 (Fed. Cir.
2010); *Elan Pharmaceuticals, Inc. v. Mayo Foundation*, 346 F.3d 1051, 1054 (Fed. Cir.
2003). A publication need not be enabling to serve as evidence of obviousness, discussed
in Section 8.9.6. *See Amgen, Inc. v. Hoechst Marion Roussel, Inc.*, 314 F.3d 1313, 1357
(Fed. Cir. 2003).

the art to make and use the invention without undue experimentation.[148] If, for example, a marketing brochure boasts of the advantages of a process, but it does not include enough information to allow the process to be duplicated, the brochure lacks an enabling disclosure.[149] In deciding whether a disclosure is enabling, the knowledge that would be available to those of skill in the art can be taken into account. In other words, the publication does not have to include information that would already be known to persons of ordinary skill.[150]

8.9.1.2 Prior Applications (§ 102(e))[151]

Another category of prior art reference, not discussed in § 102(a), is a patent *application*. The circumstances under which a patent application can constitute prior art are set forth in § 102(e). Section 102(e) has evolved into a complex paragraph freighted with cross-references to other portions of the Patent Act, but the gist of it is the addition of the following to the list of potential prior art references:

1. A patent application, filed by another inventor in the United States,[152] before the applicant's date of invention, *if* (eventually) the application issued as a patent or it was published.

If Inventor A had a patent application on file before Inventor B conceived of the same invention, then Inventor A's application would be prior art to Inventor B, even if Inventor A's application neither issued as a patent nor was published as an application until some later date. Note that § 102(e) does not apply to patent applications that are *never* made public.

---

[148] The enabling disclosure requirement also applies to patent applications. *See* Section 8.6. One difference is that a prior art reference is enabling if it discloses the invention but does not tell one how to use it. Patent applications must enable a substantial utility. *See* Rasmusson v. Smithkline Beecham Corp., 413 F.3d 1318, 1325–26 (Fed. Cir. 2005).

[149] *See* Helefix Ltd. v. Blok-Lok, Ltd., 208 F.3d 1339, 1346–48 (Fed. Cir. 2000).

[150] *In re* Donohue, 766 F.2d 531, 533 (Fed. Cir. 1985).

[151] There is no apparent logic to the ordering of paragraphs in § 102. They will therefore be discussed in the order that seems easiest to understand rather than in the order in which they appear in the statute. As before, we are discussing here the version of § 102 that applies to patents and patent applications with an effective filing date before March 16, 2013.

[152] Under certain circumstances, an "international application" may qualify. *See* 35 U.S.C. § 102(e)(1).

8.9.1.3   Prior Inventions (§ 102(g))

Section 102(g) establishes another category of prior art reference:

A person shall be entitled to a patent unless—
(g)(2) before the applicant's invention thereof, the invention was made in this country by another inventor who had not abandoned, suppressed, or concealed it. . . .

Here we are looking for a second inventor—a second inventor who, before the applicant's own date of invention, made the same invention in this country. Two inventors can conceive of the same invention, even if they are working independently. The telephone, for example, is said to have been invented independently, and almost simultaneously, by Alexander Graham Bell and Elisha Gray.[153] Other countries award priority to the first inventor to file a patent application, but in the United States the patent has traditionally gone the first to *invent.* That will change as the United States transitions to a first-to-file system following the adoption of the America Invents Act. But with respect to patents and patent applications having an effective filing date before March 16, 2013, § 102(g) denies a patent to an inventor who was not the first to invent.[154]

There is an important exception. The first invention does not count against a later inventor if the first invention was "abandoned, suppressed, or concealed." An invention is "abandoned, suppressed, or concealed if, within a reasonable time after completion, no steps are taken to make the invention publicly known."[155] Abandonment, suppression, and concealment can be inferred if, after a reasonable period of time, the first inventor has not filed a patent application, used the invention in public,

---

[153] Although a recent book claims that Bell stole essential information from Gray's own patent application, thanks to some chicanery at the Patent Office. *See* SETH SHULMAN, THE TELEPHONE GAMBIT: CHASING ALEXANDER GRAHAM BELL'S SECRET (2008).

[154] Section 102(g)(2) may be invoked in litigation to invalidate an issued patent. *See, e.g.,* Flex-Rest, LLC v. Steelcase, Inc., 455 F.3d 1351, 1358 (Fed. Cir. 2006); Dow Chemical Co. v. Astro-Valcour, Inc., 267 F.3d 1334, 1339 (Fed. Cir. 2001); Apotex USA, Inc. v. Merck & Co., 254 F.3d 1031, 1035 (Fed. Cir. 2001). If the contest for priority occurs in the course of prosecuting a patent application, the result can be an interference proceeding, discussed in Section 5.4. In that event, § 102(g)(1) controls. The rules are much the same, except that work in some foreign countries can suffice to establish priority, whereas § 102(g)(2) is restricted to prior invention in the United States. Interference proceedings will no longer be necessary when the America Invents Act is fully implemented. At that point, it will no longer matter which of two competing applicants invented first.

[155] *Apotex,* 254 F.3d at 1039; Correge v. Murphy, 705 F.2d 1326, 1330 (Fed. Cir. 1983).

embodied the invention in a product for sale, or described the invention in a publication.[156] This exception to the "first to invent" rule rewards those who make inventions available to the public and penalizes those who hide or abandon inventions.[157]

If the delay in publicizing an invention, or applying for a patent, is more than a few years, abandonment may be presumed.[158] The presumption can be overcome by evidence that efforts to perfect the invention caused the delay.[159] On the other hand, efforts to *commercialize* the invention cannot excuse an applicant's failure to file promptly.[160] In *Lutzker v. Plet*,[161] where the invention was a device for making canapés, the first inventor (Lutzker) waited more than four years after completing the invention before disclosing it to the public at a trade show. By the time of the trade show, the second inventor (Plet) had invented the device independently and filed a patent application. Lutzker argued that the delay should be excused because it had been due to efforts to perfect the invention. The Patent Office, affirmed by the court, disagreed. The delay was attributed to the development of a recipe book, packaging, and other things unrelated to the invention itself. Lutzker was therefore found to have abandoned, suppressed, or concealed the invention, and his activities did not prevent the issuance of a patent to Plet.[162]

Two points should be mentioned about the timing of an abandonment. First, the abandonment can be nullified if the first inventor renews his or her efforts to patent the invention, or to make it available to the public,

---

[156] *See Flex-Rest*, 455 F.3d at 1359; *Dow Chemical*, 267 F.3d at 1342.

[157] *See* Checkpoint Sys., Inc. v. U.S. Int'l Trade Comm'n, 54 F.3d 765, 761 (Fed. Cir. 1995).

[158] *See* Lutzker v. Plet, 843 F.2d 1364, 1367 (Fed. Cir. 1988) (discussing cases in which delays of 29 months to four years were held sufficient to show abandonment, suppression, or concealment). There is no period of time that is unreasonable *per se*. *See Flex-Rest*, 455 F.3d at 1359; *Dow Chemical*, 267 F.3d at 1342–43. "Rather a determination of abandonment, suppression or concealment has 'consistently been based on equitable principles and public policy as applied to the facts of each case.'" *Checkpoint*, 54 F.3d at 761.

[159] *See Lutzker*, 843 F.2d at 1367.

[160] If the prior inventor never intended to file a patent application but, instead, meant to introduce the invention to the public by a product, courts are far more tolerant of commercial activities as an excuse for delay. *See Flex-Rest*, 455 F.3d at 1360; *Dow Chemical*, 267 F.3d at 1343; *Checkpoint*, 54 F.3d at 762. This means, oddly enough, that the prior inventor who never filed a patent application himself may be better off because he can more easily invalidate the subsequent patent of someone else.

[161] 843 F.2d 1364 (Fed. Cir. 1988).

[162] The court was influenced by the fact that the recipe book and other items accounting for the delay were not related to the disclosure in Lutzker's patent application. *Lutzker*, 843 F.2d at 1367–68.

before the second inventor "enters the field."[163] The first inventor would be credited with the date of renewed activity as his or her "date of invention." Thus, if Lutzker had begun work on a patent application before Plet entered the field, his earlier inactivity could have been overlooked. Second, § 102(g) refers to prior inventions that "had" not been abandoned, suppressed, or concealed, implying that an invention abandoned, suppressed, or concealed *after* the entry into the field of the second inventor would still be effective as prior art.[164]

8.9.1.4 *Date of Invention*

When applying the version of § 102 that governs patents and patent applications filed before March 16, 2013, an important step is determining the patentee's (or applicant's) "date of invention." A patent, patent application, or other reference is not *prior* art under §§ 102(a) or (e) unless it predates the patentee's or applicant's date of invention. Applying § 102(g) requires consideration of the dates of invention of both the patentee or patent applicant and an alleged prior inventor. As can be seen in the discussion that follows, determining the date of invention is no simple task. One of the virtues of the America Invents Act is that the *new* version of § 102, governing patents and applications filed after March 16, 2013, does not hinge on the date of invention. As discussed in Section 8.9.2, the *filing* date of a patent or patent application, rather than the invention date, is the critical question, and it is a question that can be answered quite easily. Nevertheless, courts will have to apply the original date-of-invention rules when testing the validity of older patents.

"Invention" involves two steps: "conception" and "reduction to practice."[165] Conception is the mental act of invention–the moment of insight when the inventor imagines the thing that ultimately will be claimed. As formally defined by the Federal Circuit, conception requires the formation in the inventor's mind of "a definite and permanent idea of the invention,

---

[163] *See Lutzker*, 843 F.2d at 1368; Paulik v. Rizkalla, 760 F.2d 1270, 1275–76 (Fed. Cir. 1985).

[164] The language of the statute seems clear. However, the Federal Circuit has not ruled on this issue, and it could be argued that ignoring a later abandonment would hinder the policy of making inventions available to the public.

[165] The Supreme Court regards conception as the more important of the two. *See* Pfaff v. Wells Electronics, Inc., 525 U.S. 55, 60 (1998) ("The primary meaning of the word 'invention' in the Patent Act unquestionably refers to the inventor's conception rather than to a physical embodiment of that idea."). However, as discussed below, reduction to practice still plays an important role in establishing priority.

including every feature of the subject matter sought to be patented."[166] If the inventor has done no more than recognize a problem, the conception of the invention is still incomplete.[167] Conception is complete only when the inventor finds the *solution* to a problem, and the solution is worked out in sufficient detail, in the inventor's mind, that persons of ordinary skill in the art could put the inventor's ideas to practice without extensive research or undue experimentation.[168]

"Reduction to practice" means reducing the idea to a physical embodiment and, in most cases, testing it to confirm that it will work.[169] In the case of an apparatus, reduction to practice means that the apparatus was assembled, at least in prototype. In the case of a method, reduction to practice means that the method was actually performed.[170] A patent claim is

---

[166] Sewall v. Walters, 21 F.3d 411, 415 (Fed. Cir. 1994); *see also* Solvay S.A. v. Honeywell Int'l, Inc., 622 F.3d 1367, 1377 (Fed. Cir. 2010) ("Conception is the 'formation, in the mind of the inventor, of a definite and permanent idea of the complete and operative invention, as it is hereafter to be applied in practice.'"); Shum v. Intel Corp., 499 F.3d 1272, 1277 (Fed. Cir. 2007); Stern v. Trustees of Columbia University, 434 F.3d 1375, 1378 (Fed. Cir. 2006). A mere research plan coupled with a vague hope of success does not amount to a conception. *See In re* Jolley, 308 F.3d 1317, 1323 (Fed. Cir. 2002); Hitzeman v. Rutter, 243 F.3d 1345, 1356–57 (Fed. Cir. 2001); Burroughs Wellcome Co. v. Barr Labs., Inc., 40 F.3d 1223, 1228 (Fed. Cir. 1994) ("An idea is definite and permanent when the inventor has a specific, settled idea, a particular solution to the problem at hand, not just a general goal or research plan he hopes to pursue."). An inventor who has stumbled across a patentable invention must recognize it, though the inventor need not appreciate that it is, in fact, patentable. *See* Invitrogen Corp. v. Clontech Labs., Inc., 429 F.3d 1052, 1074 (Fed. Cir. 2005); Rosco, Inc. v. Mirror Lite Co., 304 F.3d 1373, 1381 (Fed. Cir. 2002); *Hitzeman*, 243 F.3d at 1358–59. The word "invention" means that the idea must be original to the inventor, not copied from somewhere else, even if the work from which it was copied occurred in another country. *Solvay*, 622 F.3d at 1377–78 (conception must be "an original idea of the inventor").

[167] *See* Morgan v. Hirsch, 728 F.2d 1449 (Fed. Cir. 1994).

[168] *See Solvay*, 622 F.3d at 1377 ("The test for conception is whether the inventor had an idea that was definite and permanent enough that one skilled in the art could understand the invention."); Brand v. Miller, 487 F.3d 862, 870 n.4 (Fed. Cir. 2007); *Stern*, 434 F.3d at 1378. Conception does not, however, require proof that the invention works "to a scientific certainty." University of Pittsburgh v. Hedrick, 573 F.3d 1290, 1299 (Fed. Cir. 2009).

[169] *See Solvay*, 622 F.3d at 1376 ("[a]ctual reduction to practice requires that the claimed invention work for its intended purpose"); Z4 Technologies, Inc. v. Microsoft Corp., 507 F.3d 1340, 1352 (Fed. Cir. 2007); Slip Track Sys., Inc. v. Metal-Lite, Inc., 304 F.3d 1256, 1265 (Fed. Cir. 2002) (reduction to practice "may require testing, depending on the character of the invention and the problem that it solves").

[170] *See Z4*, 507 F.3d at 1352 ("'the inventor must prove that . . . he constructed an embodiment or performed a process that met all of the [claim] limitations'"); *Slip Track*, 304 F.3d at 1265.

not reduced to practice until there is a physical embodiment that includes all of the elements of the claim.[171]

The amount of testing of the physical embodiment necessary for reduction to practice varies considerably depending on the nature of the invention. The courts are instructed to employ a "common sense approach."[172] Some devices are so simple, and their effectiveness so obvious, that no testing at all is required.[173] On the other hand, some inventions require careful evaluation under conditions that duplicate, or simulate, the intended working environment of the invention. The testing required is whatever is reasonably necessary to demonstrate that the invention will work.[174] Even where testing is required, it is not necessary to demonstrate that the invention is so refined that it is ready to market.[175] A prototype that is not yet of commercial quality may be sufficient to show that the principle of the invention is sound.[176] Moreover, "[t]esting need not show utility beyond a possibility of failure, but only utility beyond a probability of failure."[177]

In a few cases, an invention is so unpredictable that it cannot be fully *conceived* until experiments have been performed and the results evaluated. Conception and reduction to practice are, in these cases, simultaneous. This is most likely to occur in the fields of chemistry and biotechnology, where useful combinations can sometimes be discovered only by trial and error.[178] In *Smith v. Bousquet*,[179] for example, the court held that the

---

[171] *See* Eaton v. Evans, 204 F.3d 1094, 1097 (Fed. Cir. 2000).

[172] Scott v. Finney, 34 F.3d 1058, 1061 (Fed. Cir. 1994).

[173] *See Slip Track*, 304 F.3d at 1265.

[174] "[The] common sense approach prescribes more scrupulous testing under circumstances approaching actual use conditions when the problem includes many uncertainties. On the other hand, when the problem to be solved does not present myriad variables, common sense similarly permits little or no testing to show the soundness of the principles of operation of the invention." *Scott*, 34 F.3d at 1063; *see also* Taskett v. Dentlinger, 344 F.3d 1337, 1341 (Fed. Cir. 2003).

[175] "Reduction to practice does not require 'that the invention, when tested, be in a commercially satisfactory stage of development.'" *Scott*, 34 F.3d at 1061; *see also* Loral Fairchild Corp. v. Matsushita Elec. Indus. Co., 266 F.3d 1358, 1362–63 (Fed. Cir. 2001) ("Once the invention has been shown to work for its intended purpose, reduction to practice is complete.... Further efforts to commercialize the invention are simply not relevant....").

[176] *See Scott*, 34 F.3d at 1062.

[177] *Id.*

[178] *See* Mycogen Plant Science , Inc. v. Monsanto Co., 243 F.3d 1316, 1330 (Fed. Cir. 2001) ("The doctrine of simultaneous conception and reduction to practice is somewhat rare but certainly not unknown, especially in the unpredictable arts such as chemistry and biology."), *vacated on other grounds*, 535 U.S. 1109 (2002).

[179] 111 F.2d 157 (C.C.P.A. 1940).

effectiveness of a chemical as an insecticide, on particular species and under particular conditions, could not be predicted until realistic experiments were carried out. Until then, plans to use the chemical as an insecticide were mere hope or speculation, not an invention.[180]

The reduction to practice discussed so far is *actual* reduction to practice. Filing a patent application effects a "*constructive* reduction to practice."[181] "Constructive" is a word often used in the law when an act is treated as though it were one thing when it is actually something else.[182] Although filing a patent application is not a reduction to practice at all, it is treated as though it were for purposes of fixing the date of invention. Consequently, an inventor who never produces a physical embodiment of the invention, or who does so only later, will be considered to have reduced to practice on his filing date.[183]

If "date of invention" were always synonymous with "date of reduction to practice," life would be simpler. In fact, the date of conception must also be taken into account because of the following complication introduced by § 102(g):

> In determining priority of invention under this subsection, there shall be considered not only the respective dates of conception and reduction to practice of the invention, but also the reasonable diligence of one who was first to conceive and last to reduce to practice, from a time prior to conception by the other.

In other words, when two inventors contend for the title of "first to invent," either in the context of an interference proceeding or a prior art challenge to an issued patent, the inventor who was first to conceive but last to reduce

---

[180] More recently, the concept of simultaneous conception and reduction to practice has been applied to inventions involving DNA. *See, e.g., Mycogen*, 243 F.3d at 1330–31; Amgen, Inc. v. Chugai Pharmaceutical Co., 927 F.2d 1200, 1206–7 (Fed. Cir. 1991).

[181] *Solvay*, 622 F.3d at 1376; Frazer v. Schlegel, 498 F.3d 1283, 1287 (Fed. Cir. 2007); Hoffman-La Roche, Inc. v. Promega Corp., 323 F.3d 1354, 1377 (Fed. Cir. 2003).

[182] See the discussion of "constructive notice" in Section 11.8.3.2.

[183] Treating the filing of a patent application as equivalent to producing a physical embodiment of the invention is not so far-fetched; the application should include all of the information necessary to allow one skilled in the art to complete such an embodiment without undue experimentation. If it does not include that information, the patent will be invalid for lack of enablement. *See* Section 8.6.

to practice will prevail, if, but only if, the inventor who was first to conceive was "diligent" in reducing the invention to practice.[184]

The easiest cases to resolve are those in which the first inventor to conceive of the invention is also the first to reduce it to practice. Suppose, for example, that Inventor A, who has received a patent, sues an infringer. The infringer argues that the invention of Inventor B is prior art to Inventor A's patent under § 102(g). If Inventor A's date of conception precedes Inventor B's date of conception *and* Inventor's A's date of reduction to practice precedes Inventor B's date of reduction to practice, Inventor B's work is not prior art. If the situation is reversed (Inventor B's dates of conception and reduction to practice precede Inventor A's respective dates), then Inventor B's invention is prior art to Inventor A. In neither case is anyone's diligence an issue. When, however, the first inventor to conceive was last to reduce to practice, diligence comes into play. To return to the example, if Inventor A was the first to conceive of the invention, but before Inventor A could reduce the invention to practice Inventor B both conceived and reduced to practice, the patent to Inventor A would be valid only if Inventor A had been diligent from a time *prior* to B's date of conception.[185]

The rules can be more easily visualized with the aid of a timeline. In the following examples, "C" stands for the date of conception and "RTP" for the date of reduction to practice. Time progresses from left to right. Assume that Inventor A has received a patent. Inventor B developed the same invention independently, and his work is alleged to be prior art under § 102(g). In the first example, B's invention is not prior art because he was last to conceive and last to reduce to practice:

---

[184] *See Pfaff*, 525 U.S. at 61 ("[A]ssuming diligence on the part of the applicant, it is normally the first inventor to conceive, rather than the first to reduce to practice, who establishes the right to patent."); Brand v. Miller, 487 F.3d 862, 869 (Fed. Cir. 2007); Medichem, S.A. v. Rolabo, S.L., 437 F.3d 1157, 1169 (Fed. Cir. 2006). The Federal Circuit has applied the diligence principle in the context of § 102(a). *See In re* Mulder, 716 F.2d 1542, 1545 (Fed. Cir. 1983) (printed publication); Loral Fairchild Corp. v. Matsushita Elec. Indus. Co., 266 F.3d 1358, 1365-66 (Fed. Cir. 2001) (Newman, J., dissenting). However, the subsequent addition of the phrase "under this subsection" suggests that it is only appropriate in the prior invention context of § 102(g).

[185] *See* Singh v. Brake, 317 F.3d 1334, 1340 (Fed. Cir. 2003); *Jolley*, 308 F.3d at 1326. The time period that begins just before a rival's conception and ends with one's own reduction to practice is frequently called the "critical period" for diligence. *See, e.g.*, Scott v. Koyama, 281 F.3d 1243, 1247 (Fed. Cir. 2002); Bey v. Kollonitsch, 806 F.2d 1024, 1025–26 (Fed. Cir. 1986). Earlier lapses in diligence can be overlooked.

```
A: C --------- RTP
B:           C ------------ RTP
```

In the second example, B's invention is prior art because he was first to conceive and first to reduce to practice:

```
A:           C ------------ RTP
B: C --------- RTP
```

In the third example, A was first to conceive, but B was first to reduce to practice. B's invention is not prior art *if* A was diligent, though not as swift as B, in reducing his invention to practice:

```
A: C ------------------- RTP (diligent?)
B:        C ----- RTP
```

In the last example, B was first to conceive, but A was first to reduce to practice. B's invention is prior art *if* B was diligent in reducing his invention to practice:

```
A:      C ----- RTP
B: C ------------------- RTP (diligent?)
```

The purpose of this rather confusing set of rules is to reward inventors who are the first to conceive of an idea, while encouraging inventors to bring their ideas to a practical end, or a public disclosure, as soon as possible.

"Diligence" in this context means reasonable efforts to reduce the invention to practice or to file a patent application. Diligent effort must be relatively continuous. Some excuses have been recognized for lapses of effort —most notably the need to complete some other invention before the first can be reduced to practice.[186] The courts will also consider "the reasonable everyday problems and limitations encountered by an inventor," including illness, poverty, the need for an occasional vacation, or the need to make a living by other means.[187] Efforts to fund or commercialize the invention,

---

[186] *See, e.g.,* Keizer v. Bradley, 270 F.2d 396 (C.C.P.A. 1959).

[187] *See* Griffith v. Kanamaru, 816 F.2d 624, 626–27 (Fed. Cir. 1987). If the reduction to practice had been a constructive reduction to practice, accomplished by filing a patent application, the patent attorney's need to work on other applications can be considered an adequate excuse for delay if the applications were handled in the order received or if there was a need to work on related applications as a group. *See Bey,* 806 F.2d at 1028–30.

or time devoted to an unrelated invention, are not considered adequate excuses for delay.[188]

Although diligence seems the inverse of abandonment or concealment, and the factual considerations are similar, remember that they are distinct issues under § 102(g). Abandonment can negate a prior art reference that was both conceived *and* reduced to practice before the patentee entered the scene. Diligence is an issue only in the rarer circumstance that the first inventor to conceive was the last to reduce to practice.

8.9.1.5   Burdens of Proof–Conception, Reduction to Practice, and Diligence

If a question of priority turns on the filing date of a patent application or the publication date of a technical journal, the proof is relatively straightforward. The filing date of a patent application is a matter of public record, and the publication date of a journal is usually easy to verify. If, however, priority depends on dates of conception and reduction to practice, the facts can be much harder to establish. A conception date, in particular, can be a difficult thing to prove because the essential activity occurs entirely in the mind of the inventor.

Whenever there is a successful invention, there are sure to be those who purport to have had the same idea first. By the same token, it is easy for any patentee faced with prior art to claim an earlier conception date. The courts have therefore established certain rules governing the proof required to establish conception and reduction to practice.

First, the application filing date is presumed to be the applicant's date of invention in the absence of other evidence.[189] During prosecution of a patent application, if the applicant needs to establish an earlier date of invention in order to predate a potential prior art reference, this can be accomplished under certain circumstances by means of a sworn affidavit from the inventor establishing prior conception and reduction to practice.[190] This is known as "swearing behind" a reference. In litigation, such claims must be subject to

---

[188] *See Griffith,* 816 F.2d at 627–28. As in the case of abandonment or concealment, the line between work on the invention and unrelated commercial activity can be difficult to draw. "Precedent illustrates the continuum between, on the one hand, ongoing laboratory experimentation, and on the other hand, pure money-raising activity that is entirely unrelated to practice of the process." *Scott,* 281 F.3d at 1248 (holding that construction of facilities for large-scale practice of the claimed process sufficed to show diligence).

[189] *See* Ecolochem, Inc. v. Southern California Edison Co., 227 F.3d 1361, 1371 (Fed. Cir. 2000); Bausch & Lomb, Inc. v. Barnes-Hind/Hydrocurve, Inc., 796 F.2d 443, 449 (Fed. Cir. 1986).

[190] *See* 37 C.F.R. § 1.131.

proof. A party challenging a patent must establish prior conception and reduction to practice by "clear and convincing evidence,"[191] and a patentee claiming an invention date prior to the filing date must introduce evidence to support it.[192]

A date of conception cannot be established entirely by the inventor's own testimony, which is likely to be untrustworthy.[193] The date must be *corroborated*, usually by the testimony of a noninventor who was made aware of the inventor's work soon after the date in question.[194] For this reason, engineers involved in organized research programs often have their laboratory notebooks periodically reviewed, signed, and dated by a colleague.[195] A witnessed notebook can be the best evidence of what was conceived and when.[196] Dates of reduction to practice and allegations of diligence also must be corroborated by evidence independent of the inventor.[197] Although eyewitness testimony is often best, corroboration is subject to a "rule of reason" that allows the inventor's claims to be substantiated by any evidence sufficient

---

[191] Solvay S.A. v. Honeywell Int'l, Inc., 622 F.3d 1367, 1374 (Fed. Cir. 2010); Apotex, USA, Inc. v. Merck & Co., 254 F.3d 1031, 1036 (Fed. Cir. 2001).

[192] *See In re* NTP, 654 F.3d 1279, 1291 (Fed. Cir. 2011). The ultimate burden of proof on validity, however, always remains with the party challenging the patent. *See* Innovative Scuba Concepts, Inc. v. Feder Indus., Inc., 26 F.3d 1112, 1115 (Fed. Cir. 1994).

[193] *See* Lazare Kaplan Int'l, Inc. v. Photoscribe Technologies, Inc., 628 F.3d 1359, 1374 (Fed. Cir. 2010); Martek Biosciences Corp. v. Nutrinova, Inc., 579 F.3d 1363, 1374–75 (Fed. Cir. 2009) ("The purpose of the corroboration requirement is to prevent fraud, namely to 'provide[] an additional safeguard against courts being deceived by inventors who may be tempted to mischaracterize the events of the past through their testimony.' "); Medichem, S.A. v. Rolabo, S.L., 437 F.3d 1157, 1170 (Fed. Cir. 2006).

[194] *See NTP*, 654 F.3d at 1291; *Lazare*, 628 F.3d at 1374; *Martek*, 579 F.3d at 1374–75; Sandt Technology, Ltd. v. Resco Metal and Plastics Corp., 264 F.3d 1344, 1350 (Fed. Cir. 2001).

[195] The colleague, however, cannot be a co-inventor. See *Medichem*, 437 F.3d at 1171.

[196] *Sandt Technology*, 264 F.3d at 1350–51 ("Documentary or physical evidence that is made contemporaneously with the inventive process provides the most reliable proof that the inventor's testimony has been corroborated."); *see also Lazare*, 628 F.3d at 1374; *Martek*, 579 F.3d at 1375. In comparison, "post-invention oral testimony is more suspect, as there is more of a risk that the witness may have a litigation-inspired motive to corroborate the inventor's testimony, and that the testimony may be inaccurate." *Sandt*, 264 F.3d at 1351.

[197] *See Medichem*, 437 F.3d at 1169 (corroboration of reduction to practice); Brown v. Barbacid, 436 F.3d 1376, 1380 (Fed. Cir. 2006) (corroboration of diligence). The Federal Circuit has described the standard for corroborating reduction to practice as "more stringent." *Martek*, 579 F.3d at 1376; Singh v. Brake, 222 F.3d 1362, 1370 (Fed. Cir. 2000). Perhaps that is because reduction to practice requires the inventor to take things farther than conception. *See Martek*, 579 F.3d at 1376 ("a notebook page may well show that the inventor *conceived* what he wrote on the page, whereas it may not show that the experiments were *actually performed*, as required for a reduction to practice" (emphasis in original)).

to establish credibility.[198] For example, testimony regarding a reduction to practice might be corroborated by dated invoices for the parts that were used to build an embodiment of the invention.[199]

8.9.1.6 Prior Work by the Same Inventor

The kinds of prior art listed in §§ 102(a), (e), and (g) are limited, expressly or by implication, to prior inventions, patents, patent applications, printed publications, public knowledge, or public use attributable to persons *other than the inventor*.[200] This limitation can be difficult to apply in cases where a patent names two or more joint inventors.[201] For example, is a publication by A alone prior art to the joint invention of A and B? In these cases, courts resort to the concept of the "inventive entity," which is simply a way of referring to a specific group of inventors. A reference can be considered prior art to a patent or patent application if it is attributable to a different inventive entity.[202] This is true whether the prior inventive entity is composed of

[198] *See NTP*, 654 F.3d at 1291; *Lazare*, 628 F.3d at 1374; *Medichem*, 437 F.3d at 1170–71 (" '[I]t is not necessary to produce an actual over-the-shoulder observer. Rather, sufficient circumstantial evidence of an independent nature can satisfy the corroboration requirement.' "); *Sandt Technology*, 264 F.3d at 1350 ("rule of reason" test, examining "all pertinent evidence"). In *Woodland Trust v. Flowertree Nursery, Inc.*, 148 F.3d 1368, 1371 (Fed. Cir. 1998), the court listed a number of factors relevant to whether the testimony of a corroborating witness satisfies the rule of reason. These include the interest of the corroborating witness in the subject matter of the suit and the amount of time that has elapsed since the events in question. *See also Lazare*, 628 F.3d at 1374.

[199] *See* Lacotte v. Thomas, 758 F.2d 611, 613 (Fed. Cir. 1985).

[200] *In re* Katz, 687 F.2d 450, 454 (C.C.P.A. 1982); *see also* Invitrogen Corp. v. Biocrest Mfg., L.P., 424 F.3d 1374, 1381 (Fed. Cir. 2005); Rapoport v. Dement, 254 F.3d 1053, 1056 (Fed. Cir. 2001) (report cannot be cited as prior art against its author). Section 102(a) refers to an invention "patented or described in a printed publication . . . before the invention thereof by the applicant." While there is no explicit exception for the applicant's own work, clearly the applicant himself cannot patent or describe an invention in a printed publication before he has at least conceived it. It might be possible for the applicant to produce a patent or publication in comparison to which his later invention is *obvious* (see Section 8.9.4), but the courts have generally ruled out the use of an inventor's own work as the basis for an obviousness challenge. *See Katz*, 687 F.2d at 454. The statutory bar provisions (*see* Section 8.9.1.7) create an important exception. A statutory bar, based either on anticipation or obviousness, can be triggered by the inventor's own activities if they occur more than one year before an application is filed. *See Invitrogen*, 424 F.3d at 1381. A prior patent by the same inventor can raise issues of double patenting. *See* Section 8.10.

[201] *See* Section 6.1.

[202] For patents and patent applications filed after March 16, 2013, disclosures in patent applications and patents are not prior art if the subject matter was "owned by the same person or subject to an assignment to the same person." 35 U.S.C. § 102(b)(2).

entirely different individuals or whether some individuals are common to both inventive entities. Thus, a publication by A, describing his work alone, could invalidate the subsequent patent of A and B together.[203] A publication describing the work of A and B together could invalidate a subsequent patent to A alone. But a publication describing the work of A and B together would not be prior art to the subsequent patent of A and B.[204] Note that the question is not who *wrote* the publication but rather whose *invention* the publication describes. A publication by A and B describing the work of A alone would not be § 102(a) prior art to A's subsequent patent.[205]

Section 103(c) provides another twist. Even if a prior invention is attributable to a different inventive entity, if the invention is *only* a potential reference under § 102(e), (f), or (g), and if the prior invention and the subsequent application are owned by the *same person* (or both are subject to an obligation to assign to the same person), the prior invention cannot render the subsequent patent invalid for obviousness.[206] This provision applies most often where several people are working on a project for the same corporation,[207] and it prevents the work of one person from invalidating the work of a colleague, recognizing that both are generally working under the same direction and toward the same goal.

8.9.1.7 Statutory Bars

Section 102(b), as applied to patents or patent applications filed before March 16, 2013, provides as follows:

A person shall be entitled to a patent unless—
　(b) the invention was patented or described in a printed publication in this or a foreign country or in public use or on sale in this country, more than one year prior to the date of the application for patent in the United States. . . .

Section 102(b) is similar to 102(a) in that both refer to prior patents, printed publications, and public use. However, § 102(b) differs

---

[203] This is one occasion on which A and B might reconsider whether B was properly named as a joint inventor. If B's contribution did not rise to the level of invention, and if B was named as an inventor only accidentally, it would be possible to correct the patent to name only A as the inventor, thereby removing the prior publication as a potential prior art reference. *See* Section 6.1.

[204] Unless, again, it could suffice for a statutory bar under § 102(b). *See* Section 8.9.1.7.

[205] *See Katz,* 687 F.2d at 455.

[206] *See* Section 8.9.4.

[207] The law generally treats a corporation as a "person." People are "natural persons."

fundamentally from § 102(a) in three respects. First, § 102(b) adds the "on sale" language. Second, a § 102(b) issue often arises from the actions of the applicant, whereas a § 102(a) issue can only arise from the acts of a third party. Finally, the important date for § 102(b) is not the date of the invention but a date exactly one year before the patent application was filed.[208] This date is known as the application's "critical date." The purpose of § 102(b) is to ensure that the applicant did not delay too long in filing a patent application after the occurrence of certain key events.

Imagine the following scenario. On January 1, 2010, an inventor conceived of a better mousetrap and reduced the invention to practice by constructing a prototype in his workshop. January 1, 2010, is the date of the invention, and that date is corroborated by a witnessed laboratory notebook. The inventor submitted a complete description of the mousetrap to the *Inventor's Newsletter*, which published the description on January 1, 2011. On January 2, 2012, the inventor filed a patent application, and the application matured into an issued patent. The "critical date" of the patent, under § 102(b), is January 2, 2011. The publication in the *Inventor's Newsletter* on January 1, 2011, is not prior art under § 102(a) because it did not occur before the applicant's date of invention. However, the publication did occur before the critical date. Consequently, if the publication included a complete and enabling description of the invention, the patent would be invalid under § 102(b). In essence, § 102(b) provides a one-year grace period after the first patent, publication, public use, or offer to sell that relates to the claimed invention.[209] An inventor has that long to file a patent application, or the right to a patent is lost.

The rationale for § 102(b) is threefold. First, and most generally, it encourages diligence by penalizing inventors who are lazy or inclined to suppress their inventions, or who for some other reason delay in filing a patent application.[210] Second, it prevents the public from being misled

---

[208] When prosecution results in a chain of related applications, a later application may be entitled to the effective filing date of a preceding application for purposes of § 102(b). *See* Section 5.2.

[209] *See* Gemmy Indus. Corp. v. Chrisha Creations Ltd., 452 F.3d 1353, 1358 (Fed. Cir. 2006); Woodland Trust v. Flowertree Nursery, Inc., 148 F.3d 1368, 1370 (Fed. Cir. 1998).

[210] *See* August Technology Corp. v. Camtek, Ltd., 655 F.3d 1278, 1288 (Fed. Cir. 2011) ("[s]ection 102(b) encourages prompt disclosure of new inventions"); Special Devices, Inc. v. OEA, Inc., 270 F.3d 1353, 1357 (Fed. Cir. 2001); La Bounty Mfg., Inc., v. U.S. Int'l Trade Comm'n, 958 F.2d 1066, 1071 (Fed. Cir. 1992) ("The general purpose behind [the] section 102(b) bars is to require inventors to assert with due diligence their right to a patent through the prompt filing of a patent application.").

where the availability of the invention to the public, without evidence that the inventor intends to obtain a patent, might create the impression that the invention is up for grabs.[211] Finally, it prevents what could be an unwarranted extension of the inventor's monopoly powers beyond the 20 years contemplated by the patent system.[212] Without some limitation, an inventor might delay seeking patent protection indefinitely, and the mere threat that the inventor would do so eventually could prevent others from daring to compete. On the other hand, an inventor does need a certain amount of time to perfect the invention, judge whether it is worth pursuing, and prepare a patent application.[213] Section 102(b) establishes one year as the period that most effectively balances the needs of the inventor against the needs of the public.

The prohibitions of § 102(b) are commonly known as "statutory bars." A statutory bar can prevent the issuance of a claim in a patent application, or it can be used to challenge the validity of an issued patent in subsequent infringement litigation. A reference that qualifies under § 102(b) can also be used as the basis for a finding of obviousness.[214] In some cases, a reference can qualify as prior art under either § 102(a) or § 102(b). If so, § 102(b) can provide the simpler analysis because it relies on the easily determined critical date of the patent application rather than the often difficult to determine date of invention.

The most frequently encountered statutory bar is probably the "on sale bar" created when the inventor, or a third party,[215] takes steps to commercialize the claimed invention more than one year before the filing date of

---

[211] *See* Continental Plastic Containers v. Owens Brockway Plastic Prods., Inc., 141 F.3d 1073, 1079 (Fed. Cir. 1998) ("[t]he primary policy underlying the 'public use' case is that of detrimental public reliance"); Baxter Int'l, Inc. v. Cobe Labs., Inc., 88 F.3d 1054, 1058 (Fed. Cir. 1996).

[212] *See* Atlanta Attachment Co. v. Leggett & Platt, Inc., 516 F.3d 1361, 1365 (Fed. Cir. 2008) ("The overriding concern of the on-sale bar is an inventor's attempt to commercialize his invention beyond the statutory term."); *Continental Plastic*, 141 F.3d at 1079.

[213] *See Baxter Int'l*, 88 F.3d at 1058 (policies behind § 102(b) include " 'allowing the inventor a reasonable amount of time following sales activity to determine the potential economic value of a patent' ").

[214] *See* Dippin' Dots, Inc. v. Mosey, 476 F.3d 1337, 1344 (Fed. Cir. 2007); Elmer v. ICC Fabricating, Inc., 67 F.3d 1571, 1574 (Fed. Cir. 1995).

[215] *See Special Devices*, 270 F.3d at 1355 ("By phrasing the statutory bar in the passive voice, Congress indicated that it does not matter who places the invention 'on sale'; it only matters that someone—inventor, supplier or other third party—placed it on sale.").

the patent application.[216] A single sale, or a single offer to sell, is sufficient to invoke the statutory bar.[217]

Disputes frequently arise over whether certain activity did or did not constitute a sale or definite offer to sell. For example, an inventor may contend that a commercial relationship with a potential customer was not related to a bona fide sale of the patented product but rather to joint development effort. In *Continental Can Co. v. Monsanto Co.*,[218] a plastics company entered into an agreement with the Coca-Cola Company to develop a plastic bottle. Under the agreement, the companies would work together to produce a suitable bottle, with the plastics company making the bottles and Coca-Cola testing them. If a satisfactory bottle were developed, Coca-Cola would purchase the bottles from the plastics company under terms that were partially negotiated. The plastics company produced bottles in a variety of shapes, including one that allegedly embodied the patent claim in question, but the project was abandoned when tests proved unsuccessful.[219] Although the trial court found that the relationship had placed the patented bottle "on sale" before the critical date, the Federal Circuit disagreed and reversed:

> Although Admiral Plastic's hope was surely commercial sales, and the record shows that prices and quantities were discussed, this does not of itself place the subject matter "on sale" in the sense of § 102(b).

---

[216] *See Atlanta Attachment*, 516 F.3d at 1365 ("Our patent laws deny a patent to an inventor who applies for a patent more than one year after making an attempt to profit from his invention by putting it on sale."); Honeywell Int'l Inc. v. Universal Avionics Sys. Corp., 488 F.3d 982, 998 (Fed. Cir. 2007).

[217] Electromotive Div. of General Motors Corp. v. Transportation Sys. Div. of General Electric Co., 417 F.3d 1203, 1209 (Fed. Cir. 2005). An offer to sell must be so definite and final that, applying traditional principles of contract law, acceptance of that offer would form a binding contract. *See* MEMC Electronic Materials, Inc. v. Mitsubishi Materials Silicon Corp., 420 F.3d 1369, 1376 (Fed. Cir. 2005) (emails with technical data did not include price terms); Lacks Indus., Inc. v. McKechnie Vehicle Components USA, Inc., 322 F.3d 1335, 1347–48 (Fed. Cir. 2003); Group One, Ltd. v. Hallmark Cards, Inc., 254 F.3d 1041, 1046 (Fed. Cir. 2001). A sale need not be profitable to invalidate a patent. *In re* Cygnus Telecommunications Technology, LLC, 536 F.3d 1343, 1355 (Fed. Cir. 2008). An *offer* itself is sufficient even if no sale was completed. Cargill, Inc. v. Canbra Foods, Ltd., 476 F.3d 1359, 1370 (Fed. Cir. 2007); Scaltech, Inc. v. Retec/Tetra, L.L.C., 269 F.3d 1321, 1328 (Fed. Cir. 2001).

[218] 948 F.2d 1264 (Fed. Cir. 1991).

[219] *See id.* at 1269.

The . . . bottle was a part of a terminated development project that never bore commercial fruit and was cloaked in confidentiality. While the line is not always bright between development and being on sale . . . in this case the line was not crossed.[220]

A transaction does not constitute a bar under § 102(b) if it is part of an "experimental use"–that is, if the primary object of the "sale" was not to profit from the invention but to test it in the field as a prelude to filing a patent application.[221] Although a court will consider a variety of factors in deciding if a sale was for purposes of commerce or of experiment,[222] at a minimum the seller must inform the purchaser that the goods are experimental, and the seller must retain sufficient control over the goods to conduct the required monitoring or tests.[223]

[220] *Id.* at 1270. A sale or offer to sell must be to a separate entity. A transaction between related corporations completed purely for accounting purposes would not constitute a genuine sale, at least if the selling entity "so controls the purchaser that the invention remains out of the public's hands." *See* Ferag AG v. Quipp, Inc., 45 F.3d 1562, 1567 (Fed. Cir. 1995). On the other hand, sales *to the patentee* by an independent supplier, not for purposes of experiment or development but in preparation for release to the general public, can invalidate a patent. *Special Devices,* 270 F.3d at 1355–57; *but cf.* Trading Technologies Int'l, Inc. v. Espeed, Inc., 595 F.3d 1340, 1361–62 (Fed. Cir. 2010) (contract to supply inventor with a finished copy of patented software "for his own secret, personal use" did not trigger § 102(b)). Licensing someone to practice the invention (*see* Section 6.3) is not a sale that triggers § 102(b). Elan Corp. v. Andrx Pharmaceuticals, Inc. 366 F.3d 1336, 1341 (Fed. Cir. 2004); *In re* Kollar, 286 F.3d 1326, 1330–34 (Fed. Cir. 2002).

[221] *See* Pfaff v. Wells Electronics, Inc., 525 U.S. 55, 64 (1998) ("[A]n inventor who seeks to perfect his discovery may conduct extensive testing without losing his right to obtain a patent for his invention–even if such testing occurs in the public eye. The law has long recognized the distinction between inventions put to experimental use and products sold commercially."); *Electromotive,* 417 F.3d at 1210; EZ Dock, Inc. v. Schafer Sys., Inc., 276 F.3d 1347, 1352–53 (Fed. Cir. 2002) (sale may have been primarily to test dock in rougher waters). To qualify as experimental, the transaction must have been primarily for purposes of experimentation rather than profit. *Electromotive,* 417 F.3d at 1210; Allen Eng'g Corp. v. Bartell Indus., Inc., 299 F.3d 1336, 1352–53 (Fed. Cir. 2002). Sales may have been experimental even though they did not result in any changes to the claimed invention. *Honeywell,* 488 F.3d at 997.

[222] *See Electromotive,* 417 F.3d at 1213 (listing 13 nonexclusive factors); Clock Spring, L.P. v. Wrapmaster, Inc., 560 F.3d 1317, 1327 (Fed. Cir. 2009) (invoking the same factors in the context of a public use bar).

[223] *See Electromotive,* 417 F.3d. at 1213–14; Paragon Podiatry Lab., Inc. v. KLM Labs., Inc. 984 F.2d 1182, 1186–87 (Fed. Cir. 1993); La Bounty Mfg., Inc. v. U.S. Int'l Trade Comm'n, 958 F.2d 1066, 1071–72 (Fed. Cir. 1992).

A court will also consider whether payment was made, whether the seller kept the kind of records that would suggest experimentation, and whether the seller required the purchaser to keep the activities confidential.[224] Keeping track of customer responses and complaints after sale of a new product is not sufficient to show that the sales were primarily experimental.[225] Moreover, the experiments have to relate to the claimed invention. If the experiments relate to some other aspect of a product, or if they are nothing more than marketing tests to gauge consumer demand, the sale is not within the experimental use exception.[226]

One issue that long divided opinion is the extent to which the invention must be complete before it can be offered for sale in a manner triggering § 102(b).[227] The Supreme Court eventually decreed, in *Pfaff v. Wells Electronics, Inc.*,[228] that the invention must be "ready for patenting" before the critical date in order for a sale or offer to sell to be invalidating.[229]

---

[224] *See* Eli Lilly & Co. v. Zenith Goldline Pharmaceuticals, Inc., 471 F.3d 1369, 1381 (Fed. Cir. 2006); *Allen Eng'g*, 299 F.3d at 1353–55; U.S. Environmental Prods. Inc. v. Westall, 911 F.2d 713, 717 (Fed. Cir. 1990). An inventor's subjective intent to experiment is not relevant. *See Electromotive*, 417 F.3d at 1212.

[225] *See Paragon*, 984 F.2d at 1187–88.

[226] *See Dippin' Dots*, 476 F.3d at 1344; Smithkline Beecham Corp. v. Apotex Corp., 365 F.3d 1306, 1317 (Fed. Cir. 2004); *In re* Smith, 714 F.2d 1127, 1135–36 (Fed. Cir. 1983). Testing features that are not mentioned in the claim but inherent to the invention–like durability–may suffice. *See Electromotive*, 417 F.3d at 1211–12. On the other hand, an experimental use requires that "claimed features or overall workability are being tested for purposes of the filing of a patent application." *Clock Spring*, 560 F.3d at 1327 (discounting claim that public use of underground pipe-installation technique was for testing durability when pipes were not dug up and checked until almost a year *after* a patent application had been filed). A sale or public use cannot be experimental if the invention is already reduced to practice, and therefore "ready for patenting." *In re* Omeprazole Patent Litigation, 536 F.3d 1361, 1372 (Fed. Cir. 2008); *Cygnus*, 536 F.3d at 1356 (" 'experimental use cannot occur after a reduction to practice' ").

[227] *See, e.g.*, UMC Electronics Co. v. U.S., 816 F.2d 647 (Fed. Cir. 1987) (where the majority held that an invention need not be reduced to practice to be offered for sale, and Judge Smith penned a sharp dissent).

[228] 525 U.S. 55 (1998).

[229] *Id.* at 67; *see also August Technology*, 655 F.3d at 1288. The court speaks of the invention being "ready for patenting" *before the critical date* rather than before the date of the offer to sell. *Pfaff*, 525 U.S. at 67. This suggests that the event triggering the commencement of the one-year grace period could be the event which makes the invention ready for patenting (such as a reduction to practice), if that event occurs subsequent to the offer. The Federal Circuit has ruled that this is correct interpretation. *August Technology*, 655 F.3d at 1289 (the invention must be ready for patenting before the critical date, but it need not be ready for patenting when the invalidating offer was made).

Once the invention is ready for patenting, there is no excuse to delay (more than one year) filing a patent application. One way to demonstrate that the invention was ready for patenting is an actual reduction to practice.[230] An inventor who has reduced the invention to practice—building the claimed apparatus or performing the claimed method—should be ready to prepare the kind of enabling disclosure required in a patent application.[231] Alternatively, one can demonstrate that an invention was ready for patenting through "drawings or other descriptions of the invention that were sufficiently specific to enable a person skilled in the art to practice the invention."[232] If these descriptions were available to the inventor, they could have been incorporated in a patent application. Consequently, an offer to sell an invention that has yet to be built can bar or invalidate a subsequent patent. In *Pfaff* the inventor had such confidence in his ability to proceed directly from an engineering drawing to a finished product that he offered to sell the product in large quantities before any had been made.[233] The drawing showed that the invention was ready for patenting, so the offer, before the critical date, invalidated the patent.

Public use of the claimed invention before the patent's critical date can also operate as a bar under § 102(b).[234] A use of the invention by any

---

[230] *Id.*; *Atlanta Attachment*, 516 F.3d at 1366–67; *Honeywell*, 488 F.3d at 997. An invention cannot be offered for sale before the date on which it was conceived. *August Technology*, 655 F.3d at 1289 ("an invention cannot be offered for sale until its conception date"); Sparton Corp. v. U.S., 399 F.3d 1321, 1324 (Fed. Cir. 2005). However, if a preconception offer to sell *remained open*, then the invention would be offered for sale as soon as conception occurred. *August Technology*, 655 F.3d at 1289. Because conception in patent law requires something more specific than a general idea, *see* Section 8.9.1.4, the counterintuitive sequence of offer to sell followed by conception might sometimes occur. *See id.* at 1289 ("the seller is offering to sell the invention once he has conceived of it").

[231] *See* Section 8.6.

[232] *Pfaff*, 525 U.S. at 67. An invention may be fully conceived but not yet ready for patenting if the development necessary for putting the invention to practice is incomplete. *See* Space Sys./Loral, Inc. v. Lockheed Martin Corp., 271 F.3d 1076, 1080–81 (Fed. Cir. 2001). On the other hand, the invention can be ready for patenting even if the inventor does not yet have perfect confidence that it will work. *See* Robotic Vision Sys., Inc. v. View Eng'g, Inc., 249 F.3d 1307, 1312 (Fed. Cir. 2001) ("It will be a rare case indeed in which an inventor has no uncertainty concerning the workability of his invention before he has reduced it to practice.").

[233] *See Pfaff*, 525 U.S. at 58. As the inventor testified at his deposition: "Q. It was in a drawing. Is that correct? A. Strictly in a drawing. Went from the drawing to the hard tooling. That's the way I do my business. Q. Boom-boom? A. You got it. Q. You are satisfied, obviously, when you come up with some drawings that it is going to go—'it works'? A. I know what I am doing, yes, most of the time." *Id.* at 58 n.3.

[234] Star Scientific, Inc. v. R.J. Reynolds Tobacco Co., 655 F.3d 1364, 1377 (Fed. Cir. 2011); *Clock Spring*, 560 F.3d at 1325.

person, other than the inventor, who is under no obligation of secrecy may constitute a public use of the invention.[235] It is public use even if not communicated to a wider public, as was likely true in the celebrated case of a corset steel used by the lady friend of the man who invented it.[236] On the other hand, because § 102(b) refers to "public" use, a use that is observed only by persons under an obligation of secrecy does not invoke the statutory bar.[237] The public use bar is subject to the same experimental use exception as the on-sale bar.[238] Some inventions must be tested in a more-or-less public environment, and if it is clear that the use is experimental it will not invalidate a claim.[239]

When the inventor demonstrates the invention to a few friends or associates, the determination of whether such use was "public" can be difficult. In *Moleculon Research Corp. v. CBS, Inc.*,[240] the inventor displayed a model of his cube puzzle to a few university colleagues. The "personal relationships and surrounding circumstances" were sufficient for the court to find that the inventor had retained control over the invention and the distribution of information concerning it, even though there was no express agreement of confidentiality.[241] In contrast, a jury in *Beachcombers v. Wildwood Creative Products, Inc.*[242] found that a demonstration of an improved kaleidoscope to party guests was a public use, and the Federal Circuit affirmed. The

---

[235] *Star Scientific,* 655 F.3d at 1377; *Clock Spring,* 560 F.3d at 1325; American Seating Co. v. USSC Gp., Inc., 514 F.3d 1262, 1267 (Fed. Cir. 2008); Motionless Keyboard Co. v. Microsoft Corp., 486 F.3d 1376, 1384 (Fed. Cir. 2007). The public use bar is said to "discourage 'the removal of inventions from the public domain which the public justifiably comes to believe are freely available.' " *American Seating,* 514 F.3d at 1267.

[236] Egbert v. Lippman, 104 U.S. 333 (1881); *see also Motionless Keyboard,* 486 F.3d at 1384.

[237] *See Motionless Keyboard,* 486 F.3d at 1385 (keyboard tester had signed a nondisclosure agreement); Eli Lilly & Co. v. Zenith Goldline Pharmaceuticals, Inc., 471 F.3d 1369, 1381 (Fed. Cir. 2006) (restricted access to information on drug tests).

[238] *See Clock Spring,* 560 F.3d at 1326; *Honeywell,* 488 F.3d at 998; *Eli Lilly,* 471 F.3d at 1381. The "ready for patenting" test of *Pfaff* applies here as well. Invitrogen Corp. v. Biocrest Mfg., LP, 424 F.3d 1374, 1379 (Fed. Cir. 2005).

[239] *See Pfaff,* 525 U.S. at 64; Netscape Communications Corp. v. Konrad, 295 F.3d 1315, 1320 (Fed. Cir. 2002); Allied Colloids Inc. v. American Cyanamid Co., 64 F.2d 1570, 1574 (Fed. Cir. 1995).

[240] 793 F.2d 1261 (Fed. Cir. 1986).

[241] *Id.* at 1266; *see also American Seating,* 514 F.3d at 1268 (limited group who saw the invention "shared a general understanding of confidentiality"); *Invitrogen,* 424 F.3d at 1381 (confidentiality obligations need not be express); Bernhardt, L.L.C. v. Collezione Europa USA, Inc., 386 F.3d 1371, 1381 (Fed. Cir. 2004).

[242] 31 F.3d 1154 (Fed. Cir. 1994).

purpose of the demonstration was "getting feedback on the device," and the host made no efforts toward secrecy.[243]

Although it does not fit neatly in the categories of public use or on sale, a commercial use of the invention by the applicant before the critical date, even if that use does not make the invention itself a matter of public knowledge, is considered sufficient to invoke the statutory bar.[244] Suppose that an applicant invented a more efficient method of manufacturing copper wire. If the finished product resembled any other copper wire, no one outside of the factory might know anything of the improved process. Nevertheless, if the applicant used that process, and profited from it, prior to the critical date of the patent application, the Federal Circuit has held that such use forfeits the right to obtain a patent.[245] Here there is a difference between the activities of the patent applicant and unrelated third parties. If a third party made commercial use of the method before the applicant's critical date, but such use did not disclose the invention to the public, § 102(b) does not apply.[246] Perhaps the distinction exists because an inventor's own secret but commercial use, or a third party's nonsecret commercial use, can put the inventor on notice of the need to file promptly.[247] A secret third-party use, on the other hand, could catch the inventor off guard.

---

[243] *Id.* at 1160.

[244] *See American Seating,* 514 F.3d at 1267 (bar applies if invention is publicly accessible *or* "commercially exploited"); *Invitrogen,* 424 F.3d at 1382 ("secrecy of use alone is not sufficient to show that existing knowledge has not been withdrawn from public use: commercial exploitation is also forbidden"); *Special Devices,* 270 F.3d at 1357; *Woodland Trust,* 148 F.3d at 1370–71. Sometimes the bar is characterized as an on-sale bar, sometimes as a public use bar. *See Special Devices,* 270 F.3d at 1357 (characterizing *Woodland Trust* as referring to the on-sale bar); *Woodland Trust,* 148 F.3d at 1998 (citing cases referring to "public use"). In the paradoxical words of *Kinzenbaw v. Deere & Co.,* 741 F.2d 383, 390 (Fed. Cir. 1984), "[a] commercial use is a public use even if it is kept secret."

[245] *See* D.L. Auld Co. v. Chroma Graphics Corp., 714 F.2d 1144, 1147–48 (Fed. Cir. 1983) (secret commercial use by "applicant for patent or his assignee" triggers § 102(b)). Sale of a product that *embodies* the patented invention without, somehow, disclosing it triggers § 102(b) regardless of who sold it. *In re* Epstein, 32 F.3d 1559, 1568 (Fed. Cir. 1994); J.A. LaPorte, Inc. v. Norfolk Dredging Co., 787 F.2d 1577, 1583 (Fed. Cir. 1986). Perhaps that is because the sale of the claimed invention itself does not straddle the public use and on-sale bars as problematically as the sale of a product made by a secret process.

[246] *See* Resqnet.com, Inc. v. Lansa, Inc., 594 F.3d 860, 866 (Fed. Cir. 2010); *Woodland Trust,* 148 F.3d at 1371 ("when an asserted prior use is not that of the applicant, § 102(b) is not a bar when that prior use or knowledge is not available to the public").

[247] *See Special Devices,* 270 F.3d at 1355.

Another type of statutory bar is created by 35 U.S.C. § 102(d), which provides as follows:

A person shall be entitled to a patent unless–

(d) the invention was first patented or caused to be patented, or was the subject of an inventor's certificate, by the applicant or his legal representatives or assigns in a foreign country prior to the date of the application for patent in this country on an application for patent or inventor's certificate filed more than twelve months before the filing of the application in the United States. . . .

Simply put, an inventor who applied for a patent in a foreign country, waited more than 12 months before filing in the United States, and received the foreign patent before filing in the United States will be denied a U.S. patent.[248] As in the case of § 102(b), § 102(d) promotes diligence in filing and prevents the extension of the patent monopoly.[249]

8.9.2 Defining Prior Art (Patents Filed after March 16, 2013)

The America Invents Act redesigned § 102 for patents or patent applications with an effective filing date after March 16, 2013. Whether a potential reference counts as prior art no longer depends on the applicant's date of invention. Now the *filing date* assumes that critical role. Henceforth, inventors will no longer be denied patents simply because someone else invented first. In settling rights between competing inventors, the race to invent will be replaced, to some extent, by a race to the patent office. Whether this is fair to inventors, or the right way to spur innovation, remains subject to debate. Critics worry that corporations with large resources will win the race to file at the expense of individuals or small entities. If patent applications are filed in haste, their disclosures may be less useful as teaching documents. Whether these fears are borne out remains to be seen. At least the new system should produce more predictable

---

[248] *See* Bayer AG v. Schein Pharmaceuticals, Inc., 301 F.3d 1306, 1312 (Fed. Cir. 2002).

[249] *See In re* Kathawala, 9 F.3d 942, 947 (Fed. Cir. 1993). One other rarely used form of statutory bar arises from § 102(c), which provides that an inventor is not entitled to a patent if "he has abandoned the invention." *See* Oddzon Prods., Inc. v. Just Toys, Inc., 122 F.2d 1396, 1402 (Fed. Cir. 1997). "Abandoning the invention" means abandoning the right to *patent* the invention. Mere delay in filing a patent application does not show that the invention was abandoned. *See* Paulik v. Rizkalla, 760 F.2d 1270, 1272 (Fed. Cir. 1985) (" 'the mere lapse of time' will not prevent the inventor from receiving a patent"). If an inventor were, for example, to announce to the public that he would not patent his invention, such an announcement might constitute an abandonment.

outcomes at a lower administrative cost. Compared to determining who was first to invent, determining who was first to file is a simple matter.

The new version of § 102(a) provides that a person shall be entitled to a patent unless:

> (1) the claimed invention was patented, described in a printed publication, or in public use, on sale, or otherwise available to the public before the effective filing date of the claimed invention . . .

Much of the language here is familiar, and it is likely that terms such as "printed publication" and "public use" will be interpreted to have the same meaning as they did in the original version of § 102.[250] What is new is that § 102(a)(1) refers to the filing date—not the date of invention or the critical date—as the watershed moment. If, before the effective filing date,[251] the claimed invention was patented, described in a printed publication, used in public, offered for sale, or "otherwise [made] available to the public,"[252] a patent application will be denied, subject to the exceptions discussed below. If a patent issues, the accused infringer can challenge the validity of the patent on the same grounds.[253]

Section 102(a)(2) also denies a patent if the claimed invention was described in an issued patent, or a published patent application, that names another inventor and that has an earlier effective filing date.[254] This replaces the former § 102(g), with its rules governing conception, reduction to

---

[250] The new § 102(a) no longer distinguishes between activity in the United States and abroad.

[251] "Effective" filing date is an important distinction. An application may be entitled to the filing date of an earlier application to which it bears some relation. See Sections 5.2 and 5.3.

[252] This is a catch-all category that may correspond to the more ambiguous "known," construed by the courts to mean *publicly* known, that used to appear in § 102(a). The word "otherwise" suggests that all of the other categories in § 102(a)–like "on sale"–must also make the invention "available to the public," a qualification that might turn out to be significant.

[253] *See* 35 U.S.C. § 282.

[254] The precise language is "[unless] the claimed invention was described in a patent issued under section 151[the general section on issuing a patent following a successful examination], or in an application for patent published or deemed published under section 122(b) [governing the publication of patent applications], in which the patent or application, as the case may be, names another inventor and was effectively filed before the effective filing date of the claimed invention." Although the use of verb tenses is somewhat confusing, the intention seems to be to count as prior art any patent or published application with an earlier effective filing date so long as its disclosures are eventually made public. The rules for determining the effective filing date of a potential prior art patent or application are spelled out in § 102(d).

practice, and diligence,[255] with a much simpler rule—subject to the exceptions discussed below, in a contest between independent inventors, the inventor who files first wins. Interference proceedings,[256] which decide whether one competing inventor or another invented first, are no longer necessary.

Section 102(b) includes some important exceptions to the categories of prior art established in § 102(a). First, public disclosure of the claimed subject matter *by the inventor*, or by someone who obtained the subject matter *from the inventor*, is not disqualifying prior art so long as it occurred *one year or less* before the effective filing date.[257] If Inventor A files an application on an improved mousetrap on August 1, 2013, his public announcement of the same invention on June 1, 2013, will not deny him a patent. The same would be true if the disclosure came from A's research assistant or from an industrial spy who infiltrated A's laboratory. To a limited extent this preserves the one-year grace period for public disclosures established in the former version of § 102(b).[258] It does not, however, apply to disclosures by third parties who discovered the same invention independently. Such a disclosure, even one day before the effective filing date of the application, would bar the issuance of a patent.

Similar protections extend to patents and patent applications by other inventors. If an earlier-filed application discloses the same invention, but the subject matter came, directly or indirectly, from the inventor named in the later-filed application, then the earlier-filed application is not prior art. If Inventor B files an application disclosing Inventor A's mousetrap before Inventor A has a chance to file, *and* Inventor B derived the subject matter from Inventor A (perhaps Inventor B is the industrial spy, or he encountered Inventor A's work legitimately), then Inventor B's application, even though it was filed first, is not prior art. This avoids the embarrassing situation of Inventor B "borrowing" Inventor A's work and beating him in the race to the patent office. Although contests between inventors will no longer be resolved by determining who invented first, it will still matter whether the first inventor to file worked independently or derived the subject matter from the other inventor. Interference

---

[255] *See* Section 8.9.1.4.

[256] *See* Section 5.4.

[257] The relevant part of § 102(b) reads: "A disclosure made one year or less before the effective filing date of a claimed invention shall not be prior art to the claimed invention . . . if –(A) the disclosure was made by the inventor or joint inventor or by another who obtained the subject matter from the inventor or a joint inventor. . . ."

[258] *See* Section 8.9.1.7.

proceedings will be replaced by (more limited) "derivation proceedings" to determine precisely that issue.[259]

Section 102(b) also provides an exception that works to the benefit of inventors who make early public disclosures of their inventions. If the disclosure that would otherwise be prior art was made less than one year before the effective filing date, and *after* the same subject matter had been disclosed *by the inventor* or by someone who obtained the subject matter from the inventor, then it will not count as prior art. Suppose that Inventor A and Inventor B, working independently, devise the same mousetrap invention, and Inventor A files a patent application on August 1, 2013. If Inventor B published a description of the same mousetrap on July 1, 2013, this would normally bar Inventor A from obtaining a patent. However, if Inventor A published *his own* description of the mousetrap on June 1, 2013, Inventor B's subsequent description would not count as prior art, even though it came before Inventor A's filing date. This rule encourages public disclosure of inventions as a defensive strategy —a development that should generally benefit the public. To a certain extent, the race to the patent office is accompanied by a race to publicize.

Comparable safeguards apply to potentially invalidating patents and patent applications having earlier filing dates. If Inventor B filed a patent application on July 1, 2013, it would not count as prior art to Inventor A, who filed on August 1, 2013, if Inventor A had already publicly disclosed the invention in June.[260]

Under these rules, it is a bit simplistic to characterize the new system as a first-to-file system. In the scenario described above, Inventors A and B worked independently and B filed first, but A's earlier public disclosure, in the end, counts for more. Inventor A's public disclosure, coming before B's filing date, bars B from obtaining a patent. Inventor B's earlier application, because of the protective effect of A's disclosure, does not bar A from obtaining a patent so long as everything occurred less than one year before A's filing date. What we have is a modified first-to-file system that rewards public disclosure.

---

[259] *See* Section 5.4.

[260] Inventor A's application is also saved if the subject matter claimed in A's application and disclosed in B's were owned by the same person or subject to an assignment to the same person. 35 U.S.C. § 102(b)(2)(C). This would prevent problems where, for example, A and B were employees of the same company, which owned rights to the inventions of either. Section 102(c) provides a similar exception where inventors are operating under a joint research agreement.

8.9.3 Anticipation

Establishing that a patent, patent application, publication, or other potential reference falls within one of the categories of prior art is only a first step. Next one must ask whether or not the claimed invention is novel when compared to the reference. If the claim includes subject matter identical to that disclosed or embodied in a prior art reference, the claim is "anticipated" and invalid for lack of novelty.[261]

Testing for anticipation is much like testing for infringement.[262] First, one construes the claim to determine exactly what it means.[263] The same claim construction must be used for all issues of infringement and validity. After construing the claim, one compares the claim to the reference.[264] The claim serves as a checklist, and if every element of the claim finds an exact match in the reference, the claim is anticipated.[265] Anticipation requires

---

[261] *See* Sanofi-Synthelabo v. Apotex, Inc., 550 F.3d 1075, 1082 (Fed. Cir. 2008) ("Claimed subject matter is 'anticipated' when it is not new; that is, when it was previously known."); Net MoneyIN, Inc. v. Verisign, Inc., 545 F.3d 1359, 1369 (Fed. Cir. 2008). "[D]ifferences between the prior art reference and the claimed invention, however slight, invoke the question of obviousness, not anticipation." *Net MoneyIN*, 545 F.3d at 1371.

[262] *See* Chapter 10.

[263] *See* Chapter 7.

[264] *See* Teleflex, Inc. v. Ficosa North America Corp., 299 F.3d 1313, 1335 (Fed. Cir. 2000) (describing the "two-step procedure").

[265] *See* ClearValue, Inc. v. Pearl River Polymers, Inc., 668 F.3d 1340, 1344 (Fed. Cir. 2012); Bard Peripheral Vascular, Inc. v. W.L. Gore & Assoc., Inc., 670 F.3d 1171, 1184 (Fed. Cir. 2012); Orion IP, LLC v. Hyundai Motor America, 605 F.3d 967, 975 (Fed. Cir. 2010); *Sanofi-Synthelabo*, 550 F.3d at 1082. The reference must not merely mention the elements individually; they must be combined or "arranged" in the manner claimed as an invention. Therasense, Inc. v. Becton, Dickinson & Co., 593 F.3d 1325, 1332 (Fed. Cir. 2010); *Sanofi-Synthelabo*, 550 F.3d at 1083; *Net MoneyIN*, 545 F.3d at 1369–70. On the other hand, a reference can be anticipating even if it discourages, or "teaches away," from the invention that it discloses. Krippelz v. Ford Motor Co., 667 F.3d 1261, 1269 (Fed. Cir. 2012) ("teaching away is not relevant to an anticipation analysis; it is only a component of an obviousness analysis"); Leggett & Platt, Inc. v. Vutek, Inc., 537 F.3d 1349, 1356 (Fed. Cir. 2008); Celeritas Technologies, Ltd. v. Rockwell Int'l Corp., 150 F.3d 1354, 1361 (Fed. Cir. 1998) ("A reference is no less anticipatory if, after disclosing the invention, the reference then disparages it."). The tests of anticipation and literal infringement (*see* Section 10.5) are so similar it is sometimes said that whatever would literally infringe a claim if it came later in time would anticipate if it came before. *See* Upsher-Smith Labs., Inc. v. Pamlab, L.L.C., 412 F.3d 1319, 1322 (Fed. Cir. 2005) (referring to the "century-old axiom"). However, because anticipation can be based on references that would not infringe (for example, the description of an invention in a publication), the "infringement test" of anticipation may be more confusing than helpful.

that all claim elements appear in a *single* reference.[266] This is because combining the teachings of one reference with the teachings of another reference might be sufficiently inventive to warrant a patent.[267] The question, in such a case, is whether the combination was nonobvious, a separate issue discussed in the next section.

If the prior art reference is a patent or printed publication, it anticipates only if it discloses or "teaches" each and every element of the claimed invention when read by a person skilled in the art.[268] A particular claim element can be mentioned *explicitly* in the reference,[269] or it can be *inherent.*[270]

---

[266] *Bard,* 670 F.3d at 1184; *Orion,* 605 F.3d at 975; *Net MoneyIN,* 545 F.3d at 1369. If one document incorporates by reference another, the combination may be treated as a single disclosure for purposes of an anticipation analysis. *See* Callaway Golf Co., v. Acushnet Co., 576 F.3d 1331, 1346 (Fed. Cir. 2009). The "host document" must " 'clearly identify[] the subject matter which is incorporated and where it is to be found.' " *Id.* A bare mention of another document does not incorporate by reference the contents of that document. *See id.*

[267] *See* Clearstream Wastewater Sys., Inc. v. Hydro-Action, Inc., 206 F.3d 1440, 1445 (Fed. Cir. 2000) (combination claims "can consist of new combinations of old elements;" individual elements of those combinations "may, and often do, read on the prior art").

[268] Like a patent disclosure, an anticipating reference must be enabling. *See ClearValue,* 668 F.3d at 1344 (an anticipating reference " 'must describe . . . each and every claim limitation and enable one of skill in the art to practice an embodiment of the claimed invention without undue experimentation' "); *Bard,* 670 F.3d at 1184; *Orion,* 605 F.3d at 975; Elan Pharmaceuticals, Inc. v. Mayo Foundation for Medical Education and Research, 346 F.3d 1051, 1054 (Fed. Cir. 2003) ("It is insufficient to name or describe the desired subject matter, if it cannot be produced without undue experimentation."). On the other hand, a reference can be enabling, and anticipating, even if what it describes has not actually been attempted. *See Elan,* 346 F.3d at 1055. For anticipation, a reference may be enabling even if it does not describe how the invention can be usefully applied. *See* Impax Labs., Inc. v. Aventis Pharmaceuticals Inc., 468 F.3d 1366, 1381–82 (Fed. Cir. 2006).

[269] The reference does not have to describe a claim element in precisely the same words used in the patent claim. *See In re* Bond, 910 F.2d 831, 832 (Fed. Cir. 1990) (anticipation is not an "ipsissimis verbis" test).

[270] *See Bard,* 670 F.3d at 1184 ("A 'single prior art reference must expressly or inherently disclose each claim limitation to anticipate a claim.' "); King Pharmaceuticals, Inc. v. Eon Labs., Inc., 616 F.3d 1267, 1275 (Fed. Cir. 2010) (a reference anticipates if the claimed invention is "the natural result" of the disclosed process); Marrin v. Griffin, 599 F.3d 1290, 1295 (Fed. Cir. 2010); Telemac Cellular Corp. v. Topp Telecom, Inc., 247 F.3d 1316, 1327 (Fed. Cir. 2001) (" 'Under the principles of inherency, if the prior art necessarily functions in accordance with, or includes, the claimed limitation, it anticipates.' "). Inherency cannot be " 'established by probabilities or possibilities,' " nor is it enough that " 'a certain thing may result from a given set of circumstances.' " Bettcher Indus., Inc. v. Bunzl USA, Inc., 661 F.3d 629, 639 (Fed. Cir. 2011); *see also Therasense,* 593 F.3d at 1332. Although anticipation requires that every claim element be found in a single reference, other references can be used to prove the fact of inherency. *Teleflex,* 299 F.3d at 1335; Continental Can Co. v. Monsanto Co., 948 F.2d 1264, 1268–69 (Fed. Cir. 1991).

Suppose, for example, that a claim to a mousetrap required a "flexible" spring, and a prior publication disclosed a mousetrap with a steel spring of certain dimensions. Even if the publication did not refer to the flexibility of the spring, the spring described might be inherently flexible because of its materials and design. In this situation, the flexible spring element of the claim would be met by the reference, even though it was not explicit.[271]

Although anticipation requires that all of the elements of a claim be found in one reference, it may be proper to look to other references as an aid to understanding the anticipatory reference.[272] It is not proper to look to other references to fill in claim elements missing in the primary reference.[273] This relatively clear distinction was blurred somewhat by the decision in *In re Graves*.[274] There the Federal Circuit held that a reference

---

[271] The Federal Circuit has issued conflicting statements on whether an inherent characteristic must have been *recognized* in order to count for anticipation. Some opinions state that the inherent characteristic must be "necessarily present" and "so recognized by persons of ordinary skill." Finnegan Corp. v. International Trade Comm'n, 180 F.3d 1354, 1365 (Fed. Cir. 1999); *see also* Crown Operations Int'l, Ltd. v. Solutia Inc., 289 F.3d 1367, 1377 (Fed. Cir. 2002). On other occasions, the court has observed that "[i]nherency is not necessarily coterminous with the knowledge of those of ordinary skill in the art," and "[a]rtisans of ordinary skill may not recognize the inherent characteristics of functioning of the prior art." *In re* Cruciferous Sprout Litigation, 301 F.3d 1343, 1349 (Fed. Cir. 2002). The more recent decisions disavow the requirement of recognition. *See, e.g., Leggett & Platt*, 537 F.3d at 1355; Abbott Labs. v. Baxter Pharmaceutical Prods., Inc., 471 F.3d 1363, 1367–68 (Fed. Cir. 2006); Prima Tek II, L.L.C. v. Polypap, S.A.R.L., 412 F.3d 1284, 1289 (Fed. Cir. 2005). Recognition may be superfluous if beneficial characteristics were present in the prior art and the advantages were enjoyed whether anyone knew it or not. *See King Pharmaceuticals*, 616 F.3d at 1275 ("'merely discovering and claiming a new benefit of an old process cannot render the process again patentable'"). If certain vegetable sprouts always included cancer-preventing chemicals, the people who ate them reaped the benefits, even if unknowingly. *See Cruciferous Sprout*, 301 F.3d at 1350 (the inherent characteristics "have existed as long as the sprouts themselves.... It matters not that those of ordinary skill heretofore may not have recognized these inherent characteristics of the sprouts"). In some instances, however, failure to recognize an inherent characteristic may negate the benefits. For example, if a diet described in a publication could cure cancer but no one realized it, the diet would not be prescribed to those who could profit from it. The Federal Circuit has not explained things in quite this fashion, but it seems a plausible approach.

[272] *See Teleflex*, 299 F.3d at 1335; Bristol-Meyers Squibb Co. v. Ben Venue Labs., Inc., 246 F.3d 1368, 1379 (Fed. Cir. 2001). When used in that limited fashion, the additional references need not be *prior* art. *See Bristol-Meyers*, 246 F.3d at 1379.

[273] *Teleflex*, 299 F.3d at 1335.

[274] 69 F.3d 1147 (Fed. Cir. 1995).

lacking a claim element could still be held to anticipate if the missing element was "within the knowledge of a skilled artisan."[275] This sounds suspiciously close to an obviousness test, rather than the classic test of anticipation, and it is not clear how far in this direction the Federal Circuit is willing to go.[276]

If a patent claims a broad genus, a reference that includes a single species of the genus will anticipate the claim.[277] For example, a claim that specified a fuel composed of (among other things) "10 to 50 percent methane" would be anticipated by a prior fuel that met all of the other claim elements and that was composed of 25 percent methane. The claim is anticipated because it would otherwise prevent the practice of at least one fuel combination already in use. The converse, however, is not true. If a claim called for a fuel composed of exactly 25 percent methane, and a prior publication discussed such a fuel with a methane concentration of anywhere from 10 to 50 percent, the claim requiring exactly 25 percent may not be anticipated.[278]

8.9.4 Obviousness (§ 103)

Obviousness is a concept drawn from the following language of 35 U.S.C. § 103:

A patent for a claimed invention may not be obtained, notwithstanding that the claimed invention is not identically disclosed as set forth

---

[275] *Id.* at 1152.

[276] *See Net MoneyIN*, 545 F.3d at 1371 ("it is not enough that the prior art reference discloses part of the claimed invention, which an ordinary artisan might supplement to make the whole, or that it includes multiple, distinct teachings that the artisan might somehow combine to achieve the claimed invention"); *Teleflex*, 299 F.3d at 1334–35 (rejecting an argument based on *Graves* and reiterating that additional prior art references cannot fill gaps in the allegedly anticipating reference).

[277] *See* Eli Lilly & Co. v. Barr Labs., Inc. 251 F.3d 955, 971 (Fed. Cir. 2001) ("Our case law firmly establishes that a later genus claim limitation is anticipated by, and therefore not patentably distinct from, an earlier species claim."); Atlas Powder Co. v. Ireco, Inc., 190 F.3d 1342, 1346 (Fed. Cir. 1999) ("[I]f granting patent protection on the disputed claim would allow the patentee to exclude the public from practicing the prior art, then that claim is anticipated, regardless of whether it also covers subject matter not in the prior art.").

[278] *See Sanofi-Synthelabo*, 550 F.3d at 1083; Atofina v. Great Lakes Chemical Corp., 441 F.3d 991, 999 (Fed. Cir. 2006); *Upsher-Smith*, 412 F.3d at 1323. Disclosure of a sufficiently limited genus might anticipate a species of the genus, even if the prior art did not name that species specifically. *See Bristol-Meyers*, 246 F.3d at 1380. The detailed description of a small genus might be equivalent to an explicit description of each of its members. *See Atofina*, 441 F.3d at 999; *but cf. Impax*, 468 F.3d at 1381 (disclosure in reference of "hundreds of compounds" did not allow a person skilled in the art to separately envision each member of the class).

in section 102, if the differences between the claimed invention and the prior art are such that the claimed invention as a whole would have been obvious before the effective filing date of the claimed invention to a person having ordinary skill in the art to which the claimed invention pertains.

Like anticipation, obviousness is a ground for rejecting a patent claim in the course of prosecution or invalidating a patent claim in the course of infringement litigation. Obviousness, however, does not require that the claimed invention be identical to the prior art. Instead, obviousness focuses on the differences between the claim and the prior art and asks whether those differences are really inventive, or whether they are differences that might have occurred to anyone of ordinary skill.[279] Like § 102, § 103 prevents a patent claim from taking from the public what, in a sense, it already possesses.

Obviousness must be judged from the perspective of the "person of ordinary skill in the art."[280] For patents and patent applications before March 16, 2013, we ask whether the invention was obvious at the time it was made. For patents and patent applications filed after March 16, 2013,

---

[279] "Determining obviousness requires considering whether two or more pieces of prior art could be combined, or a single piece of prior art could be modified, to product the claimed invention." Comaper Corp. v. Antec, Inc., 596 F.3d 1343, 1351–52 (Fed. Cir. 2010). Obvious inventions include "those modest, routine, everyday, incremental improvements of an existing product or process that confer commercial value (otherwise they would not be undertaken) but do not involve sufficient inventiveness to merit patent protection." Ritchie v. Vast Resources, Inc., 563 F.3d 1334, 1337 (Fed. Cir. 2009). A typical example of an obvious invention would be the use of a different material in an existing product to take advantages of the known properties of that material. *See id.* (smoother borosilicate glass substituted for conventional soda-lime glass). Patents for such modest, inevitable advancements would actually hinder technological development. *See* KSR Int'l Co. v. Teleflex Inc., 550 U.S. 398, 419 (2007) ("[g]ranting patent protection to advances that would occur in the ordinary course without real innovation retards progress"). Although obviousness looks to the differences between the claimed invention and the prior art, the invention still must be viewed as a whole. *See* 35 U.S.C. § 103; Princeton Biochemicals, Inc. v. Beckman Coulter, Inc., 411 F.3d 1332, 1337 (Fed. Cir. 2005); Para-Ordnance Mfg., Inc. v. SGS Imports Int'l, Inc., 73 F.3d 1085, 1087 (Fed. Cir. 1995).

[280] *See* 35 U.S.C. § 103; Star Scientific, Inc. v. R.J. Reynolds Tobacco Co., 655 F.3d 1364, 1374 (Fed. Cir. 2011); Arkie Lures, Inc. v. Gene Larew Tackle, Inc., 119 F.3d 953, 956 (Fed. Cir. 1997) (obviousness must be approached "not from the viewpoint of the inventor, but from the viewpoint of a person of ordinary skill in the field of the invention"); Custom Accessories, Inc. v. Jeffrey-Allan Indus., Inc., 807 F.2d 955, 962 (Fed. Cir. 1986) ("obvious" means obvious to a person of ordinary skill–"not to the judge, or to a layman, or to those skilled in remote arts, or to geniuses in the art").

we ask whether the invention was obvious before the application was filed.[281]

The "person of ordinary skill in the art" is a mythical everyman whose viewpoint is often called upon in patent law, not only in context of obviousness but also, for example, in deciding whether a patent specification enables the practice of the claimed invention.[282] The person of ordinary skill is not an inventor or innovator but a person of ordinary competence who does the expected thing.[283] The level of expertise and education required of the person of ordinary skill varies depending on the art. In a very sophisticated art, a person of ordinary skill might have a Ph.D. and years of hands-on experience. In a less sophisticated art, the person of ordinary skill might be a shade-tree mechanic.[284] A court must decide what level of skill represents ordinary skill in the art at the relevant time.[285]

---

[281] The change reflects the centrality of the filing date of a patent rather than the invention date, following adoption of the America Invents Act.

[282] *See* Section 8.6.

[283] Life Technologies, Inc. v. Clontech Labs., Inc., 224 F.3d 1320, 1325 (Fed. Cir. 2000); Standard Oil Co. v. American Cyanamid Co., 774 F.2d 448, 454 (Fed. Cir. 1985) ("A person of ordinary skill in the art is . . . presumed to be one who thinks along the lines of conventional wisdom in the art and is not one who undertakes to innovate, whether by patient, and often expensive, systematic research or by extraordinary insights. . . ."). On the other hand, a person of ordinary skill is not a machine, incapable of exercising any ingenuity whatsoever. *KSR*, 550 U.S. at 420 ("A person of ordinary skill is also a person of ordinary creativity, not an automaton.").

[284] A higher level of ordinary skill in the art means that fewer inventions are nonobvious. *See* Innovention Toys, LLC v. MGA Entertainment, Inc., 637 F.3d 1314, 1314 (Fed. Cir. 2011) ("A less sophisticated level of skill generally favors a determination of nonobviousness, and thus the patentee, while a higher level of skill favors the reverse.").

[285] *See KSR*, 550 U.S. at 406; Abbott Labs. v. Andrx Pharmaceuticals, Inc., 452 F.3d 1331, 1336 (Fed. Cir. 2006); Ruiz v. A.B. Chance Co., 234 F.3d 654, 666 (Fed. Cir. 2000). Factors that may be considered include " '(1) the educational level of the inventor; (2) [the] type of problems encountered in the art; (3) prior art solutions to those problems; (4) [the] rapidity with which innovations are made; (5) [the] sophistication of the technology; and (6) [the] educational level of active workers in the field.' " Daiichi Sankyo Co. v. Apotex, Inc., 501 F.3d 1254, 1256 (Fed. Cir. 2007). What is obvious to a layperson is necessarily obvious to a person of ordinary skill in the art. *Innovention*, 637 F.3d at 1323. On the other hand, an invention that would be obvious to an inventor can still be patentable. Inventors and patentees are often assumed to be persons of extraordinary skill. *See Life Technologies*, 224 F.3d at 1325; Kloster Speedsteel AB v. Crucible Inc., 793 F.2d 1565, 1574 (Fed. Cir. 1986). The "person of ordinary skill" is someone who *makes* things, not someone who only *uses* the technology supplied by others. *See* Dystar Textilfarben GmbH v. C.H. Patrick Co., 464 F.3d 1356, 1362–63 (Fed. Cir. 2006) (person skilled in the art of dyeing would be someone familiar with chemistry, not the high-school-educated equipment operator who merely "flips the switches").

Nonobviousness should not be confused with complexity. Sometimes the simplest inventions are the most innovative.[286] Nor must the invention embrace a "flash of genius"–the kind of sudden inspiration that led Archimedes to shout "Eureka!" An invention that is the product of patient experimentation, or that is discovered entirely by accident, is just as patentable as one that arises from pure mental effort.[287] The only requirement is that the invention would not have occurred to a person of ordinary skill. This principle accounts for the last sentence of § 103, which provides, rather cryptically, that "[p]atentability shall not be negated by the manner in which the invention was made."[288]

While anticipation requires that all the elements of the claimed invention be found in a single prior art reference, obviousness can be based on the combination of more than one reference. If some elements of the claimed invention were found in one place, and the remaining elements were found in another, the combination might have been obvious to a person of ordinary skill. Courts sometimes imagine this hypothetical person standing in a workshop, surrounded by all of the relevant patents, publications, and other prior art references.[289] The question then becomes, would such a person, confronting the problem solved by the invention and aware of all of these references, have found it obvious to make the claimed combination?

---

[286] *See* Gentry Gallery, Inc. v. Berkline Corp., 134 F.3d 1473, 1478 (Fed. Cir. 1998) ("simplicity alone is not determinative of obviousness"); *In re* Oetiker, 977 F.2d 1443, 1447 (Fed. Cir. 1992); Demaco Corp. v. F. Von Langsdorff Licensing Ltd., 851 F.2d 1387, 1390–91 (Fed. Cir. 1988).

[287] *See* Graham v. John Deere Co., 383 U.S. 1, 15 (1966); *Life Technologies*, 224 F.3d at 1325 ("the path that leads an inventor to the invention is . . . irrelevant to patentability"); *In re* Dow Chemical Co., 837 F.2d 469, 472 (Fed. Cir. 1988) ("[m]ost technological advance is the fruit of methodical, persistent investigation").

[288] An invention may have been obvious from a technological point of view but not from a business point of view. Because patents are meant to encourage the technological arts, even an advancement ingenious from a marketing perspective is unpatentable if it is obvious from a technological perspective. *See* Media Technologies Licensing, LLC v. Upper Deck Co., 596 F.3d 1334, 1339 (Fed. Cir. 2010); Orthopedic Equipment Co. v. U.S., 702 F.2d 1005, 1013 (Fed. Cir. 1983) ("[T]he fact that the two disclosed apparatus would not be combined by businessmen for economic reasons is not the same as saying that it could not be done because skilled persons in the art felt that there was some technological incompatibility that prevented their combination.").

[289] *See Para-Ordnance*, 73 F.3d at 1088. However, the visual image of the art "tableau" was criticized by the judge who first created it, perhaps because it suggests the use of hindsight in selecting the references to "hang in the workshop." *See* Standard Oil Co. v. American Cynamid Co., 774 F.2d 448, 454 n.3 (Fed. Cir. 1985) (referring to the "unfortunate popularity" of the tableau imagery).

The references that may be considered include any of the kinds of prior art set forth in § 102 as long as they are "analogous art."[290] A reference qualifies as analogous art if (1) it "is from the same field of endeavor, regardless of the problem addressed" or (2) it is "reasonably pertinent to the particular problem with which the inventor is involved."[291] The latter includes material from another field that, as a source of ideas, "logically would have commended itself to an inventor's attention in considering his problem"[292] For example, in *In re Paulsen*,[293] the claimed invention concerned a case for a portable computer hinged in such a way that it could be closed tight for carrying or latched in an upright position for viewing the display screen. The court found it appropriate to consider references concerning hinges and latches, even if they were not in the portable computer field:

> The problems encountered by the inventors . . . were problems that were not unique to portable computers. They concerned how to connect and secure the computer's display housing to the computer while meeting certain size constraints and functional requirements. . . . We agree with the Board that given the nature of the problems confronted by the inventors, one of ordinary skill in the art "would have consulted the mechanical arts for housings, hinges, latches, springs, etc."[294]

---

[290] *In re* Klein, 647 F.3d 1343, 1348 (Fed. Cir. 2011); *Innovention*, 637 F.3d at 1321.

[291] *Klein*, 647 F.3d at 1348; *see also Innovention*, 637 F.3d at 1321; Wyers v. Master Lock Co., 616 F.3d 1231, 1237 (Fed. Cir. 2010); *Comaper*, 596 F.3d at 1351. If the subject matter disclosed in a prior art reference serves the same purpose as the claimed invention and addresses the same problem, it is likely to commend itself to the attention of a person of ordinary skill. *Klein*, 647 F.3d at 1348. The pertinent art should be defined in terms of the *problem* faced by the inventor, not the *solution* embodied in the patented invention. The latter would introduce inappropriate hindsight. *See* Monarch Knitting Machinery Corp. v. Sulzer Morat GmbH, 139 F.3d 877, 881 (Fed. Cir. 1998). Sometimes it is difficult to define the "field of the inventor's endeavor." In one case, the Federal Circuit affirmed findings by the PTO that toothbrushes and hairbrushes are in the same field of endeavor. *In re* Bigio, 381 F.3d 1320 (Fed. Cir. 2004). Their construction is similar, and a small hairbrush (perhaps for a moustache) would be much like a toothbrush. *Id.* at 1325–27. Judge Newman, dissenting, wrote that "[a] brush for hair has no more relation to a brush for teeth than does hair resemble teeth." *Id.* at 1327.

[292] *Klein*, 647 F.3d at 1348; *see also Innovention*, 637 F.3d at 1321; *In re* Icon Health & Fitness, Inc., 496 F.3d 1374, 1379–80 (Fed. Cir. 2007); *Princeton Biochemicals*, 411 F.3d at 1339.

[293] 30 F.3d 1475 (Fed. Cir. 1994).

[294] *Id.* at 1481–82. In *Icon Health* the court found that an inventor designing a folding treadmill might have considered earlier work on folding beds. Even though beds and treadmills are in different fields of endeavor, the invention had more to do with the problem of folding than with treadmills per se. *Icon Health*, 496 F.3d at 1380.

In *In re Oetiker*,[295] on the other hand, the court found insufficient evidence that a person working on hose clamps would have been motivated to consider fasteners used in clothing.[296]

Sometimes a prior reference "teaches away" from the claimed invention. To teach away means to suggest that the claimed combination should be avoided as undesirable or ineffective.[297] This is one factor to consider in deciding whether certain references render a claimed invention obvious. Nevertheless, sufficient disclosure can render an invention obvious and unpatentable even if the reference suggests that the invention is an inferior approach.[298]

It is no easy task to adopt the perspective of a different person (a person of ordinary skill in the art) at a different time (the time the invention was made, or when the application was filed). One can easily fall prey to hindsight. Once you have seen the invention and how it solves a problem, it may seem like the obvious thing to do[299]–particularly if, as is often the case, the *ingredients* of the solution were already available. Concerned that worthy inventions might, in retrospect, be held obvious simply because their component parts already existed,[300] the Federal Circuit held that a combination can be found obvious only if there was some "teaching, suggestion or motivation" to support it.[301] In other words, one cannot prove

---

[295]   977 F.2d 1443 (Fed. Cir. 1992).

[296]   *Id.* at 1447.

[297]   *See* Crocs, Inc. v. Int'l Trade Comm'n, 598 F.3d 1294, 1308–09 (Fed. Cir. 2010); *Icon Health*, 496 F.3d at 1381 (" 'A reference may be said to teach away when a person of ordinary skill, upon reading the reference, would be discouraged from following the path set out in the reference, or would be led in a direction divergent from the path that was taken by the applicant.' "); *In re* Kahn, 441 F.3d 977, 990 (Fed. Cir. 2006). "Teaching away" is not relevant to anticipation. Krippelz v. Ford Motor Co., 667 F.3d 1261, 1269 (Fed. Cir. 2012).

[298]   *See In re* Gurley, 27 F.3d 551, 553 (Fed. Cir. 1994) ("A known and obvious composition does not become patentable simply because it has been described as somewhat inferior to some other product for the same use.").

[299]   "Good ideas may well appear 'obvious' after they have been disclosed, despite having been previously unrecognized." *Arkie Lures*, 119 F.3d at 956; *see also KSR*, 550 U.S. at 421 (warning against "the distortion caused by hindsight"); *Star Scientific*, 655 F.3d at 1357 ("the great challenge of the obviousness judgment is proceeding without any hint of hindsight").

[300]   *See* Crown Operations Int'l, LTD v. Solutia Inc., 289 F.3d 1367, 1376 (Fed. Cir. 2002) (" 'Determination of obviousness cannot be based on the hindsight combination of components selectively culled from the prior art to fit the parameters of the patented invention.' "); *Life Technologies*, 224 F.3d at 1326 ("It is axiomatic that a claimed invention is not obvious solely because it is composed of elements that are all individually found in the prior art."); *In re* Gorman, 933 F.2d 982, 987 (Fed. Cir. 1991).

[301]   Pfizer, Inc. v. Apotex, Inc., 480 F.3d 1348, 1362 (Fed. Cir. 2007); *Kahn*, 441 F.3d at 986; *In re* Fulton, 391 F.3d 1195, 1200 (Fed. Cir. 2004).

the obviousness of combination A plus B simply by showing that A already existed and so did B. One has to show that persons of ordinary skill would have been led, in some fashion, to combine A with B to solve the problem at hand.[302] In a similar vein, the Federal Circuit emphasized that the standard of obviousness is not whether something would have been "obvious to try."[303] Instead, one has to show that the invention was obvious to *do*.

These rules, when strictly applied, made obviousness difficult to establish—too difficult, in the end, for the Supreme Court to approve. In one of the more important patent cases of recent years, *KSR Int'l Co. v. Teleflex Inc.*,[304] the court considered the obviousness of a height-adjustable accelerator pedal equipped with an electronic sensor. Height-adjustable pedals already existed, as did electronic sensors for pedals that were not adjustable, but no one had combined them as the patentee did. Finding no "teaching, suggestion or motivation" to support the combination, the Federal Circuit reversed the district court's judgment that the invention was obvious. On appeal, the Supreme Court found that the "teaching, suggestion or motivation" test had been applied too woodenly in this case.[305] There may have been no explicit teaching encouraging persons skilled in the art to combine a height-adjustable pedal with an electronic sensor, yet the course of the industry made the combination inevitable, even with ordinary levels of ingenuity.[306] Electronic sensors were becoming

---

[302] *See Crown*, 289 F.3d at 1376 ("There must be a teaching or suggestion within the prior art, within the nature of the problem to be solved, or within the general knowledge of a person of ordinary skill in the field of the invention, to look to particular sources, to select particular elements, and to combine them as combined by the inventor.").

[303] *Pfizer*, 480 F.3d at 1365 (it is a "truism" that "obvious to try" is not the correct standard of obviousness); Novo Nordisk A/S v. Becton Dickinson & Co., 304 F.3d 1216, 1220 (Fed. Cir. 2002).

[304] 550 U.S. 398 (2007).

[305] *Id.* at 419 ("The obviousness analysis cannot be confined by a formalistic conception of the words teaching, suggestion, and motivation, or by overemphasis on the importance of published articles and the explicit content of issued patents."). However, the "teaching, suggestion or motivation test," if flexibly applied, can still be a useful tool. *See Comaper*, 596 F.3d at 1352; Ortho-McNeil Pharmaceutical, Inc. v. Mylan Labs., Inc., 520 F.3d 1358, 1364 (Fed. Cir. 2008) ("a flexible TSM test remains the primary guarantor against a non-statutory hindsight analysis").

[306] *See KSR*, 550 U.S. at 420 ("familiar items may have obvious uses beyond their primary purposes, and in many cases a person of ordinary skill will be able to fit the teachings of multiple patents together like pieces of a puzzle"); *Comaper*, 596 F.3d at 1352.

standard, so eventually persons skilled in the art would add them to adjustable pedals–just as the patentee had done.[307]

Although it recognized the need to avoid hindsight, the Supreme Court endorsed "common sense" as a better guide to obviousness than any rigid formula.[308] Even the "obvious to try" approach can be useful. If there were only a few options to try, and one could have tried them with a fair expectation of success, then the solution might be considered obvious.[309] The court also observed that combinations are more likely to be obvious if

---

[307] *See KSR,* 550 U.S. at 419. In some fields, "market demand, rather than scientific literature, will drive design trends." *Id.* Obviousness still cannot be found simply by identifying all of the elements of the claimed invention separately in the prior art. *See id.* at 418 ("a patent composed of several elements is not proved obvious merely by demonstrating that each of its elements is, independently, known in the prior art"); Power-One, Inc. v. Artesyn Technologies, Inc., 599 F.3d 1343, 1352 (Fed. Cir. 2010).

[308] *KSR,* 550 U.S. at 421; *see also Wyers,* 616 F.3d at 1240 ("in appropriate cases, the ultimate inference as to the existence of a motivation to combine references may boil down to a question of 'common sense' "); Perfect Web Technologies, Inc. v. InfoUSA, Inc., 587 F.3d 1324, 1328 (Fed. Cir. 2009) ("Common sense has long been recognized to inform the analysis of obviousness if explained with sufficient reasoning."); Leapfrog Enterprises, Inc. v. Fisher-Price, Inc., 485 F.3d 1157, 1161 (Fed. Cir. 2007).

[309] A "design need or market pressure" may lead persons skilled in the art to consider both the problem and its plausible solutions. If the possibilities are "finite" and "predictable," then "a person of ordinary skill has good reason to pursue the known options within his or her technical grasp." *KSR,* 550 U.S. at 421. If this leads to "the anticipated success," the solution to the problem is "likely the product not of innovation but of ordinary skill and common sense." *Id.* In this case, "the fact that a combination was obvious to try might show that it was obvious under § 103." *Id.; see also In re* Brimonidine Patent Litigation, 643 F.3d 1366, 1375 (Fed. Cir. 2011) ("Where 'the problem is known, the possible approaches to solving the problem are known and finite, and the solution is predictable through use of a known option,' a solution that is obvious to try may indeed be obvious."); *Perfect Web,* 587 F.3d at 1331; Takeda Chemical Indus., Ltd. v. Alphapharm Pty., Ltd., 492 F.3d 1350, 1359 (Fed. Cir. 2007). Certainty of success is not required; only a "reasonable expectation of success." *In re* Kubin, 561 F.3d 1351, 1360 (Fed. Cir. 2009). If a person of ordinary skill would have had to try *everything* before finding the claimed solution, the solution may not have been obvious. *See* Bayer Schering Pharma AG v. Barr Labs., Inc., 575 F.3d 1341, 1347 (Fed. Cir. 2009) (the number of options to try must have been " 'small or easily traversed' "); *Kubin,* 561 F.3d at 1359 ("where a defendant merely throws metaphorical darts at a board filled with combinatorial prior art possibilities, courts should not succumb to hindsight claims of obviousness"); Abbott Labs. v. Sandoz, Inc., 544 F.3d 1341, 1352 (Fed. Cir. 2008) ("The Court in *KSR* did not create a presumption that all experimentation in fields where there is already a background of useful knowledge is 'obvious to try,' without considering the nature of the science or technology."). If a person of ordinary skill would have expected "roadblocks" rather than success, then a potential solution may not even have been "obvious to try." *See Brimonidine,* 643 F.3d at 1376. The same is true if "vague prior art does not guide an inventor towards a particular solution." *Bayer,* 575 F.3d at 1347.

they consist of known components performing their usual functions—for example, a known perfume added to a known sunblock, each behaving as one would expect.[310] On the other hand, a combination might be non-obvious if it creates some unexpected synergy—perhaps a perfume combined with a sunblock producing an unexpected mosquito repellent. In *KSR*, the sensor and pedal in combination produced nothing more than the sum of the parts. Common sense showed, in the end, that the improvement did not rise to the level of a patentable invention.[311]

Although obviousness determinations are highly fact-specific,[312] two additional examples will give the reader some flavor for how the decisions are made. In *In re Gorman*,[313] the claimed invention was a novelty lollipop in the shape of a thumb. The elements of the claimed invention included a thumb-shaped candy core; a protective covering, also thumb-shaped, which served first as a mold for the candy core and then as a "toy and novelty item for placement upon the thumb of the user;" a lollipop stick; a plug of chewing gum or similar edible material to seal the bottom of the candy; and a plastic or cardboard disk at the base of the "thumb."

The prior art located by the Patent Office included 13 references. Some showed candy or ice cream formed in a rubbery mold, which served double duty as a wrapper for the product. One ice cream product on a stick included a similar cardboard base. Other references (believe it or not) disclosed thumb-shaped candies and confections. Edible plugs also had been disclosed for sealing liquid inside of candy and ice cream products.

---

[310] *KSR,* 550 U.S. at 416 ("The combination of familiar elements according to known methods is likely to be obvious when it does no more than yield predictable results."); *see also* Ecolab, Inc. v. FMC Corp., 569 F.3d 1335, 1349 (Fed. Cir. 2009); Monolithic Power Sys., Inc. v. O2 Micro Int'l Ltd., 558 F.3d 1341, 1352 (Fed. Cir. 2009); *Leapfrog,* 485 F.3d at 1161.

[311] Another case illustrating common-sense improvement is *Ball Aerosol and Specialty Container, Inc. v. Limited Brands, Inc.,* 555 F.3d 984 (Fed. Cir. 2009). The invention concerned a candle enclosed in a metal can—a potentially dangerous situation because of the propensity of metal to conduct heat from the candle to the surface on which it rests. The patentee added small "feet" to the bottom of the can, to provide some insulating space, and a cap that could be removed and used as a base. Because the prior art taught similar arrangements to minimize scorching, the claimed invention would have been simple and routine for any person of ordinary skill. *Id.* at 993 (the "decreased heat transfer—would have been entirely predictable and grounded in common sense").

[312] *See Pfizer,* 480 F.3d at 1366. Once the facts are determined, the ultimate decision on obviousness is a "question of law." *See Star Scientific,* 655 F.3d at 1374; *Innovention,* 637 F.3d at 1320.

[313] 933 F.2d 892, 897 (Fed. Cir. 1991).

Although Gorman's claim was very detailed, and none of the references included all of the things that Gorman claimed, the Patent Office found that the combination still would have been obvious to any person of ordinary skill. The Federal Circuit affirmed: "The various elements Gorman combined . . . are all shown in the cited references in various subcombinations, used in the same way, for the same purpose as in the claimed invention."[314]

In *Moleculon Research Corp. v. CBS, Inc.,*[315] on the other hand, the Federal Circuit upheld the determination of the trial court that the claimed invention was not obvious. There the invention was a cube puzzle of the kind popularized by Rubik's Cube. In fact, Rubik's Cube was the product accused of infringement. The claims described a puzzle in the shape of a subdivided cube, the pieces of which could be scrambled and restored by rotating the facets of the cube. CBS, which owned the rights to Rubik's Cube, argued that the claims were obvious in light of a prior patent, to one Gustafson, disclosing a spherical puzzle with a subdivided, rotating shell. A person skilled in the art might have *considered* converting Gustafson's sphere puzzle into a cube with rotating faces, but nothing in the art suggested that such a change would have been desirable. On the contrary, the evidence showed that Gustafson, while considering other shapes, had dismissed a cube as inadequate.[316] Moreover, one expert described the cube as a "quantum leap" from the sphere.[317] On the basis of this evidence, the lower court properly concluded that even someone aware of Gustafson's sphere would not have found it obvious to make the cube.

Even these two examples are enough to prove the Federal Circuit's observation that "[t]he obviousness standard, while easy to expound, is sometimes difficult to apply."[318] It is not hard to imagine *Gorman* or *Moleculon* reaching an opposite conclusion.

8.9.4.1 *Secondary Considerations*

Because the obviousness determination is such a difficult and subjective one, courts have increasingly emphasized the importance of "secondary considerations"—factors thought to provide objective evidence of

---

[314] *Gorman,* 933 F.2d at 987.
[315] 793 F.2d 1261 (Fed. Cir. 1986).
[316] *Id.* at 1268.
[317] *Id.*
[318] Uniroyal, Inc. v. Rudkin-Wiley Corp., 837 F.2d 1044, 1050 (Fed. Cir. 1988).

nonobviousness. In *Graham v. John Deere Co.*,[319] the Supreme Court suggested that these "secondary considerations," including "commercial success, long felt but unsolved needs, failure of others, etc.,"[320] might be illuminating. Under subsequent Federal Circuit precedent, secondary considerations have become a mandatory aspect of the obviousness analysis.[321]

Secondary considerations include the following:

- Commercial success
- Long-felt need
- Failure of others
- Industry recognition
- Expressions of skepticism or disbelief
- Unexpected results
- Copying
- Near-simultaneous invention

The secondary consideration most frequently encountered is commercial success. Commercial success means evidence that a product covered by a patent claim has earned substantial profits in the marketplace. In theory, an invention that has been successful in the marketplace could not have been an obvious one. Otherwise, someone else would have stepped ahead of the inventor in order to reap the available rewards.[322] One problem with this theory is that the commercial success of a product can be due to any number of factors other than the claimed invention–

---

[319] 383 U.S. 1 (1966).

[320] *Id.* at 17–18. The factors specifically mentioned in *Graham* may be given greater weight than others subsumed in the "etc." *See* Ecolochem, Inc. v. Southern California Edison Co., 227 F.3d 1361, 1380 (Fed. Cir. 2000).

[321] *See* Star Scientific, Inc. v. R.J. Reynolds Tobacco Co., 655 F.3d 1364, 1375 (Fed. Cir. 2011) ("secondary considerations 'may often be the most probative and cogent evidence [of nonobviousness] in the record' "); In re Huai-Hung Kao, 639 F.3d 1057, 1067 (Fed. Cir. 2011) ("when secondary considerations are present, though they are not always dispositive, it is error not to consider them"); Hybritech, Inc. v. Monoclonal Antibodies, Inc., 802 F.2d 1367, 1380 (Fed. Cir. 1986) (secondary considerations are more than "icing on the cake").

[322] *See* Syntex (USA) LLC v. Apotex, Inc., 407 F.3d 1371, 1383 (Fed. Cir. 2005) ("commercial success permits the inference that others have tried and failed"); Dickey-John Corp. v. Int'l Tapetronics Corp., 710 F.2d 329, 346–47 (7th Cir. 1983) ("If individuals believe there is 'a fortune waiting in the wings' for the person who solves the problem, we infer that with such an incentive, many artisans were actually attempting to find the solution. The longer they failed to do so, the stronger the inference that it took extraordinary skill to solve the problem.").

including marketing know-how, advertising, manufacturing techniques, quality control, price, or features of the product other than those covered by the claim. In order to meet this objection, a "nexus" must exist between the success and the claimed invention.[323] Nexus means a logical, cause-and-effect relationship between the success of the product and the claimed invention. Such a connection might be shown in a number of ways, including consumer surveys, comparisons to similar products, or testimony concerning the relative advantages of the claimed invention.[324]

Commercial success is useful as a secondary consideration to patentees or applicants who have marketed a product covered by the claim. Commercial success can also be premised on a product marketed by someone else—even an infringer—as long as there is a nexus between the success of the product and the invention claimed.[325] Success in licensing[326] may also be offered as evidence of commercial success.[327]

The other secondary considerations are relatively straightforward. If there had been a long-felt need for an invention, or if others had tried and failed to solve the problem addressed by the invention, it is reasonable to infer that the invention was not an obvious one. Otherwise the problem

---

[323] *See* Tokai Corp. v. Easton Enterprises, Inc., 632 F.3d 1358, 1369 (Fed. Cir. 2011); Geo M. Martin Co. v. Alliance Machine Sys. Int'l LLC, 618 F.3d 1294, 1304 (Fed. Cir. 2010) (no nexus where success was actually due to advantage of preexisting market share); Wyers v. Master Lock Co., 616 F.3d 1231, 1246 (Fed. Cir. 2010); Iron Grip Barbell Co. v. USA Sports, Inc., 392 F.3d 1317, 1324 (Fed. Cir. 2004). A similar nexus may be required of any secondary consideration. *See Huai-Hung Kao*, 639 F.3d at 1068 ("Where the offered secondary consideration actually results from something other than what is both claimed and *novel* in the claim, there is no nexus to the merits of the claimed invention.").

[324] *See* Demaco Corp. v. F. Von Langsdorff Licensing Ltd., 851 F.2d 1387, 1392–93 (Fed. Cir. 1988). "[I]f the marketed product embodies the claimed features, and is coextensive with them, then a nexus is presumed and the burden shifts to the party asserting obviousness to present evidence to rebut the presumed nexus." Brown & Williamson Tobacco Corp. v. Philip Morris Inc., 229 F.3d 1120, 1130 (Fed. Cir. 2000). One way to rebut the presumption might be to show that other products embodying the patented invention were commercial failures; hence, the successful product must owe its success to something other than the invention. *See id.* To demonstrate commercial success, the patentee need not sell every possible embodiment within the scope of the claim; it is enough to sell one embodiment if its success can be attributed to "the merits of the claimed invention." *Huai-Hung Kao*, 639 F.3d at 1069.

[325] *See Brown & Williamson*, 229 F.3d at 1130.

[326] *See* Section 6.3.

[327] *See In re* GPAC Inc., 57 F.3d 1573, 1580 (Fed. Cir. 1995). Here the nexus requirement is essential because the reason for a license may be nothing more than avoidance of litigation. *See Iron Grip*, 392 F.3d at 1324.

would have been solved before and the need already satisfied.[328] Reactions to the invention by persons skilled in the art can also be important. If experts in the field praised the invention, or, even better, if they expressed skepticism or disbelief that anyone had solved the problems overcome by the invention, this also serves as evidence of nonobviousness.[329] Unexpected results can be useful in showing that an invention was not an obvious one, particularly where the results are unexpectedly good.[330] Finally, because imitation is the sincerest form of flattery, copying of the invention can be taken as objective evidence that the invention was not obvious.[331]

---

[328] *See Geo M. Martin,* 618 F.3d at 1304–05; Perfect Web Technologies, Inc. v. InfoUSA, Inc., 587 F.3d 1324, 1332 (Fed. Cir. 2009); Advanced Display Sys., Inc. v. Kent State University, 212 F.3d 1272, 1285 (Fed. Cir. 2000) (failure of others); *In re* Dow Chemical Co., 837 F.2d 469, 472 (Fed. Cir. 1988) ("Recognition of need, and difficulties encountered by those skilled in the field, are classical indicia of unobviousness."). On the other hand, "mere passage of time without the claimed invention" does not prove nonobviousness. *In re* Kahn, 441 F.3d 977, 990 (Fed. Cir. 2006).

[329] *See* Rolls-Royce, PLC v. United Technologies Corp., 603 F.3d 1325, 1339–40 (Fed. Cir. 2010) (industry prizes and recognition); Pressure Prods. Medical Supplies, Inc. v. Greatbatch Ltd., 599 F.3d 1308, 1319 (Fed. Cir. 2010) (other companies refused to license because they did not believe the invention could work); Power-One, Inc. v. Artesyn Technologies, Inc., 599 F.3d 1343, 1352 (Fed. Cir. 2010) (acclamation); Ortho-McNeil Pharmaceutical, Inc. v. Mylan Labs., Inc., 520 F.3d 1358, 1365 (Fed. Cir. 2008) (expert skepticism); Monarch Knitting Machinery Corp. v. Sulzer Morat GmbH, 139 F.3d 877, 885 (Fed. Cir. 1998) ("general skepticism"); Gillette Co. v. S.C. Johnson & Son, Inc., 919 F.2d 720, 726 (Fed. Cir. 1990) (skepticism toward "new-fangled approach"). "Teaching away" can be one form of expressing skepticism. *See Monarch Knitting,* 139 F.3d at 885 ("[i]n effect, 'teaching away' is a more pointed and probative form of skepticism").

[330] *See Ortho-McNeil,* 520 F.3d at 1365; Kao Corp. v. Unilever U.S., Inc., 441 F.3d 963, 970 (Fed. Cir. 2006); Richardson-Vicks Inc. v. Upjohn Co., 122 F.3d 1476, 1483 (Fed. Cir. 1997). Unexpected results should be "reasonably commensurate with the scope of the claims." *Huai-Hung Kao,* 639 F.3d at 1068. Unexpected results for only a subset of a claimed range may not support the nonobviousness of the entire claimed invention. *See In re* Harris, 409 F.3d 1339, 1344 (Fed. Cir. 2005); *In re* Peterson, 315 F.3d 1325, 1330–31 (Fed. Cir. 2003). A finding of unexpected technical results, rather than unexpected success in the marketplace, is the relevant consideration. *See* Media Technologies Licensing, LLC v. Upper Deck Co., 596 F.3d 1334, 1339 (Fed. Cir. 2010).

[331] *Ortho-McNeil,* 520 F.3d at 1365; *Advanced Display,* 212 F.3d at 1285–86; Diversitech Corp. v. Century Steps, Inc., 850 F.2d 675, 679 (Fed. Cir. 1988); *but cf. Ecolochem,* 227 F.3d at 1380 (copying "is only equivocal evidence of non-obviousness" and may have occurred because of " 'a general lack of concern for patent property' "). "Copying" means a deliberate effort to duplicate a patented product, not coincidental similarity, even if it results in infringement. *See Tokai,* 632 F.3d at 1370; *Wyers,* 616 F.3d at 1246 ("Not every competing product that arguably falls within the scope of a patent is evidence of copying; otherwise, 'every infringement suit would automatically confirm the nonobviousness of the patent.' ").

All of the secondary considerations discussed so far are potential evidence of *nonobviousness.*[332] Near-simultaneous invention is one secondary consideration that is positive evidence of obviousness. If an invention is made independently by another inventor, at nearly the same time as the applicant or patentee, this is evidence that the invention was not the result of uncommon effort or insight. Rather, the art may simply have progressed to the point where the claimed invention was the obvious next step.[333] Note that an independent near-simultaneous invention can serve as objective evidence of obviousness even if that invention occurred shortly after the date that is the dividing line for prior art under § 102.

8.9.5 Derivation

One rule of patentability that almost goes without saying is that an applicant cannot claim someone else's invention. For patents and patent applications filed before March 16, 2013, this principle is embodied in 35 U.S.C. § 102(f), which states that a patent cannot be obtained if the applicant "did not himself invent the subject matter sought to be patented." If the purported inventor took the idea from someone else, the claim is unpatentable or, if already issued, invalid. A defense based on § 102(f) is usually referred to as a "derivation" defense because the claim is said to be derived from someone else's invention.[334] A derivation defense requires proof, by clear and convincing evidence, (1) that the invention was fully conceived by another person before it had been conceived by the purported inventor and (2) that the conception was communicated to the purported inventor.[335] The information communicated must have been an

---

[332] The absence of commercial success, long-felt need, and the other indicia of nonobviousness has generally been held a "neutral factor" rather than positive evidence of obviousness. *See* Gentry Gallery, Inc. v. Berkline Corp., 134 F.3d 1473, 1478 (Fed. Cir. 1998).

[333] *See Geo M. Martin*, 618 F.3d at 1305 ("Independently made, simultaneous inventions, made 'within a comparatively short space of time,' are persuasive evidence that the claimed apparatus 'was the product only of ordinary mechanical or engineering skill.' "); *Ecolochem*, 227 F.3d at 1379; *In re* Merk & Co., 800 F.2d 1091, 1098 (Fed. Cir. 1986).

[334] *See* Eaton Corp. v. Rockwell Int'l Corp., 323 F.3d 1332, 1344 (Fed. Cir. 2003); Price v. Symsek, 988 F.2d 1187, 1190 (Fed. Cir. 1993).

[335] Creative Compounds, LLC v. Starmark Labs., 631 F.3d 1303, 1313 (Fed. Cir. 2011); International Rectifier Corp. v. Ixys Corp., 361 F.3d 1363, 1276 (Fed. Cir. 2004); *Eaton*, 323 F.3d at 1344; Gambro Lundia AB v. Baxter Healthcare Corp., 110 F.3d 1573, 1576 (Fed. Cir. 1997). The claim of prior conception must be corroborated (*see* Section 8.9.1.5). *Creative*, 651 F.3d at 1313; Lacks Indus., Inc. v. McKechnie Vehicle Components USA, Inc., 322 F.3d 1335, 1349 (Fed. Cir. 2003).

"enabling disclosure" of the invention,[336] not merely information that could have made the invention obvious.[337]

Even though the America Invents Act places new emphasis on the filing date of a patent application, if Inventor A's application actually reflects the work of Inventor B, Inventor A still cannot obtain a patent even if Inventor A filed first. Inventor A would not, in fact, be an inventor of the claimed subject matter at all. Section 135 of the revised Patent Act provides for derivation proceedings, which take the place of the interference proceedings formerly used to determine which competing inventor invented first.[338] Here the issue is more limited—did the inventor named in an earlier patent application derive the invention from someone else? Although the case law has yet to develop, it is likely that "derivation" will mean in this context, as is did before, a situation where another inventor conceived of the invention first and that conception was communicated to the person who claimed the right to patent it. If two inventors conceived of the same invention working *independently*, it would not be accurate to say that the second derived the invention from the first. In that case, the last to invent but first to file may well be entitled to a patent.

8.10 DOUBLE PATENTING

An inventor is entitled to one patent on one invention.[339] If more than one patent could be obtained on the same invention, an inventor could extend the period of exclusivity beyond what the law intends.[340] Or each patent could be assigned to a different party, subjecting potential licensees

---

[336] *Eaton*, 323 F.3d at 1344. Enabling disclosures are discussed in Section 8.6.

[337] *Gambro*, 110 F.3d at 1577–78. *Gambro* suggests that one could never base a finding of obviousness on the kind of disclosure contemplated in § 102(f). However, the Federal Circuit later decided that a § 102(f) disclosure, combined with other references, *can* lead to a finding of obviousness. Oddzon Prods., Inc. v. Just Toys, Inc., 122 F.3d 1396, 1403–4 (Fed. Cir. 1997).

[338] *See* Section 5.4. Section 291(a) allows a civil action by the owner of one patent who contends that another patent, claiming the same invention, was the product of derivation. Such an action must be filed within one year of the issuance of the challenged patent. 35 U.S.C. § 291(b).

[339] Perricone v. Medicis Pharmaceutical Corp., 432 F.3d 1368, 1373 (Fed. Cir. 2005); Geneva Pharmaceuticals, Inc. v. Glaxosmithkline PLC, 349 F.3d 1373, 1377 (Fed. Cir. 2003).

[340] *See* Sun Pharmaceutical Indus., Ltd. v. Eli Lilly & Co. 611 F.3d 1381, 1384 (Fed. Cir. 2010); *In re* Basell Poliolefine Italia S.P.A., 547 F.3d 1371, 1375 (Fed. Cir. 2008); AstraZeneca AB v. KV Pharmaceutical Co., 494 F.3d 1011, 1016 (Fed. Cir. 2007).

to multiple overlapping claims.[341] To prevent this result, a claim can be held unpatentable or invalid if it duplicates the subject matter of a claim in an earlier patent to the same inventor. This is known as "double patenting." Double patenting can also be found where the claims are attributable to different inventors but are owned by a common assignee.[342]

Double patenting comes in two forms. The first is "same invention" double patenting, which means that the later claim is substantially identical in scope to the earlier claim.[343] The prohibition against same invention double patenting is said to have a statutory basis in 35 U.S.C. § 101, which states that "[w]hoever invents or discovers any new and useful process . . . may obtain *a* patent therefor."[344] The more common form of double patenting is "obviousness-type" double patenting, which means that the later claim, though not identical, is only an obvious variation of the earlier claim.[345] The reasoning behind this prohibition is that once a patent has expired, the public should be at liberty to use not only the precise invention claimed but also variations that would be obvious to one of ordinary skill.[346]

Issues of obviousness-type double patenting often arise where an inventor seeks to patent both a broad genus and a narrow species of that genus. For example, an inventor might conceive of both a generic design for a new mousetrap and a specific variation of that design using a particularly sensitive trigger. If the inventor obtained a patent on the broad invention first and then sought a patent on the variation or improvement, the question would be whether the variation was obvious in light of the more general design. If not, the inventor would be entitled to both patents.[347] On the other hand, if the inventor obtained the narrower patent first and the broader patent second, the second patent would almost certainly be held

---

[341] *See In re* Fallaux, 564 F.3d 1313, 1319 (Fed. Cir. 2009).

[342] *See AstraZeneca,* 494 F.3d at 1016; *In re* Longi, 759 F.2d 887, 893 (Fed. Cir. 1985).

[343] *See In re* Lonardo, 119 F.3d 960, 965 (Fed. Cir. 1997); *In re* Goodman, 11 F.3d 1046, 1052 (Fed. Cir. 1993); *Longi,* 759 F.2d at 892.

[344] *See Sun,* 611 F.3d at 1384; *Perricone,* 432 F.3d at 1372–73.

[345] *See Sun,* 611 F.3d at 1384; *AstraZeneca,* 494 F.3d at 1016; *Perricone,* 432 F.3d at 1373.

[346] *See Geneva Pharmaceuticals,* 349 F.3d at 1378; *Lonardo,* 119 F.3d at 965; *Longi,* 759 F.2d at 892–93.

[347] The combination of both patents, issued at different times, might prevent anyone from making the specific mousetrap for a period of more than 20 years. This is not improper. If one product embodies several distinct patentable inventions, each such invention can result in a patent. When a particular patent expires, that invention is available to the public *as long as* it is practiced in a way that does not violate some other patent. *See In re* Kaplan, 789 F.2d 1574, 1577–78 (Fed. Cir. 1986).

obvious in light of the first.[348] This result conforms with the rule derived in the context of § 102 that a claim to a genus is anticipated if a single species of that genus is found in the prior art.[349]

Obviousness-type double patenting can be cured, in a sense, by filing a "terminal disclaimer" with the Patent Office.[350] A terminal disclaimer is a binding statement that (1) a later patent will expire at the same time as a prior patent and (2) the later patent will be enforceable only as long as it and the prior patent are commonly owned.[351] The voluntary curtailment of the term of the second patent removes any concern that the existence of two similar patents will improperly extend the duration of the patent monopoly. The requirement of common ownership eliminates the additional risk that the two similar patents might be assigned to different parties, each of whom could press duplicative and harassing claims against a potential infringer.[352]

The terminal disclaimer mechanism provides inventors with some incentive to further develop their patented ideas, even in ways that might be considered obvious, and to disclose those developments to the public

---

[348] *See Perricone*, 432 F.3d at 1374 (double patenting where second patent claimed a treatment for skin damage, and the earlier patent claimed the same treatment for sunburn— a species of skin damage).

[349] *See* Section 8.9.3. Although this is classified as an instance of obviousness-type double patenting, *see Goodman*, 11 F.3d at 1052–53, one can conceive of cases in which the full scope of a genus is not obvious merely from the disclosure of a species of the genus. Perhaps this would be better classified as "anticipation-type" double patenting. *See Sun*, 611 F.3d at 1385 (claim in second patent is not " 'patentably distinct' " if the later claim " 'is obvious over[] or anticipated by' " the earlier claim). On rare occasions the inventor actually filed the application for the broader patent *first*, and it issued second only because of delays in prosecution over which the inventor had no control. Under these circumstances, the second patent has been denied only if each claimed invention would be obvious in light of the other—a so-called two-way test of obviousness. *See Fallaux*, 564 F.3d at 1316. While this can result in an extension of the patent monopoly beyond the contemplated period, where it was not the patentee's fault the extension is not "unjustified." *In re* Braat, 937 F.2d 589, 595 (Fed. Cir. 1991). The two-way test is not appropriate if the applicant is even partially responsible for the delay in issuing the first-filed application. *See Fallaux*, 564 F.3d at 1316; *Basell*, 547 F.3d at 1376. Nor is it appropriate if the applicant could have filed all of the claims in one application. *See In re* Berg, 140 F.3d 1428, 1434 (Fed. Cir. 1998). A two-way approach for obviousness-type double patenting is also adopted whenever when one of the patents at issue is a utility patent and the other is a design patent. *See In re* Dembiczak, 175 F.3d 994, 1002 (Fed. Cir. 1999).

[350] *See* 35 U.S.C. § 253; *Perricone*, 432 F.3d at 1375; *Goodman*, 11 F.3d at 1052; *Longi*, 759 F.2d at 894.

[351] *See* 37 C.F.R. § 1.321(c).

[352] *See Fallaux*, 564 F.3d at 1319; *In re* Van Ornum, 696 F.2d 937, 944–45 (C.C.P.A. 1982).

through additional patents.[353] This procedure applies only to obviousness-type double patenting; same-invention double patenting cannot be remedied by a terminal disclaimer. A terminal disclaimer is also no protection against grounds of invalidity other than double patenting.[354]

Sometimes related patents can be attributed to a "restriction requirement."[355] A restriction requirement results when the patent examiner, during prosecution, finds that an application claims two or more distinct inventions. The applicant must elect which invention to pursue in the pending application, and if the applicant wishes to pursue one of the other inventions, the applicant must file a divisional application. That application and the original application may each result in a patent. Because, in this case, the existence of two separate patents is attributable to the Patent Office's determination that each application represents a distinct invention, the patents are immune from a challenge of double patenting.[356] A different result would be unfair to the applicant. But if the claims of the separate applications evolve during the course of prosecution, as they sometimes do, the applicant must maintain "consonance"–that is, the claims cannot be changed in such a way that what was formerly patentably distinct is no longer so. If consonance is lost, so is the immunity from double patenting.[357]

---

[353] *See* Quad Environmental Technologies Corp. v. Union Sanitary Dist., 946 F.2d 870, 873 (Fed. Cir. 1991).

[354] *See id.* at 874.

[355] *See* Section 5.3.

[356] *See* 35 U.S.C. § 121; *Geneva Pharmaceuticals*, 349 F.3d at 1378; Applied Materials, Inc. v. Advanced Semiconductor Materials America, Inc., 98 F.3d 1563, 1568 (Fed. Cir. 1996); Gerber Garment Technology, Inc. v. Lectra Sys., Inc., 916 F.2d 683, 687 (Fed. Cir. 1990).

[357] *See Geneva Pharmaceuticals*, 349 F.3d at 1381; *Gerber*, 916 F.2d at 688.

CHAPTER 9

Enforceability Defenses

Certain defenses to a claim of patent infringement produce, if successful, a holding that the patent is "unenforceable" rather than invalid. The most important of these are the inequitable conduct and misuse defenses.[1] If a patent is unenforceable, it cannot be the basis of an infringement claim.

9.1 INEQUITABLE CONDUCT

In court proceedings, the adversarial system keeps litigants honest. If a party shades the truth or withholds important evidence from the court, the other party will expose the error, if it can. As discussed in Section 5.1, patent prosecution is *ex parte*, meaning that persons who might oppose the issuance of a patent have no opportunity to participate. The Patent Office must rely heavily on information provided by applicants, and if applicants misrepresent the facts, there is no one to contradict them. Because applicants could take advantage of this situation, they are charged with a duty of candor and fair dealing.[2]

---

[1] Transferring ownership of a patent subject to a terminal disclaimer, contrary to the requirement that patents linked by a terminal disclaimer remain commonly owned, might also create an unenforceability defense.

[2] *See* Advanced Magnetic Closures, Inc. v. Rome Fastener Corp., 607 F.3d 817, 829 (Fed. Cir. 2010 ("Patent applicants 'have a duty to prosecute patent applications in the [PTO] with candor, good faith, and honesty.'"); Honeywell Int'l Inc. v. Universal Avionics Sys. Corp., 488 F.3d 982, 999 (Fed. Cir. 2007).

Applicants must disclose to the patent examiner any information that is "material" to the issuance of the patent.[3] Usually, applicants do not have to *search* for such information. They do not, for example, have to scour the prior art for invalidating references.[4] But an applicant aware of such a reference must inform the patent examiner. This duty extends to the applicant, to the applicant's attorneys, and to anyone else who is substantively involved in the application process.[5] Failure to meet the required duty of candor is known as "inequitable conduct."

Inequitable conduct may be raised as a defense in patent infringement litigation, and, if it is proven by clear and convincing evidence, the patent will be held unenforceable.[6] Unenforceability is like invalidity with one important exception. If a single claim of a patent is invalid, the remaining claims of the patent survive if they do not suffer the same defect.[7] In contrast, if an applicant obtained a single patent claim through inequitable conduct, the *entire patent* is unenforceable.[8] This result often makes inequitable conduct a more

---

[3] 37 C.F.R. § 1.56.

[4] *See* Frazier v. Roessel Cine Photo Tech., Inc., 417 F.3d 1230, 1238 (Fed. Cir. 2005); Brasseler, U.S.A. I, L.P. v. Stryker Sales Corp., 267 F.3d 1370, 1382 (Fed. Cir. 2001); FMC Corp. v. Hennessy Indus., Inc., 836 F.2d 521, 526 n.6 (Fed. Cir. 1987). The "possibility that material information may exist" is not enough to trigger a duty to inquire; there must be some clue "suggest[ing] the existence of specific information the materiality of which may be ascertained with reasonable inquiry." *Brasseler*, 267 F.3d at 1382. On the other hand, an applicant cannot cultivate ignorance if there are sufficient warnings of invalidating prior art. *See* Hewlett-Packard Co. v. Bausch & Lomb Inc., 882 F.2d 1556, 1562 (Fed. Cir. 1989) (wrongful intent may be inferred from evidence of "studied ignorance"). Usually an attorney can rely on information provided by the applicant unless there is reason to doubt its accuracy or completeness. *See Brasseler*, 267 F.3d at 1382–83 ("[t]here is no need for an attorney to pursue a fishing expedition"). Although applicants generally do not have to search for relevant prior art, those who petition for accelerated examination must submit the results of a preexamination search and an explanation of how the claimed invention differs from the closest references. *See* M.P.E.P. § 708.02(a).

[5] Avid Identification Sys., Inc. v. Crystal Import Corp., 603 F.3d 967, 973 (Fed. Cir. 2010); Evident Corp. v. Church & Dwight Co., 399 F.3d 1310, 1315–16 (Fed. Cir. 2005). "Substantive involvement" does not include involvement that is merely "administrative or secretarial in nature." *Avid*, 603 F.3d at 974. Even an "innocent" inventor cannot enforce the patent if a co-inventor, or the inventor's attorney, committed inequitable conduct. *See Advanced Magnetic*, 607 F.3d at 828 ("One bad apple spoils the entire barrel."). Note that "inventors represented by counsel are presumed to know the law." *Id.* at 1385.

[6] Liquid Dynamics Corp. v. Vaughan Co., Inc., 449 F.3d 1209, 1226 (Fed. Cir. 2006).

[7] 35 U.S.C. § 288.

[8] Therasense, Inc. v. Becton, Dickinson & Co., 649 F.3d 1276, 1288 (Fed. Cir. 2011) (en banc); Impax Labs., Inc. v. Aventis Pharmaceuticals Inc., 468 F.3d 1366, 1375 (Fed. Cir. 2006); Baxter Int'l, Inc. v. McGaw, Inc., 149 F.3d 1321, 1332 (Fed. Cir. 1998) ("It is . . . settled law that inequitable conduct with respect to one claim renders the entire patent unenforceable."). Unenforceability can even extend to another patent if the patents are sufficiently related. This is sometimes called "infectious unenforceability." *See Baxter*, 149 F.3d at 1327.

formidable defense than, for example, anticipation, even though both defenses could rely on the same prior art reference.[9] In fact, the Federal Circuit recently dubbed inequitable conduct the " 'atomic bomb' of patent law."[10]

An inequitable conduct defense can be based on a misrepresentation made to the Patent Office or a withholding of information.[11] In either case, two elements must be proven: *materiality* and *intent.*[12] Both standards have been subject to conflicting definitions over the years.[13]

"Materiality" means that the information withheld or misrepresented was important enough to warrant the severe penalties associated with inequitable conduct. For many years, the test of materiality endorsed by the Federal Circuit was whether there was a substantial likelihood that a reasonable patent examiner would have considered the information important in deciding whether the application should issue as a patent.[14] Information could be "important" to a reasonable examiner even if, ultimately, the patent would have issued anyway.[15] However, in the 2011 *Therasense* case,[16] the Federal Circuit abandoned the important-to-a-reasonable-examiner standard in favor of a

---

[9] *See Therasense,* 649 F.3d at 1288–89 (observing that inequitable conduct "may endanger a substantial portion of a company's patent portfolio").

[10] *Id.* at 1288. Courts can also award the prevailing party its attorneys' fees in an "exceptional case." Inequitable conduct before the PTO, like misconduct in litigation, is a proper basis for finding a case to be exceptional. *See* Taltech Ltd. v. Esquel Enterprises Ltd., 604 F.3d 1324, 1328 (Fed. Cir. 2010).

[11] *See* Lazare Kaplan Int'l, Inc. v. Photoscribe Technologies, Inc., 628 F.3d 1359, 1378 (Fed. Cir. 2010) (inequitable conduct possible where the applicant " 'made an affirmative misrepresentation of material fact, failed to disclose material information, or submitted false material information' "); Ring Plus, Inc. v. Cingular Wireless Corp., 614 F.3d 1354, 1358 (Fed. Cir. 2010); Cancer Research Technology Ltd. v. Barr Labs., Inc., 625 F.3d 724, 732 (Fed. Cir. 2010).

[12] Aventis Pharma S.A. v. Hospira, Inc., 675 F.3d 1324, 1334 (Fed. Cir. 2012); *Therasense,* 649 F.3d at 1290; Golden Hour Data Sys., Inc. v. emsCharts, Inc., 614 F.3d 1367, 1373 (Fed. Cir. 2010); *Honeywell,* 488 F.3d at 999. The party challenging the patent must prove both materiality and intent by "clear and convincing evidence." Dippin' Dots, Inc. v. Mosey, 476 F.3d 1337, 1345 (Fed. Cir. 2007); Flex-Rest, LLC v. Steelcase, Inc., 455 F.3d 1351, 1363 (Fed. Cir. 2006).

[13] *See Therasense,* 649 F.3d at 1287 ("the standards for intent to deceive and materiality have fluctuated over time").

[14] *Golden Hour,* 614 F.3d at 1373–74; *Advanced Magnetic,* 607 F.3d at 829; Astrazeneca Pharmaceuticals LP v. Teva Pharmaceuticals USA, Inc., 583 F.3d 766, 773 (Fed. Cir. 2009) (noting four competing standards of materiality but calling the important-to-a-reasonable-examiner standard the "most often employed"); Larson Mfg. Co. v. Aluminart Prods. Ltd., 559 F.3d 1317, 1326 (Fed. Cir. 2009).

[15] *See Larson,* 559 F.3d at 1327; Cargill, Inc. v. Canbra Foods, Ltd., 476 F.3d 1359, 1366 (Fed. Cir. 2007); Digital Control, Inc. v. Charles Machine Works, 437 F.3d 1309, 1318 (Fed. Cir. 2006).

[16] Therasense, Inc. v. Becton, Dickinson & Co., 649 F.3d 1276 (Fed. Cir. 2011) (en banc).

"but-for" standard of materiality. Under this standard, withheld information is material only if it would have prevented the PTO from allowing the claim.[17]

The court explained that "inequitable conduct hinges on basic fairness," and the severe penalties could be justified only if the patentee had received "the unfair benefit of . . . an unwarranted claim."[18] The tightened standard is also meant to curtail the glut of inequitable conduct claims that have "plagued not only the courts but also the entire patent system."[19] The court recognized an exception to the but-for materiality standard where "the patentee has engaged in affirmative acts of egregious misconduct."[20] Acts of this sort–like the filing of "an unmistakably false affidavit"–are inherently material, in contrast to a mere failure to disclose prior art.[21] If an applicant actually lies to the patent examiner, it will not matter that the patent could have been obtained honestly.

The intent threshold of inequitable conduct is as important as the materiality threshold. If the applicant withheld or misrepresented information because of an innocent mistake, the applicant did not commit inequitable conduct, no matter how material the information may have been.[22] At one

---

[17] *Id.* at 1291; *see also Aventis*, 675 F.3d at 1334. "When an applicant fails to disclose prior art to the PTO, that prior art is but-for material if the PTO would not have allowed the claim had it been aware of the undisclosed prior art." *Therasense*, 649 F.3d at 1291. When deciding if withheld information would have prevented issuance of the claim, "the court should apply the preponderance of the evidence standard and give claims their broadest reasonable construction," as would be the case in the PTO. *Id.* at 1291–92; *see also, Aventis*, 675 F.3d at 1334. Information cannot be material if it is cumulative of, or less material than, other information available to the examiner. *Astrazeneca*, 583 F.3d at 773; *Larson*, 559 F.3d at 1327; Technology Licensing Corp. v. Videoteck, Inc., 545 F.3d 1316, 1337 (Fed. Cir. 2008). Nor is it material if the applicant withheld information that the examiner discovered independently. Molins PLC v. Textron, Inc., 48 F.3d 1172, 1185 (Fed. Cir. 1995); Scripps Clinic Research Foundation v. Genentech, Inc., 927 F.2d 1565, 1582 (Fed. Cir. 1991). These distinctions were probably more important before the standard of materiality became a but-for standard.

[18] *Therasense*, 649 F.3d at 1292. "After all, the patentee obtains no advantage from misconduct if the patent would have issued anyway." *Id.*

[19] *Id.* at 1289. An easily triggered inequitable conduct defense was said to overburden patent examiners by encouraging the disclosure of "a deluge of prior art references, most of which have marginal value." *Id.*

[20] *Id.* at 1292.

[21] *Id.* at 1292–93.

[22] *See Aventis*, 675 F.3d at 1334–35; *Therasense*, 649 F.3d at 1292 ("the accused infringer must prove by clear and convincing evidence that the applicant knew of the reference, knew that it was material, and made a deliberate decision to withhold it"); *Cargill*, 476 F.3d at 1364; *Liquid Dynamics*, 449 F.3d at 1227 ("Intent is a subjective inquiry into whether the inventor knew the information was material and chose not to disclose it."). Although "subjective good faith can support a defense to inequitable conduct . . . there is no such thing as a good faith intent to deceive." *Cargill*, 476 F.3d at 1367–68.

time, some courts considered gross negligence to be sufficient intent to warrant a finding of inequitable conduct.[23] However, in *Kingsdown Medical Consultants v. Hollister Inc.*,[24] the Federal Circuit, resolving conflicting precedent, held that inequitable conduct can only occur if the applicant or attorney made a *deliberate decision* to deceive the Patent Office. A lapse that is the result of carelessness, even gross carelessness, does not amount to inequitable conduct.[25]

Intent to deceive can be proven by indirect or circumstantial evidence.[26] It is rare that inequitable conduct will be proven by an applicant's admission or a "smoking gun" document referring to a planned deception. Rather, the proof is likely to be found in circumstances where the information was so important, and the situation so devoid of any possibility of an excuse, that one must conclude that the deception was deliberate.[27] If there are other reasonable ways to explain the nondisclosure, then the evidence is not enough to demonstrate intent to deceive.[28] Moreover, one cannot

---

[23] *See, e.g.*, Driscoll v. Cebalo, 731 F.2d 878, 885 (Fed. Cir. 1984).

[24] 863 F.2d 867 (Fed. Cir. 1988) (resolution of conflicting precedent decided en banc).

[25] *Id.; see also Therasense*, 649 F.3d at 1290 (no "should have known" standard); *Ring Plus*, 614 F.3d at 1361; *Golden Hour*, 614 F.3d at 1378 ("Gross negligence is not inequitable conduct."); *Brasseler*, 267 F.3d at 1382 ("a finding of deceptive intent may not be based solely on gross negligence"). In *Therasense*, the Federal Circuit disavowed earlier suggestions that materiality and intent may be judged on a "sliding scale" where lesser evidence of intent may be adequate for a withheld reference of greater materiality. 649 F.3d at 1290; *see also Aventis*, 675 F.3d at 1334. It is not clear whether a "balancing" of materiality and intent, often mentioned by the Federal Circuit prior to *Therasense, see, e.g., Taltech*, 604 F.3d at 1328 ("a greater showing of one allows a lesser showing of the other"), still contributes to the ultimate conclusion that the patent should or should not be held unenforceable.

[26] *Therasense*, 649 F.3d at 1290 ("Because direct evidence of deceptive intent is rare, a district court may infer intent from indirect and circumstantial evidence."); *see also Ring Plus*, 614 F.3d at 1361; *Golden Hour*, 614 F.3d at 1377.

[27] *See Impax*, 468 F.3d at 1375 ("intent to deceive is generally inferred from the facts and circumstances surrounding the applicant's overall conduct"); *Dippin' Dots*, 476 F.3d at 1345 (" '[S]moking gun' evidence is not required in order to establish an intent to deceive. . . ."); Hoffman-La Roche, Inc. v. Promega Corp., 323 F.3d 1354, 1371 (Fed. Cir. 2003) ("a finding of intent does not require a confession from the stand by the inventor or the prosecuting attorney"). If the circumstantial evidence is sufficient to infer the necessary intent, "a mere denial of intent to mislead (which would defeat every effort to establish inequitable conduct) will not suffice [to rebut that evidence]." GFI, Inc. v. Franklin Corp., 265 F.3d 1268, 1275 (Fed. Cir. 2001).

[28] *See Aventis*, 675 F.3d at 1335 ("the specific intent to deceive must be 'the single most reasonable inference able to be drawn from the evidence' "); *Therasense*, 649 F.3d at 1290–91; *Ring Plus*, 614 F.3d at 1361; *Golden Hour*, 614 F.3d at 1377. If the applicant published the information for the benefit of the scientific community, it is more difficult to conclude that it was deliberately withheld from the PTO. *See Cancer Research*, 625 F.3d at 734.

infer from the materiality of the reference alone that the applicant intended to deceive by failing to disclose it.[29]

9.2 MISUSE

The patent system strikes a delicate balance between, on the one hand, the desire to encourage innovation by rewarding inventors with exclusive rights to their inventions and, on the other hand, the desire to promote healthy competition in the marketplace. While the essence of the patent system is the grant of a monopoly, it is still a monopoly of limited scope and duration. If a patent owner attempts to leverage the advantage of a patent into something beyond its intended boundaries, the patent owner may be held to have committed "misuse."[30] Like the inequitable conduct defense, the misuse defense leads, if successful, to a holding that the patent is unenforceable.

An early example of overreaching by a patent owner can be found in *Morton Salt Co. v. G.S. Suppiger.*[31] Suppiger obtained a patent on a machine used in the canning industry for adding salt tablets to the contents of the cans. Only the machine was patented; the salt tablets were not. Nevertheless, when Suppiger leased its machines to canneries, it licensed the canneries to use the machines only if they agreed to buy all of their salt tablets from a Suppiger subsidiary. The Supreme Court viewed this extension of the patent grant as improper and held that a patent owner guilty of

---

[29] *See Therasense,* 649 F.3d at 1290 ("a district court may not infer intent solely from materiality"); *Ring Plus,* 614 F.3d at 1361; *Cancer Research,* 625 F.3d at 733 ("intent to deceive cannot be found based on materiality alone ... [a] district court must find some other evidence that indicates that the applicant appreciated the information's materiality"); Optium Corp. v. Emcore Corp., 603 F.3d 1313, 1321 (Fed. Cir. 2010) (no inference even in cases of "high materiality").

[30] *See* Monsanto Co. v. Scruggs, 459 F.3d 1328, 1339 (Fed. Cir. 2006) ("In order for competitive behavior to amount to patent misuse, one must 'impermissibly broaden[] the scope of the patent grant with anticompetitive effect.' "); Monsanto Co. v. McFarling, 363 F.3d 1336, 1341 (Fed. Cir. 2004); C.R. Bard, Inc. v. M3 Sys., Inc., 157 F.3d 1340, 1372 (Fed. Cir. 1998) ("Patent misuse relates primarily to a patentee's actions that affect competition in unpatented goods or that otherwise extend the economic effect beyond the scope of the patent grant."); Windsurfing Int'l, Inc. v. AMF, Inc., 782 F.2d 995, 1001 (Fed. Cir. 1986) (a misuse defense "requires that the alleged infringer show that the patentee has impermissibly broadened 'the physical or temporal scope' of the patent grant with anticompetitive effect"). "In cases in which the restriction is reasonably within the patent grant, the patent misuse defense can never succeed." *Monsanto,* 363 F.3d at 1341.

[31] 314 U.S. 488 (1941).

such practices could not look to a court for relief.[32] Today such conduct might be characterized as misuse.

Although there is no exhaustive list of the kinds of behavior that constitute misuse, the following may raise questions:

- A patent license, such as that discussed in *Morton Salt*, that compels the licensee to purchase separate, unpatented goods from the patent owner. This is called a "tying" arrangement.[33]
- A patent license that forbids the licensee from dealing with the patent owner's competitors. This is sometimes called "tying-out" in contrast the "tying-in" found in *Morton Salt*.
- A patent license granted only on the condition that *other* patents are also licensed, even though the other patents may be undesired or even invalid.[34]
- Extending the collection of royalty payments past the expiration of the patent term.[35]
- Charging royalties on products that do not use the patented invention.[36]

The misuse defense covers some of the same territory as the federal antitrust laws,[37] at least where the challenged activity takes the form of a threat

---

[32] *Id.* at 492–94.

[33] *See Monsanto*, 363 F.3d at 1341; Virginia Panel Corp. v. Mac Panel Co., 133 F.3d 860, 869 (Fed. Cir. 1997) (referring to tying of "staple good[s]" as an example of "*per se* patent misuse"). It is not misuse to demand that licensees purchase from the patent owner goods that, if purchased from someone else, could supply the basis of a claim of contributory infringement—for example, goods useful only in practicing the patented invention. *See* 35 U.S.C. § 271(d). Contributory infringement is discussed in Section 10.4.

[34] It is common for patent owners to license a group of related patents as a package—an arrangement that may be convenient for the licensee as well as for the patent owner. *See* U.S. Philips Corp. v. Int'l Trade Comm'n, 424 F.3d 1179, 1192–93 (Fed. Cir. 2005). The *U.S. Philips* case casts some doubt on whether package licensing can ever be anticompetitive, even if the licensee has no alternative. The negotiated price for the package will reflect the value of the technology that the licensee *does* need, and the "extra" licenses do not compel the licensee to use those technologies instead of others. *See* 424 F.3d at 1190–91.

[35] *See* Brulotte v. Thys Co., 379 U.S. 29, 33 (1964); *Virginia Panel*, 133 F.3d at 869.

[36] *See U.S. Philips*, 424 F.3d at 1184.

[37] The federal antitrust laws (e.g., the Sherman Antitrust Act, 15 U.S.C. §§ 1–7) are designed to protect competition in the marketplace. Because a patent is a *legal* form of monopoly, efforts to enforce a patent within its legitimate scope do not violate the antitrust laws. *See In re Independent Service Organizations Antitrust Litigation*, 203 F.3d 1322, 1326 (Fed. Cir. 2000) (generally a patent owner who brings suit to enforce right to exclude is exempt from antitrust laws). Antitrust concerns should arise only if the patent was obtained by fraud or was known to be invalid, or if the suit for infringement was a "mere sham." *See id.*; Atari Games Corp. v. Nintendo of America, Inc., 897 F.2d 1572, 1576 (Fed. Cir. 1990).

to competition. Conduct may rise to the level of misuse without violating the antitrust laws,[38] but similar considerations of "market power," anticompetitive effects, and business justifications appear in either context,[39] particularly after changes to 35 U.S.C. § 271. The latter now states that it is misuse to condition a patent license on the sale of a separate, unpatented product only if the patent owner has "market power" in the relevant market.[40] The same limitation applies to patent licenses offered only as a group.[41]

"Market power" is a concept developed in the setting of antitrust law, and perhaps only an economist could provide a thorough definition. In general terms, market power means the ability to alter the conditions of trade, and in particular to raise prices, beyond what could be accomplished in a competitive market. Whether a company has market power depends on the availability of acceptable substitutes for whatever goods or services that company controls. Thus, if *Morton Salt* had applied the current version of § 271, the court might have considered whether Suppiger's patented salt-depositing machines were so superior that it could compel canneries to obtain a patent license, even at the cost of having to purchase unpatented salt tablets from Suppiger's subsidiary. If the canneries could easily have chosen another machine without such restrictions, Suppiger would not have had the power to restrain competition.

Even where a misuse defense is dependent on a demonstration of anticompetitive effects, it is not necessary that the party raising the defense have suffered those anticompetitive effects personally. Protection of the public from abusive practices, and denial of relief to those undeserving of the court's protection, are sufficient reasons to hold a patent unenforceable, no matter what effect the challenged conduct has had on the litigants in a particular case.[42]

Some conduct that might seem anticompetitive is not considered misuse. For example, it is not misuse to grant only a limited number of licenses to a patent, to grant no licenses to a patent, or to completely suppress an

---

[38] *U.S. Philips,* 424 F.3d at 1185–86; *Monsanto,* 459 F.3d at 1339.

[39] *See Virginia Panel,* 133 F.3d at 869 (discussing "rule of reason" applied to some practices alleged to be misuse); *Windsurfing,* 782 F.2d at 1002 (unless conduct has been deemed per se anticompetitive, there must be a showing that it "tends to restrain competition unlawfully in an appropriately defined market").

[40] 35 U.S.C. § 271(d). A patent does not confer market power automatically, nor can a court presume that a patent confers such power. Illinois Tool Works Inc. v. Independent Ink, Inc., 547 U.S. 28, 45–46 (2006).

[41] 35 U.S.C. § 271(d).

[42] *Morton Salt,* 314 U.S. at 493–94.

invention by neither practicing it nor licensing it.[43] Generally, it is up to the patentee to decide whether the invention will be exploited during the term of the patent. On the other hand, recent decisions give courts some leeway to deny an injunction even after a successful suit for infringement. One factor courts may consider is the impact on the public if the patentee does not permit the invention to be made available for use.[44]

Unlike invalidity or unenforceability resulting from inequitable conduct, unenforceability resulting from misuse is reversible. The patent can be enforced again as soon as the objectionable conduct has ceased and any lingering effects have "dissipated."[45]

---

[43] *See* 35 U.S.C. § 271(d) (stating that "refus[al] to license or use any rights to the patent" is not an act of misuse); *Independent Service Organizations*, 203 F.3d at 1326; Cygnus Therapeutics Sys. v. Alza Corp., 92 F.3d 1153, 1160 (Fed. Cir. 1996) ("a patentee may, if it wishes, do nothing with the subject matter of the patent"); King Instruments Corp. v. Perego, 65 F.3d 941, 950 (Fed. Cir. 1995) ("The market may well dictate that the best use of a patent is to exclude infringing products, rather than to market the invention.").

[44] *See* eBay Inc. v. MercExchange, L.L.C., 547 U.S. 388, 391 (2006).

[45] *Morton Salt* 314 U.S. at 493; *see also* Qualcomm Inc. v. Broadcom Corp., 548 F.3d 1004, 1025 (Fed. Cir. 2008) ("the successful assertion of patent misuse may render a patent unenforceable until the misconduct can be purged; it does not render the patent unenforceable for all time"); Senza-Gel Corp. v. Seiffhart, 803 F.2d 661, 668 n.10 (Fed. Cir. 1986).

CHAPTER 10

Infringement

The owner of a patent has the exclusive right to make, use, sell, offer to sell, or import into the United States the invention described by the claims.[1] Anyone else who engages in those activities without the permission of the patent owner is an "infringer." An infringer can be sued for money damages[2] and can be compelled by a court to cease the infringing activities.

10.1 PATENT TERM

Generally speaking, the exclusive rights conferred by a patent begin on the date the patent issues and expire 20 years after the *filing date* of the application (or any earlier application cited for purposes of priority).[3] Consequently, the term of the patent will vary depending on how long it takes for the application to make its way through the Patent Office. A patent issued in 2005 on an application filed in 2000 would last only 15 years, expiring in 2020.[4]

---

[1] *See* 35 U.S.C. § 271(a).

[2] *See* Section 11.8.

[3] 35 U.S.C. § 154(2).

[4] The 20-year term applies to utility patents. Design patents, discussed in Section 12.1, have a term of 14 years from the date of issue. 35 U.S.C. § 173. Owners of utility patents must pay "maintenance fees" periodically to keep their patents from expiring prematurely. *See* 35 U.S.C. § 41(b) (maintenance fees due at 3 years, six months after the grant; 7 years, six months after the grant; and 11 years, six months after the grant). Maintenance fees are substantial, and some patent owners who are not making money from their patents simply allow them to expire.

The term of a patent used to be 17 years from the date of *issue*.[5] Consequently, long delays in prosecution,[6] sometimes due to maneuvering by the applicant, occasionally resulted in patents issuing on inventions that had already been in public use for decades.[7] In 1990, for example, computer chip manufacturers learned that a patent had been issued to Gilbert Hyatt claiming the basic concept of the microprocessor—already the subject of a long-established and lucrative industry. This patent appeared at such a late date because it took 21 years and the prosecution of a long chain of related applications before the patent issued. Because the application process was conducted in secret, none of the chip manufacturers knew of the patent until, from their perspective, it was too late to do anything about it. The current practice of measuring the effective term of a patent from its filing date reduces the incentive for applicants to delay prosecution and surprise an industry with a so-called "submarine patent."

Under the current rules, if the examination is unduly delayed and the PTO bears the blame, the term of the patent may be extended accordingly.[8] The term may also be extended if a successful appeal,[9] an interference proceeding,[10] or certain kinds of regulatory delay,[11] such as FDA review of the patented product, prevent the patentee from enjoying the full term of its commercial monopoly.

In the event a patent application is published before its date of issue,[12] the patentee enjoys "provisional rights," meaning the right to demand a reasonable royalty from anyone who practiced the patented invention in the interval.[13] These rights apply only against parties with actual notice of the patent application,[14] and they can be collected only after the patent

---

[5] Due to the change from a 17-year to a 20-year term, patents applied for prior to June 8, 1995, are entitled to the greater of the 20-year term provided by the current statute or the term of 17 years from issue provided by the former statute. 35 U.S.C. § 154(c).

[6] The record holder in this respect might be U.S. Patent No. 6,130,946, disclosing a cryptography machine resembling the German Enigma device. The patent issued on October 10, 2000, based on an application filed on October 23, 1936.

[7] Calculated delay may allow an accused infringer to raise the defense of "prosecution laches." *See* Section 11.8.3.3.

[8] *See* 35 U.S.C. § 154(b).

[9] *See* 35 U.S.C. § 154(b)(1)(C).

[10] *See id.* Interference proceedings are discussed in Section 5.4.

[11] *See* 35 U.S.C. §§ 155–56.

[12] *See* Section 5.1.

[13] 35 U.S.C. § 154(d). The invention claimed in the issued patent must be "substantially identical" to the invention claimed in the published application. *Id.*

[14] 35 U.S.C. § 154(d)(1)(B).

has issued. Such rights are one incentive for applicants to publish their applications, even when the law does require it.[15] Except for these provisional rights, an applicant with a "patent pending" has no exclusive rights until the patent issues. On the other hand, with certain exceptions,[16] the patentee can demand that infringing activity cease when the patent issues, even if it had already begun. Warnings of a "patent pending" advise potential infringers that they should not begin what they may not be permitted to continue. On the other hand, one should remember that many pending applications result in narrow patent claims or are denied altogether.

10.2 GEOGRAPHIC LIMITATIONS

United States patent law does not apply to activities that take place entirely in another country.[17] The sale or use of a patented product in Japan, for example, is not an infringement of a United States patent, although it could be an infringement of a corresponding Japanese patent.[18] The law also provides an explicit exception for inventions built into vehicles, such as aircraft, that may enter the United States temporarily. If a United States patent covered a design for landing gear, and a Japanese airliner with the claimed landing gear flew into the United States to deliver passengers, the use of the landing gear in the United States would not infringe the patent.[19]

---

[15] *See* Section 5.1.

[16] One exception involves a prior commercial use defense created by the America Invents Act. *See* Section 10.10. Although prior use does not, in this case, render the patent invalid, it does permit the party who used the claimed invention more than one year before the filing date of the patent (or the patentee's public disclosure of the invention) to continue such use. *See* 35 U.S.C. § 273. Another exception involves the "intervening rights" that may arise in the context of reissued patents. *See* Section 5.5.

[17] *See* Microsoft Corp. v. AT&T Corp., 550 U.S. 437, 441 (2007) ("It is the general rule under United States patent law that no infringement occurs when a patented product is made and sold in another country."); Transocean Offshore Deepwater Drilling, Inc. v. Maersk Contractors USA, Inc., 617 F.3d 1296, 1309 (Fed. Cir. 2010); Rotec Indus., Inc. v. Mitsubishi Corp., 215 F.3d 1246, 1251 (Fed. Cir. 2000) (" '[t]he right conferred by a patent under our law is confined to the United States and its territories, and infringement of this right cannot be predicated of acts wholly done in a foreign country' ").

[18] An offer to sell an article to be delivered and used in the United States is an offer to sell in this country, even if the negotiations were conducted abroad. *Transocean*, 617 F.3d at 1309 ("The focus should not be on the location of the offer, but rather the location of the future sale that would occur pursuant to the offer.").

[19] *See* 35 U.S.C. § 272; National Steel Car, Ltd. v. Canadian Pacific Railway, Ltd., 357 F.3d 1319, 1326 (Fed. Cir. 2004). The exception applies to countries offering reciprocal privileges.

In two respects, United States patent law does take notice of activities occurring in another country. First, supplying the components of a patented invention from the United States to a foreign country, where they will be assembled into the claimed combination, can be an infringement of a United States patent.[20] The legal analysis mirrors that of "contributory infringement" or "inducement" of infringement in the United States, topics discussed in Section 10.4. Second, it can be an infringement of a United States patent to import, use, sell, or offer to sell in the United States a product made in a foreign country by a process patented in the United States.[21] This prevents the evasion of United States patents by moving production overseas.[22]

The latter provision does not apply if the product is "materially changed by subsequent processes" or if the product "becomes a trivial and

---

[20] *See* 35 U.S.C. § 271(f); Cardiac Pacemakers, Inc. v. St. Jude Medical, Inc., 576 F.3d 1348, 1360 (Fed. Cir. 2009) (en banc). The components must be supplied with the intent that they be combined in an infringing manner. *See* Liquid Dynamics Corp. v. Vaughan Co., 449 F.3d 1209, 1222 (Fed. Cir. 2006). The *intention* is what counts. Proof that they were actually combined is unnecessary. Waymark Corp. v. Porta Sys. Corp., 245 F.3d 1364, 1367–68 (Fed. Cir. 2001). In that respect, § 271(f) differs from contributory infringement or inducement. *See id.* In *Microsoft Corp. v. AT&T Corp.*, 550 U.S. 437 (2007), the Supreme Court held that sending software code to a foreign country does not qualify as supplying a "component" of a patented combination. A component is a tangible thing. Software is more like a construction blueprint—something not covered by § 271(f). *Id.* at 1755 ("A blueprint may contain precise instructions for the construction and combination of the components of a patented device, but it is not itself a combinable component of that device."); *see also* Pellegrini v. Analog Devices, Inc., 375 F.3d 1113, 1118 (Fed. Cir. 2004). Section 271(f) does not apply to process claims. *Cardiac Pacemakers*, 576 F.3d at 1365 (overruling an earlier case in which a catalyst to perform a patented method had been treated as a "component" of that process); *see also* NTP, Inc. v. Research in Motion, Ltd., 418 F.3d 1282, 1322 (Fed. Cir. 2005) (U.S. sales of BlackBerry devices did not violate § 271(f), even if used abroad in a patented process).

[21] 35 U.S.C. § 271(g); Kinik Co. v. Int'l Trade Comm'n, 362 F.3d 1359, 1361–62 (Fed. Cir. 2004); Biotec Biologische Naturverpackungen GmbH v. Biocorp, Inc., 249 F.3d 1341, 1351–52 (Fed. Cir. 2001). The patent must be in force when the steps of the process are performed abroad. Monsanto Co. v. Syngenta Seeds, Inc., 503 F.3d 1352, 1360 (Fed. Cir. 2007). Section 271(g) applies only to physical products made abroad; it does not apply to intangible products like information. *NTP*, 418 F.3d at 1323; Bayer AG v. Housey Pharmaceuticals, Inc. 340 F.3d 1367, 1377 (Fed. Cir. 2003). When the process was used abroad, the patentee may have difficulty proving that it was used at all. Under § 295 of the Patent Act, if there is a "substantial likelihood" that the process was used to make an imported product, and the patentee has made reasonable, but unsuccessful, efforts to determine what process was actually used, the court shall presume that the patented process was used. The burden to prove otherwise then rests with the defendant.

[22] *See* Eli Lilly & Co. v. American Cyanamid Co., 82 F.3d 1568, 1571–72 (Fed. Cir. 1996).

nonessential component of another product."[23] So, for example, if the patent claimed a process for refining aluminum, it would probably not be an infringement to import an automobile having an aluminum ashtray, even if the material from which the ashtray was made could be traced back to the patented process. At some point, the imported product becomes too far removed from the claimed process to regard the importation of that product as an infringement.

10.3 STATE OF MIND

Generally speaking, the intentions of the infringer are irrelevant to infringement. A patent can be infringed even by someone who is unaware that the patent exists.[24] On the other hand, infringement that *is* intentional, referred to as "willful infringement," can result in an award of increased damages, up to three times the amount of damages that could be recovered from an innocent infringer, together with attorneys' fees. These increased awards, intended as a penalty or deterrent, are discussed in Section 11.8.2.

Indirect infringement, discussed in Section 10.4, is an exception to the general rule. "Inducement" of infringement and "contributory infringement," both forms of indirect infringement, do require an awareness of the patent and knowledge of the infringing acts.

10.4 DIRECT AND INDIRECT INFRINGEMENT

One who, without authority, makes, uses, sells, offers to sell, or imports into the United States a product covered by a patent is a direct infringer. One who is not a direct infringer may be held equally liable for encouraging

---

[23] 35 U.S.C. § 271(g); *see also Biotec,* 249 F.3d at 1352; *Eli Lilly,* 82 F.3d at 1572; Bio-Technology General Corp. v. Genentech, Inc., 80 F.3d 1553, 1560 (Fed. Cir. 1996).

[24] Hilton Davis Chemical Co. v. Warner-Jenkinson Co., 62 F.3d 1512, 1519 (Fed. Cir. 1995) (en banc) ("Intent is not an element of infringement. . . . A patent may exclude others from practicing the claimed invention, regardless of whether the infringers even know of the patent."), *rev'd on other grounds,* Warner-Jenkinson Co. v. Hilton-Davis Chemical Co., 520 U.S. 17 (1997); *see also* Florida Prepaid Postsecondary Education Expense Board v. College Savings Bank, 527 U.S. 627, 645 (1999) ("Actions predicated on direct patent infringement . . . do not require any showing of intent to infringe."); Jurgens v. CBK, Ltd., 80 F.3d 1566, 1570 n.2 (Fed. Cir. 1996) (infringement is "a strict liability offense").

or contributing to infringement by someone else. This is sometimes referred to as "indirect" or "dependent" infringement.[25]

Indirect infringement comes in two forms—inducement of infringement and contributory infringement. The concept of inducement is the simpler one. Anyone who "actively induces" the infringement of a patent by another may be held liable as an infringer.[26] Consider the case of *Moleculon Research Corp. v. CBS, Inc.*[27] CBS sold the popular toy known as Rubik's Cube, a product that Moleculon believed to infringe its patent on a rotating-cube puzzle. Some of the claims, rather than describing the puzzle as a physical object, instead set out a method of solving the puzzle by rotating the facets of the cube. These method claims could be directly infringed only by someone performing the steps of the method—that is, by someone using the puzzle—but it would have been impractical to file suit against every consumer who purchased Rubik's Cube. Even though CBS did not directly infringe those method claims, the court found that it could be held liable for inducing infringement by purchasers, largely because it sold puzzles and instruction sheets that would lead purchasers to practice the method.[28]

---

[25] *See* RF Delaware, Inc. v. Pacific Keystone Technologies, Inc., 326 F.3d 1255, 1268 (Fed. Cir. 2003) ("dependent infringement"); Moba, B.V. v. Diamond Automation, Inc., 325 F.3d 1306, 1318 (Fed. Cir. 2003) ("indirect infringement"). Cases of indirect infringement generally require evidence of a related direct infringement by someone else. *See* i4i Ltd. Partnership v. Microsoft Corp., 598 F.3d 831, 850 (Fed. Cir. 2010); Ricoh Co., Ltd. v. Quanta Computer Inc., 550 F.3d 1325, 1341 (Fed. Cir. 2008); Acco Brands, Inc. v. ABA Locks Mfrs. Co., 501 F.3d 1307, 1312–13 (Fed. Cir. 2007). That direct infringement can be shown by circumstantial evidence. *See* Lucent Technologies, Inc. v. Gateway, Inc., 580 F.3d 1301, 1318–19 (Fed. Cir. 2009); Golden Blount, Inc. v. Robert H. Peterson Co., 438 F.3d 1354, 1362 (Fed. Cir. 2006). Usually it is not enough circumstantial evidence to show that a product *could* be used in an infringing manner if it could be used in other ways as well. Fujitsu Ltd. v. Netgear Inc., 620 F.3d 1321, 1329 (Fed. Cir. 2010). In a recent case, the Federal Circuit held that one can induce infringement of a method claim by encouraging the performance of all of the steps of the method, even if no one person performed all of them. In this case, there is no individual who can be identified as a direct infringer. Akamai Technologies, Inc. v. Limelight Networks, Inc., 692 F.3d 1301, 1309 (Fed. Cir. 2012) (en banc). *See* Section 10.5.

[26] 35 U.S.C. § 271(b).

[27] 793 F.2d 1261 (Fed. Cir. 1986).

[28] *Id.* at 1272. Under a theory of inducement, it is possible to hold officers or directors of a corporation liable for an infringement by their corporation if they "actively assisted" in that infringement. *See* Manville Sales Corp. v. Paramount Sys., Inc., 917 F.2d 544, 553 (Fed. Cir. 1990); Orthokinetics, Inc. v. Safety Travel Chairs, Inc., 806 F.2d 1565, 1578– 79 (Fed. Cir. 1986). This is one instance in which the corporate form will not shield officers or directors from personal liability for the acts of their corporation. However, such liability is rare because it is seldom possible to prove the necessary intent. *See* Al-Site Corp. v. VSI Int'l, Inc., 174 F.3d 1308, 1331 (Fed. Cir. 1999).

Although a direct infringer can be completely unaware of the existence of the patent, one who induces infringement must do so knowingly.[29] In *Global-Tech Appliances, Inc. v. SEB S.A.*,[30] the Supreme Court held that liability for inducement requires either actual awareness of the resulting infringement, or a case of "willful blindness."[31] Willful blindness means more than just "deliberate indifference to a known risk."[32] It means that the defendant, knowing there was a "high probability" that its actions would lead to patent infringement, took deliberate actions to avoid learning the truth.[33] In *Global-Tech*, the defendant directly copied a successful "cool touch" deep fryer, chose as its model a product made for overseas markets that would not include United States patent markings, and failed to inform its patent counsel about the source of its design. The court found in these facts evidence of "willful blindness."[34]

A "contributory infringer" is one who imports, sells, or offers to sell a component of a patented combination, or a material or apparatus to be used in a patented process, if all of the following conditions are met:[35]

- The item is a "*material part* of the patented invention."[36]
- The item is imported, sold or offered for sale with *knowledge* that the item was "*especially made or especially adapted*" for use in an infringing manner.[37]
- The item is *not* a "staple article or commodity of commerce suitable for substantial noninfringing use."

Many patented combinations include individual elements that themselves are common and unpatentable. The Oviatt mousetrap design

---

[29] *See ACCO*, 501 F.3d at 1312; *Moba*, 325 F.3d at 1318 ("Although § 271(b) does not use the word 'knowingly,' this court has uniformly imposed a knowledge requirement.").

[30] 131 S.Ct. 2060 (2011).

[31] *Id.* at 2069.

[32] *Id.* at 2068.

[33] *Id.* at 2070.

[34] *Id.* at 2071–72.

[35] 35 U.S.C. § 271(c); *Fujitsu*, 620 F.3d at 1326; *i4i*, 598 F.3d at 850–51; *Lucent*, 580 F.3d at 1320; *Ricoh*, 550 F.3d at 1337.

[36] *See Fujitsu*, 620 F.3d at 1331.

[37] Although it is not apparent on the face of the statute, contributory infringement requires both knowledge that the component is adapted to a particular use and knowledge of the patent that proscribes that use. Hewlett-Packard Co. v. Bausch & Lomb Inc., 909 F.2d 1464, 1469 (Fed. Cir. 1990); *see also Fujitsu*, 620 F.3d at 1330 (defendant must have known "that the combination for which its components were especially made was both patented and infringing"); *Lucent*, 580 F.3d at 1320. The Supreme Court's recent statements on willful blindness are broad enough that future cases may extend the principle to the context of contributory infringement.

(see Appendix A) includes an ordinary ping-pong ball. The Oviatt patent cannot prevent anyone from making, using, importing, selling, or offering to sell ping-pong balls, which have obvious uses unrelated to the mouse-trap invention. The inventor's legitimate monopoly extends only to the claimed combination. Suppose, however, that someone sold the remaining components of the Oviatt mousetrap without the ping-pong ball. Because all of the claims of the Oviatt patent require a ball, selling the remaining pieces would not directly infringe the patent.[38] However, it is likely that anyone who purchased the incomplete trap would eventually supply the missing ball, thereby forming an infringing combination. If the patent owner were forced to sue only those who formed that combination–consumers who purchased an incomplete trap and supplied their own ping-pong ball–enforcement of the Oviatt patent would be impractical.

Patent law treats as contributory infringement the importation, sale, or offer to sell a component of a claimed combination if the component is "especially made" for use in the patented combination (like the tubed structure depicted in the Oviatt patent) and not a "staple article or commodity of commerce suitable for substantial noninfringing use" (like a ping-pong ball). Originally, the law made no distinction between contributory infringement and inducement, and it is still useful to con-sider contributory infringement in the inducement context. The sale of a ping-pong ball could not, by itself, be regarded as an inducement to infringe the Oviatt patent because the ping-pong ball could be used for something else. The sale of the single-purpose apparatus could, however, be viewed as an inducement to infringe because the apparatus has no other plausible use.[39]

The concept of a "staple article of commerce" most obviously applies to basic materials sold in large quantities and useful in numerous applications. Ordinary nuts and bolts and common chemicals would be considered sta-ples, and their sale would not trigger contributory infringement.[40] But in this context "staple" also applies to goods having even one "substantial"

---

[38] *See* Section 10.5.

[39] *See* Spansion, Inc. v. Int'l Trade Comm'n, 629 F.3d 1331, 1355 (Fed. Cir. 2010); *Ricoh*, 550 F.3d at 1338 ("When a manufacturer includes in its product a component that can *only* infringe, the inference that infringement is intended is unavoidable.").

[40] There might be a legitimate claim of inducement if the sale were accompanied by instruc-tions telling the purchaser how to use the goods in an infringing manner. *See* Dynacore Holdings Corp. v. U.S. Philips Corp., 363 F.3d 1263, 1277 n.6 (Fed. Cir. 2004).

noninfringing use.[41] If it did not, in practical effect the patentee's monopoly would extend to unpatented uses and combinations. If Oviatt could prevent the unlicensed sale of ping-pong balls, he would have an effective monopoly not only on his own invention but also on the game of ping-pong.

10.5 LITERAL INFRINGEMENT

Determining if a patent is infringed is a two-step process.[42] First, one must examine the language of the claims at issue and determine what the claims mean. This step, referred to as claim construction or claim interpretation, proceeds according to the rules discussed in Chapter 7. Although it is a principle difficult to apply in practice, claims are supposed to be construed without reference to the thing that has been accused of infringing.[43] Once the claims have been properly construed, they must be compared to the accused product or method

---

[41] *See id.* at 1275; Preemption Devices, Inc. v. Minnesota Mining & Mfg. Co., 803 F.2d 1170, 1174 (Fed. Cir. 1986). If a particular feature of a product has only infringing uses, it does not matter if the product as a whole has other, noninfringing uses. *Fujitsu,* 620 F.3d at 1330-31 (" 'separate and distinct' " features should be analyzed individually); *Lucent,* 580 F.3d at 1320–21; *Ricoh,* 550 F.3d at 1337. A "substantial noninfringing use" does not include a use that is " 'unusual, far-fetched, illusory, impractical, occasional, aberrant, or experimental.' " *i4i,* 598 F.3d at 851. When determining if a noninfringing use is substantial, a court can consider "not only the use's frequency, but also the use's practicality, the invention's intended purpose, and the intended market." *Id.*

[42] Absolute Software, Inc. v. Stealth Signal, Inc., 659 F.3d 1121, 1129 (Fed. Cir. 2011); Elbex Video, Ltd. v. Sensormatic Electronics Corp., 508 F.3d 1366, 1370 (Fed. Cir. 2007); Stumbo v. Eastman Outdoors, Inc., 508 F.3d 1358, 1361 (Fed. Cir. 2007); Wilson Sporting Goods Co. v Hillerich & Bradsby Co., 442 F.3d 1322, 1326 (Fed. Cir. 2006).

[43] SRI Int'l v. Matsushita Electric Corp., 775 F.2d 1107, 1118 (Fed. Cir. 1985) (en banc) ("[C]laims are not construed 'to cover' or 'not to cover' the accused device. That procedure would make infringement a matter of judicial whim. It is only *after* the claims have been *construed without reference to the accused device* that the claims, as so construed, are applied to the accused device to determine infringement." (emphasis in original)); *see also* Cohesive Technologies, Inc. v. Waters Corp., 543 F.3d 1351, 1367 (Fed. Cir. 2008). On the other hand, the accused product can provide the necessary context for claim construction by focusing the court on issues relevant to the case. *See* Typhoon Touch Technologies, Inc. v. Dell, Inc., 659 F.3d 1376, 1383 (Fed. Cir. 2011) ("It is not inappropriate for a court to consider the accused devices when construing claim terms, for the purpose of 'claim construction' is to resolve issues of infringement."); Serio-US Indus., Inc. v. Plastic Recovery Technologies Corp., 459 F.3d 1311, 1319 (Fed. Cir. 2006) ("a trial court may consult the accused device for context that informs the claim construction process"); Vivid Technologies, Inc. v. American Science & Eng'g, Inc., 200 F.3d 795, 803 (Fed. Cir. 1999) ("although the claims are construed objectively and without reference to the accused device, only those terms need be construed that are in controversy, and only to the extent necessary to resolve the controversy"); Scripps Clinic & Research Found. v. Genentech, Inc., 927 F.2d 1565, 1580 (Fed. Cir. 1991) ("Of course the particular accused product (or process) is kept in mind, for it is efficient to focus on the construction of only the disputed elements or limitations of the claims.").

to see if the claims are infringed. A patent is said to be "literally infringed" if the claims literally or "exactly" describe the thing accused of infringement.[44]

A claim cannot be literally infringed if any claim element is missing entirely from the accused product.[45] This is so even if the missing element seems insignificant in comparison to the invention as a whole. If a mousetrap claim refers to a hook for hanging the trap on a wall when the trap is not in use, a trap that has no hook does not literally infringe. This principle is often called the "all-elements" rule. It can be helpful to think of a patent claim as a kind of checklist of features, every one of which must be found in the accused product in order for the claim to be infringed.[46]

---

[44] DeMarini Sports, Inc. v. Worth, Inc., 239 F.3d 1314, 1331 (Fed. Cir. 2001); General American Transportation Corp. v. Cryro-Trans, Inc., 93 F.3d 766, 770 (Fed. Cir. 1996); Southwall Technologies, Inc. v. Cardinal IG Co., 54 F.3d 1570, 1575 (Fed. Cir. 1995).

[45] *See* Star Scientific, Inc. v. R.J. Reynolds Tobacco Co., 655 F.3d 1364, 1378 (Fed. Cir. 2011); TIP Sys., LLC v. Phillips & Brooks/Gladwin, Inc., 529 F.3d 1364, 1379 (Fed. Cir. 2008); BMC Resources, Inc. v. Paymentech, L.P., 498 F.3d 1373, 1378 (Fed. Cir. 2007); Techsearch, L.L.C. v. Intel Corp., 286 F.3d 1360, 1371 (Fed. Cir. 2002) ("To establish literal infringement, all of the elements of the claim, as correctly construed, must be present in the accused system.").

[46] Infringement of a method claim requires performing *each* of the recited steps. Centillon Data Sys., LLC v. Qwest Communications Int'l, Inc., 631 F.3d 1279, 1286 (Fed. Cir. 2011); Lucent Technologies, Inc. v. Gateway, Inc., 580 F.3d 1301, 1317 (Fed. Cir. 2009). This can present problems when some steps are performed by one party and some by another. Similarly, it may be difficult to prove that a claimed system was "used" in an infringing manner if some components are used by one party and some by another. *See Centillon*, 631 F.3d at 1284 (" 'use' of a system claim 'requires a party . . . to use each and every . . . element of a claimed [system]' "). If one party "puts the system as a whole into service, *i.e.*, controls the system and obtains benefit from it," as a customer might use a communications system, that party satisfies the definition of "use" even without direct physical control *See id.* at 1285. The party that provides the system for use by another but that does not use the entire system itself is not a direct infringer, though it may be liable for inducing infringement (*see* Section 10.4). *See id.* at 1286. With respect to method claims, if different parties perform different steps of the claimed invention, liability may be found on a theory of "joint infringement" only if "one party exercised 'control or direction' over the entire process such that all steps of the process can be attributed to the controlling party, *i.e.*, the 'mastermind.' " Golden Hour Data Sys., Inc. v. emsCharts, Inc., 614 F.3d 1367, 1380 (Fed. Cir. 2010); *see also* Miniauction, Inc. v. Thomson Corp., 532 F.3d 1318, 1329 (Fed. Cir. 2008) ("At the other end of this multi-party spectrum, mere 'arms-length cooperation' will not give rise to direct infringement by any party."). On the other hand, the Federal Circuit recently held that a party who induces others to perform a patented method is liable as an infringer, even if no *one* individual performs all of the steps of the method (meaning that no individual directly infringes). Akamai Technologies, Inc. v. Limelight Networks, Inc., 692 F.3d 1301, 1309 (Fed. Cir. 2012) (en banc). A party that performs some of the steps of a patented method and induces others to perform the remainder is also liable as an infringer. *Id.* ("It would be a bizarre result to hold someone liable for inducing another to perform all of the steps of a method claim but to hold harmless one who goes further by actually performing some of the steps himself.").

On the other hand, infringement is not avoided by adding things that are not described in the claim.[47] Suppose that a first inventor claims a mouse-trap comprising the combination of a spring, a latch, a mouse-trapping jaw, and a trigger that releases the latch and closes the jaw. A later inventor improves the combination by adding an audible alarm that sounds when the trap has sprung. The improved trap would still literally infringe as long as it had the spring, latch, jaw, and trigger recited in the claim.[48]

Some accused infringers mistakenly believe that if they have obtained a patent covering their own product, they are immune from charges of infringing another patent. This is simply not the case. A patent only conveys the right to *exclude others;* it does not convey a right to produce or sell the invention claimed.[49] Even if the inventor of the trap-with-alarm had obtained a patent on the improvement (which is perfectly feasible as long

---

[47] *See* Free Motion Fitness, Inc. v. Cybex Int'l, Inc., 423 F.3d 1343, 1353 (Fed. Cir. 2005) ("Basic patent law holds that a party may not avoid infringement of a patent claim using an open transitional phrase, such as comprising, by adding additional elements."); Suntiger, Inc. v. Scientific Research Funding Gp., 189 F.3d 1327, 1336 (Fed. Cir. 1999); Northern Telecom, Inc. v. Datapoint Corp., 908 F.2d 931, 945 (Fed. Cir. 1990) ("Nor is infringement avoided if a claimed feature performs not only as shown in the patent, but also performs an additional function."). The same principle applies to method claims. *See* Smith & Nephew, Inc. v. Ethicon, Inc., 276 F.3d 1304, 1311 (Fed. Cir. 2001) ("Infringement arises when all of the steps of a claimed method are performed, whether or not the infringer also performs additional steps."). There is an exception if the claim is limited by its terms to the recited elements *and no others. See Suntiger,* 189 F.3d at 1336 ("If a claim is specific as to the number of elements and the addition of an element eliminates an inherent feature of the claim, then that additional element will prevent a finding of literal infringement."). When a claim preamble ends with the words "consisting of" (rather than the more common "comprising"), the claim is limited to only the elements recited.

[48] *See* Innogenetics, N.V. v. Abbott Labs., 512 F.3d 1363, 1371–72 (Fed. Cir. 2008) ("Abbott argues that a patent can never be literally infringed by embodiments that did not exist at the time of the filing. Our case law allows for after-arising technology to be captured within the literal scope of valid claims that are drafted broadly enough."); JVW Enterprises, Inc. v. Interact Accessories, Inc., 424 F.3d 1324, 1333 (Fed. Cir. 2005) (additional features and improvements do not avoid infringement).

[49] General Electric Co. v. Int'l Trade Comm'n, 670 F.3d 1206, 1218 (Fed. Cir. 2012) ("a separately patented invention may indeed be within the scope of the claims of a dominating patent"); Bio-Technology General Corp. v. Genentech, Inc., 80 F.3d 1553, 1559 (Fed. Cir. 1996) (" '[T]he existence of one's own patent does not constitute a defense to infringement of someone else's patent. It is elementary that a patent grants only the right to *exclude others* and confers no right on its holder to make, use, or sell.' " (emphasis in original)); Atlas Powder Co. v. E.I. Du Pont de Nemours & Co., 750 F.2d 1569, 1580 (Fed. Cir. 1984).

as the improvement is nonobvious), the product would still infringe.[50] However, the new patent would prevent the first inventor from adding an alarm to his invention without a license from the second inventor.

The concept of literal infringement is relatively straightforward—a patent is literally infringed if the accused product is exactly what the claims describe. But this is not the end of the infringement inquiry. Even if the accused product is *not* exactly what the claims describe, it can still be found infringing under the doctrine of equivalents. Alternatively, if an accused product *is* exactly what the claims describe, it can still theoretically be found noninfringing under the reverse doctrine of equivalents. These doctrines are discussed in the sections that follow.

10.6 THE DOCTRINE OF EQUIVALENTS

The doctrine of equivalents is one of the most important doctrines in patent law and one of the most perplexing. It is not based on the patent statutes passed by Congress but is entirely a product of judicial reasoning. Some critics view the doctrine as inconsistent with other fundamental principles of patent law. However, the doctrine has a long history, and, having survived recent criticisms, it is clearly here to stay.

10.6.1 *Winans v. Denmead*

Winans v. Denmead,[51] an ancient but important case in the evolution of the doctrine of equivalents, provides a useful introduction. Winans obtained a patent on a coal-carrying railroad car shaped like the base (or "frustum") of a cone, with the smaller end extending below the level of the axles. The circular cross section and tapered dimensions of the car equalized the pressures on the load-bearing surfaces, with the result that a lighter car could carry a relatively larger burden without damage. The patent claim specifically referred to a car "in the form of a frustum of a cone." The car accused of infringing the patent was similarly tapered, but it had an octagonal rather than a circular cross section. Rather than the "frustum of

---

[50] *See Atlas Powder,* 750 F.2d at 1580 ("if Atlas patents A+B+C and Du Pont then patents the improvement A+B+C+D, Du Pont is liable to Atlas for any manufacture, use, or sale of A +B+C+D because the latter directly infringes claims to A+B+C"). A second patent can bear on whether an improvement is equivalent to the original if there is no literal infringement. *See* Section 10.6.

[51] 56 U.S. 330 (1853).

a cone," the shape of the car was closer to an octagonal pyramid. The accused car did not fall within the literal language of the claim, but it provided similar (though reduced) benefits in equalizing the pressures exerted by the load.

Even though the accused car was outside of the literal language of the claim, the court found that it employed the principle of the invention. The differences were merely differences of "form," and the court held these differences insufficient to avoid infringement.

> The exclusive right to the thing patented is not secured, if the public are at liberty to make substantial copies of it, varying its form or proportions. And, therefore, the patentee, having described his invention, and shown its principles, and claimed it in that form which most perfectly embodies it, is, in contemplation of law, deemed to claim every form in which his invention may be copied, unless he manifests an intention to disclaim some of those forms.[52]

A dissenting justice rejected this "substance over form" approach to infringement and emphasized the importance of definite claims in informing the public of the limits of the patentee's monopoly. A patentee, he felt, should be held to the limitations made explicit in the claims. He also warned that nothing could be "more mischievous, more productive of oppressive and costly litigation, or exorbitant and unjust pretensions and vexatious demands" than relaxation of the requirement that patentees be bound by definite claims.[53]

10.6.2 *Graver Tank*

The modern history of the doctrine of equivalents begins in 1950 with *Graver Tank & Mfg. Co. v. Linde Air Prods. Co.*[54] The patent at issue claimed a material to be used in an electric welding process, including as a principal ingredient an "alkaline earth metal" such as magnesium. The accused product used manganese instead of magnesium, and while the names of the ingredients are nearly the same, manganese is *not* an alkaline earth metal as specifically required by the patent claims. Nevertheless, invoking the doctrine of equivalents as expressed in *Winans v. Denmead*, the court

---

[52] *Id.* at 343.
[53] *Id.* at 347 (Campbell, J., dissenting).
[54] 339 U.S. 605 (1950).

found the patent infringed. The following paragraph summed up the majority's support for the doctrine:

> [T]o permit imitation of a patented invention which does not copy every literal detail would be to convert the protection of the patent grant into a hollow and useless thing. Such a limitation would leave room for–indeed encourage–the unscrupulous copyist to make unimportant and insubstantial changes and substitutions in the patent which, though adding nothing, would be enough to take the copied matter outside the claim, and hence outside the reach of law. . . . Outright and forthright duplication is a dull and very rare type of infringement. To prohibit no other would place the inventor at the mercy of verbalism and would subordinate substance to form.[55]

The court declined to establish any definite test of whether something outside of the literal scope of a patent claim is still equivalent. "Equivalence," said the court, "is not the prisoner of a formula."[56] Rather, the judgment must be made in the context of the particular invention, the functions performed by the claimed and the substituted element, and the knowledge available to those skilled in the art. In addition, "[a]n important factor is whether persons reasonably skilled in the art would have known of the interchangeability of an ingredient not contained in the patent with one that was."[57] The court also referred to an earlier case inquiring whether the accused product performs " 'substantially the same function in substantially the same way to obtain the same result,' "[58] reasoning that " 'if two devices do the same work in substantially the same way, and accomplish substantially the same result, they are the same, even though they differ in name, form or shape.' "[59]

Applying these principles to the case before it, the court found the patent infringed, even though the accused welding material did not include the alkaline earth metal apparently required by the claim. The manganese served the same purpose as an alkaline earth metal, and persons skilled in the art knew the two ingredients to be interchangeable. The substitution was nothing more than a slight and obvious variation of the invention literally described.[60]

---

[55] *Id.* at 607.

[56] *Id.* at 609.

[57] *Id.*

[58] *Id.* at 608 (quoting Sanitary Refrigerator Co. v. Winters, 280 U.S. 30, 42 (1929)).

[59] *Id.* at 608 (quoting Union Paper-Bag Machine Co. v. Murphy, 97 U.S. 120, 125 (1877)).

[60] *Id.* at 612.

10.6.3 Challenges to the Doctrine

The doctrine of equivalents is intended to free the infringement inquiry from excessive literalism and elevate substance over form.[61] From that perspective, the doctrine seems an enlightened policy. On the other hand, the doctrine is at odds with the requirement of claims "particularly pointing out and distinctly claiming the subject matter which the applicant regards as his invention."[62] Ideally, claims notify the public of what can or cannot be done without risk of infringing the patent.[63] But when the doctrine of equivalents applies, claims can be positively misleading by seeming to include restrictions that, in the end, a court will disregard. Attempting to honor the "competitor's need for precise wording as an aid in avoiding infringement" while avoiding "the risk of injustice that may result from a blindered focus on words alone,"[64] *Graver Tank* committed courts to a narrow and difficult path.

Recognizing the tension between the doctrine of equivalents and fair notice to potential infringers, the Federal Circuit has warned that

> [a]pplication of the doctrine of equivalents is the exception . . . not the rule, for if the public comes to believe (or fear) that the language of patent claims can never be relied on, and that the doctrine of equivalents is simply the second prong of every infringement charge, regularly available to extend protection beyond the scope of the claims, then claims will cease to serve their intended purpose. Competitors will never know whether their actions infringe a granted patent.[65]

Yet in practice, allegations of infringement under the doctrine of equivalents have become the rule, not the exception. Wherever there is any doubt as to literal infringement, patent owners routinely invoke the

---

[61] "Unfortunately, the nature of language makes it impossible to capture the essence of a thing in a patent application. . . . If patents were always interpreted by their literal terms, their value would be greatly diminished. Unimportant and insubstantial substitutes for certain elements could defeat the patent, and its value to inventors could be destroyed by simple acts of copying." Festo Corp. v. Shoketsu Kinzoku Kogyo Kabushiki Co., 535 U.S. 722, 731 (2002).

[62] 35 U.S.C. § 112.

[63] *See* Slimfold Mfg. Co., Inc. v. Kinkead Indus., Inc., 932 F.2d 1453, 1457 (Fed. Cir. 1991) ("Inherent in our claim-based patent system is also the principle that the protected invention is what the claims say it is, and thus that infringement can be avoided by avoiding the language of the claims.").

[64] Laitram Corp. v. Cambridge Wire Cloth Co., 863 F.2d 855, 856–57 (Fed. Cir. 1988).

[65] London v. Carson Pirie Scott & Co., 946 F.2d 1534, 1538 (Fed. Cir. 1991).

doctrine of equivalents as a fall-back position. Indeed, attorneys representing patent owners would be remiss if they failed to take advantage of the
opportunities the doctrine provides.

Eventually, critics began to suggest ways in which application of the
doctrine of equivalents might be limited. For example, because *Graver
Tank* had alluded to the "pirating" of an invention, or a "fraud on the
patent" by an "unscrupulous copyist," some critics suggested that the doctrine of equivalents ought to be applied only in such egregious circumstances.[66] Had this approach been adopted, it would have significantly
changed the prevailing practice of applying the doctrine even against
"innocent infringers."

In *Warner-Jenkinson Co. v. Hilton Davis Chemical Co.*,[67] the Supreme
Court entered the debate for the first time since *Graver Tank*. Although
the court "share[d] the concern . . . that the doctrine of equivalents . . . has
taken on a life of its own, unbounded by the patent claims,"[68] it declined
the invitation to abolish the doctrine of equivalents or limit it to "unscrupulous copyists."[69] Instead, it reaffirmed the principles of *Graver Tank*
and the generalized application of the doctrine, with some refinements
discussed below. Unless Congress enacts new legislation, which seems
very unlikely, the doctrine of equivalents will be with us for the foreseeable future.[70]

---

[66] *See, e.g.*, International Visual Corp. v. Crown Metal Mfg. Co., 991 F.2d 768, 773–75 (Fed.
Cir. 1993) (Lourie, J., concurring). Note, however, that one person's "piracy" is another
person's "designing around" a patent claim. The latter, which refers to the deliberate
avoidance of a patent claim when engineering a product, is encouraged as a means of fur-
thering the "useful arts" promoted by patent law. *See* State Indus., Inc. v. A.O. Smith
Corp., 791 F.2d 1226, 1235–36 (Fed. Cir. 1985) ("One of the benefits of a patent system
is its so-called 'negative incentive' to 'design around' a competitor's products, even when
they are patented, thus bringing a steady flow of innovations to the marketplace."). As the
Supreme Court remarked in rejecting an "equitable" distinction, "one wonders how ever
to distinguish between the intentional copyist making minor changes to lower the risk of
legal action, and the incremental innovator designing around the claims, yet seeking to
capture as much as is permissible of the patented advance." Warner-Jenkinson Co. v.
Hilton Davis Chemical Co., 520 U.S. 17, 36 (1997).

[67] 520 U.S. 17 (1997).

[68] *Id.* at 28–29.

[69] *Id.* at 34–36.

[70] In 2002, the Supreme Court reaffirmed the doctrine of equivalents while acknowledging
the costs of the uncertainty it creates. *See Festo*, 535 U.S. at 732.

10.6.4 Tests of Equivalence

One of the most intractable problems raised by the doctrine of equivalents is how a court, or in many cases a jury, can decide what is equivalent and what is not. Fulfilling the prophecy of the dissenting justice in *Winans v. Denmead,* the issue of equivalence has been as "productive of oppressive and costly litigation" as any other, primarily because the results are unpredictable.[71] In virtually any case, the patentee can produce evidence of similarities between the accused product and the invention described in the claims, seemingly leading to a conclusion of equivalence. At the same time, the defendant can produce evidence of dissimilarities, seemingly leading to a conclusion of nonequivalence. How is a judge or jury to decide?

Although the *Graver Tank* court declined to reduce equivalence to a formula, its reference to equivalence based on performing "substantially the same function in substantially the same way to obtain the same result" was adopted in many subsequent Federal Circuit decisions as the touchstone of infringement.[72] Indeed, this function-way-result test of equivalence (also referred to as the "three-prong" test or "triple identity" test of equivalence) took on a significance that the *Graver Tank* court may not have intended or foreseen. The Federal Circuit went so far as to require that a patentee produce independent evidence on *each* part of the three-prong test—in other words, evidence that the substituted ingredient or apparatus (1) performs substantially the same function in (2) substantially the same way to (3) achieve substantially the same result as that which is literally claimed.[73] Without such close adherence to the three-prong test, the court feared that juries would be "put to sea without guiding charts."[74] Still, the debate commonly boils down to the second prong of the test—whether the accused product and the claimed invention function in "substantially the same way"[75]—and the answer to that question is rarely straightforward.

---

[71] *See* Paper Converting Machine Co. v. Magna-Graphics Corp., 745 F.2d 11, 19 (Fed. Cir. 1984) ("In view of [the doctrine of equivalents], a copier rarely knows whether his product 'infringes' a patent or not until a district court passes on the issue.").

[72] *See, e.g.,* Malta v. Schulmerich Carillons, Inc., 952 F.2d 1320, 1327 (Fed. Cir. 1991); Lear Siegler, Inc. v. Sealy Mattress Co., 873 F.2d 1422, 1425 (Fed. Cir. 1989).

[73] *See Malta,* 952 F.2d at 1327; *Lear Siegler,* 873 F.2d at 1425.

[74] *Lear Siegler,* 873 F.2d at 1426–27. The patentee must offer specific evidence, not "generalized testimony as to the overall similarity." American Calcar, Inc. v. American Honda Motor Co., 651 F.3d 1318, 1338–39 (Fed. Cir. 2011); Paice LLC v. Toyota Motor Co., 504 F.3d 1293, 1304–05 (Fed. Cir. 2007).

[75] *See* Slimfold Mfg. Co., Inc. v. Kinkead Indus., Inc., 932 F.2d 1453, 1457 (Fed. Cir. 1991).

Another important consideration is whether the item found in the accused product is known to be interchangeable with the item literally claimed.[76] This is not a definitive test of equivalence.[77] Things may be interchangeable in the broadest sense if they produce similar results but still operate in substantially different ways. A word processor may be interchangeable with a ballpoint pen for the purpose of preparing a grocery list, but the two may not be equivalent in an infringement analysis.[78] On the other hand, a physical incompatibility that would complicate the substitution of one thing for another (e.g., using a three-pronged instead of a two-pronged plug) may not prevent those things from being equivalent in a more conceptual sense.[79]

In recent years, the trend has been to downplay the function-way-result test as the conclusive test of equivalency.[80] Instead, the three-prong test has been described as one approach to the fundamental inquiry, which is whether the differences between the claimed and the accused product are

---

[76] *See* Graver Tank & Mfg. Co. v. Linde Air Prods. Co., 339 U.S. 605, 609 (1950); Vulcan Eng'g Co. v. Fata Aluminium, Inc., 278 F.3d 1366, 1374 (Fed. Cir. 2002) ("Known interchangeability is an important factor in determining equivalence.").

[77] *See* Warner-Jenkinson Co. v. Hilton Davis Chemical Co., 520 U.S. 28, 37 (1997) (known interchangeability "is not relevant for its own sake, but rather for what it tells the fact-finder about the similarities or differences between those elements"); Abraxis Bioscience, Inc. v. Mayne Pharma (USA) Inc., 467 F.3d 1370, 1382 (Fed. Cir. 2006) (absence of known interchangeability is "only one factor to consider in a doctrine of equivalents analysis"); Key Mfg. Gp., Inc. v. Microdot, Inc., 925 F.2d 1444, 1449 (Fed. Cir. 1991) ("an interchangeable device is not necessarily an equivalent device"); Perkin-Elmer Corp. v. Westinghouse Electric Corp., 822 F.2d 1528, 1535 (Fed. Cir. 1987) (interchangeable devices "still must perform substantially the same function in substantially the same way to obtain the same result").

[78] *See Perkin-Elmer,* 822 F.2d at 1535 (devices were "interchangeable" only in "entirely different and unrelated environments" and were not interchangeable for performing certain functions).

[79] *See* Interactive Pictures Corp. v. Infinite Pictures, Inc., 274 F.3d 1371, 1383 (Fed. Cir. 2001) ("Rather than focusing on physical or electronic compatibility, the known interchangeability test looks to the knowledge of a skilled artisan to see whether that artisan would contemplate the interchange as a design choice."); *but cf.* Frank's Casing Crew & Rental Tools, Inc. v. Weatherford Int'l, Inc., 389 F.3d 1370, 1378 (Fed. Cir. 2004) (mechanical incompatibility "underscored" a finding of substantial differences).

[80] *See Warner-Jenkinson,* 520 U.S. at 39–40 ("[W]hile the triple identity test may be suitable for analyzing mechanical devices, it often provides a poor framework for analyzing other products or processes."); Toro Co. v. White Consolidated Indus., Inc., 266 F.3d 1367, 1370 (Fed. Cir. 2001) (the function-way-result test "offers additional guidance" in "appropriate cases").

"insubstantial."[81] Yet to ask whether a difference is substantial or insubstantial seems a rephrasing of the equivalence question, more than a clarification.[82] For its part, the Supreme Court in *Warner-Jenkinson* declined to endorse any particular "linguistic framework" for deciding the ultimate question of equivalence.[83] In short, the question of equivalence is likely to remain a perennial source of confusion and difficulty.

10.6.5 Improvements

Equivalency calls on the perspective of the person of ordinary skill in the art at the time of the alleged infringement.[84] Consequently, variations that the patentee had not even imagined, much less enabled, can be held infringing under the doctrine of equivalents. For example, if a flash memory chip were substituted for the disk drive referenced in a patent claim, that claim might still be infringed under the doctrine of equivalents even if, when the patent application was filed, flash memory had not been invented yet. If the rule were otherwise, technological advancements would allow competitors to take the substance of an invention but still avoid infringement. This does not mean, however, that technological advancements are irrelevant when judging equivalency. Flash memory chips might be such an advancement over disk drives that, in the context of a particular invention, the differences between the two would be thought substantial even at the time of infringement.

---

[81] *See American Calcar*, 651 F.3d at 1338; Siemens Medical Solutions, Inc. v. Saint-Gobain Ceramics & Plastics, Inc., 637 F.3d 1269, 1279 (Fed. Cir. 2011); Stumbo v. Eastman Outdoors, Inc., 508 F.3d 1358, 1364 (function-way-result test is "one way" to show that the differences are insubstantial); Upjohn Co. v. Mova Pharmaceutical Corp., 225 F.3d 1306, 1309 (Fed. Cir. 2000) (three-prong test is "[t]he usual test of the substantiality of the differences"); *but cf.* Absolute Software, Inc. v. Stealth Signal, Inc., 659 F.3d 1121, 1139-40 (Fed. Cir. 2011) (whether differences are "insubstantial" is "a question that turns on whether the element of the accused product 'performs substantially the same function in substantially the same way to obtain the same result' as the claim limitation").

[82] *See Warner-Jenkinson*, 520 U.S. at 40 ("the insubstantial differences test offers little additional guidance as to what might render a given difference 'insubstantial'"). However, "[i]n some cases, the change in the accused device is so facially 'unimportant and insubstantial' that little additional guidance is needed." *Toro*, 266 F.3d at 1370.

[83] *Warner-Jenkinson*, 520 U.S. at 40.

[84] Warner-Jenkinson Co. v. Hilton Davis Chemical Co., 520 U.S. 28, 37 (1997) ("[T]he proper time for evaluating equivalency–and thus knowledge of interchangeability between elements–is at the time of infringement, not at the time the patent was issued."); Lighting World, Inc. v. Birchwood Lighting, Inc., 382 F.3d 1354, 1357 (Fed. Cir. 2004).

One factor that bears on whether an improvement is still an equivalent is whether the improvement is itself the subject of a patent. If we limit equivalence to "insubstantial variations," a change worthy of its own patent seems beyond reach. However, while it is a factor to be considered and given "due weight,"[85] it cannot be said categorically that a patented improvement is never equivalent.[86]

Texas Instruments, Inc. v. U.S. Int'l Trade Comm'n[87] illustrates the difficulty of applying the equivalency concept in fields subject to rapid technological change.[88] Texas Instruments obtained the first patent ever issued on a pocket calculator. The court acknowledged it as a "pioneering invention"[89] and noted that the prototype had become part of the permanent collection at the Smithsonian's Museum of History and Technology. In essence, the claims of the patent called for the basic combination of a keyboard, a processing circuit, memory, and a display, but because the claims were drafted in "means-plus-function" format,[90] the claims literally incorporated

---

[85] National Presto Indus., Inc. v. West Bend Co., 76 F. 3d 1185, 1192 (Fed. Cir. 1996); *see also* Zygo Corp. v. Wyko Corp. 79 F.3d 1563, 1570 (Fed. Cir. 1996) ("The nonobviousness of the accused device, evidenced by the grant of a United States patent, is relevant to the issue of whether the change therein is substantial.").

[86] Fiskars, Inc. v. Hunt Mfg. Co., 221 F.3d 1318, 1324 (Fed. Cir. 2000) ("it is well established that separate patentability does not avoid equivalency as a matter of law"); *National Presto*, 76 F.3d at 1192; Atlas Powder Co. v. E.I. Du Pont de Nemours & Co., 750 F.2d 1569, 1580 (Fed. Cir. 1984). In *Festo Corp. v. Shoketsu Kinzoku Kogyo Kabushiki Co.*, 493 F.3d 1368 1379 (Fed. Cir. 2007), the court observed that while "[w]e have not directly decided whether a device—novel and separately patentable because of the incorporation of an equivalent feature—may be captured by the doctrine of equivalents," there remains "a strong argument that an equivalent cannot be both non-obvious and insubstantial." *Id.* at 1380. In a subsequent case, *Siemens Medical Solutions, Inc. v. Saint-Gobain Ceramics & Plastics, Inc.*, 637 F.3d 1269 (Fed. Cir. 2011), the court declined to hold that "equivalence is tantamount to obviousness." *Id.* at 1282. It did suggest that a separate patent can make equivalence "considerably more difficult to make out." *Id.* at 1280. Just as an improvement is sometimes still an equivalent, an inferior variation may also be equivalent. *See* Whapeton Canvas Co. v. Frontier, Inc., 870 F.2d 1546, 1548 n.2 (Fed. Cir. 1989) ("inferior infringement is still infringement"). The question, as before, is whether or not the differences are insubstantial.

[87] 805 F.2d 1558 (Fed. Cir. 1986). Also see the opinion on denial of rehearing en banc, 846 F.2d 1369 (Fed. Cir. 1988).

[88] The opinion deals with equivalence under 35 U.S.C. § 112(f), discussed in Section 10.7, and under the doctrine of equivalents. At the time the court treated the analysis as essentially the same. *See Texas Instruments*, 805 F.2d at 1571. More recently, the court has suggested a difference—confining § 112(f) equivalence to structures that existed in the art when the patent was filed, and equivalence under the doctrine of equivalents to later-developed structures. *See* Section 10.7.

[89] *See* Section 10.6.7.

[90] *See* Section 7.7.4.

only the particular keyboard, processing circuit, memory, and display described in the patent specification and their equivalents.

About 17 years after filing its patent application, and 10 years after the patent issued, Texas Instruments brought an action to prevent the importation of pocket calculators by foreign manufacturers. During those years, the field had advanced in significant ways. Metal-oxide semiconductor transistors had replaced bipolar transistors, liquid crystal displays had replaced thermal printer displays, and so forth. The Federal Circuit found that each substitution, by itself, might be considered the substitution of an equivalent, but when considered *as a whole*, all of the technological changes were sufficient to take the accused devices beyond the protection of the doctrine of equivalents.[91] The decision was a controversial one, even among the judges of the Federal Circuit.

Years later, and in spite of the result in *Texas Instruments*, the Federal Circuit announced in *Chiuminatta Concrete Concepts, Inc. v. Cardinal Indus., Inc.*[92] that the unpredictability of technological developments is the primary reason, perhaps the *only* reason, to invoke the doctrine of equivalents. "The doctrine of equivalents is necessary," the court observed, "because one cannot predict the future."[93] If the applicant knew about the unclaimed equivalent (because it is "technology that predates the invention itself"), and *could* have claimed it in the patent, the court knew of "no policy-based reason why a patentee should get two bites at the apple."[94] In other words, unless the failure to claim the full scope of the invention explicitly can be excused by historical necessity, the court may refuse to apply the doctrine of equivalents.

Chiuminatta's emphasis on later-developed technology may be over-done.[95] The Supreme Court has justified the doctrine of equivalents, at least in part, by reference to the inherent imprecision of language[96]— a problem that goes beyond that of advancing technologies. *Graver Tank* itself dealt with an equivalent known at the time the patent application was filed. Later cases have interpreted *Chiuminatta's* "two bites at the

---

[91] *Texas Instruments*, 805 F.2d at 1570–72.

[92] 145 F.3d 1303 (Fed. Cir. 1998).

[93] *Id.* at 1310.

[94] *Id.* at 1311.

[95] The paragraphs discussing the "after-developed technology" rationale for the doctrine of equivalents are uncharacteristically free of citations to precedent. *See id.* at 1310–13.

[96] "[T]the nature of language makes it impossible to capture the essence of a thing in a patent application." Festo Corp. v. Shoketsu Kinzoku Kogyo Kabushiki Co., 535 U.S. 722, 731 (2002).

apple" reasoning as applying only to means-plus-function claims, where equivalence of structure is already an issue for literal infringement.[97] Except in those cases, "the mere fact that the asserted equivalent structure was pre-existing technology does not foreclose a finding of infringement under the doctrine of equivalents."[98] The rhetoric of *Chiuminatta* is, however, representative of efforts by the Federal Circuit to confine the doctrine of equivalents to situations where the uncertainty it creates is easiest to justify.[99]

10.6.6 Impact of the All-Elements Rule on Equivalence

One of the most important refinements of the principles announced in *Graver Tank* involves the all-elements rule, which states that each and every element of the claimed invention must be found in an infringing product.[100] In *Pennwalt Corp. v. Durand-Wayland, Inc.*,[101] the Federal Circuit considered whether the doctrine of equivalents could be applied if the claimed invention and the accused product were similar *as a whole*, even though individual claim elements were entirely absent in the accused product. The invention in *Pennwalt* was a machine used to sort fruit by color and weight. One of the claimed components of the machine was a "position indicating means," which kept track of the physical location of a piece of fruit as it passed through the sorter. The accused product–also a sorting device–produced comparable results. However, it did so without any means for keeping track of the physical location of a piece of fruit. The court held that an accused product cannot infringe a claim under the doctrine of equivalents unless each and every claim element, or its equivalent, can be found in the accused product. Overall similarity is insufficient if any claim element is entirely

---

[97] See Section 10.7.

[98] Kraft Foods, Inc. v. International Trading Co., 203 F.3d 1362, 1373 (Fed. Cir. 2000).

[99] A more specific application of the *Chiuminatta* reasoning is the Federal Circuit's refusal to recognize equivalents that were actually *disclosed* in the application without being explicitly claimed. *See* Section 10.6.9.

[100] *See* Star Scientific, Inc. v. R.J. Reynolds Tobacco Co., 655 F.3d 1364, 1378 (Fed. Cir. 2011); TIP Sys., LLC v. Phillips & Brooks/Gladwin, Inc., 529 F.3d 1364, 1379 (Fed. Cir. 2008); Cook Biotech Inc. v. Acell, Inc., 460 F.3d 1365, 1379 (Fed. Cir. 2006).

[101] 833 F.2d 931 (Fed. Cir. 1987) (en banc).

missing.[102] In *Warner-Jenkinson Co. v. Hilton Davis Chemical Co.*,[103] the Supreme Court reaffirmed the rule established in *Pennwalt*, stating that a strict, element-by-element application of the doctrine would ensure fair notice to potential infringers.[104]

As a corollary to the all-elements rule, courts resist any argument, even couched in terms of equivalence, that seems to ignore completely a very clear claim limitation. As the Supreme Court stated, "[i]t is important to ensure that the application of the doctrine, even as to an individual element, is not allowed such broad play as to effectively eliminate that element in its entirety."[105]

---

[102] *Pennwalt*, 833 F.2d at 935, 939; *see also* Absolute Software, Inc. v. Stealth Signal, Inc., 659 F.3d 1121, 1139 (Fed. Cir. 2011) (" 'Infringement under the doctrine of equivalents requires that the accused product contain each limitation of the claim or its equivalent.' "); American Calcar, Inc. v. American Honda Motor Co., Inc., 651 F.3d 1318, 1338 (Fed. Cir. 2011); Wavetonix LLC v. EIS Electronic Integrated Sys., 573 F.3d 1343, 1360 (Fed. Cir. 2009); E-Pass Technologies, Inc. v. 3Com Corp., 473 F.3d 1213, 1221 (Fed. Cir. 2007) ("Under the 'all elements' rule, 'the doctrine of equivalents must be applied to individual elements of the claim, not to the invention as a whole.' "). On the other hand, there need not be a "one-to-one correspondence" between the claim and the accused product. A single component of an accused product can be the equivalent of multiple components set forth in a claim. Dolly, Inc. v. Spalding & Evenflo Co., 16 F.3d 394, 398 (Fed. Cir. 1994); Sun Studs, Inc. v. ATA Equipment Leasing, Inc., 872 F.2d 978, 989 (Fed. Cir. 1989) ("elements or steps may be combined without *ipso facto* loss of equivalency"). Conversely, two components in the accused product, functioning together, can be the equivalent of one claimed component. *Wavetronix*, 573 F.3d at 1361. This principle allows greater flexibility in applying the doctrine of equivalents than the all-elements rule might suggest.

[103] 520 U.S. 17 (1997).

[104] *Id.* at 29–30. Interestingly, the Supreme Court did not mention *Pennwalt* and discussed the all-elements approach as though it were a newly discovered compromise solution to the problems posed by the doctrine of equivalents.

[105] *Warner-Jenkinson*, 520 U.S. at 29; *see also Wavetronix*, 573 F.3d at 1360; Planet Bingo, LLC v. Gametech Int'l, Inc., 472 F.3d 1338, 1344 (Fed. Cir. 2006); Primos, Inc. v. Hunter's Specialties, Inc., 451 F.3d 841, 850 (Fed. Cir. 2006) ("The 'all limitations rule' restricts the doctrine of equivalents by preventing its application when doing so would vitiate a claim limitation."). There is "no set formula" for deciding if a broad reading of equivalence would actually "vitiate" the relevant claim limitation. "Rather, courts must consider the totality of the circumstances of each case and determine whether the alleged equivalent can be fairly characterized as an insubstantial change . . . without rendering the pertinent limitation meaningless." Freedman Seating Co. v. American Seating Co., 420 F.3d 1350, 1359 (Fed. Cir. 2005); *see also* Trading Technologies Int'l, Inc. v. Espeed, Inc., 595 F.3d 1340, 1355 (Fed. Cir. 2010) ("Claim vitiation applies when there is a 'clear, substantial difference or a difference in kind' between the claim limitation and the accused product. . . . It does not apply when there is a 'subtle difference in degree.' "). Finding that something excluded by a claim limitation is still an equivalent does not, in every case, "vitiate" that limitation. Otherwise, the all-elements rule would " 'swallow the doctrine of equivalents entirely.' " *See* Abbott Labs. v. Andrx Pharmaceuticals, Inc., 473 F.3d 1196, 1212 (Fed. Cir. 2007); Depuy Spine, Inc. v. Medtronic Sofamor Danek, Inc., 469 F.3d 1005, 1018 (Fed. Cir. 2006) (the doctrine of equivalents " '*necessarily* deals with subject matter that is 'beyond,' 'ignored' by, and not included in the literal scope of the claim' " (emphasis in original)).

When a claim limitation specifically excludes an alternative, a court may refuse to find them equivalent.[106] For example, in *Moore U.S.A., Inc. v. Standard Register Co.,*[107] the patent claims described a "business type mailer form" having adhesive strips extending "the majority of the lengths" of the margins.[108] The accused product had adhesive strips covering only a minority of the margins, but the plaintiff argued that the product was still equivalent. The court rejected that argument in part because "it would defy logic to conclude that a minority—the very antithesis of a majority—could be insubstantially different from a claim limitation requiring a majority."[109] Of course, whether something is an opposite or "antithesis" as opposed to an insignificant difference is sometimes a matter of perspective. "Majority" seems the opposite of "minority," but, as a dissenting judge in *Moore* pointed out, just under 50 percent might differ insubstantially from just over 50 percent.[110]

10.6.7 Impact of Prior Art on Equivalence

The prior art imposes another limitation on the doctrine of equivalents.[111] The doctrine of equivalents cannot expand the scope of a claim so far that it encompasses or "ensnares" the prior art.[112] One method of analyzing the problem (though it is not an exclusive method) is to imagine a "hypothetical

---

[106] *See* Cordis Corp. v. Boston Scientific Corp., 561 F.3d 1319, 1330 (Fed. Cir. 2009) (no equivalency where " 'the accused device contain[s] the antithesis of the claimed structure' "); *Cook Biotech*, 460 F.3d at 1379 (" 'the concept of equivalency cannot embrace a structure that is specifically excluded from the scope of the claims' "); Scimed Life Sys., Inc. v. Advanced Cardiovascular Sys., Inc., 242 F.3d 1337, 1345 (Fed. Cir. 2001) ("Having specifically identified, criticized, and disclaimed the dual lumen configuration, the patentee cannot now invoke the doctrine of equivalents to 'embrace a structure that was specifically excluded from the claims.' "). A detailed claim may be read to exclude alternatives implicitly. *See* Bicon, Inc. v. Straumann Co., 441 F.3d 945, 955 (Fed. Cir. 2006).

[107] 229 F.3d 1091 (Fed. Cir. 2000).

[108] *Id.* at 1095.

[109] *Id.* at 1106; *see also American Calcar*, 651 F.3d at 1339 ("finding a signal from one source to be equivalent to 'signals from a plurality of sources' would vitiate that claim limitation by rendering it meaningless"); Asyst Technologies, Inc. v. Emtrak, Inc., 402 F.3d 1188, 1195 (Fed. Cir. 2005) ("the term 'mounted' can fairly be said to specifically exclude objects that are 'unmounted' "); *but cf.* Adams Respiratory Therapeutics, Inc. v. Perrigo Co., 616 F.3d 1283, 1291-93 (Fed. Cir. 2010) (a quantity less than 3,500 may be equivalent to the claim limitation "at least 3500").

[110] *See Moore*, 229 F.3d at 1119 (Newman, J., concurring in part and dissenting in part).

[111] Section 8.9 discusses prior art.

[112] Tate Access Floors, Inc. v. Interface Architectural Resources, Inc., 279 F.3d 1357, 1367 (Fed. Cir. 2002); Interactive Pictures Corp. v. Infinite Pictures, Inc., 274 F.3d 1371, 1380 (Fed. Cir. 2001) ("It is well settled law that a patentee cannot assert a range of equivalents that encompasses the prior art.").

claim" that would be *literally* infringed by the product at issue.[113] If the patentee could not have obtained such a claim—because it would have been anticipated by the prior art or rendered obvious[114]—then the accused product does not infringe. The purpose of this limitation is to ensure that patentees do not achieve indirectly, through the doctrine of equivalents, a monopoly that could not have been obtained directly by prosecution of a broader claim.[115]

The restrictions imposed by the prior art create, in effect, a "safe harbor" insofar as the doctrine of equivalents is concerned, if the accused product in all relevant respects is identical to an invention in the prior art. No hypothetical claim could encompass such a product yet avoid invalidity. The restriction applies only to the claim as a whole, so there is no immunity from infringement by equivalence unless all of the relevant features of the accused product are found in the prior art, either in one reference or in several that, together, made the combination obvious. Because patents are often granted to novel combinations of known elements, one cannot escape infringement, either literal or under the doctrine of equivalents, merely by identifying isolated features of the accused product in the prior art.[116]

The prior art also influences the doctrine of equivalents in a subtler fashion through the concept of the "pioneer patent." Whereas most patents are granted to incremental improvements of inventions that have gone before, a pioneer patent is one that breaks with the past so distinctly that it creates an entirely new field. Patents such as Bell's on the telephone, or the Texas Instruments calculator patent, have staked claims to "pioneering" status. Some cases have held that a pioneer patent, as a very basic advancement in technology, should be given a correspondingly broad scope of equivalence. A patent on a narrow improvement, on the other hand, should be held more strictly to the language of the claims.[117] Of

---

[113] Abbott Labs. v. Dey, L.P., 287 F.3d 1097, 1105 (Fed. Cir. 2002); *Interactive Pictures,* 274 F.3d at 1380; Wilson Sporting Goods Co. v. David Geoffrey & Assoc., 904 F.2d 677, 684 (Fed. Cir. 1990).

[114] *See* Sections 8.9.3 and 8.9.4.

[115] *See Tate Access Floors,* 279 F.3d at 1367 ("the doctrine of equivalents is an equitable doctrine and it would not be equitable to allow a patentee to claim a scope of equivalents encompassing material that had been previously disclosed by someone else, or that would have been obvious in light of others' earlier disclosures"); *Wilson Sporting Goods,* 904 F.2d at 684 ("The doctrine of equivalents exists to prevent fraud on a patent . . . *not* to give a patentee something which he could not lawfully have obtained from the PTO had he tried.").

[116] *See Abbott Labs.,* 287 F.3d at 1106; Corning Glass Works v. Sumitomo Electric U.S.A., Inc., 868 F.2d 1251, 1261 (Fed. Cir. 1989).

[117] *See* Sun Studs, Inc. v. ATA Equipment Leasing, Inc., 872 F.2d 978, 987 (Fed. Cir. 1989) ("The concept of the 'pioneer' arises from an ancient jurisprudence, reflecting judicial appreciation that a broad breakthrough invention merits a broader scope of equivalents than does a narrow improvement in a crowded technology").

course, whether or not a patent deserves to be called pioneering will often be a subject for debate.[118]

For the most part, the Federal Circuit has declined to divide patents into "pioneering" and "nonpioneering" categories. Instead, it has treated pioneering patents as just one end of a spectrum that embraces various degrees of inventiveness.[119] Moreover, it has emphasized that pioneer patents are not subject to different legal standards than other patents, as a reward for merit or otherwise.[120] A pioneering patent merely enjoys a potentially broader scope of equivalence because it is not hemmed in by large numbers of similar inventions in the prior art, as is generally true of an incremental improvement in an already crowded field.[121]

10.6.8 Prosecution History Estoppel

One of the most important limitations on the doctrine of equivalents is "prosecution history estoppel." The prosecution history is the written record of an applicant's dealings with the Patent Office, including any actions taken by the examiner and any statements, arguments, or modifications of the claims made by the applicant.[122] "Estoppel" means that a claim is barred because the claimant's prior actions are inconsistent with that claim. Simply put, prosecution history estoppel prevents a patent owner

---

[118] "That an improvement enjoys commercial success and has some industry impact, as many do, cannot compel a finding that an improvement falls within the pioneer category." Perkin-Elmer Corp. v. Westinghouse Electric Corp., 822 F.2d 1528, 1532 (Fed. Cir. 1987). Even the pioneering status of Texas Instruments' calculator patent was challenged. *See* Texas Instruments, Inc. v. U.S. Int'l Trade Comm'n, 846 F.2d 1369, 1370 (Fed. Cir. 1988).

[119] *See Sun Studs,* 872 F.2d at 987 ("[T]he 'pioneer' is not a separate class of invention, carrying a unique body of law. The wide range of technological advance between pioneering breakthrough and modest improvement accommodates gradations in scope of equivalency."); *Texas Instruments,* 846 F.2d at 1370 ("[t]here is not a discontinuous transition from 'mere improvement' to 'pioneer'").

[120] *See* Augustine Medical, Inc. v. Gaymar Indus., Inc., 181 F.3d 1291, 1301 (Fed. Cir. 1999) ("no objective legal test separates pioneers from non-pioneers").

[121] *See Abbott Labs.,* 287 F.3d at 1105 ("A pioneer patent by definition will have little applicable prior art to limit it, whereas an improvement patent's scope is confined by the existing knowledge on which the improvement is based."); *Augustine Medical,* 181 F.3d at 1301 ("Without extensive prior art to confine and cabin their claims, pioneers acquire broader claims than non-pioneers who must craft narrow claims to evade the strictures of a crowded art field."); *Texas Instruments,* 846 F.2d at 1370 (the "liberal" scope of equivalency afforded to pioneer patents "flows directly from the relative sparseness of prior art in nascent fields of technology").

[122] *See* Section 5.1.

from contradicting the prosecution history by claiming as an equivalent subject matter given up during prosecution in order to obtain the patent.[123]

Brenner v. United States[124] illustrates the principle. The patented invention in *Brenner* concerned a system for coding and sorting mail. The claims described a means for applying a "codable" material, such as a magnetic strip, to an article of mail. The material would carry the information needed for sorting. Initially, the claims referred to a "coded" rather than "codable" material, implying that the information was encoded beforehand. However, the applicant changed the claim language to "codable," telling the examiner that the new language more accurately described the invention " 'since when the material is placed on the mail it is not yet coded.' "[125] When compelled to distinguish certain prior art, the applicant stressed this distinction and also emphasized that the material could be erased after encoding.

The system accused of infringing used an ink jet printer to spray bar codes directly on the mail to be sorted. The only article applied to the mail was the ink itself, and the ink was not literally "codable." By the time the ink hit the paper, it was fixed in a predetermined pattern, and it could not be altered or erased afterward. The trial court, affirmed by the Federal Circuit, found that the accused system could not be held equivalent to the system claimed because the applicant, during prosecution, had clearly limited the invention to "codable" material.[126]

---

[123] *See* Festo Corp. v. Shoketsu Kinzoku Kogyo Kabushiki Co., 535 U.S. 722, 741 (2002); Honeywell Int'l, Inc. v. Hamilton Sunstrand Corp., 523 F.3d 1304, 1312 (Fed. Cir. 2008); Regents of the University of California v. Dakocytomation California, Inc., 517 F.3d 1364, 1376 (Fed. Cir. 2008); Cross Medical Prods., Inc. v Medtronic Sofamor Danek, Inc., 480 F.3d 1335, 1341 (Fed. Cir. 2007). While the clearest cases of estoppel arise when the applicant narrows a claim by amendment, *see Cross Medical*, 480 F.3d at 1341 ("a narrowing amendment classically invokes the doctrine"), estoppel can also result when the applicant argues in favor of a narrow claim interpretation. *See* Spine Solutions, Inc. v. Medtronic Sofamor Danek USA, Inc., 620 F.3d 1305, 1317 (Fed. Cir. 2010); Pods, Inc. v. Porta Stor, Inc., 484 F.3d 1359, 1368 (Fed. Cir. 2007); Conoco, Inc. v. Energy & Environmental Int'l, L.C., 460 F.3d 1349, 1363 (Fed. Cir. 2006). As the Supreme Court has observed, "the doctrine of equivalents is premised on language's inability to capture the essence of innovation"–a premise "undercut" when the applicant specifically abandoned material now urged to be equivalent. *Festo*, 535 U.S. at 734. Applicant arguments and amendments may create an estoppel even if they were unnecessary to secure the issuance of the patent. *See* Felix v. American Honda Motor Co., 562 F.3d 1167, 1184 (Fed. Cir. 2009); *Pods*, 484 F.3d at 1368. However, estoppel does require that the prosecution history demonstrate a "clear and unmistakable surrender of subject matter." *Pods*, 484 F.3d at 1367; *Conoco*, 460 F.3d at 1364.

[124] 773 F.2d 306 (Fed. Cir. 1985).

[125] *Id.* at 307.

[126] *Id.* at 308.

Prosecution history estoppel checks the inclination of some patent owners to treat claims as a "nose of wax" to be twisted in one direction to avoid invalidity and another to ensure infringement. An applicant who represents the invention as one thing in prosecution must be prepared to live with that interpretation in litigation. There can be no "second bite at the abandoned apple."[127] The doctrine also provides better notice to a patentee's competitors of the scope of the patented invention, at least in those cases where the competitors have an opportunity to review the prosecution history.[128] Most importantly, the doctrine of prosecution history estoppel prevents applicants from circumventing the process of patent examination. If the scope of equivalence were not limited by the prosecution history, an applicant could narrow the claims as much as necessary to satisfy the examiner while resorting to the doctrine of equivalents to preserve what amounts to a broader claim. Prosecution history estoppel helps to ensure that a patent claim is no broader in scope than the examiner understood it to be.[129]

Although the theory is sound, it may be difficult to determine how much the patent applicant actually surrendered. In *Festo Corp. v. Shoketsu Kinzoku Kogyo Kabushiki Co.*,[130] the Federal Circuit simplified matters by holding that the doctrine of equivalents cannot be applied *at all* to a claim element added during prosecution for reasons related to patentability.[131] For example, if an applicant added a two-spring limitation to a mousetrap claim in order to distinguish it from a prior art trap with one spring, the patent cannot later be enforced against a trap with *three* springs, even though the differences between two and three springs may be insignificant. This strict approach offered predictability and respect for the notice function of claims,[132] but the decision confounded the expectations of many patent attorneys who had routinely amended claims during prosecution, unaware of the consequences.[133]

---

[127] Lemelson v. General Mills, Inc., 968 F.2d 1202, 1208 (Fed. Cir. 1992).

[128] *See id.* at 1208 ("Other players in the marketplace are entitled to rely on the record made in the Patent Office in determining the meaning and scope of the patent.").

[129] *See* Genentech, Inc. v. Wellcome Foundation Ltd., 29 F. 3d 1555, 1564 (Fed. Cir. 1994) ("An applicant should not be able deliberately to narrow the scope of examination to avoid during prosecution scrutiny by the PTO of subject matter ... and then, obtain in court, either literally or under the doctrine of equivalents, a scope of protection which encompasses that subject matter.").

[130] 234 F.3d 558 (Fed. Cir. 2000) (en banc).

[131] *Id.* at 574.

[132] *Id.* at 575–77.

[133] *See Festo*, 234 F.3d at 638 (Newman, J., concurring in part and dissenting in part).

On appeal, the Supreme Court reversed.[134] The court reaffirmed the principle of prosecution history estoppel whenever a claim is narrowed for a "substantial reason related to patentability."[135] In such cases, the patentee is *presumed* to have given up all of the subject matter excluded from the claim–like the three-spring mousetrap of our hypothetical.[136] On the other hand, the court rejected the absolute bar imposed by the Federal Circuit. Language remains "an imperfect fit for invention."[137] An amendment "may demonstrate what the claim is not; but it may still fail to capture precisely what the claim is."[138] Accordingly, a patentee who narrowed a claim during prosecution can overcome the presumption in three ways, each demonstrating that the applicant could not have drafted a claim literally covering the alleged equivalent.[139]

First, the patentee can show that "the rationale underlying the amendment [bore] no more than a tangential relation to the equivalent in question."[140] If the amendment in our example had depended on a

---

[134] Festo Corp. v. Shoketsu Kinzoku Kogyo Kabushiki Co., 535 U.S. 722 (2002).

[135] *Id.* at 735–36. Amendments are presumed to have been made for reasons related to patentability. *Id.* at 739–40; Warner-Jenkinson, Inc. v. Hilton Davis Chemical Co., 520 U.S. 17, 33 (1997). The patent owner can rebut that presumption by showing that the amendment had another explanation. It might have been, for example, a "truly cosmetic" or clarifying amendment, having no impact on the scope of the claim. *See Festo,* 535 U.S. at 736–37.

[136] *Id.* at 740; *see also Felix,* 562 F.3d at 1182; Lucent Technologies, Inc. v. Gateway, Inc., 525 F.3d 1200, 1218 (Fed. Cir. 2008). If the applicant adds a narrowing limitation to one claim, and that same term was already present in another claim, the estoppel may limit the range of equivalents available to *both* claims, a phenomenon dubbed "infectious estoppel" by one litigant. *See Felix,* 562 F.3d at 1183; Glaxo Wellcome Inc. v. Impax Labs. Inc., 356 F.3d 1348, 1356 (Fed. Cir. 2004) ("[S]ubject matter surrendered via claim amendments during prosecution is also relinquished for other claims containing the same limitation. . . . This court follows this rule to ensure consistent interpretation of the same claim terms in the same patent.").

[137] *Festo,* 535 U.S. at 738.

[138] *Id.*

[139] *See id.* at 740; Intervet Inc. v. Merial Ltd., 617 F.3d 1282, 1291 (Fed. Cir. 2010); *Felix,* 562 F.3d at 1182.

[140] *Festo,* 535 U.S. at 740; *see also* Funai Electric Co. v. Daewoo Electronics Corp., 616 F.3d 1357, 1369 (Fed. Cir. 2010); *Honeywell,* 523 F.3d at 1315; O2 Micro Int'l Ltd. v. Beyond Innovation Technology Co., 521 F.3d 1351, 1364 (Fed. Cir. 2008). The Federal Circuit has warned that the "tangential relation criterion for overcoming the *Festo* presumption is very narrow." *Honeywell,* 523 F.3d at 1315; *Cross Medical,* 480 F.3d at 1342. There is no "hard-and-fast test" for identifying a tangential relationship, but "an amendment made to avoid prior art that contains the equivalent in question is not tangential." *Intervet,* 617 F.3d at 1291; *see also Felix,* 562 F.3d at 1184.

fundamental distinction between a single spring and multiple springs (perhaps it had been questioned whether any single spring could generate the force required), the patentee might argue that the one-spring-versus-two-spring rationale had been, at best, tangential to the issue of equivalence between two springs and three. Second, the patentee can demonstrate that the alleged equivalent was unforeseeable at the time of the amendment.[141] If a three-spring mousetrap had been inconceivable, perhaps because of some technical barrier in the art that no one expected to overcome, the applicant could not have anticipated the limiting effect of the amendment, nor might an objective observer, equally skilled in the art, have expected such an effect. Generally, if the alleged equivalent embodies technology unknown in the art at the time of the claim amendment—for example, a variant with flash memory unimaginable when disc drives were the state of the art—the equivalent will be considered unforeseeable.[142] Old technology, particularly if found in prior art in the field of the invention, is likely to be considered foreseeable.[143] Finally, the patentee may overcome the presumption by showing "some other reason" why it could not have been expected to express the claim amendment in such a way as to still include what is now argued to be equivalent.[144] This catch-all category is necessarily vague, but it might include arguments based on a "shortcoming of language."[145]

---

[141] *Festo*, 535 U.S. at 740; *see also Honeywell*, 523 F.3d at 1312–13. Foreseeability is an objective inquiry from the perspective of a person of ordinary skill in the art at the time of the amendment. *Honeywell*, 523 F.3d at 1312. Patentees who argue, for purposes of infringement, that the alleged equivalent was a known substitute (*see* Section 10.6) may have a particularly difficult time arguing that unforseeability rebuts the presumption of estoppel. *See* Ranbaxy Pharmaceuticals Inc. v. Apotex, Inc. 350 F.3d 1235, 1241 (Fed. Cir. 2003). In a subsequent opinion still related to the *Festo* dispute, the Federal Circuit held that a known technology is not unforeseeable merely because a person skilled in the art would not have expected it to be a functional equivalent. Festo Corp. v. Shoketsu Kinzoku Kogyo Kabushiki Co., 493 F.3d 1368, 1382 (Fed. Cir. 2007) ("An equivalent is foreseeable if one skilled in the art would have known that the alternative existed . . . even if the suitability of the alternative for the particular purposes defined by the amended claim scope were unknown."). Judge Newman penned a strong dissent, arguing that unknown capabilities produce unforeseeable equivalents. *See id.* at 1385.

[142] *See Honeywell*, 523 F.3d at 1312.

[143] *Id.*

[144] *Festo*, 535 U.S. at 741.

[145] Amgen Inc. v. Hoechst Marion Roussel, Inc. 457 F.3d 1293, 1313–16 (Fed. Cir. 2006). The Federal Circuit cautions that this third category of excuse is, like the tangential relation argument, "a narrow one." *Id.* at 1313.

If *Festo* is not the watershed it might have been had the original Federal Circuit decision been allowed to stand, it does at least promise a more predictable analysis for prosecution history estoppel. The focus on foreseeability recognizes both the difficulties of patent applicants, who hope to reap the rewards of their efforts for years to come, and the interests of potential infringers, who deserve fair warning of prohibited conduct.[146]

10.6.9 Disclosure of Unclaimed Embodiments

An alleged equivalent that is beyond the literal scope of the claims may be discussed in the specification as an alternative. In some ways this seems to bolster the patentee's argument in favor of infringement. At least it shows that the patentee was aware of the equivalent, and it suggests the possibility of substituting that equivalent for the matter literally claimed. But the effect of the disclosure can be quite the opposite, as illustrated in the case of *Maxwell v. J. Baker, Inc.*[147]

Maxwell was a store employee who invented a system for tying together pairs of shoes for display. Previous systems had relied on plastic filaments strung through the eyelets of the shoes, but this only worked for shoes that *had* eyelets. Some retailers punched holes in the shoes just to provide a way of tying them together. Maxwell's idea was to anchor plastic tabs inside the shoes and use holes or loops in the tabs as the attachment point for the filament. The figures in Maxwell's patent specification showed the tabs anchored between the inner and outer soles of the shoes, and the claims explicitly referred to this construction, but the specification also observed that the tabs could be stitched into the lining of the shoes. The Federal Circuit held that shoes having tabs sewn into the lining did not infringe Maxwell's patent under the doctrine of equivalents, precisely because that option had been disclosed *but not claimed* in Maxwell's patent. Such unclaimed disclosures are "dedicated to the public" and cannot be recaptured through the doctrine of equivalents.[148]

The court's position tends to penalize applicants for making their disclosures more thorough and informative. If Maxwell had kept silent about the unclaimed alternative, it might well have been found infringing. On the other hand, if viewed from the perspective of a competitor trying to avoid infringement, it may be reasonable to conclude that things discussed in

---

[146] *See Honeywell,* 523 F.3d at 1313.

[147] 86 F.3d 1098 (Fed. Cir. 1996).

[148] *Id.* at 1106–07; *see also* Unique Concepts, Inc. v. Brown, 939 F.2d 1558, 1562–63 (Fed. Cir. 1991).

the patent, but specifically excluded from the claims, were not meant to be covered. In addition, the Supreme Court has stressed the inability of language to capture the essence of an invention as the rationale for the doctrine of equivalents.[149] A patentee who described an alleged equivalent in the specification can hardly be said to have "lacked the words to describe the subject matter in question."[150] Finally, the "dedication to the public" of unclaimed embodiments forces applicants to subject to the rigors of PTO examination claims as broad as the monopoly they ultimately attempt to enforce.

For a time, it was uncertain whether the principle of *Maxwell* would find broad application,[151] but in 2002, the Federal Circuit's en banc opinion in *Johnson & Johnston Assoc., Inc. v. R.E. Service Co.*[152] reaffirmed the rule that "when a patent drafter discloses but declines to claim subject matter . . . this action dedicates that unclaimed subject matter to the public."[153] In this case, the patentee whose claims called for an "aluminum sheet" could not argue that a steel sheet was equivalent when the patent specifically disclosed, without claiming, the steel alternative.[154] The court cited the usual concerns regarding the primacy of claims and the desirability of fair notice to the public.[155] Like its unsuccessful attempt in *Festo,*[156] the "disclosure-

---

[149] *See* Festo Corp. v. Shoketsu Kinzoku Kogyo Kabushiki Co., 535 U.S. 722, 734–38 (2002).

[150] *Festo,* 535 U.S. at 734 (applying the same reasoning where claims were narrowed to exclude the alleged equivalent).

[151] *See* YBM Magnex, Inc. v. Int'l Trade Comm'n, 145 F.3d 1317 (Fed. Cir. 1998) (holding that *Maxwell* creates no "blanket rule" regarding disclosed but unclaimed embodiments but offering little to clarify the limits of the *Maxwell* principle).

[152] 285 F.3d 1046 (Fed. Cir. 2002).

[153] *Johnson & Johnston,* 285 F.3d at 105; *see also* PSC Computer Prods. Inc. v. Foxconn Int'l Inc., 355 F.3d 1353, 1357–60 (Fed. Cir. 2004). Although in the landmark Supreme Court case of *Graver Tank* the equivalent alternative of manganese was disclosed in the specification, the Federal Circuit distinguished that case as one in which the applicant at least *tried* to obtain the broader claim, though it failed when the PTO rejected it. That reasoning presents some difficulties, but at least the *Graver Tank* situation is less likely an instance of a patentee attempting to "game the system." *See Johnson & Johnston,* 285 F.3d at 1060 (Dyk, J., concurring).

[154] *Id.* at 1055.

[155] *Id.* at 1052. In order to be "dedicated to the public," the unclaimed alternative must be described in the patent with sufficient specificity that it can be identified by a person of ordinary skill in the art as a variation disclosed but not claimed. *PSC,* 355 F.3d at 1360; *see also* Pfizer, Inc. v. Teva Pharmaceuticals, USA, Inc., 429 F.3d 1364, 1379 (Fed. Cir. 2005) (the dedicated subject matter must have been "identified by the patentee as an alternative to a claim limitation"). Whether the patentee subjectively intended to disclaim is not a factor. Toro Co. v. White Consolidated Indus., Inc., 383 F.3d 1326, 1333 (Fed. Cir. 2004).

[156] *See* Section 10.6.8.

dedication rule" can be seen as an effort by the Federal Circuit to rein in the doctrine of equivalents and restore some certainty to the patent system.

10.7 EQUIVALENCE IN THE CONTEXT OF MEANS-PLUS-FUNCTION CLAIMS

Patent law would be less confusing if equivalence were an issue arising solely in connection with the doctrine of equivalents. However, equivalence is also an issue affecting *literal* infringement if the claim is a means-plus-function claim drafted in accordance with § 112(f).[157] Section 7.7.4 discusses means-plus-function claims. To summarize, literal infringement where a claim element recites a "means" for performing a specified function requires (1) that the accused product perform that function, and (2) that it use a structure identical or equivalent to the corresponding structure disclosed in the patent specification.[158]

Suppose that a mousetrap claim includes "a means for snapping the trap shut," and the specification discloses a steel spring to perform that function. The first step in addressing infringement is to see if the accused mousetrap has *any* means for "snapping the trap shut." If no component of the accused mousetrap performs that function, the claim is not literally infringed.[159] If the accused mousetrap does have some means for "snapping the trap shut," we then ask whether the structure performing that function is identical or equivalent to the steel spring. If the accused mousetrap uses a rubber band,

---

[157] "An element in a claim for a combination may be expressed as a means or step for performing a specified function without the recital of structure, material, or acts in support thereof, and such claim shall be construed to cover the corresponding structure, material or acts described in the specification and equivalents thereof." Before the America Invents Act added subsection headings to § 112, courts referred to the quoted language as § 112, ¶ 6.

[158] General Protecht Gp., Inc. v. Int'l Trade Comm'n, 619 F.3d 1303, 1312 (Fed. Cir. 2010); Hearing Components, Inc. v. Shure Inc., 600 F.3d 1357, 1370 (Fed. Cir. 2010); Minks v. Polaris Indus., Inc., 546 F.3d 1364, 1378 (Fed. Cir. 2008); Welker Bearing Co. v. PHD, Inc., 550 F.3d 1090, 1099 (Fed. Cir. 2008). The same kind of two-part comparison must be made if a prior art reference is alleged to anticipate a claim with means-plus-function elements. *See* Fresenius USA, Inc. v. Baxter Int'l, Inc., 582 F.3d 1288, 1299 (Fed. Cir. 2009).

[159] One might inquire, however, whether it performs an equivalent function sufficient to apply the doctrine of equivalents. *See* Interactive Pictures Corp. v. Infinite Pictures, Inc., 274 F.3d 1371, 1382 (Fed. Cir. 2001) ("[I]nfringement under the doctrine of equivalents may be premised on the accused and the patented component having *substantially* the same function, whereas structure corresponding to the disclosed limitation in a means-plus-function clause must perform the *identical* function." (emphasis in original)).

we have to decide whether a rubber band and a steel spring are equivalent in the context of the invention.

Paradoxically, this is one case in which literal infringement does not involve taking the language of the claims literally. Literally, a claim requiring a "means for snapping the trap shut" would be satisfied by *any* means performing that function. The compromise embodied in § 112(f) is that patentees are allowed to express a claim element as a "means" (which otherwise might be considered indefinite), but literal infringement is restricted to equivalents of the corresponding structure shown in the specification.[160]

Equivalency under § 112(f) should not to be confused with equivalency under the doctrine of equivalents. The contexts are different because the latter is a specialized subset of the *literal* infringement inquiry.[161] The basis for comparison is also different. Section 112(f) requires comparison of the accused product to the structures disclosed in the *specification*, while the doctrine of equivalents requires comparison of the accused product to the *claims*. But the tests of equivalence are generally similar. Equivalency, in each case, "invokes the familiar concept of an insubstantial change which adds nothing of significance."[162] Whether structures were known to be interchangeable is an important consideration.[163] Although the accused device must perform the same function recited in the claim (not *substantially* the same function), the other elements of the familiar three-part test of equivalence (whether the claimed and the accused device perform in substantially the same way to achieve substantially the same result)

---

[160] *See* Warner-Jenkinson Co. v. Hilton Davis Chemical Co., 520 U.S. 17, 28 (1997) (equivalence under § 112(f) is "an application of the doctrine of equivalents in a restrictive role, narrowing the application of broad literal claim elements"); Al-Site Corp. v. VSI Int'l, Inc.,174 F.3d 1308, 1320 (Fed. Cir. 1999); Johnston v. IVAC Corp., 885 F.2d 1574, 1580 (Fed. Cir. 1989) (§ 112(f) "operates to *cut back* on the types of *means* which could literally satisfy the claim language" (emphasis in original)).

[161] *See* Valmont Indus., Inc. v. Reinke Mfg. Co., 983 F.2d 1039, 1043 (Fed. Cir. 1993) ("The doctrine of equivalents has a different purpose and application than section 112.").

[162] *Valmont*, 983 F.2d at 1043; *see also Welker*, 550 F.3d at 1099 (each is based on " 'similar analyses of insubstantiality of the differences' "); Chiuminatta Concrete Concepts, Inc. v. Cardinal Indus., Inc., 145 F.3d 1303, 1310 (Fed. Cir. 1998) (each "protect[s] the substance of a patentee's right to exclude by preventing mere colorable differences or slight improvements from escaping infringement").

[163] *Hearing Components*, 600 F.3d at 1370; *Minks*, 546 F.3d at 1379. Whether the structures are "structurally equivalent"—that is, physically similar—is less important than whether they operate in a similar way and achieve a similar result. *Minks*, 546 F.3d at 1379; *but cf. Fresenius*, 582 F.3d at 1299 ("a structural analysis is required when means-plus-function limitations are at issue; a functional analysis alone will not suffice").

may be employed in the means-plus-function analysis.[164] Equivalence under § 112(f), like equivalence under the doctrine of equivalents, is "not the prisoner of a formula" but depends on the circumstances of each case.[165]

In *Chiuminatta Concrete Concepts, Inc. v. Cardinal Indus., Inc.,*[166] the Federal Circuit distinguished between the rationales for the doctrine of equivalents and equivalency under § 112(f). The reason for the doctrine of equivalents, the court said, is that unforeseen technological advances may allow minor variations in what the applicant has literally described.[167] It would not be fair to an applicant whose claims required a "vacuum tube" to allow the substitution of its modern equivalent, the solid-state transistor.[168] In cases of newly developed technology, the court seemed willing to permit a broader range of equivalents than would be permitted under § 112(f).[169] If, on the other hand, the alleged equivalent is "technology that predates the invention itself" rather than a newly developed variation, a finding of nonequivalence under 112(f) should preclude a finding of equivalence under the doctrine of equivalents.[170]

The *Chiuminatta* opinion is not a model of clarity, and it seems to overstate the differences in rationale between the doctrine of equivalents and § 112(f). Arguably, each is a remedy for the inherent inability of language

---

[164] *See General Protecht,* 619 F.3d at 1312 (structure in the accused device must perform "the identical function 'in substantially the same way, with substantially the same result' "); *Minks,* 546 F.3d at 1378 (judging equivalence under 112(f) involves " 'a reduced version of the well-known tripartite test' "); IMS Technology, Inc. v. Haas Automation, Inc., 206 F.3d 1422, 1435 (Fed. Cir. 2000).

[165] *See IMS Technology,* 206 F.3d at 1436 ("the context of the invention should be considered when performing a [§ 112(f)] equivalence analysis just as it is in a doctrine of equivalents determination"); Intel Corp. v. U.S. Int'l Trade Comm'n, 946 F.2d 821, 842–43 (Fed. Cir. 1991) ("[A]ids for determining a structural equivalent to the structure disclosed in the patent specification are the same as those used in interpreting any other type of claim language, namely, the specification, the prosecution history, other claims in the patent, and expert testimony.").

[166] 145 F.3d 1303 (Fed. Cir. 1998).

[167] *See* Section 10.6.5.

[168] *See Chiuminatta,* 145 F.3d at 1310.

[169] *See id.* at 1310 ("Even if [a later-developed] element is found not to be a [§ 112(f)] equivalent because it is not equivalent to the structure disclosed in the patent, this analysis should not foreclose it from being an equivalent under the doctrine of equivalents.").

[170] *Id.* at 1311; *see also Welker,* 550 F.3d at 1099–100; Frank's Casing Crew & Rental Tools, Inc. v. Weatherford Int'l, Inc., 389 F.3d 1370, 1379 (Fed. Cir. 2004) (the difference between § 112(f) and the doctrine of equivalents is "a question of timing;" after-arising technology should be analyzed under the doctrine of equivalents, but existing technology under § 112(f) (into which the doctrine of equivalents analysis "collapses")).

to capture the essence of an invention, whether that inability is due to evolving technologies or to lack of foresight and suitable vocabulary.[171] Later interpretations of *Chiuminatta* suggest that an important difference is between equivalence of structure, where the issues of equivalence may merge, and equivalence of function, where only the doctrine of equivalents is relevant.[172] This line of cases, however, has produced one important distinction, which may explain how the results could differ when the tests of equivalence seem to be identical. Under the doctrine of equivalents, equivalence is judged as of the date of the alleged infringement.[173] Equivalence under § 112(f) is judged as of the date the patent issued because the literal meaning of a claim should be fixed at that time.[174] An alternative that a person skilled in the art might not have considered equivalent when the patent issued—perhaps because he or she had never heard of it—might be considered equivalent at a later date.

10.8 THE REVERSE DOCTRINE OF EQUIVALENTS

The doctrine of equivalents has a judicially devised counterpart known as the reverse doctrine of equivalents. The source of the reverse doctrine is the following language in *Graver Tank*:[175]

The wholesome realism of [the doctrine of equivalents] is not always applied in favor of a patentee but is sometimes used against him. Thus, where a device is so far changed in principle from a patented

---

[171] *See* Kraft Foods, Inc. v. International Trading Co., 203 F.3d 1362, 1372–73 (Fed. Cir. 2000) (except in the case of means-plus-function claims, where equivalent structures known at the time of the patent already literally infringe, infringement under the doctrine of equivalents is *not* limited to later-developed technologies).

[172] *See Interactive Pictures*, 274 F.3d at 1381–82; WMS Gaming, Inc. v. International Game Technology, 184 F.3d 1339, 1353 (Fed. Cir. 1999). The later cases, however, still preserve the possibility of a newly developed structure that is equivalent only under the doctrine of equivalents. *Interactive Pictures*, 274 F.3d at 1381; *Al-Site*, 174 F.3d at 1320 n.2 (because of the problem of unforeseeable technological change, "the doctrine of equivalents appropriately allows marginally broader coverage than [§ 112(f)]").

[173] *Warner-Jenkinson*, 520 U.S. at 37.

[174] *Al-Site*, 174 F.3d at 1320; *see also Welker*, 550 F.3d at 1099.

[175] Graver Tank & Mfg. Co. v. Linde Air Prods. Co., 339 U.S. 605, 608–09 (1950); *see also* Roche Palo Alto LLC v. Apotex, Inc., 531 F.3d 1372 (Fed. Cir. 2008) ("The reverse doctrine of equivalents is an equitable doctrine designed 'to prevent unwarranted extension of the claims beyond a fair scope of the patentee's invention.'"); Scripps Clinic & Research Found. v. Genentech, Inc., 927 F.2d 1565, 1581; SRI Int'l v. Matsushita Electric Corp., 775 F.2d 1107, 1123 (Fed. Cir. 1985) (en banc).

article that it performs the same or a similar function in a substantially different way, but nevertheless falls within the literal words of the claim, the doctrine of equivalents may be used to restrict the claim and defeat the patentee's action for infringement.

Thus, a product literally described by a claim can be held noninfringing if it is "so far changed in principle" that it functions in a "substantially different way" when compared to what the patentee actually invented.

The language in *Graver Tank* suggests that the doctrine of equivalents is a two-way street, but in practice the reverse doctrine has proven to be far less potent than its counterpart. Cases won on the reverse doctrine of equivalents are exceedingly rare.[176] In 2002 the Federal Circuit observed that it had never, in its 20-year history, affirmed a finding of noninfringement based on the reverse doctrine.[177] Before the legislative adoption of means-plus-function claims and their explicit limitations, the judicially created reverse doctrine of equivalents may have served to restrict the scope of overly broad claims. Today, the court found, the strictures of § 112–including the definiteness, description, and enablement requirements–left the reverse doctrine an "anachronistic exception . . . long mentioned but rarely applied."[178] Absent a problem of enablement or description, it would be difficult to persuade a court that an accused product literally described by a patent claim was still so "changed in principle" as to avoid infringement.

10.9 THE EXPERIMENTAL USE DEFENSE

A rarely invoked defense to a charge of infringement is that the challenged activity was done for purposes of experimentation rather than profit. This defense finds some support in a number of older cases in which a patented device was constructed not to sell it but to test its advantages. For example, in *Akro Agate Co. v. Master Marble Co.*,[179] the court held that the use of a patented machine to make glass marbles was not an infringement because the marbles had been made only as an experiment, the results were unsatisfactory, and the marbles themselves were not sold. In

---

[176] *See, e.g.*, Precision Metal Fabricators Inc. v. Jetstream Sys. Co., 6 U.S.P.Q.2d 1704 (N. D. Cal. 1988); Lesona Corp. v. United States, 530 F.2d 896, 905–6 (Ct. Cl. 1976).

[177] Tate Access Floors, Inc. v. Interface Architectural Resources, Inc., 279 F.3d 1357, 1368 (Fed. Cir. 2002); *see also Roche,* 531 F.3d at 1378.

[178] *Tate Access Floors,* 279 F.3d at 1368.

[179] 318 F. Supp. 305, 315, 333 (N.D.W. Va. 1937).

Kaz Mfg. Co. v. Chesebrough-Ponds, Inc.,[180] the defendant constructed a patented vaporizer solely for the purpose of a television commercial in which it compared the design unfavorably to its own (with the slogan "steam is dangerous"). The court did not view this as an infringement either.

The Federal Circuit has viewed the experimental use exception as an extremely narrow one, applicable only when the experiments were conducted "solely for amusement, to satisfy idle curiosity, or for strictly philosophical inquiry."[181] In other words, a kitchen experimenter seeking amusement on a rainy afternoon might practice a patent without infringing, but experiments conducted for commercial purposes are likely to violate a patent if they involve making or using the claimed invention.[182] Any use "in keeping with the legitimate business of the alleged infringer" fails to qualify for the limited exception,[183] including research undertaken by a university solely for purposes of education and discovery.[184]

In 35 U.S.C. § 271(e), Congress established a narrow experimental use exception to cover the testing of patented pharmaceuticals.[185] When a patent on a particular drug expires, rival manufacturers are, of course, permitted to market their own versions of the drug. But before this can happen, the new drug must undergo extensive government-required tests of safety and effectiveness. If manufacturing and using the drug for purposes of such

---

[180] 317 F.2d 679 (2d Cir. 1963).

[181] Madey v. Duke University, 307 F.3d 1351, 1362 (Fed. Cir. 2002); Embrex, Inc. v. Service Eng'g Corp., 216 F.3d 1343, 1349 (Fed. Cir. 2000).

[182] *See* Douglas v. United States, 181 U.S.P.Q. 170, 176–77 (Ct. Cl. 1974). In the former instance, the infringement is seemingly excused on the legal principle of "de minimis non curat lex," or "the law does not concern itself with trifles." *But see Embrex,* 216 F.3d at 1352–53 (Rader, J., concurring) (arguing that patent law does not permit *de minimis* infringement; "the statute leaves no leeway to excuse infringement because the infringer only infringed a little").

[183] *Madey,* 307 F.3 at 1362.

[184] *Id.* at 1362 ("[M]ajor research universities . . . often sanction and fund research projects with arguably no commercial application whatsoever. However, these projects unmistakably further the institution's legitimate business objectives, including educating and enlightening students and faculty participating in these projects. These projects also serve . . . to increase the status of the institution and lure lucrative research grants, students and faculty.").

[185] *See* Merck KGaA v. Integra Life Sciences I, Ltd., 545 U.S. 193, 202 (2005) (the statute "provides a wide berth for the use of patented drugs in activities related to the federal regulatory process"). Although the statute is not clear on this point, it has been held to cover both drugs and medical devices that must undergo government-required tests. Eli Lilly & Co. v. Medtronic, Inc., 496 U.S. 661 (1990).

tests were held to be an infringement, the tests could not *begin* until after the patent had expired. Consequently, there would be a considerable delay between the expiration of the patent and the opportunity to market a competitive drug. The patent owner would have, in effect, a patent of longer duration than the patent laws intend. Section 271(e) prevents this by allowing these tests to occur prior to the expiration of the patent without fear of liability.

10.10 THE PRIOR COMMERCIAL USE DEFENSE

The America Invents Act introduced a complex prior commercial use defense that applies to any patent issued after September 16, 2011. Under § 273 of the Patent Act, it is not an infringement to use, in a manufacturing or other commercial process, a patented method, machine, or composition of matter under the following conditions: (1) the party using it now used it before in good faith, and (2) such use began at least one year before the earlier of the effective filing date of the patent or the public disclosure of the invention by the patentee.[186] The prior use must have occurred in the United States.[187] It might be an internal use (e.g., a waste disposal method used inside a factory) or a use that led to the commercial transfer of the end result (e.g., a use of a patented machine to manufacture articles for sale).[188] Use in a nonprofit laboratory for the benefit of the public also counts.[189]

The defense is subject to significant limitations. The right to use the patented invention cannot be licensed or transferred to anyone else unless as a part of an entire line of business.[190] If the use has been transferred, it cannot be extended to additional sites.[191] A party that abandoned use of the patented invention cannot rely on uses that predate that abandonment.[192] The defense does not apply with respect to uses derived from the patentee's own efforts.[193] If an accused infringer unreasonably (and

---

[186] 35 U.S.C. § 273(a). The conditions of public disclosure are those set forth in the version of § 102(b) adopted under the America Invents Act. *See* Section 8.9.2.

[187] 35 U.S.C. § 273(a)(1).

[188] *Id.*

[189] 35 U.S.C. § 273(c)(2). Activities related to premarketing regulatory review may also suffice. 35 U.S.C. § 273(c)(1).

[190] 35 U.S.C. § 273(e)(1)(B).

[191] 35 U.S.C. § 273(e)(1)(C).

[192] 35 U.S.C. § 273(e)(4).

[193] 35 U.S.C. § 273(e)(2).

unsuccessfully) asserts the prior use defense, the case is an "exceptional" one in which the victor can recover its attorneys' fees.[194]

The prior commercial use defense, to some extent, takes the place of § 102(g) of the Patent Act, which prior to the revisions of the America Invents Act counted as prior art to a claimed invention an earlier use that, while it may not have been made public, was not abandoned, suppressed, or concealed.[195] Under the new regime, although the company that first discovered an invention may not be entitled to patent it, and it may not succeed in invalidating the patent received by someone else, it may be permitted to continue what it had been doing all along. Whether this defense will be often used remains to be seen.

---

[194] 35 U.S.C. § 273(f).
[195] *See* Section 8.9.1.3.

CHAPTER 11

Patent Litigation

A patent owner whose rights have been infringed can file a lawsuit in a federal district court.[1] If the suit is successful, the court can compel the infringer to stop the infringing activity and pay the patent owner for infringement that has already occurred. Litigation, or the threat of litigation, is what gives a patent its "teeth."

The suit may be brought by the original recipient of the patent, or its successor if rights to the patent have been transferred by assignment.[2] Either may be referred to as the "patentee." If the owner of the patent transfers "all substantial rights," the new owner may sue in its name alone.[3] A licensee who possesses an exclusive license[4] but not "all substantial rights" may sue for infringement, but he or she must join the patent owner in the suit in order to guard against the possibility of multiple judgments against

---

[1] The patent owner cannot sue in a state court because the federal courts have exclusive jurisdiction. *See* 28 U.S.C. § 1338(a). If the defendant imports infringing goods, the patent owner may initiate proceedings in the International Trade Commission in lieu of, or in addition to, a suit in a district court. *See* Section 11.9. Suits against the United States government must be brought in the Court of Claims. *See* 28 U.S.C. § 1498.

[2] *See* 35 U.S.C. §§ 281 (patentee's right to sue for infringement), 100(d) ("patentee" includes successors in title); Asymmetrx, Inc. v. Biocare Medical, LLC, 582 F.3d 1314, 1318 (Fed. Cir. 2009); Morrow v. Microsoft Corp., 499 F.3d 1332, 1339 (Fed. Cir. 2007).

[3] Alfred E. Mann Foundation for Scientific Research v. Cochlear Corp., 604 F.3d 1354, 1358–59 (Fed. Cir. 2010); *Morrow*, 499 F.3d at 1340.

[4] *See* Section 6.3.

the same infringer.[5] A licensee who does *not* have an exclusive license lacks the kind of injury necessary for "standing" to sue.[6] A nonexclusive licensee cannot expect to be the only party making, using, or selling the patented invention. On the other hand, the licensee may be disadvantaged in competition if it is paying for the right to practice the patented invention and the infringer is not, so the licensee may wish to persuade the patent owner to bring suit–something the owner should be willing to consider in order to preserve the value of a license.

A typical lawsuit concerns three issues:

1. Is the patent valid and enforceable?
2. Are the claims infringed?
3. If the claims are infringed, what relief should be awarded?

The patentee can prevail only if the patent is valid *and* infringed. On occasion, the defendant[7] will concede that the patent is valid and challenge only the charge of infringement, or it will concede infringement and argue invalidity, but it is more common for the defendant to make war on both fronts. Patent litigation may also involve related claims (e.g., breach of contract, unfair competition, or antitrust claims) if they arise from the same factual situation.

Infringement litigation is often a complicated, time-consuming, and costly process. Patent cases typically involve both subtle issues of law and complex questions of technology. In order to try such a case, both parties have to acquire a thorough understanding of, at a minimum, the patent and its file history, the accused products, and any prior art that might be used to challenge the validity of the patent. As a result, just the discovery phase of the litigation, in which both parties gather the evidence needed to try the case, often takes more than a year. It is not unusual for an infringement suit to take several years from the day it is filed until the final disposition of the case, and worse examples can be found.[8]

Patent cases are difficult for courts and juries, both because the law is unfamiliar and because an understanding of complex technology may be critical. Imagine how difficult it would be for an average juror to determine

---

[5] *Alfred E. Mann*, 604 F.3d at 1359; *Morrow*, 499 F.3d at 1340.

[6] *Id.*

[7] It is convenient to use the term "defendant" interchangeably with "accused infringer," but in a declaratory judgment action (*see* Section 11.2) the accused infringer may technically be the plaintiff.

[8] For example, in March 1999 the Supreme Court denied the last appeal in *United States v. Hughes Aircraft Co.*, a case filed in 1973. *See* 525 U.S. 1177 (1999).

whether one complex procedure in genetic engineering is "equivalent" to another. Simply mastering the vocabulary can be a daunting task. These difficulties contribute to a certain level of unpredictability in the outcome of patent litigation.

11.1 JURISDICTION AND VENUE

The geographical location where a suit for patent infringement must be filed (for example, in the Northern District of California or in the Eastern District of New York) depends on the rules of "in personam jurisdiction" and "venue." A federal court has in personam jurisdiction (or jurisdiction over the person) only if the individual or corporate defendant has had certain "minimum contacts" with the district in which that court resides.[9] If an accused infringer has had no contact whatsoever with, for example, the state of Florida, then suit cannot be filed there. The minimum-contacts doctrine has constitutional origins in the due process clause. The rules are subtle and depend in part on the jurisdictional rules of the state where the court is located.[10] If the accused infringer has an office in the district, regularly transacts business in the district, or conducts infringing activity in the district, the minimum contacts test will likely be satisfied.[11] It may even be

---

[9] *See* International Shoe Co. v. State of Washington, 326 U.S. 310, 316 (1945) (defendant must have "certain minimum contacts with [the forum] such that the maintenance of the suit does not offend 'traditional notions of fair play and substantial justice' "). The defendant's contacts with the forum must be such that "he should reasonably anticipate being haled into court there." *See* World-Wide Volkswagen Corp. v. Woodson, 444 U.S. 286, 297 (1980); LSI Indus. Inc. v. Hubbell Lighting, Inc., 232 F.3d 1369, 1375 (Fed. Cir. 2000). The emphasis is on deliberate or "purposeful" contacts rather than those that may occur by accident. *See* Beverly Hills Fan Co. v. Royal Sovereign Corp., 21 F.3d 1558, 1565 (Fed. Cir. 1994).

[10] *See* Trintec Indus., Inc. v. Pedre Promotional Prods., Inc. 395 F.3d 1275, 1279–80 (Fed. Cir. 2005) (discussing the state "long-arm statute").

[11] If the accused infringer's contacts with the forum are "continuous and systematic," the court may have "general jurisdiction" concerning *any* matter involving the accused infringer. *See* Campbell Pet Co. v. Miale, 542 F.3d 879, 883 (Fed. Cir. 2008); *Trintec,* 395 F.3d at 1279; Deprenyl Animal Health, Inc. v. University of Toronto Innovations Found., 297 F.3d 1343, 1350 (Fed. Cir. 2002). If the contacts are more sporadic but relate specifically to the subject matter of the suit, the court may exercise "specific jurisdiction" so long as that is consistent with "fair play and substantial justice." *See* Trintec, 395 F.3d at 1279; *Deprenyl,* 297 F.3d at 1350–51. A thorny issue is whether a corporate Internet website accessible in the region is sufficient to establish jurisdiction. The answer may depend on whether the site is a passive one only available to be read or an interactive one that permits business transactions. *See* Trintec, 395 F.3d at 1281.

sufficient that the infringer intended the accused products to enter the district via the "stream of commerce."[12]

If a court has jurisdiction over the defendant, the next question is one of venue. The rules of venue create further restrictions on where suit can be filed. In a patent case, venue is appropriate in the following districts:

- Where the defendant "resides," *or*
- Where the defendant has committed acts of infringement *and* has a regular and established place of business.[13]

In 1988, the federal venue statutes were altered so that corporate defendants are held to reside in any district where the corporation is subject to in personam jurisdiction—in other words, wherever it has established "minimum contacts."[14] Most patent cases are filed against corporations rather than against individuals or partnerships, so the minimum-contacts standard is generally the test of whether a suit can or cannot be filed in a particular judicial district.

Because a corporate defendant typically has minimum contacts with several states—possibly with all 50—patent owners may have a number of choices in deciding where to file suit. The choice is likely to be governed by factors such as geographical convenience, the experience of the court in dealing with patent litigation, whether the court's docket permits a speedy trial, and any perceived "home field" advantages. Within the limits set by the rules of jurisdiction and venue, the location of the lawsuit is generally within the control of the plaintiff. If, however, the defendant can show that another district would be more suitable (for the "convenience of parties and witnesses" and "in the interest of justice"[15]), the court in which the suit was filed has the power to transfer the case to another district if it is a district in which the suit could have been filed in the first instance.

---

[12] *See* Viam Corp. v. Iowa Export-Import Trading Co., 84 F.3d 424, 427–28 (Fed. Cir. 1996); *Beverly Hills Fan,* 21 F.3d at 1565 ("The allegations are that defendants purposefully shipped the accused fan into Virginia through an established distribution channel. The cause of action for patent infringement is alleged to arise out of those activities. No more is usually required to establish specific jurisdiction.").

[13] 28 U.S.C. § 1400(b).

[14] *See* 28 U.S.C. § 1391(c); *Trintec,* 395 F.3d at 1280 ("Venue in a patent action against a corporate defendant exists wherever there is personal jurisdiction."); VE Holding Corp. v. Johnson Gas Appliance Co., 917 F.2d 1574 (Fed. Cir. 1990).

[15] 28 U.S.C § 1404(a).

11.2 DECLARATORY JUDGMENT

Patent cases generally arise when a patent owner files suit against a party it accuses of infringement. However, it is also possible for the accused infringer to launch a preemptive strike by filing suit against a patentee. A suit of this kind is called an action for "declaratory judgment" because it asks the court to declare that the party filing suit is *not* liable to the patent owner, either because the patent is invalid, the patent is not infringed, or for some other reason.[16] The potential infringer, in such a case, is nominally the plaintiff and the patent owner is the defendant.[17]

If it were not for declaratory judgment actions, parties accused of infringement would have to wait until the patent owner chose to litigate before the dispute could be resolved. In the meantime, the accused infringer would have to give in to the patent owner's demands or proceed as before with the risk that investments would be lost, and accumulated damages assessed, when the patent owner finally did sue.[18] A suit for declaratory judgment allows the potential infringer to bring matters to a head. It also gives the accused infringer more control over the forum in which the case will be heard.

Federal courts generally follow a "first to file" rule in deciding where a case will be tried.[19] Suppose that a patent owner in California accused a company in Illinois of infringement. For the sake of convenience, and possibly in the hope of sympathy from a local jury, the patent owner would likely prefer that any litigation take place in California, while the accused infringer, for the same reasons, would prefer Illinois. If the accused infringer sues for declaratory judgment in Illinois before the patent owner sues in California, the first-to-file rule generally means that the case will be heard in Illinois. The first-to-file rule is not absolute, however. An exception can be made if the interests of justice or expediency require.[20]

---

[16] *See* 22 U.S.C. § 2201 (Declaratory Judgment Act).

[17] Even if the patent owner initiates the lawsuit, the accused infringer may choose to file a *counterclaim* for declaratory judgment.

[18] *See* Cardinal Chemical Co. v. Morton Int'l, Inc., 508 U.S. 83, 95 (1993) (discussing the Declaratory Judgment Act as a cure for the "scarecrow patent").

[19] *See* Electronics for Imaging, Inc. v. Coyle, 394 F.3d 1341, 1347 (Fed. Cir. 2005); Genentech, Inc. v. Eli Lilly & Co., 998 F.2d 931, 937 (Fed. Cir. 1993).

[20] *See Electronics for Imaging,* 394 F.3d at 1347–48; Serco Services Co. v. Kelley Co., 51 F.3d 1037, 1039 (Fed. Cir. 1995); *Genentech,* 998 F.2d at 937.

A federal court can only try a case if there is a genuine dispute–a "case or controversy" in constitutional terms.[21] A potential infringer cannot file an action for declaratory judgment simply because there is a hypothetical possibility that a patent owner will allege infringement.[22] The threat must be definite and concrete.[23] The Federal Circuit long applied strict standards of immediacy, including a reasonable apprehension of imminent litigation by the patentee.[24] In 2007, the Supreme Court criticized that test,[25] saying instead the dispute must be "real and substantial" and one that admits of concrete relief rather than an advisory opinion.[26] The patent owner's pattern of suing similar businesses, together with public statements that it will pursue an aggressive litigation strategy, may give a potential defendant grounds to file for declaratory judgment.[27]

A licensee who is paying royalties is in no danger of being sued by the patentee but might want to challenge the validity of the patent or its application to the licensed product. The Supreme Court has held that a licensee

---

[21] *See* 3M Co. v. Avery Dennison Corp., 673 F.3d 1372, 1376 (Fed. Cir. 2012); Streck, Inc. v. Research & Diagnostic Sys., Inc., 665 F.3d 1269, 1281–82 (Fed. Cir. 2012); Cat Tech LLC v. Tubemaster, Inc., 582 F.3d 871, 879 (Fed. Cir. 2008) ("Because of this case or controversy requirement, a court may not adjudicate 'a difference or dispute of a hypothetical or abstract character' or 'one that is academic or moot.' "); Micron Technology, Inc. v. Mosaid Technologies, Inc., 518 F.3d 897, 901 (Fed. Cir. 2008).

[22] *See* Vanguard Research, Inc. v. Peat, Inc., 304 F.3d 1249, 1254–55 (Fed. Cir. 2002) ("To invoke the court's declaratory judgment jurisdiction, a plaintiff must show 'more than the nervous state of mind of a possible infringer,' but does not have to show that the patentee is 'poised on the courthouse steps.' ").

[23] *3M*, 673 F.3d at 1376; *Streck*, 665 F.3d at 1282.

[24] *See* Phillips Plastics Corp. v. Kato Hatsujou K.K., 57 F.3d 1051, 1052–54 (Fed. Cir. 1995) (ongoing license negotiations did not create a reasonable apprehension of litigation).

[25] MedImmune, Inc. v. Genentech, Inc., 549 U.S. 118, 132 n.11 (2007).

[26] *Id.* at 127; *see also 3M*, 673 F.3d at 1376; *Streck*, 665 F.3d at 1282; *Micron*, 518 F.3d at 901. Whether the potential infringer experienced a "reasonable apprehension of suit" may still be relevant, though it is not dispositive. *Streck*, 665 F.3d at 1282.

[27] *See Micron*, 518 F.3d at 901. The Federal Circuit requires some "affirmative act by the patentee relating to the enforcement of his patent rights." *3M*, 673 F.3d at 1377. A communication from the patent owner simply calling attention to the patent and referring to the recipient's product line has not been found sufficient. *Id.* at 1379. However, in *3M*, the patent owner (allegedly) identified a specific 3M product, said that it "may infringe," announced that "licenses are available," and promised to send claim charts matching up the patent to the identified product. Those facts were enough, if proven, to establish a genuine controversy. *Id.* It was important that the communications had been initiated by the patentee, not by 3M. *See id.* at 1379–80. If the declaratory judgment plaintiff does not currently have a product that might run afoul of the patent, it may have to show at least "meaningful preparation to conduct potentially infringing activity" in order to establish an immediate controversy. *See Cat Tech*, 528 F.3d at 880 ("meaningful preparation . . . remains an important element").

in that position need not breach the license agreement simply to create the dispute necessary to seek declaratory judgment—a risky step if the challenge proved unsuccessful.[28]

11.3 BURDEN OF PROOF

The patent owner has the burden of proving infringement by a "preponderance of the evidence."[29] In other words, based on the evidence presented, it must be more likely than not that the patent is infringed. If the evidence on both sides is equally persuasive, the claim must fail.

If the accused infringer raises a defense of invalidity or unenforceability, the defendant bears the burden of proof with respect to that defense.[30] Moreover, the burden is one of "clear and convincing" evidence, a higher standard of proof than a mere preponderance of the evidence.[31] The evidence not only must favor the accused infringer's version of the facts, it must be sufficient to produce an "abiding conviction" that the facts are "highly probable."[32] The reason for this higher standard of proof is the presumption of validity discussed in Section 8.2.

11.4 THE ROLE OF JUDGE AND JURY

Litigants in a patent case are entitled to trial by jury.[33] This right can be waived, by consent of both parties, in favor of a bench trial in which the

---

[28] *See MedImmune*, 549 U.S at 134 (characterizing the strategy of breaching the license agreement first and risking treble damages as "bet[ting] the farm").

[29] Creative Compounds, LLC v. Starmark Labs., 651 F.3d 1303, 1314 (Fed. Cir 2011); Siemens Medical Solutions USA, Inc. v. Saint-Gobain Ceramics & Plastics, Inc., 637 F.3d 1269, 1279 (Fed. Cir. 2011); Warner-Lambert Co. v. Teva Pharmaceuticals USA, Inc., 418 F.3d 1326, 1342 (Fed. Cir. 2005).

[30] 35 U.S.C. § 282; Microsoft Corp. v. i4i L.P., 131 S.Ct. 2238, 2243 (2011); PowerOasis, Inc. v. T-Mobile USA, Inc., 522 F.3d 1299, 1303 (Fed. Cir. 2008); Adenta GmbH v. OrthoArm, Inc., 501 F.3d 1364, 1371 (Fed. Cir. 2007); Pfizer, Inc. v. Apotex, Inc., 480 F.3d 1348, 1359 (Fed. Cir. 2007).

[31] *Microsoft*, 131 S.Ct. at 2245–46; Tokai Corp. v. Easton Enterprises, Inc., 632 F.3d 1358, 1367 (Fed. Cir. 2011); Uniloc USA Inc. v. Microsoft Corp., 632 F.3d 1292, 1321 (Fed. Cir. 2011); *Pfizer*, 480 F.3d at 1359.

[32] Proctor & Gamble Co. v. Teva Pharmaceuticals USA, Inc., 566 F.3d 989, 994 (Fed. Cir. 2009); *Pfizer*, 480 F.3d at 1359 n.5; Am-Pro Protective Agency, Inc. v. United States, 281 F.3d 1234, 1239–40 (Fed. Cir. 2002) (also referring to the standard as one of "well-nigh irrefragable" proof).

[33] *See* Markman v. Westview Instruments, Inc., 517 U.S. 370, 377 (1996) ("there is no dispute that infringement cases today must be tried to a jury, as their predecessors were more than two centuries ago").

judge decides all issues.[34] Even if the trial does involve a jury, the judge will still decide certain questions. Generally speaking, a judge decides "questions of law," whereas the jury decides "questions of fact."[35] In reality, most questions have a factual aspect and a legal aspect. For example, to decide if an accused product is equivalent to a claimed invention, one has to address questions of fact (how does the accused product differ from the claimed invention?) and questions of law (how much can the accused product differ from the claimed invention before the law no longer considers them equivalent?).

Because there is no practical way to separate every nuance of fact and law, certain issues have, somewhat arbitrarily, been deemed questions of law for the judge, and others questions of fact for the jury.[36] Anticipation is a question of fact,[37] but obviousness is a question of law.[38] Compliance with the definiteness and enablement requirements are questions of law.[39] Compliance with the written description and utility requirements are questions of fact.[40] Claim interpretation is a question of law[41] while infringement is a question of fact.[42] Some questions of law, such as obviousness, depend in part on underlying issues of fact that can be submitted to the jury.[43]

---

[34] *See* Rule 38 of the Federal Rules of Civil Procedure.

[35] *See* Jurgens v. McKasy, 927 F.2d 1552, 1557 (Fed. Cir. 1991) ("In a jury trial, there are two decisionmakers, the judge and the jury. In general, the judge decides issues of law and issues committed to his discretion, and the jury decides issues of fact that are material to the case and in genuine dispute.").

[36] Frequent disagreements among the Federal Circuit judges as to whether something is a question of law or a question of fact illustrate how arbitrary the distinctions can be. *See, e.g.,* Markman v. Westview Instruments, Inc, 52 F.3d 967 (Fed. Cir. 1995) (en banc panel split on whether claim interpretation is an issue of law decided by the judge alone); Lough v. Brunswick Corp., 103 F.3d 1517 (Fed. Cir. 1997) (panel split on whether experimental use in the context of prior public use is a question of fact or law).

[37] Bard Peripheral Vascular, Inc. v. W.L. Gore & Assoc., Inc., 670 F.3d 1171, 1184 (Fed. Cir. 2012).

[38] Aventis Pharma S.A. v. Hospira, Inc., 675 F.3d 1324, 1332 (Fed. Cir. 2012).

[39] IGT v. Bally Gaming Int'l, Inc., 659 F.3d 1109, 1119 (Fed. Cir. 2011) (definiteness); Transocean Offshore Deepwater Drilling, Inc. v. Maersk Contractors. USA, Inc., 617 F.3d 1296, 1305 (Fed. Cir. 2010) (enablement).

[40] Streck, Inc. v. Research & Diagnostic Sys., 665 F.3d 1269, 1285 (Fed. Cir. 2012) (written description); *In re* Swartz, 232 F.3d 862, 863 (Fed. Cir. 2000) (utility).

[41] *Markman,* 517 U.S. at 372.

[42] Byrne v. Wood, Herron & Evans, LLP, 676 F.3d 1024, 1034 (Fed. Cir. 2012).

[43] *See* Mycogen Plant Science, Inc. v. Monsanto Co., 243 F.3d 1316, 1331 (Fed. Cir. 2001) (questions of law with underlying issues of fact can be submitted to the jury accompanied by appropriate instructions on the law).

The judge also rules on "equitable" claims and defenses. In the eighteenth century, there were two varieties of court—courts of law and courts of equity—and they differed in the kinds of claims that could be heard and the remedies that could be granted. Only courts of law provided a right to a jury trial. In the United States, courts of law and equity were merged long ago, so the distinction would be little more than an historical curiosity if not for the language of the Seventh Amendment of the Constitution. In lieu of setting forth the right to a jury trial in explicit terms, the Seventh Amendment provides that "the right of trial by jury shall be preserved" as it was under English common law. To this day courts are required to examine claims from an historical perspective and try to determine whether, applying eighteenth-century standards, the claim is "legal" or "equitable." If the latter, there is no right to a jury.[44]

For purposes of patent litigation, it is enough to know that a claim seeking *money damages* is a legal claim with a right to a jury trial, but a claim to an *injunction* is an equitable claim. In the rare instance that a patentee chooses to forgo damages and sue only for an injunction, neither party has a right to a jury trial.[45] Certain defenses are also equitable in nature and reserved to the judge to decide. These include inequitable conduct,[46] laches, and estoppel[47] (discussed in Sections 9.1, 11.8.3.3 and 11.8.3.4, respectively). The Federal Circuit has held that infringement under the doctrine of equivalents (discussed in Section 10.6), sometimes referred to as the "*equitable* doctrine of equivalents," is in fact a matter for decision by a jury.[48]

In spite of the latter development, there may be a trend toward assigning more decision-making responsibility to judges and less to juries. At least certain disapproving Federal Circuit judges perceive such a trend.[49] This shift, if there is one, may reflect a feeling that juries are overmatched by the complex and difficult issues often presented in patent cases.

---

[44] *See* Tegal Corp. v. Tokyo Electron America, Inc., 257 F.3d 1331, 1339 (Fed. Cir. 2001).

[45] *See id.* at 1341.

[46] Kingsdown Medical Consultants, Ltd. v. Hollister, Inc., 863 F.2d 867, 876 (Fed. Cir. 1988) ("the ultimate question of whether inequitable conduct occurred is equitable in nature").

[47] A.C. Aukerman Co. v. R.L. Chaides Construction Co., 960 F.2d 1020, 1028 (Fed. Cir. 1992) (en banc).

[48] Miken Composites, L.L.C. v. Wilson Sporting Goods Co., 515 F.3d 1331, 1336 (Fed. Cir. 2008).

[49] See *Lough*, 103 F.3d at 1519 (Newman, J., dissenting) ("In converting the factual question of experimental purpose into a matter of law, our court has cut another notch in the removal of patent issues from the trier of fact.").

11.5 BIFURCATION

Patent cases are often tried in phases rather than all at once. A trial divided into two phases is "bifurcated"; division into three or more phases is also possible. The purpose of holding trial in stages is to focus the issues, avoid confusion, and save unnecessary effort.

One common practice is to hold separate trials on liability and damages. If the court does not find the accused infringer liable, there is no need to proceed with the damages phase. Another option is to hold a preliminary bench trial on those issues that do not require fact finding by the jury. For example, if a patent has been challenged on grounds of inequitable conduct (an equitable defense reserved to the judge), that part of the case can be tried before any jury has been selected.

When the Supreme Court held in *Markman v. Westview Instruments*[50] that claim interpretation is a matter within the province of the judge rather than the jury, questions arose as to how and when judges should decide questions of claim interpretation and how judges should communicate their findings to the jury. Many courts have responded by scheduling a "*Markman* hearing" before the jury trial. During the hearing, the court may receive evidence and argument from all parties regarding their proposed claim interpretations. The judge's findings are then incorporated into the jury instructions so that the jury can determine whether or not the claims have been infringed.[51]

11.6 PRELIMINARY INJUNCTIONS

Patent litigation often begins with a motion for a preliminary injunction.[52] A preliminary injunction is a court order preventing the accused infringer from making, using, selling, offering to sell, or importing the accused product until the case has been decided. In effect, it forces the accused infringer to put its activities on hold. On occasion, the Federal Circuit has characterized a preliminary injunction as "a drastic and extraordinary remedy that is not to be routinely granted."[53]

---

[50] 517 U.S. 370, 372 (1996).

[51] *See* Sulzer Textile A.G. v. Picanol, N.V., 358 F.3d 1356, 1366 (Fed. Cir. 2004) ("[I]t is the duty of trial courts ... to inform jurors both of the court's claim construction rulings on all disputed claim terms and of the jury's obligation to adopt and apply the court's determined meanings of disputed claim terms to the jury's deliberation of the facts.").

[52] *See* 35 U.S.C. § 283.

[53] *See, e.g.*, National Steel Car, Ltd. v. Canadian Pacific Railway, Ltd., 357 F.3d 1319, 1324 (Fed. Cir. 2004).

The judge decides whether to grant the motion for a preliminary injunction by weighing the following factors:[54]

- The likelihood that the patent owner will ultimately prevail in the litigation–in other words, the likelihood that one or more patent claims will be held valid, enforceable, and infringed.[55] This requires the judge to make a preliminary assessment of the evidence, including any defenses that may be raised by the accused infringer.
- Whether the patent owner would suffer "irreparable harm" if the injunction were denied. Irreparable harm is harm that cannot be cured by the eventual payment of money damages. If the only harm to the patentee is a temporary loss of royalty income pending trial, this loss is one that probably can be made up, with interest, when damages are received. However, the harm might be irreparable if the accused infringer would not have the funds to pay damages after trial or if sales of infringing articles would create some form of intangible harm. For example, if the patent owner itself sold an article within the scope of the patent, the infringer's sales of a competing product pending trial might injure the patent owner's reputation and market share in ways that would be difficult to translate into a payment of money.[56] Note that if the patent owner fails to seek a preliminary injunction at the first opportunity, it may be difficult to convince the court that there is a threat of immediate harm.[57]
- The balance of hardships if the motion is granted or denied. In other words, would the harm to the patent owner if the injunction were denied outweigh the harm to the accused infringer if the injunction were granted? The harm to the accused infringer is often more tangible and immediate. If the accused product accounts for a substantial portion of the accused infringer's business, the loss of that business pending trial could result in diminished profits, employee layoffs, or even bankruptcy. A court is unlikely to grant an injunction with such severe consequences unless it is very clear that the patent owner will prevail on the merits.

---

[54] *See* Winter v. Natural Resources Defense Council, Inc. 555 U.S. 7, 20 (2008) (general standards for preliminary injunctions); Celcis In Vitro, Inc. v. CellzDirect, Inc., 664 F.3d 922, 926 (Fed. Cir. 2012); AstraZeneca LP v. Apotex, Inc., 633 F.3d 1042, 1049 (Fed. Cir. 2010); Erico Int'l Corp. v. Vutec Corp., 516 F.3d 1350, 1353–54 (Fed. Cir. 2008).

[55] *See AstraZeneca,* 633 F.3d at 1050.

[56] *See id.* at 1062–63 (introduction and subsequent withdrawal of defendant's generic pharmaceutical might cause confusion and injury to patentee's good will).

[57] *See, e.g.,* High Tech Medical Instrumentation, Inc. v. New Image Indus., Inc., 49 F.3d 1551, 1557 (Fed. Cir. 1995) ("Absent a good explanation, not offered or found here, 17 months is a substantial period of delay that militates against the issuance of a preliminary injunction by demonstrating that there is no apparent urgency to the request for injunctive relief.").

• The public interest. A court may hesitate to grant an injunction that would deny the public an important product–for example, a drug or medical device–even temporarily.[58] On the other hand, the enforcement of valid patents ultimately benefits the public by encouraging innovation.[59]

A court must weigh each of these factors and determine whether a preliminary injunction is appropriate. The stronger the patent owner's case, the lesser the showing of irreparable harm necessary to justify an injunction.[60]

11.7 SUMMARY JUDGMENT

Sometimes the merits of a case are so clear that it is unnecessary to conduct a full-blown jury trial. The mechanism for cutting short such a case is known as "summary judgment." The judge grants summary judgment when there is no "genuine issue of material fact" for decision by a jury.[61] In other words, the evidence is so one-sided that the outcome of the case cannot reasonably be disputed, and a competent jury could reach only one decision.[62] Either party to a patent infringement suit may bring a motion for summary judgment, supported by evidence in its favor (usually in the form of documents and sworn testimony) or pointing out the absence of evidence supporting claims on which the other party bears the burden of proof.[63] The opposing party naturally submits its own evidence in an attempt to convince the judge that there is, at least, a "genuine issue of material fact" to be decided.

---

[58] *See* Hybritech Inc. v. Abbott Labs., 849 F.2d 1466, 1458 (Fed. Cir. 1988).

[59] *See Celsis,* 664 F.3d at 931–32.

[60] *See* New England Braiding Co. v. A.W. Chesterton Co., 970 F.2d 878, 883 n.5 (Fed. Cir. 1992).

[61] Rule 56(c) of the Federal Rules of Civil Procedure states that summary judgment "shall be rendered forthwith if the pleadings, depositions, answers to interrogatories, and admissions on file, together with the affidavits, if any, show that there is no genuine issue as to any material fact and that the moving party is entitled to a judgment as a matter of law." A dispute as to an immaterial fact–one that need not be decided to render a decision–does not preclude summary judgment. "A disputed fact is material to the outcome of the suit if a finding of that fact is necessary and relevant to the proceeding." Madey v. Duke University, 307 F.3d 1351, 1358 (Fed. Cir. 2002).

[62] *See id.* at 1358 ("Issues of fact are genuine only 'if the evidence is such that a reasonable jury could return a verdict for the nonmoving party.' ").

[63] *See* Celotex Corp. v. Catrett, 477 U.S. 317, 325 (1986); Exigent Technology, Inc. v. Atrana Solutions, Inc., 442 F.3d 1301, 1308–09 (Fed. Cir. 2006); Golan v. Pingel Enterprise, Inc., 310 F.3d 1360, 1367–68 (Fed. Cir. 2002). The party opposing the motion "must show more than a mere metaphysical doubt regarding the material facts" and must produce more than "a mere scintilla of evidence." *Golan,* 310 F.3d at 1368.

An entire matter may be decided by summary judgment, or the judge may determine that individual questions raise no genuine issue of fact even if they do not resolve the entire case.[64] For example, a court might grant summary judgment (or "summary adjudication") finding that a particular invention predates the patentee's invention while leaving to the jury the genuinely disputed question of whether the prior invention anticipates the claims at issue. Sometimes courts grant summary judgment that a patent is infringed,[65] but usually the accused infringer can at least raise a "genuine issue of fact" regarding alleged differences between the accused product and the claimed invention. More frequently a court holds a patent *not* infringed on summary judgment.[66] Sometimes courts grant summary judgment that patents are invalid or unenforceable.[67] Because liability can be found only if a patent is valid, enforceable, *and* infringed, a negative judgment on one of these issues can dispose of the entire case.

11.8 REMEDIES

When a court determines that a patent is both valid and infringed, it must decide what remedies to grant the patentee. Permanent injunctions against further infringement were once granted to victorious patent owners almost automatically.[68] But in *eBay Inc. v. MercExchange, L.L.C.,*[69] the Supreme Court held that courts should not enter injunctions routinely simply because infringement has been proven. Instead, the plaintiff must

---

[64] *See* Rule 56(d) of the Federal Rules of Civil Procedure.

[65] *See, e.g.,* IGT v. Bally Gaming Int'l, Inc., 659 F.3d 1109, 1121 (Fed. Cir. 2011); Solvay S.A. v. Honeywell Int'l, Inc., 622 F.3d 1367, 1386 (Fed. Cir. 2010); Monsanto Co. v. Scruggs, 459 F.3d 1328, 1332 (Fed. Cir. 2006); Amgen Inc. v. Hoechst Marion Roussel, Inc., 314 F.3d 1313, 1351 (Fed. Cir. 2003).

[66] *See, e.g.,* American Calcar, Inc. v. American Honda Motor Co., 651 F.3d 1318, 1337 (Fed. Cir. 2011); American Piledriving Equipment, Inc. v. Geoquip, Inc., 637 F.3d 1324, 1340 (Fed. Cir. 2011); PSN Illinois, LLC v. Ivoclar Vivadent, Inc., 525 F.3d 1159 (Fed. Cir. 2008); Schwarz Pharma, Inc. v. Paddock Labs., Inc., 504 F.3d 1371, 1378 (Fed. Cir. 2007).

[67] *See, e.g.,* Tokai Corp. v. Easton Enterprises, 632 F.3d 1358, 1361 (Fed. Cir. 2011) (obviousness); Clock Spring, L.P. v. Wrapmaster, Inc., 560 F.3d 1317, 1321 (Fed. Cir. 2009) (public use bar); Automotive Technologies Int'l, Inc. v. BMW of North America, Inc., 501 F.3d 1274, 1276 (Fed. Cir. 2007) (enablement); Ferring B.V. v. Barr Labs., Inc., 437 F.3d 1181, 1183 (Fed. Cir. 2006) (inequitable conduct).

[68] *See* Richardson v. Suzuki Motor Co., 868 F.2d 1226, 1246–47 (Fed. Cir. 1989) ("Infringement having been established, it is contrary to the laws of property, of which the patent law partakes, to deny the patentee's right to exclude others from use of his property.... It is the general rule that an injunction will issue when infringement has been adjudged, absent a sound reason for denying it.").

[69] 547 U.S. 388 (2006).

demonstrate the following conditions traditionally required in other types of lawsuit: (1) that it has suffered irreparable injury, (2) that monetary damages cannot compensate for the injury, (3) that the balance of hardships warrants injunctive relief, and (4) that the public interest would not be disserved by a permanent injunction.[70] If these conditions do not prevail, a court may decide to impose what amounts to a compulsory license; the infringer may continue but owes the patentee an ongoing royalty payment in an amount fixed by the court.[71] This new approach may benefit the public, perhaps ensuring the supply of products needed by consumers or preventing economic disruptions like unemployment. On the other hand, patent owners have lost a significant bargaining chip because it is no longer certain that infringing activity must cease following a successful lawsuit.

11.8.1 Damages

The other remedy available to a patentee is an award of money damages to compensate for past infringement. While injunctions are a matter within the discretion of the judge, the calculation of damages is a question of fact for the jury.[72] A patentee can elect to pursue damages in either of two forms. One is *lost profits* attributable to the infringement.[73] This form of recovery is appropriate if the infringer competed with the patentee in the marketplace

---

[70] *Id.* at 391; *see also* Robert Bosch LLC v. Pylon Mfg. Corp., 659 F.3d 1142, 1148 (Fed. Cir. 2011). There is no presumption of irreparable injury in cases of patent infringement. *Robert Bosch,* 659 F.3d at 1149. On the other hand, courts deciding whether to impose an injunction "should [not] entirely ignore the fundamental nature of patents as property rights granting the owner the right to exclude." *Id.* A patentee who competes with the infringer in the marketplace may be irreparably harmed if an injunction is denied, even if the infringer is not the patentee's only competitor. *See id.* at 1151; Pfizer, Inc. v. Teva Pharmaceuticals USA, Inc., 429 F.3d 1364, 1381 (Fed. Cir. 2005) ("Picking off one infringer at a time is not inconsistent with being irreparably harmed."). Irreparable harm need not be harm that affects the "core" of the patentee's business. *See Robert Bosch,* 659 F.3d at 1152. Where there is evidence that the infringer does not have the resources to pay royalties, an injunction is particularly appropriate. *See id.* at 1155–56.

[71] *See* Paice LLC v. Toyota Motor Corp., 504 F.3d 1293, 1313–14 (Fed. Cir. 2007).

[72] Utah Medical Prods., Inc. v. Graphic Controls Corp., 350 F.3d 1376, 1381 (Fed. Cir. 2003); Micro Chemical, Inc. v. Lextron, Inc., 317 F.3d 1387, 1394 (Fed. Cir. 2003). "A court is not at liberty to supplant its own judgment on the damages amount for the jury's findings." Oiness v. Walgreen Co., 88 F.3d 1025, 1030 (Fed. Cir. 1996). The award can be rejected by the court only if "the amount is grossly excessive or monstrous, clearly not supported by the evidence or based only on speculation or guesswork." Monsanto Co. v. McFarling, 488 F.3d 973, 981 (Fed. Cir. 2007). If the parties waived their right to a jury trial, the judge would determine all issues of fact, including the amount of damages.

[73] The infringer cannot be compelled to turn over *its* profits in lieu of calculating the *patentee's* lost profits, except where the infringed patent is a design patent. *See* 35 U.S.C. § 289.

and it can be shown that sales made by the infringer were sales lost to the patentee.[74] The standard of proof is one of "reasonable probability."[75]

The calculation of lost profits is often complicated by disputes over collateral sales that the patentee might have lost together with sales of the patented item. Suppose, for example, that the patent covered a component of a larger item—perhaps an improved lens for a flashlight. The patentee might demand the profits that could have been made from the sale of flashlights if the infringer had not misappropriated the lens design. The patentee might argue further that lost flashlight sales led to lost sales of accessories and spare parts—for example, spare bulbs, batteries, and so forth. The infringer, on the other hand, might attempt to apportion the profits in some way so that only profits from the patented *lens* could be recovered.

These disputes are resolved by the "entire market value rule," which "allows calculation of damages based on the value of an entire apparatus containing several features, when the patent-related feature in the 'basis for customer demand.' "[76] The patented and unpatented features must constitute "components of a single assembly or parts of a complete machine," or together they must operate as "a single functional unit."[77] Recovery cannot be had for functionally unrelated items sold together with the patented invention as a matter of convenience or to satisfy customer demand for a package deal.[78] Returning to the example, the entire flashlight would likely be held the appropriate base for calculating lost profits because the patented lens

---

[74] *See* American Seating Co. v. USSC Gp., Inc., 514 F.3d 1262, 1268 (Fed. Cir. 2008); Stryker Corp. v. Intermedics Orthopedics, Inc., 96 F.3d 1409, 1417 (Fed. Cir. 1996). Lost profits are most easily proven in a two-supplier market, but they can also be based on suppositions relating to market share. *See* King Instruments Corp. v. Perego, 65 F.3d 941, 953 (Fed. Cir. 1995). In the two-supplier situation (the two suppliers being the patentee and the infringer), proof of lost profits typically focuses on the following factors: (1) the demand for the patented product; (2) the absence of acceptable substitutes; (3) the capacity of the patentee to exploit the demand had there been no infringement; and (4) the amount of profit the patentee would have made if the patentee, rather than the infringer, had made the sales. *See* Siemens Medical Solutions USA, Inc. v. Saint-Gobain Ceramics & Plastics, Inc., 637 F.3d 1269, 1287 (Fed. Cir. 2011); *Stryker*, 96 F.3d at 1418.

[75] *See* Wechsler v. Macke Int'l Trade, Inc., 486 F.3d 1286, 1297 (Fed. Cir. 2007).

[76] Imonex Services, Inc. v. W.H. Munzprufer Dietmar Trenner GmbH, 408 F.3d 1374, 1380 (Fed. Cir. 2005); *see also* Marine Polymer Technologies, Inc. v. Hemcon, Inc., 672 F.3d 1350, 1360 (Fed. Cir. 2012) (en banc); Uniloc USA, Inc. v. Microsoft Corp., 632 F.3d 1292, 1318 (Fed. Cir. 2011); Lucent Technologies, Inc. v. Gateway, Inc., 580 F.3d 1301, 1336 (Fed. Cir. 2009).

[77] *American Seating*, 514 F.3d at 1268; Rite-Hite Corp. v. Kelley Co., 56 F.3d 1538, 1550 (Fed. Cir. 1995) (en banc).

[78] *See American Seating*, 514 F.3d at 1268; *Rite-Hite*, 56 F.3d at 1550.

together with the unpatented bulb and housing form a "single functional unit." On the other hand, if the flashlights were sold as part of a tool kit, the other tools would likely be excluded from the calculation of lost profits because their use and function are unrelated to the patented lens.[79]

Another issue is whether a patentee can recover profits lost on sales of an unpatented item that competes with sales of an infringing item. Suppose, for example, that the inventor of the improved flashlight lens decided, for whatever reason, to market only flashlights that are *not* covered by the patent. Meanwhile, the infringer marketed flashlights that *are* covered by the patent. Can the patentee recover the profits that it would have made on unpatented flashlights if not for the sales of the infringing ones? According to the Federal Circuit, those profits can be recovered as long as it can be shown that the sales of the unpatented flashlights would have been made if not for the infringement.[80]

In many cases lost profits are difficult to calculate, or the patentee did not lose any profits through competition because the patentee did not sell a product of its own. In these situations, the patentee may choose to pursue a *reasonable royalty* as the measure of damages. This is, by statute, the minimum that a patentee can be awarded.[81] A reasonable royalty is the amount that the infringer would have paid the patentee if, instead of infringing the patent, it had obtained a license. This is generally assessed as a percentage of the sales price of the infringing goods multiplied by total sales.

The best guide to calculating a reasonable royalty is evidence of an established royalty.[82] If there is no established royalty, then a reasonable

---

[79] The flashlight batteries might be a close call. They are a necessary part of a functioning flashlight but are often sold separately. The infringer might argue that when batteries are sold with a flashlight, it is done only as a matter of "convenience and business advantage." *Rite-Hite*, 56 F.3d at 1550. Alternatively, a distinction might be drawn between the original batteries, which are sold as a part of the flashlight, and replacement batteries, which the patentee could not have expected to sell. *See* Kaufman Co. v. Lantech, Inc., 926 F.2d 1136, 1144 (Fed. Cir. 1991) (whether "accessories" should be included in the calculation of lost profits depends on whether there is a reasonable probability that the patentee would have made the sale if not for the infringement). The entire-market-value rule can also be used to determine the base for calculating a reasonable royalty.

[80] *Rite-Hite*, 56 F.3d at 1548–49.

[81] 35 U.S.C. § 284 ("Upon finding for the claimant the court shall award the claimant damages adequate to compensate for the infringement, but in no event less than a reasonable royalty for the use made of the invention by the infringer, together with interest and costs as fixed by the court.").

[82] Monsanto Co. v. McFarling, 488 F.3d 973, 978–79 (Fed. Cir. 2007) ("An established royalty is usually the best measure of a 'reasonable' royalty for a given use of an invention because it removes the need to guess at the terms to which parties would hypothetically agree."); Nickson Indus., Inc. v. Rol Mfg. Co., 847 F.2d 795, 798 (Fed. Cir. 1988).

royalty must be determined through a difficult mental exercise. One must imagine what would have occurred if, at the time the infringement began, the patentee and the infringer sat down together and negotiated the terms of a patent license. The amount that the patentee would have been willing to accept, and that the infringer would have been willing to pay, is the amount of a reasonable royalty.[83]

The courts have identified a number of factors that should be considered in the context of this "hypothetical negotiation." These are commonly known as "*Georgia-Pacific* factors"—a reference to one of the first opinions to set them down.[84] The *Georgia-Pacific* factors include the following:[85]

- Any evidence of an established royalty rate
- Rates paid by the infringer for rights to similar patents
- Whether the patentee had a policy of refusing licenses
- Whether the patentee and the infringer were competitors
- Whether sales of the patented item would generate (for the infringer or the patentee) additional sales of nonpatented items, including such things as accessories and spare parts[86]
- The time remaining before the patent expired
- The established success and profitability of items within the scope of the patent
- The advantages of the patented invention over available substitutes
- The portion of both selling price and profits that could be attributed to the patented invention rather than to other product components or features

The hypothetical negotiation exercise is difficult and imprecise, in part because it requires the jury, or the judge in a bench trial, to imagine the state of affairs as they existed when the infringement began, putting aside

---

[83] *See* Powell v. Home Depot U.S.A., Inc., 663 F.3d 1221, 1238 (Fed. Cir. 2011); *Lucent*, 580 F.3d at 1324; Mitutoyo Corp. v. Central Purchasing, LLC, 499 F.3d 1284, 1292 (Fed. Cir. 2007); *Rite-Hite*, 56 F.3d at 1554. Some courts have accepted a 25 percent "rule of thumb" as the starting point for a reasonable royalty, but the Federal Circuit has rejected this as "fundamentally flawed." *Uniloc*, 632 F.3d at 1315.

[84] Georgia-Pacific Corp. v. United States Plywood Corp., 318 F. Supp. 1116 (S.D.N.Y. 1970); *see also Powell*, 663 F.3d at 1239; Parental Guide of Texas, Inc. v. Thomson, Inc., 446 F.3d 1265, 1270 (Fed. Cir. 2006); *Micro-Chemical*, 317 F.3d at 1393; Interactive Pictures Corp. v. Infinite Pictures, Inc., 274 F.3d 1371, 1385–86 (Fed. Cir. 2001).

[85] *See Georgia-Pacific*, 318 F. Supp. at 1120.

[86] These additional sales are known as "convoyed sales" or "derivative sales."

knowledge of subsequent events.[87] It also requires that the patentee and the infringer be pictured as a willing licensor and a willing licensee, respectively, when the reality may have been very different.[88]

Even if the hypothetical negotiation could be imagined perfectly, basing a damages figure on the result would seem to make infringement a "no-lose" proposition.[89] The potential infringer who would otherwise pay for a license might decide to take its chances, knowing that, at worst, it would be forced to pay after litigation no more than would have been required for a license. In reality, things are not so easy for the would-be infringer. First, courts recognize that the hypothetical negotiation is only a mental exercise. In the end, an infringer may be compelled to pay more than an actual licensee would have paid.[90] More importantly, if the infringement was willful, damages can be increased as a punishment.

11.8.2 Willful Infringement

Although unintentional infringement is still infringement, the law recognizes a difference in culpability between the innocent infringer and the deliberate infringer. A court can as much as triple the damages assessed against a "willful" infringer.[91] Willfulness is a question of fact,[92] and the

---

[87] *See* Unisplay, S.A. v. American Electronic Sign Co., 69 F.3d 512, 518 (Fed. Cir. 1995); Hanson v. Alpine Ski Area, Inc., 718 F.2d 1075, 1079 (Fed. Cir. 1983) (" 'The key element in setting a reasonable royalty . . . is the necessity for return to the date when the infringement began.' "). In seeming contradiction to this rule, some cases have approved the use of later information to suggest what a reasonable royalty might have been. *See Lucent,* 580 F.3d at 1333 ("factual developments occurring after the date of the hypothetical negotiation can inform the damages calculation"); Fromson v. Western Litho Plate & Supply Co., 853 F.2d 1568, 1575 (Fed. Cir. 1988) (the law "permits and often requires a court to look to events and facts that occurred thereafter and that could not have been known to or predicted by the hypothesized negotiators").

[88] *See Rite Hite,* 56 F.3d at 1554 n.13 (imagining the patentee as a willing licensor is "inaccurate, and even absurd").

[89] *See Fromson,* 853 F.2d at 1574–75.

[90] *See King Instruments,* 65 F.3d at 951 n.6; *Fromson,* 853 F.2d at 1575 n.11 ("Courts have on occasion recognized the need to distinguish between royalties payable by infringers and non-infringers.").

[91] *See* 35 U.S.C. § 284 ("the court may increase the damages up to three times the amount found or assessed"). Although the statute does not specify the circumstances under which damages may be increased, the courts have held that "an award of enhanced damages requires a showing of willful infringement." *In re* Seagate Technology, LLC, 497 F.3d 1360, 1368 (Fed. Cir. 2007) (en banc).

[92] Bard Peripheral Vascular, Inc. v. W.L. Gore & Assoc. Inc., 670 F.3d 1171, 1189 (Fed. Cir 2012); Powell v. Home Depot U.S.A., Inc., 663 F.3d 1221, 1228 (Fed. Cir. 2011); Biotec Biologische Naturverpackungen GmbH v. Biocorp, Inc., 249 F.3d 1341, 1356 (Fed. Cir. 2001) (willful infringement "is quintessentially a question of fact, for it depends on findings of culpable intent and deliberate or negligent wrongdoing").

standard of proof is one of clear and convincing evidence.[93] Whether or not to increase the damages, and by how much, is a decision left to the discretion of the trial judge.[94]

The standard of conduct that is judged willful has evolved in recent years. At one time, the Federal Circuit held that potential defendants had an affirmative duty of "due care" to avoid infringing–suggesting that carelessness alone might justify an award of enhanced damages. In the en banc *Seagate* decision,[95] the Federal Circuit abandoned the due-care standard in favor of a recklessness standard–in other words, a willful infringer is one who proceeds in spite of a "high likelihood" of infringing a valid patent.[96] The risk must have been one that would have been apparent to an objectively reasonable observer, and the danger of liability must have been known, "or so obvious that it should have been known," to the infringer.[97]

Willfulness depends on the totality of the circumstances.[98] Traditionally, an important consideration has been whether the infringer sought out and relied on competent advice of counsel. Here too, much has changed in recent years. In *Seagate*, the Federal Circuit retreated from earlier suggestions that one must always, or almost always, seek legal advice, even when such precautions seem unnecessary.[99] In *Knorr-Bremse*, also an en banc decision, the Federal Circuit abolished the inference, commonly observed before,[100] that infringers who did not rely on advice of counsel must have received no advice or advice that was unfavorable.[101] Today, § 298 of the Patent Act, introduced by the America Invents Act, flatly states

---

[93] *Seagate*, 497 F.3d at 1371.

[94] *See* Electro Scientific Indus., Inc. v. General Scanning Inc., 247 F.3d 1341, 1353 (Fed. Cir. 2001) ("A finding of willfulness does not mandate enhanced damages."); Graco, Inc. v. Binks Mfg. Co., 60 F.3d 785, 792 (Fed. Cir. 1995).

[95] *In re* Seagate Technology, LLC, 497 F.3d 1360 (Fed. Cir. 2007) (en banc).

[96] *Id.* at 1371; *see also Bard*, 670 F.3d at 1189; *Powell*, 663 F.3d at 1236; Transocean Offshore Deepwater Drilling, Inc. v. Maersk Contractors USA, Inc., 617 F.3d 1296, 1312 (Fed. Cir. 2010).

[97] *Seagate*, 497 F.3d at 1371; *see also Bard*, 670 F.3d at 1190; *Powell*, 663 F.3d at 1236; *Transocean*, 617 F.3d at 1312. Because of the objective and subjective elements, the *Seagate* approach has been called a "two-pronged analysis." *Powell*, 663 F.3d at 1236.

[98] Liquid Dynamics Corp. v. Vaughan Co., Inc., 449 F.3d 1209, 1225 (Fed. Cir. 2006); Knorr-Bremse Systeme Fuer Nutzfahrzeuge GmbH v. Dana Corp., 383 F.3d 1337, 1342 (Fed. Cir. 2004) (en banc).

[99] *See Seagate*, 497 F.3d at 1371 ("Because we abandon the affirmative duty of due care, we also reemphasize that there is no affirmative obligation to obtain opinion of counsel.").

[100] *See* Electro Medical Sys., S.A. v. Cooper Life Sciences, Inc., 34 F.3d 1048, 1056 (Fed. Cir. 1994); L.A. Gear, Inc. v. Thom McAn Shoe Co., 988 F.2d 1117, 1126 (Fed. Cir. 1993).

[101] *Knorr-Bremse*, 383 F.3d at 1344.

that failure to obtain advice of counsel, or to present such advice to the court, may not be used to prove willful infringement.[102]

Advice of counsel can be used by the infringer to demonstrate that the infringement was *not* willful.[103] An attorney may have predicted–reasonably, if incorrectly–that the patent in question would be found invalid or not infringed, giving the client a reasonable basis to proceed. However, a defendant who relies on advice of counsel must be willing to waive the attorney-client privilege that would otherwise protect confidential communications. This can be a difficult choice, but the Federal Circuit in *Seagate* limited the scope of the waiver, making reliance on advice of counsel less costly for potential infringers. The waiver allows the patentee to examine attorney-client communications between the infringer and the counsel who rendered the advice, to make sure that the advice was what the infringer claims it to have been. But in most cases the patentee cannot inquire into communications between the infringer and its *trial* counsel, who are often different attorneys than those offering prelitigation advice.[104]

Another potential remedy against a willful infringer is an award of reasonable attorneys' fees. The general rule in the United States is that each litigant must bear its own legal costs, regardless of the outcome of the case, but § 285 of the Patent Act provides for an award of attorneys' fees in an "exceptional case." Willful infringement may create such an exceptional case,[105] though it is still a matter for the judge's discretion.[106] On occasion

---

[102] 35 U.S.C. § 298. After willfulness is established according to *Seagate*'s standard of recklessness, the infringer's failure obtain advice of counsel might still be relevant to the question of how much damages should be increased. *See* Spectralytics, Inc. v. Cordis Corp., 649 F.3d 1336, 1348 (Fed. Cir. 2011).

[103] There may be some legal advice so lacking in substance or preparation that one could not reasonably rely upon it. *See* Comark Communications, Inc. v. Harris Corp., 156 F.3d 1182, 1191 (Fed. Cir. 1998). Competent advice is advice from a qualified attorney, based on a thorough investigation, with support for its conclusions spelled out in reasonable detail.

[104] *Seagate*, 497 F.3d at 1374.

[105] *See* Martec, LLC v. Johnson & Johnson, 664 F.3d 907, 916 (Fed. Cir. 2012); Serio-US Indus. v. Plastic Recovery Technologies Corp., 459 F.3d 1311, 1321 (Fed. Cir. 2006) ("[e]xceptional cases usually feature some material, inappropriate conduct related to the matter in litigation, such as willful infringement"); Tate Access Floors, Inc. v. Maxcess Technologies, Inc., 222 F.3d 958, 972 (Fed. Cir. 2000). Even if the infringement was not willful, "vexatious conduct" by the infringer in the course of the litigation may justify an award of attorneys' fees. *See* Beckman Instruments, Inc. v. LKB Produkter AB, 892 F.2d 1547, 1551–52 (Fed. Cir. 1989).

[106] Odetics, Inc. v. Storage Technology Corp., 185 F.3d 1259, 1274 (Fed. Cir. 1999). Where the jury has found willful infringement, a judge's *unexplained* failure to treat the case as "exceptional" may be an abuse of discretion. *See Tate Access Floors*, 222 F.3d at 972.

courts award attorneys' fees to the accused infringer, generally when the patentee committed inequitable conduct or the claim of infringement was frivolous.[107] It is by no means proper to award attorneys' fees to the prevailing party as a matter of routine.[108]

11.8.3 Limitations

Recovery of damages for patent infringement can be limited under certain circumstances. Some of the most important limiting factors are the statute of limitations, failure to properly mark products or give notice of infringement, laches, and equitable estoppel.

11.8.3.1 Statute of Limitations

35 U.S.C. § 286 provides that no damages may be recovered for infringement that occurred more than six years prior to the filing of a claim. This statute of limitations is equivalent to those found in many other areas of the law, and the purpose is the usual one of encouraging the prompt disposition of potential claims. Section 286 does not prevent the filing of a suit unless the only relief that could be granted is damages for infringement more than six years ago. If, for example, the defendant had infringed continuously for the past eight years, the patentee could still sue to recover damages for the most recent six years of infringement and could obtain an injunction against future infringement.[109]

11.8.3.2 Notice and Marking

Many manufactured articles bear markings referring to a specific patent or patents. These are the result of 35 U.S.C. § 287, which states such markings provide "notice to the public" that the article is patented. They may not

---

[107] *See Martec*, 664 F.3d at 916–21 (baseless suit and litigation misconduct); Monsanto Co. v. Bayer Bioscience N.V., 514 F.3d 1229, 1242 (Fed. Cir. 2008) (inequitable conduct); Haynes Int'l, Inc. v. Jessop Steel Co., 8 F.3d 1573, 1579 (Fed. Cir. 1993) (a "frivolous" lawsuit justifying an award of attorneys' fees is one which "the patentee knew or, on reasonable investigation, should have known, was baseless"). A patentee's failure to investigate thoroughly before bringing an unsuccessful claim of infringement may render the case "exceptional." *See* Superior Fireplace Co. v. Majestic Prods. Co., 270 F.3d 1358, 1378 (Fed. Cir. 2001) ("From the record on appeal, it is unclear if Superior inspected the allegedly infringing products, prepared claim charts, construed the claims at issue, or even read those claims.").

[108] *See* Revlon, Inc. v. Carson Prods. Co., 803 F.2d 676, 679 (Fed. Cir. 1986).

[109] *See* Teva Pharmaceuticals USA, Inc. v. Novartis Pharmaceuticals Corp., 482 F.3d 1330, 1341 (Fed. Cir. 2007).

provide *actual notice* to a particular individual who has never seen the article, but the law considers them "constructive notice" to anyone.[110] Where it is not practical to mark a patent number on the article itself, it can be displayed on packaging.[111] If a patent owner or licensee makes, sells, offers to sell, or imports into the United States articles covered by the patent but not marked in this fashion, no damages for infringement can be recovered until (1) marking begins or (2) the infringer receives from the patent owner actual notice of the infringement.[112] The damages limitation encourages patent owners to mark their goods and provide at least that much notice to the public.[113]

The marking of goods must be "substantially consistent and continuous."[114] If the patentee sells a large shipment of unmarked goods, this resets the damages clock, so to speak. The obligation to mark applies to goods made or sold by the patent owner *or* licensee (express or implied).[115] Patent owners therefore have to make sure that licensees are properly marking their goods, or the patent owner's ability to recover damages for infringement will be impaired.[116] Section 287 does not apply to patents with just method claims, for the simple reason that a method cannot be marked.[117] If neither the patent owner nor the patent owner's licensees have sold any products covered by the patent, no marking or other notice is required to begin the accumulation of damages for infringement.

---

[110] *See* Syngenta Seeds, Inc. v. Delta Cotton Coop., Inc., 457 F.3d 1269, 1276 (Fed. Cir. 2006); Sentry Protection Prods., Inc. v. Eagle Mfg. Co., 400 F.3d 910, 918 (Fed. Cir. 2005).

[111] 35 U.S.C. § 287(a). The America Invents Act allows patentees to mark their goods with an Internet address in lieu of patent numbers. The designated website must be accessible to the public, and it must associate the product with the relevant patent numbers. *See id.*

[112] *See id.*; Crown Packaging Technology, Inc. v. Rexam Beverage Can Co., 559 F.3d 1308, 1316 (Fed. Cir. 2009); SRI Int'l, Inc. v. Advanced Technology Labs, Inc., 127 F.3d 1462, 1469 (Fed. Cir. 1997); Maxwell v. J. Baker, Inc., 86 F.3d 1098, 1111 (Fed. Cir. 1996).

[113] *See Crown Packaging*, 559 F.3d at 1316; Nike, Inc. v. Wal-Mart Stores, Inc., 138 F.3d 1437, 1443 (Fed. Cir. 1998).

[114] *Maxwell*, 86 F.3d at 1111; American Medical Sys., Inc. v Medical Eng'g Corp., 6 F.3d 1523, 1537 (Fed. Cir. 1993).

[115] *Maxwell*, 86 F.3d at 1111; Amstead Indus. Inc. v. Buckeye Steel Castings Co., 24 F.3d 178, 185 (Fed. Cir. 1994).

[116] This obligation is subject to a "rule of reason," and "substantial compliance" may be held sufficient. *See Maxwell*, 86 F.3d at 1111–12 (patentee's reasonable efforts were sufficient, even though a "numerically large number" of goods–still a small percentage of the total–were not properly marked).

[117] *Crown Packaging*, 559 F.3d at 1316–17; *American Medical*, 6 F.3d at 1538. If a patent includes method and apparatus claims, and the method relates to an apparatus that can be marked, damages will be limited if the patentee asserts both method and apparatus claims. In such a case, it may be better strategy to assert the method claims only. *See Crown Packaging*, 559 F.3d at 1317; *American Medical*, 6 F.3d at 1538–39.

If products have not been properly marked, the patentee can provide *actual notice* to the infringer.[118] The notice can come in the form of a warning letter from the patentee or without ceremony in the form of a suit for infringement.[119] Once such notice has been provided, damages with respect to that infringer can begin to accrue. The notice must come from the patent owner; it is not enough that the accused infringer discovered the infringement on its own or through a third party.[120] Moreover, the notice must identify the patent, and it must specifically charge the recipient with infringement of that patent.[121] In *Amstead Indus. Inc. v. Buckeye Steel Castings Co.*,[122] the infringer (Buckeye) received a form letter from the patent owner mentioning the patent and warning it not to infringe. The same letter had been sent to other companies throughout the industry. The court found that this was not actual notice of infringement to Buckeye because it did not specifically charge Buckeye with infringement, nor did it identify any infringing device.[123]

11.8.3.3 Laches

The equitable principle of "laches" may also bar recovery of damages accrued before suit was filed. As explained by the Federal Circuit in *A.C. Aukerman Co. v. R. L. Chaides Construction Co.*,[124] laches may bar the recovery of prefiling damages if (1) the patentee unreasonably and inexcusably delayed in filing suit and (2) the accused infringer was materially harmed

---

[118] *See* U.S. Philips Corp. v. Iwasaki Electric Co., 505 F.3d 1371, 1375 (Fed. Cir. 2007).

[119] *See American Medical,* 6 F.3d at 1537.

[120] *U.S. Philips,* 505 F.3d at 1375; Lans v. Digital Equipment Corp., 252 F.3d 1320, 1327 (Fed. Cir. 2001).

[121] *See U.S. Philips,* 505 F.3d at 1375 (actual notice "requires the affirmative communication of a specific charge of infringement by a specific accused product or device"). It is immaterial whether the patent owner "threatens suit, demands cessation of infringement, or offers a license under the patent." *SRI,* 127 F.3d at 1470. The important thing is that "the recipient is notified, with sufficient specificity, that the patent holder believes that the recipient of the notice may be an infringer." *Id.*

[122] 24 F.3d 178, 185–87 (Fed. Cir. 1994).

[123] *Id.* at 187. Somewhat clouding the picture, the Federal Circuit has stated that the notice of infringement must be specific but not necessarily an "unqualified charge of infringement." Gart v. Logitech, Inc., 254 F.3d 1334, 1344 (Fed. Cir. 2001). Specific reference to the patent and the potentially infringing product, together with advice that the recipient seek an opinion of counsel to determine "whether a non-exclusive license under the patent is needed," is sufficient to warn the recipient that it is believed to infringe. *Id.*

[124] 960 F.2d 1020 (Fed. Cir 1992) (en banc).

by the delay.[125] If the patentee delayed filing suit for more than six years, measured from the time it first knew or should have known of the alleged infringement,[126] laches is presumed, though that presumption can be overcome with the introduction of contrary evidence.[127]

 The harm to the accused infringer can be either "economic" or "evidentiary."[128] Economic harm means the loss of investments or the incurring of additional damages that could have been avoided if suit had been filed earlier. For example, during the period of delay the accused infringer might have made unrecoverable investments in a factory to manufacture the accused product. A patentee cannot delay unreasonably while such investments are made, nor can it "lie silently in wait watching damages escalate."[129] Evidentiary prejudice refers to the loss of evidence that the accused infringer might have used in its defense had the case been brought sooner. Such prejudice can arise where, for example, important documents have been lost, memories have faded, or witnesses have died.[130]

---

[125] *Aukerman*, 960 F.2d at 1032; *see also* Hearing Components, Inc. v. Shure Inc., 600 F.3d 1357, 1375 (Fed. Cir. 2010); Symantec Corp. v. Computer Associates Int'l, Inc., 522 F.3d 1279, 1294 (Fed. Cir. 2008). Enforcement of the laches defense is still left to the judge's discretion and sense of fairness. *See* Gasser Chair Co. v. Infanti Chair Mfg. Corp., 60 F.3d 770, 773 (Fed. Cir. 1995). If the infringer itself has behaved unfairly (perhaps by deliberately copying the patentee's invention), the court may decline to exercise its equitable powers. *See id.*

[126] *See Hearing Components*, 600 F.3d at 1375; Wanless v. General Electric Co., 148 F.3d 1334, 1337 (Fed. Cir. 1998) ("The period of delay begins at the time the patentee had actual or constructive knowledge of the defendant's potentially infringing activities."). Because laches can arise based on what the patentee *should* have known, patentees are, in effect, required to "police their rights" by keeping themselves reasonably informed of potentially infringing activity. *Wanless*, 148 F.3d at 1338. A patentee cannot remain "negligently or willfully oblivious" where the potentially infringing activity is so "pervasive, open, and notorious" that a reasonable patentee would investigate. *Id.*

[127] *Hearing Components*, 600 F.3d at 1375; *Symantec*, 522 F.3d at 1294; *Aukerman*, 960 F.2d at 1028, 1037–39; *Wanless*, 148 F.3d at 1337 ("A delay of more than six years raises a presumption that it is unreasonable, inexcusable, and prejudicial.").

[128] State Contracting & Eng'g Corp. v. Condotte America, Inc., 346 F.3d 1057, 1066 (Fed. Cir. 2003); *Aukerman*, 960 F.2d at 1033.

[129] *Aukerman*, 960 F.3d at 1033. The court must find that the potential infringer would have acted differently if the infringer had made its claim more promptly. In other words, the losses must have been *caused* by the delay. *See State Contracting*, 346 F.3d at 1066; *Gasser*, 60 F.3d at 775. Also, the losses must be more than the additional damages owed simply because infringement took place over a longer period. Otherwise economic harm could be demonstrated in every case. *Hearing Components*, 600 F.3d at 1376.

[130] *Aukerman*, 960 F.2d at 1033; *see also Hearing Components*, 600 F.3d at 1376.

Laches is an equitable defense that depends on the exercise of the judge's discretion in view of all the circumstances.[131] Those circumstances include the length of the delay and any excuses or justifications offered by the patentee. Excuses for delay that may be acceptable include the demands of other litigation, negotiations with the accused infringer, and disputes over ownership of the patent.[132] Fairness may sometimes require that the patentee notify the accused infringer of the reason for its delay.[133]

The effect of a successful laches defense is to bar recovery of damages incurred *before* the lawsuit was filed.[134] The patentee can still recover damages for subsequent infringement as well as an injunction against future infringement.

The Federal Circuit has also endorsed the concept of "prosecution laches," which bars enforcement of a patent issuing after unreasonable and unexplained delays in prosecution, even though the applicant complied with the relevant PTO regulations.[135] The defense prevents an applicant from unreasonably delaying the issuance of a patent simply to put itself in a more advantageous position with respect to others who, not knowing of the pending application, may be investing in infringing technology. In this instance, a successful laches defense appears to render the claims generally unenforceable.[136] A severe remedy, prosecution laches "should be applied only in egregious cases of misuse of the statutory patent system."[137] Intentional delays in prosecuting a patent application were more likely to occur before 1995, when the term of a patent was measured

---

[131] *Aukerman*, 960 F.2d. at 1032.

[132] *Id.* at 1033. Poverty or inability to find an attorney willing to work for a contingent fee have not been recognized as valid excuses for delay. *See* Hall v. Aqua Queen Mfg., Inc., 93 F.3d 1548, 1554 (Fed. Cir. 1996).

[133] *See Aukerman*, 960 F.2d at 1033; Vaupel Textilmaschinen KG v. Meccanica Euro Italia S.P.A., 944 F.2d 870, 877 (Fed. Cir. 1991) (for the "other litigation" excuse to apply, the patentee must inform the accused infringer of the other litigation and of its intention to enforce the patent when the other litigation concludes).

[134] Odetics, Inc. v. Storage Technology Corp., 185 F.3d 1259, 1272–73 (Fed. Cir. 1999); *Aukerman*, 960 F.2d at 1041.

[135] *See* Symbol Technologies, Inc. v. Lemelson Medical, Education & Research Found., LP, 277 F.3d 1361, 1363–65 (Fed. Cir. 2002).

[136] *See id.* at 1364.

[137] Symbol Technologies, Inc. v. Lemelson Medical, Education & Research Found., LP, 422 F.3d 1378, 1385 (Fed. Cir. 2005). An example of such egregious misuse is "refiling an application solely containing previously-allowed claims for the business purpose of delaying their issuance," particularly when it is done repeatedly. *Id.* The tactics employed by the patentee in *Symbol Technologies* resulted in gaps of 18 to 39 years between filing and issue. *Id.* at 1386.

from its issue date rather than its filing date. Today, such delays would shorten the period during which the patent could be enforced.

11.8.3.4   Equitable Estoppel

Equitable estoppel is an equitable defense similar to laches, but it depends on a somewhat different set of circumstances. In order for this defense to apply, the patentee must somehow have *communicated* to the potential infringer the idea that the patentee would not press a claim.[138] This communication can be in the form of words, conduct, or even silence if, under the circumstances, one would expect the patentee to voice any objections to the potential infringer's activities.[139] In addition, the potential infringer must have *relied* on the communication and suffered material harm as a result of that reliance.[140] Equitable estoppel is most easily applied where, for example, the patentee told the potential infringer that it would not interfere, the potential infringer relied on that communication and invested in a new factory, and the patentee then reversed itself and filed suit.[141] The more difficult cases are those where the patentee did nothing and the potential infringer interpreted that inaction as tacit permission.

As in applying the laches defense, the court must weigh all of the circumstances and determine what fairness dictates.[142] If the defense of equitable estoppel applies, it bars *any* relief to the patentee.[143] In this

---

[138] Vanderlande Indus. Nederland BV v. Int'l Trade Comm'n, 366 F.3d. 1311, 1324 (Fed. Cir. 2004); A.C. Aukerman Co. v. R.L. Chaides Construction Co., 960 F.2d 1020, 1042 (Fed. Cir. 1992) (en banc).

[139] Aspex Eyewear Inc. v. Clariti Eyewear, Inc., 605 F.3d 1305, 1310 (Fed. Cir. 2010); *Aukerman*, 960 F.2d at 1041–42. If the "communication" is in the form of inaction, then there must have been some contact or relationship with the patentee that would allow the inaction to be reasonably interpreted as a sign of abandonment. *Aukerman*, 960 F.3d at 1042. For example, the patentee might have threatened immediate enforcement of its patents and then failed to follow through, which could reasonably be interpreted as a change of heart. *See Aspex*, 605 F.3d at 1310; Meyers v. Asics Corp., 974 F.2d 1304, 1309 (Fed. Cir. 1993). Ironically, the patentee who insists most emphatically that it will enforce its patent rights is the patentee most likely to be found to have abandoned those rights by its subsequent inaction.

[140] *See Aspex*, 605 F.3d at 1311; *Vanderlande*, 366 F.3d. at 1324; *Aukerman*, 960 F.2d at 1042–43.

[141] Unlike the laches defense, equitable estoppel does not require any element of delay. *Aukerman*, 960 F.2d at 1041–42.

[142] *Aspex*, 605 F.3d at 1313; *Aukerman*, 960 F.2d at 1043.

[143] *Aukerman*, 960 F.2d at 1041.

respect, the consequences are more severe than those of the traditional laches defense, which prevents only the recovery of past damages.

11.9 THE INTERNATIONAL TRADE COMMISSION

If allegedly infringing products are being imported into the United States, a patent owner can request an investigation by the International Trade Commission (ITC). In many ways, an ITC investigation is similar to a suit for patent infringement in a district court, but there are important differences.

First, the matter will be handled by an administrative law judge (ALJ) rather than a conventional judge or jury. The decision of the ALJ is reviewed by the ITC commissioners and, if an exclusion of infringing goods is ordered, by the president of the United States.[144] Second, the patent owner must demonstrate that importation of infringing articles threatens a "domestic industry" in those articles–in other words, there must be significant business activity in the United States, either under way or imminent, that will be injured by the illicit competition of infringing goods.[145] Third, the ITC can award no money damages for past infringement; it can only order that the importation of infringing goods be stopped.[146] Finally, although an ITC investigation involves much of the same effort as does a suit in a district court, the schedule is generally more compressed. An ITC investigation, from start to finish, is generally completed in a little more than a year.

11.10 JUDGMENTS OF INVALIDITY

When a court has held a patent invalid, and all avenues of appeal have been exhausted, the patent cannot in the future be asserted against any potential infringer.[147] In a sense, a patent owner has only one chance to defend the validity of the patent. On the other hand, an unsuccessful attempt by one accused infringer to challenge the validity of a patent generally does not preclude another accused infringer from raising similar arguments.

---

[144] *See* 19 U.S.C. § 1337(c), (j).

[145] *See* 19 U.S.C. § 1337(a)(2)–(3).

[146] *See* 19 U.S.C. § 1337(d).

[147] Assuming that the patent owner had a "full and fair opportunity" to defend the patent. *See* Blonder-Tongue Labs., Inc. v. Univ. of Illinois Found., 402 U.S. 313, 328 (1971).

CHAPTER 12

Special Topics

This final chapter covers two specialized topics outside of the mainstream of patent law but still worthy of discussion: design patents and plant patents.

12.1 DESIGN PATENTS

Throughout this book, the term "patent" generally refers to a *utility patent*. A utility patent is a patent on a device, method, or composition of matter having a practical use.[1] Most of the inventions one would commonly think of—from mousetraps to communications satellites—are things properly the subject of a utility patent. However, the Patent Office also issues *design patents*. A design patent is a curious hybrid similar in some respects to an ordinary utility patent but applied to the kinds of artistic (or at any rate decorative) expression that are also the subject of copyright or trademark protection.[2] Whereas utility patents exist to promote the "useful arts," design patents exist to promote the "decorative arts."[3]

The PTO issues design patents to new, original, and ornamental designs embodied in manufactured objects.[4] The design can be a surface ornament, such as a pattern on a cream pitcher, or it can derive from the shape and

---

[1] "Utility" is defined broadly and can be applied to inventions such as toys that have minimal practical value. *See* Section 8.4.

[2] *See* Sections 2.1–2.2.

[3] Avia Group Int'l, Inc. v. L.A. Gear California, Inc., 853 F.2d 1557, 1563 (Fed. Cir. 1988).

[4] 35 U.S.C. § 171.

configuration of the object itself. A sleek new shape for a cell phone, for example, could be the subject of a design patent. Copies of three design patents can be found in Appendix B. They depict designs for a belt buckle, a flower pot, and a waffle. A design patent cannot be awarded to an entirely abstract design not associated with any particular utilitarian object. One could not, for example, obtain a design patent on a painting of sunflowers.[5] But one could obtain a design patent on a vase that bears the same painting as a decoration.

Although a design patent must claim an article of manufacture, the design cannot be dictated by functional considerations.[6] If the shape of a new tennis racket served to enlarge the "sweet spot," that shape should not be the subject of a design patent. Instead, the shape should be protected by a utility patent, assuming that it meets the criteria of patentability. One factor to consider in judging whether a design is functional or ornamental is whether the same functions could be accomplished by designs of significantly different appearance.[7]

Although neither the Patent Office nor the courts are well suited to judge artistic merit, a design must be "ornamental" before it can be granted a design patent. The design need not be a fine example of artistic expression, but it must, in some way, appeal to the aesthetic sense. On occasion, design patents have been denied because the depicted article failed to meet this criterion.[8] On the other hand, design patents have been granted to objects that would

---

[5] *See* M.P.E.P. § 1504.01.

[6] *See* Richardson v. Stanley Works, Inc., 597 F.3d 1288, 1293 (Fed. Cir. 2010) ("a design patent, unlike a utility patent, limits protection to the ornamental design of the article"); Door-Master Corp. v. Yorktowne, Inc., 256 F.3d 1308, 1312 (Fed. Cir. 2001) ("only 'the non-functional aspects of an ornamental design as shown in a patent' are proper bases for design patent protection"); L.A. Gear, Inc. v. Thom McAn Shoe Co., 988 F.2d 1117, 1123 (Fed. Cir. 1993). If the design is "primarily functional rather than ornamental," the design patent is invalid. *Richardson*, 597 F.3d at 1294; PHG Technologies, LLC v. St. John Co., 469 F.3d 1361, 1366 (Fed. Cir. 2006).

[7] *See PHG*, 469 F.3d at 1366–37; Rosco, Inc. v. Mirror Lite Co., 304 F.3d 1373, 1378 (Fed. Cir. 2002) ("[I]f other designs could produce the same or similar functional capabilities, the design of the article in question is likely ornamental, not functional."); *L.A. Gear*, 988 F.2d at 1123. Even if every element of the design has a function, the overall configuration may be a matter of patentable aesthetic expression. *See L.A. Gear*, 988 F.2d at 1123; *Avia*, 853 F.2d at 1563.

[8] *See, e.g.*, Blisscraft of Hollywood v. United Plastics Co., 294 F.2d 694, 696 (2d Cir. 1961) (finding a pitcher design insufficiently ornamental: "Plaintiff's pitcher has no particularly aesthetic appeal in line, form, color, or otherwise. . . . The reaction which the pitcher inspires is simply that of the usual, useful and not unattractive piece of kitchenware."). In more recent cases, designs are unlikely to be criticized for failing to look attractive. Instead, the debate is likely to center on whether aesthetic aspirations (however successful) or functional necessity dictated the design. *See* Seiko Epson Corp. v. Nu-Kote Int'l, Inc., 190 F.3d 1360, 1368 (Fed. Cir. 1999) ("Nor need the design be aesthetically pleasing. . . . The design may contribute distinctiveness or consumer recognition to the [product], but an absence of artistic merit does not mean that the design is purely functional.").

not ordinarily be thought of as having an ornamental aspect—for example, a hip prosthesis.[9] Apparently, a physician selecting a hip prosthesis might be moved to select the one that appeals to the eye.

Because design patents protect visually appealing designs, they may be denied to objects hidden from view.[10] A vacuum cleaner bag was denied a design patent on that ground.[11] Nevertheless, a design may be sufficiently ornamental if its appearance is "a matter of concern" during some significant portion of its life cycle.[12] A hip prosthesis is not visible in use, but it is visible when displayed at a trade show or in advertising.

Whereas utility patents include many pages describing the invention in words, design patents describe the invention only through drawings.[13] This is appropriate because the purpose of the patent is to protect a visual design. Utility patents can have many claims. A design patent has only one,[14] typically in the form "The ornamental design for the [object] as shown."[15] The bracketed portion would name the kind of object depicted—for example, a belt buckle.

A patented design need not have utility, but it must be new and nonobvious.[16] Obviousness is difficult to judge in aesthetic matters,[17] and the

[9] *See In re* Webb, 916 F.2d 1553 (Fed. Cir. 1990).

[10] *See Door-Master*, 256 F.3d at 1312 ("generally concealed features are not proper bases for design patent protection because their appearance cannot be a 'matter of concern' "); *Webb*, 916 F.2d at 1557.

[11] *See* Ex Parte Fesco, 147 U.S.P.Q. 74 (Pat. Off. Bd. App. 1965).

[12] *See* Contessa Food Prods., Inc. v. Conagra, Inc., 282 F.3d 1370, 1379 (Fed. Cir. 2002); Keystone Retaining Wall Sys., Inc. v. Westrock, Inc., 997 F.2d 1444, 1451 (Fed. Cir. 1993); *Webb*, 916 F.2d at 1557–58.

[13] *See* Amini Innovation Corp. v. Anthony California, Inc., 439 F.3d 1365, 1371 (Fed. Cir. 2006) ("It is the drawings of the patent . . . that define the patented design."); Hupp v. Siroflex of America, Inc., 122 F.3d 1456, 1464 (Fed. Cir. 1997) ("A design patent contains no written description; the drawings are the claims to the patented subject matter."). Although verbal accounts of what the drawings depict can assist courts in explaining their reasoning, the Federal Circuit has cautioned lower courts against overreliance on verbal descriptions in design patent cases. *See* Crocs, Inc. v. Int'l Trade Comm'n, 598 F.3d 1294, 1302 (Fed. Cir. 2010) ("misplaced reliance on a detailed verbal description of the claimed design risks undue emphasis on particular features of the design rather than examination of the design as a whole").

[14] *See* 37 C.F.R. § 1.153(a).

[15] *See* M.P.E.P. § 1503.03.

[16] 35 U.S.C. §§ 171, 103; *L.A. Gear*, 988 F.2d at 1124; *Avia*, 853 F.2d at 1563.

[17] As in the case of a utility patent, factors to consider include the scope and content of the prior art, the differences between the prior art and the claimed subject matter, the level of ordinary skill in the art, and secondary considerations such as commercial success or copying. *Avia*, 853 F.2d at 1564. *See* Sections 8.9.4 and 8.9.4.1. In the case of a design patent, obviousness must be judged from the perspective of a designer of ordinary capabilities. Litton Sys., Inc. v. Whirlpool Corp., 728 F.2d 1423, 1443 (Fed. Cir. 1984).

prior art available for the Patent Office to consult—primarily earlier design patents and utility patents—may barely scratch the surface. Nevertheless, a design patent, like a utility patent, carries a presumption of validity.

The term of a design patent is 14 years from the date of issue.[18] An object can infringe a design patent if it presents substantially the same appearance to an ordinary observer—so much so that the ordinary observer would be deceived into believing the designs were the same.[19] Differences will not avoid infringement if the patented design and the accused product are sufficiently similar overall.[20] It is not an infringement to copy only the functional aspects of a patented design.[21]

The patentee can recover the "entire profit" of an infringer who has sold an article covered by a design patent.[22]

12.2 PLANT PATENTS

A new plant variety can be the subject of a utility patent,[23] but only if the variety is nonobvious,[24] and only if the patent disclosure satisfies the usual

---

[18] 35 U.S.C. § 173.

[19] *Crocs*, 598 F.3d at 1303 ("an ordinary observer . . . [must] be deceived into believing that the accused product is the same as the patented design"); Int'l Seaway Trading Corp. v. Walgreens Corp., 589 F.3d 1233, 1239 (Fed. Cir. 2009); *Amini*, 439 F.3d at 1371(" 'the resemblance [must be] such as to deceive such an observer, inducing him to purchase one supposing it to be the other' "). The Federal Circuit used to apply a two-part test for design patent infringement. The accused design had to present substantially the same appearance to an ordinary observer, *and* the accused design had to include whatever made the patented design different than prior designs—the patented design's "point of novelty." In the *en banc* decision *Egyptian Goddess, Inc. v. Swisa, Inc.*, 543 F.3d 665, 678 (Fed. Cir. 2008), the court abandoned the "point of novelty" prong. The prior art is still relevant for its influence on the impressions of an ordinary observer. For example, if there were many similar tennis shoe designs, it might take a high level of similarity, involving the details that set the patented design apart, before the ordinary observer would conclude that the accused product and the patented shoe were the same. *See Crocs*, 598 F.3d at 1303; *Int'l Seaway*, 589 F.3d at 1239–40; *Egyptian Goddess*, 543 F.3d at 678. Although there is a strong similarity to the test of trademark infringement, discussed in Section 2.2, here the proper comparison is between the accused product and the design depicted in the patent, not between the accused product and the patentee's own commercial embodiment, which may include features not depicted in the patent. *See* Sun Hill Indus., Inc. v. Easter Unlimited, Inc., 48 F.3d 1193, 1196 (Fed. Cir. 1995). The same ordinary observer test should be applied when comparing the patented design to the prior art to determine if the design is novel or anticipated. *Int'l Seaway*, 589 F.3d at 1240.

[20] *See Contessa*, 282 F.3d at 1376–78.

[21] *See* Lee v. Dayton-Hudson Corp., 838 F.2d 1186, 1189 (Fed. Cir. 1988).

[22] 35 U.S.C. § 289.

[23] J.E.M. AG Supply, Inc. v. Pioneer Hi-Bred Int'l, Inc., 534 U.S. 124, 127 (2001).

[24] *See* Section 8.9.4.

requirements, such as the enablement and written description requirements.[25] These are often problematic in the case of a plant variety. If the
difference between a newly discovered rose and a known variety is a subtle
difference in color and perfume, it is difficult to describe these differences
in words and equally difficult to decide if the differences are nonobvious.
Congress addressed these difficulties by providing a special form of patent
for plant varieties, thereby putting agriculture on a more even footing with
industry when it comes to encouraging and rewarding innovation.

A plant patent can be obtained by one who "invents or discovers
and asexually reproduces any distinct and new variety of plant, including
cultivated spores, mutants, hybrids, and newly-found seedlings, other than
a tuber propagated plant or a plant found in an uncultivated state."[26]
Asexual reproduction refers to reproduction by grafting, budding and similar procedures that reproduce a genetically identical plant from a portion
of the first plant or its progeny.[27] The "invention" is complete only when
the new variety has been discovered, its distinguishing characteristics have
been identified, and it has been asexually reproduced. If the asexually
reproduced plant has the distinctive characteristics of its parent, this demonstrates that the characteristics likely represent a genetic rather than an
environmental variation.

A patent cannot be granted for the discovery of a new plant in the wild—
that is, in an "uncultivated state." However, patents can be granted for varieties that arise from unplanned sports or mutations of cultivated crops.
Imazio Nursery, Inc. v. Dania Greenhouses,[28] for example, discusses a patented
variety of heather discovered as a seedling in a cultivated field. This variety, dubbed "Erica Sunset," blooms during the Christmas season, much
earlier than the ordinary heather from which it arose.

Plant patents have only one claim, which typically refers to the plant variety "shown and described" in the specification, usually with a brief recital of

---

[25] *See* Sections 8.6 and 8.8.

[26] 35 U.S.C. § 161. According to the Manual of Patent Examining Procedure, tubers (such as
potatoes) are excluded because "this group alone, among asexually reproduced plants, is
propagated by the same part of the plant that is sold as food." M.P.E.P. § 1601. The term
"plant" is used in its popular sense rather than a strict scientific sense, so species such as
bacteria are also excluded. *Id.*

[27] See M.P.E.P. § 1601. The Plant Variety Protection Act, 7 U.S.C. § 2321 *et seq.*, provides
similar legal protection for sexually reproduced plant varieties (e.g., plants grown from
seed) but not as a part of the patent system. The Plant Variety Protection Act is administered by the Department of Agriculture.

[28] 69 F.3d 1560 (Fed. Cir. 1995).

the characteristics that distinguish the new variety.[29] In contrast to a utility patent, a description found in a plant patent need only be "as complete as is reasonably possible."[30] Because of their function in identifying the patented variety, illustrations are an important part of a plant patent, and they must be "artistically and competently executed."[31]

A plant variety is patentable if it is "distinct and new"[32]–a threshold of novelty less demanding than nonobviousness. The patent confers the right to exclude others from asexually reproducing the claimed plant or from using or selling such a plant.[33] It is not an infringement of a plant patent to grow the claimed plant from seed.[34] It is also not an infringement to develop independently a variety that is indistinguishable from the patented variety. An infringement occurs only if the accused variety is an *offspring* of the original, which means that an element of proving infringement is evidence that the accused infringer had access to the original plant or its asexually reproduced progeny.[35] This is in contrast to the usual rule (applied to utility patents) that independent development is not a defense to infringement.

---

[29] *See* 35 U.S.C. § 162 ("The claim in the specification shall be in formal terms to the plant shown and described.").

[30] 35 U.S.C. § 162.

[31] M.P.E.P. § 1606. Either drawings or color photographs are acceptable. *Id.* Examples of plant patents have been omitted from the Appendix due to the difficulty of reproducing the illustrations.

[32] 35 U.S.C. § 161.

[33] 35 U.S.C. § 163.

[34] One may infringe a *utility* patent by growing the patented plant variety from saved seed. *See* Monsanto Co. v. David, 516 F.3d 1009, 1014 (Fed. Cir. 2008); Monsanto Co. v. McFarling, 302 F.3d 1291, 1299 (Fed. Cir. 2002).

[35] *See* Imazio Nursery, 69 F.3d at 1569–70.

Note on Sources

In any area of the law, there is no substitute for the original sources. In the specific case of patent law, the primary source is Title 35 of the U.S. Code, known as the Patent Act. Several one-volume references reproduce the Patent Act and other selected legislation concerning copyright and trademark law. A good example is *Selected Statutes and International Agreements on Unfair Competition, Trademark, Copyright and Patent*, edited by Paul Goldstein and Edmund W. Kitch and published by Foundation Press. Rules and regulations specifically relating to patent applications and prosecution can be found in Title 37 of the Code of Federal Regulations, published by the Office of the Federal Register and the *Manual of Patent Examining Procedure* (or MPEP), published by the Department of Commerce. All of these materials can now be conveniently located online at the PTO website: http://www.uspto.gov/main/patents.htm.

Judicial opinions cited in this book can be found in any good law library or through electronic resources like Lexis or Westlaw. Supreme Court decisions are found in the *United States Reports* (abbreviated in case citations as "U.S.") and the Supreme Court Reporter ("S.Ct.") published by West Publishing Co. Published decisions of the Federal Circuit Court of Appeals are found in West's *Federal Reporter* ("F.2d" or "F.3d"). District Court opinions are found in West's *Federal Supplement* ("F. Supp." or "F. Supp. 2d"), or BNA's *United States Patent Quarterly* ("U.S.P.Q." or "U.S.P.Q.2d").

Several multivolume treatises provide very detailed surveys of United States patent law, including its historical development. The one the author turns to most frequently is Professor Donald S. Chisum's *Chisum on Patents*, published by Matthew Bender. Professor Chisum's work would be a useful supplement to this book when greater detail is required.

Sample
Utility Patents

US005502918A

United States Patent [19]

Oviatt

[11] Patent Number: 5,502,918

[45] Date of Patent: Apr. 2, 1996

[54] **MOUSETRAP FOR CATCHING MICE LIVE**

[76] Inventor: **Bill Oviatt**, 1375 Highway 71 North, Springdale, Ark. 72764

[21] Appl. No.: **347,890**

[22] Filed: **Dec. 1, 1994**

[51] Int. Cl.⁶ **A01M 23/02**

[52] U.S. Cl. **43/61**; 43/60; 43/66

[58] Field of Search 43/66, 67, 61, 43/60, 58, 75

[56] **References Cited**

U.S. PATENT DOCUMENTS

944,926 12/1909 Turnbo 43/66
1,226,641 5/1917 Cushing 43/60
4,768,305 9/1988 Sackett 43/61

Primary Examiner—Kurt Rowan
Attorney, Agent, or Firm—Rick Martin

[57] **ABSTRACT**

A "Y" shaped mousetrap lures a mouse into an open end of the "Y" by means of smelly bait located at a closed end of the bottom of the "Y". The "Y" is pivotally supported horizontally by a stand. As the mouse walks past the pivot point, a ping pong ball rolls from the opposite short "Y" tube member and down to the entrance of the open ended tube member. The mouse is trapped alive and can be drowned by immersing the mousetrap.

8 Claims, 3 Drawing Sheets

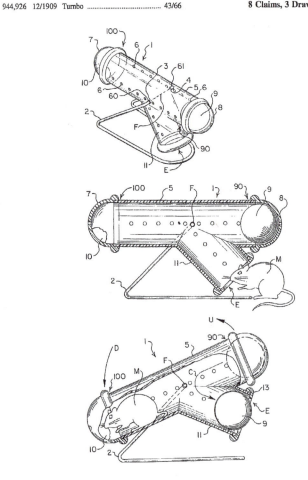

248

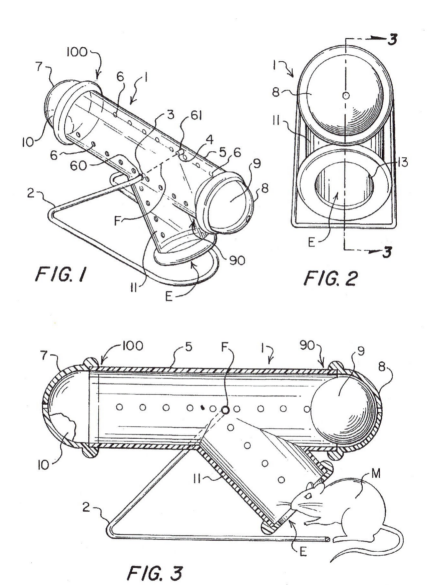

FIG. 1

FIG. 2

FIG. 3

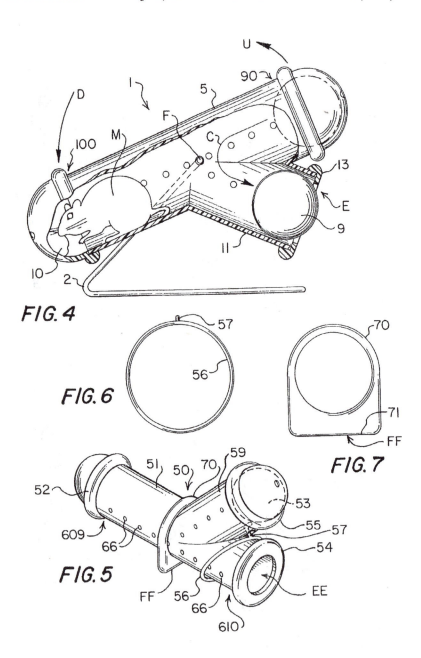

FIG. 4

FIG. 6

FIG. 7

FIG. 5

250

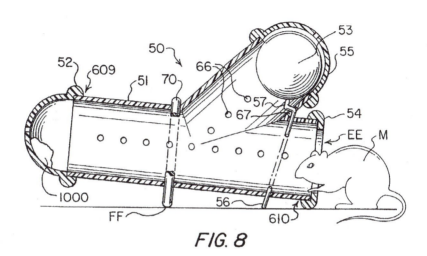

FIG. 8

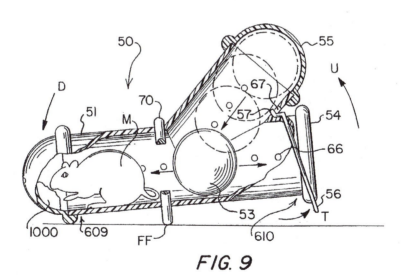

FIG. 9

1

MOUSETRAP FOR CATCHING MICE LIVE

FIELD OF INVENTION

The present invention relates to a better mousetrap.

BACKGROUND OF THE INVENTION

Mice can be a nuisance and/or a health menace. Traditional mousetraps are comprised of either a mechanical or chemical killing means. When a mouse is killed in a household, many health problems can arise. These health problems include the release of body fluids containing viruses inside the household. Parasites including worms or lice can be released. Decomposition bacteria will cause odors and cause injury to pets or children who ingest them.

The present invention eliminates these hazards by catching the mouse alive. A simple, cylindrical, teeter-totter contains bait at a closed end of the cylinder. The mouse enters the open end of the cylinder and walks toward the bait. As the mouse passes a fulcrum the cylinder tilts the bait end of the cylinder downward. The mouse becomes trapped by a downward rolling ping pong ball. The trap containing the trapped mouse can be brought outside where the entire trap can be thrown in a bucket to drown the mouse.

SUMMARY OF THE INVENTION

The main object of the present invention is to trap a mouse alive.

Another object of the present invention is to provide an inexpensive trap.

Yet another object of the present invention is to allow the trap to be easily dropped into a bucket of water to drown the mouse.

Still yet another object of the present invention is to reuse the trap.

Other objects of this invention will appear from the following description and appended claims, reference being had to the accompanying drawings forming a part of this specification wherein like reference characters designate corresponding parts in the several views.

BRIEF DESCRIPTION OF THE DRAWINGS

FIG. 1 is a top perspective view of the preferred embodiment.

FIG. 2 is a front plan view of the preferred embodiment shown in FIG. 1.

FIG. 3 is a longitudinal sectional view taken along line 3—3 of FIG. 2.

FIG. 4 is a side plan view with a partial cut-away showing the mouse of FIG. 3 trapped.

FIG. 5 is a top perspective view of an alternate embodiment.

FIG. 6 is a front plan view of the retaining ring of FIG. 5.

FIG. 7 is a front plan view of the pivot stand of FIG. 5.

FIG. 8 is a longitudinal partial sectional view of the embodiment of FIG. 5 in the process of trapping a mouse.

FIG. 9 is a partial cut-away of the embodiment shown in FIG. 8 having caught the mouse.

Before explaining the disclosed embodiment of the present invention in detail, it is to be understood that the invention is not limited in its application to the details of the particular arrangement shown, since the invention is capable

2

of other embodiments. Also, the terminology used herein is for the purpose of description and not of limitation.

DESCRIPTION OF THE PREFERRED EMBODIMENT

Referring first to FIG. 1 the trap 1 is comprised of a support stand 2 preferably made of wire. Support stand 2 has wire ends 3, 4 which form a fulcrum for the main tube 5. Main tube 5 preferably is a plastic cylinder having holes 6, 60, 61. Holes 60, 61 removably attach to the wire ends 3, 4 thereby permitting the main tube 5 to teeter-totter around the fulcrum F. Holes 6 also provide an entrance for water when the trap 1 is immersed to kill a mouse.

A pair of removable end caps 7, 8 seal the ends of main tube 5. Before the end caps 7, 8 are secured to main tube 5, the bait 10 and the ping pong ball 9 are inserted as shown at bait end 100 and ball end 90.

An entrance tube 11 forms a "Y" with the main tube 5. Entrance tube 11 depends downward from main tube 5 and points away from the bait end 100.

FIG. 2 shows a mouse eye view of the trap 1. The lure of the bait 10 emanates from entrance E. In FIG. 3 the mouse M is entering entrance E of entrance tube 11. The main tube 5 is in the loaded position which is horizontal. Thus, the ping pong ball 9 rests at ball end 90.

Referring next to FIG. 4 the mouse M has had it. He's eating the bait 10. But as he walked past the fulcrum F his weight caused the main tube 5 to pivot around fulcrum F so that the bait end 100 fell down in direction D and the ball end 90 rose up in direction U. The ping pong ball 9 urged by gravity rolled in path C to close the entrance E. A rim 13 prevents the ping pong ball 9 from rolling past the entrance E.

When finished eating mouse M will turn around and walk past fulcrum F. Main tube 5 will teeter back to a horizontal position. However, ping pong ball 9 will prevent the egress of mouse M out of entrance E. All mouse M can do is travel back and forth in main tube 5 and entrance tube 11, thereby causing the trap 1 to teeter-totter around fulcrum F. Trap 1 can then be immersed in water to drown mouse M or opened at end caps 7, 8 to release mouse M. Of course, in an alternate use one could kill mouse M with poison bait and trap him in the same manner.

Referring next to FIGS. 5, 6, 7a trap 50 is shown. FIG. 5 shows the trap 50 in the horizontal loaded position. In this alternate embodiment a main tube 51 teeter-totters around fulcrum FF. Preferably a plastic ring 70 has a flat base 71 which acts as fulcrum FF. The entrance EE is at the entrance end 610 of the main tube 51. A removable cap 52 seals the bait end 609 of the main tube 51. Holes 66 can allow water to enter main tube 51 during immersion.

The trapping mechanism is comprised of a retaining tube 59 forming a "Y" with the main tube 51. Retaining tube 59 rises obliquely from main tube 51 away from the bait end 609 of the main tube 51. The ping pong ball 53 is held up in the load position by retaining prong 57 of swivel ring 56.

Referring last to FIGS. 8, 9 mouse M is first entering in FIG. 8 entrance EE. The swivel ring 56 is resting on the ground in the cocked position. The retaining prong 57 is pivotally supported in hole 67. Retaining prong 57 is holding up the ping pong ball 53.

When the mouse M passes the fulcrum FF he becomes trapped. The main tube 51 teeters so that the bait end 609 falls in direction D, and the entrance end 610 rises in

3

direction U. The swivel ring **56** pivots in direction T because the prong **57** is urged downward by ping pong ball **53**. Hole **67** acts as a fulcrum. The ping pong ball **53** is restrained from exiting entrance EE by rim **54**. End caps **52, 55** prevent the mouse's egress.

Although the present invention has been described with reference to preferred embodiments, numerous modifications and variations can be made and still the result will come within the scope of the invention. No limitation with respect to the specific embodiments disclosed herein is intended or should be inferred.

I claim:

1. A mousetrap comprising:

a main tube having a central fulcrum means, a bait end, and a ball end;

a base stand having a means to support the main tube at the fulcrum;

said bait end further comprising mouse bait and a main tube closure;

said ball end further comprising a ball and a main tube closure;

an entrance tube depending down from the main tube at the central fulcrum means, and angled toward the ball end;

said entrance tube having a mouse entrance adjacent a supporting surface for the base stand; and

said main tube having a horizontal load position wherein said ball rests at the ball end, wherein a mouse enters the mouse entrance, walks toward the bait up the entrance tube, and passes the fulcrum means, thereby causing the main tube to teeter down at the bait end, and cause the ball to roll down the main tube then down the entrance tube, functioning to block an egress of the mouse out the mouse entrance.

2. The mousetrap of claim 1 wherein said central fulcrum means further comprise holes in the main tube.

3. The mousetrap of claim 2 wherein said means to support further comprises a pair of prong ends fittingly engaged in the holes in the main tube.

4. The mousetrap of claim 1 wherein the ball further comprises a ping pong ball.

4

5. The mousetrap of claim 3 wherein said central fulcrum means further comprises a support stand depending from the main tube.

6. A mousetrap comprising:

a main tube having a closed bait end, a mouse entrance end, and a central fulcrum means supporting the main tube on a support surface;

a ball tube angularly rising from the main tube;

said ball tube further comprising a closure, a ball, and a ball support means, functioning to hold the ball against the closure when the main tube is teetered in a cocked position;

a bait in the bait end, functioning to lure a mouse into the mouse entrance, past the central fulcrum means, thereby causing the main tube to teeter downward at the bait end, and causing the ball support means to release the ball to roll into the main tube and thereby block an egress of the mouse out the mouse entrance.

7. The mousetrap of claim 5 wherein said ball support means further comprises a swivel ring suspended from a hole in the ball tube by a prong, wherein said prong swings away from the ball, thereby releasing it when the main tube is teetered downward at the bait end.

8. A mousetrap comprising:

a "Y" shaped tube pivotally supported at a center point by a stand;

said "Y" shaped tube having a straight tube closed at both ends, and having bait at one end, and a ball at an opposing ball end, said ball end being adjacent to an open tube member;

said open tube member depending from the straight tube so as to form a mouse entrance when the straight tube is suspended horizontally, whereby a mouse attracted by a bait at the bait end passes the center point and causes the straight tube to teeter with the bait end down, thereby causing the ball to travel to the open tube member, thus trapping the mouse.

* * * * *

United States Patent [19]

Fisher

[11] **Patent Number:** **4,662,101**

[45] **Date of Patent:** **May 5, 1987**

[54] **RAT OR MOUSE TRAP**

[76] Inventor: **Harry L. Fisher,** 9336 S. 208th St., Kent, Wash. 98031

[21] Appl. No.: **880,285**

[22] Filed: **Jun. 30, 1986**

[51] Int. Cl.⁴ A01M 23/04
[52] U.S. Cl. 43/69
[58] Field of Search 43/69

[56] **References Cited**

U.S. PATENT DOCUMENTS

121,608	12/1871	Francisco	43/69
290,580	12/1883	Harwell	43/69
1,208,206	12/1916	Poynter	43/69
1,525,349	2/1925	Yamasaki	43/69

FOREIGN PATENT DOCUMENTS

81327 8/1934 Sweden 43/69

Primary Examiner—Gene P. Crosby
Attorney, Agent, or Firm—Bruce A. Kaser

[57] **ABSTRACT**

A mousetrap (10) is made of a pivoting platform (12) suspended over a pitfall (14). The platform (12) is balanced in a manner such that it normally assumes a horizontal position, thus giving a mouse an appearance of a stable bridge over the pitfall. When the mouse (42) steps onto the platform (12) for the purpose of obtaining bait placed thereon, however, the platform (12) spins and dumps the mouse into the pitfall thereby trapping it.

1 Claim, 5 Drawing Figures

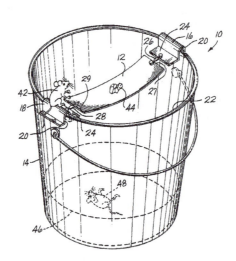

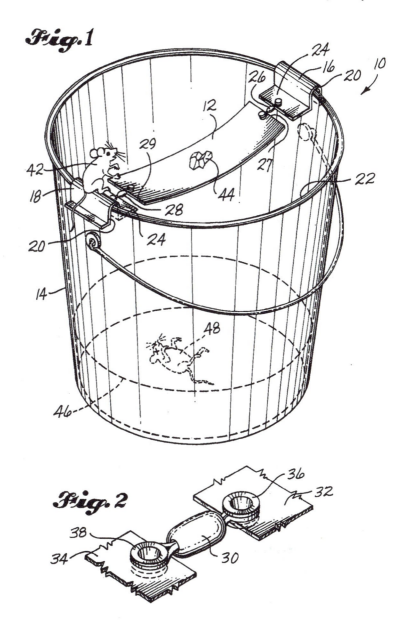

Fig.1

Fig.2

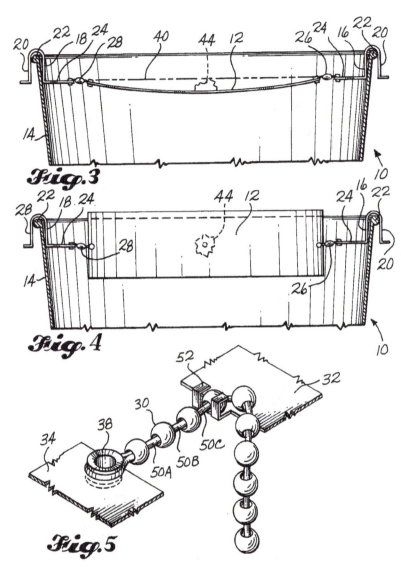

Fig.3

Fig.4

Fig.5

1

RAT OR MOUSE TRAP

TECHNICAL FIELD

This invention relates to animal traps, and in particular, traps for rats, mice and/or similar vermin.

BACKGROUND ART

The damage caused by rats and mice to agricultural products is well known. Every year these pests cause incalculable damage to crops, whether they be in the field or stored, and other foodstuffs of a similar nature. Further, the problems associated with rat or mice infestation of domestic household environments are well known.

Man has continuously engaged in war with these pests and has engaged in various attempts at eradicating and/or controlling them. The present invention provides yet another attempt which has certain advantages over previous ones. As will become apparent, the present invention is, quite literally, the better mousetrap.

DISCLOSURE OF THE INVENTION

The present invention provides a trap for rats, mice and similar vermin. This invention employs a pit or pitfall into which these pests fall and are trapped. Once there, they may be either killed or maintained in a live condition.

A platform is suitably supported over the pitfall in a manner such that the platform can freely turn or pivot about a center line axis. The platform is balanced in a manner such that it normally assumes a horizontal position thereby giving a vermin an appearance of providing a secure supporting surface over the pitfall. The vermin can access the platform from the edge of the pitfall, and when the vermin moves onto the platform, the vermin's weight causes the platform to become unbalanced and turn, thus causing the vermin to fall into the pitfall. Of course, the vermin would be enticed onto the platform by a suitable bait placed on the platform but out of reach from the edge of the pitfall's opening.

Preferably, the pitfall is made of a bucket or another suitable container of like nature. The platform is supported over the bucket's opening by a pair of supporting members hooked to the bucket's rim. One supporting member is positioned directly across the bucket's opening from the other.

The platform comprises a generally rectangular sheet of material which spans the distance between the supporting members, with each end of the platform being pivotally connected to the end's respective adjacent supporting member. These connections are symmetrical, that is, the mid-point of each end of the rectangular platform is pivotally connected to a supporting member. This makes a pair of pivot points which define the center line axis, such axis extending generally horizontally across the bucket or pitfall's opening and about which the platform is free to turn.

The rectangular platform is curved sufficiently that its center of gravity is offset from the center line axis. Since the platform can freely turn, this causes the platform to normally assume the above-mentioned horizontal position. After the weight of a mouse or rat on the platform unbalances it, causing it to turn, the platform naturally turns back to the horizontal position after the mouse or rat falls off.

Each supporting member may have an inwardly projecting ledge from the rim or edge of the bucket or

2

pitfall which provides vermin-access onto the platform. Swivel members are provided for making the pivotal connection between each ledge and the ends of the platform.

An advantage to the present invention is that it is effective in controlling vermin without using poison. Poison, of course, has been known to be one of the most effective methods of controlling vermin. However, it is undesirable to use poison in situations where the poison may get mixed into foodstuffs that are eventually to be consumed by humans. This invention is ideally suited for use in these kinds of situations.

Another advantage to the present invention is that it may be used as a live trap, or otherwise, if so desired. The bottom of the bucket may be filled with a few inches of water into which a mouse or rat will fall after being dumped by the platform. Eventually, the mouse or rat drowns. However, by leaving the bucket empty, they may be trapped alive.

BRIEF DESCRIPTION OF THE DRAWINGS

In the drawings, like reference numerals and letters refer to like parts throughout the various views, and wherein:

FIG. 1 is a pictorial view of a preferred embodiment of the invention, and shows a curved rectangular platform pivotally supported over the opening of a bucket;

FIG. 2 is an enlarged fragmentary pictorial view showing a swivel member which connects the platform shown in FIG. 1 to a supporting member connected to the rim of the bucket;

FIG. 3 is a side elevational view of the platform shown in FIG. 1;

FIG. 4 is a view like FIG. 3 but shows the platform in a pivoting or turned condition; and

FIG. 5 is a view like FIG. 2 but shows an alternative embodiment for connecting the rectangular platform in FIGS. 1, 3 and 4 to a supporting member on the bucket's rim.

BEST MODE FOR CARRYING OUT THE INVENTION

Referring now to the drawings, and first to FIG. 1, therein is shown at 10 a preferred embodiment of the invention. The invention includes a rectangular platform 12 which is suspended over the upwardly directed opening of a bucket 14. The platform 12 is attached to the bucket 14 by a pair of supporting members 16, 18. Each supporting member has a hook portion 20 that is attached to the bucket's rim 22. Further, each member 16, 18 has an inwardly projecting ledge portion 24 that provides vermin-access from the edge of the bucket 22 onto the platform 12.

The platform 12 is pivotally connected at each of its ends 27, 29 to respective adjacent supporting members 16, 18 as shown at 26, 28. These connections are better illustrated in FIG. 2 which shows a swivel member 30 interconnecting a first member 32 and a second member 34. The swivel member 30 is connected to the two members 32, 34 by rivets 36, 38, or other suitable means, and permits the first member 32 to pivot relative to the second member 34.

Referring back to FIG. 3, each swivel member 26, 28 connects the approximate center point of the platform's ends 27, 29 to the supporting members 16, 18. The swivel members 26, 28 thus define two points through which a horizontal center line axis 40 passes. The platform 12 is free to turn about this axis 40 and is curved slightly so that its center of gravity is offset from the axis. This offset causes the platform 12 to be normally balanced in the horizontal position shown in FIGS. 1 and 3.

Referring again to FIG. 1, therein is shown a mouse 42 poised on the rim 22 of the bucket 14. A suitable bait 44 is positioned on the center of the platform 12 and attracts the mouse 42. It should be understood that a suitable ramp or similar structure would be provided to permit the mouse 42 to access the bucket's rim 22. This is not shown in the drawings, however. The bait 44 would, of course, be positioned on the center of the platform 12 so that its weight would not unbalance the platform.

The horizontal position of the platform 12 gives the mouse 42 the appearance that the platform provides a bridge across the opening of the bucket 14. However, when the mouse 14 steps onto the platform 12, in its desire to obtain the bait 44, the mouse's weight unbalances the platform, causing it to turn as shown in FIG. 4, and thus dumps the mouse 42 into the bucket 14. The offset center of gravity of the platform 12 then causes the platform to return to the horizontal position after the mouse falls therefrom.

It should be appreciated that the above-described curved platform 12 could be replaced by a straight platform having a suitable counterweight attached thereto. This would not be a preferred embodiment, however.

The bottom of the bucket 14 may be filled with a few inches of water as indicated by the dashed lines 46. The mouse 42 may be able to swim in the water for a certain period of time but will eventually become tired and drown as shown at 48.

FIG. 5 shows an alternative embodiment of the swivel member 30 shown in FIG. 2. This embodiment may be used if it is desired to adapt the platform 12 to a bucket or other container having a different diameter. In this embodiment, the swivel member 30 comprises a plurality of swivel links as indicated at 50a, 50b, and 50c. The length of this alternative swivel member 30 is therefore adjustable by catching and releasing the links

50a, 50b, 50c from a link-catch 52 which is suitably connected to member 32.

The above description is presented for exemplary purposes only. This description is not meant to limit patent protection insofar as it is understood that certain departures may be taken from the above-described embodiments without departing from the overall spirit and scope of the invention. With regard to patent protection, the invention is to be limited not by the above description but only by the subjoined patent claims, in accordance with the well-established legal doctrines of patent claim interpretation.

What is claimed is:

1. A trap for mice, rats or vermin of a similar nature, and for use in connection with a pitfall having an upwardly directed opening, comprising:

a generally rectangular platform having a top surface and a bottom surface, and having a thin cross section;

a pair of platform supporting members, each of which is connected to the edge of said pitfall's opening, wherein one of said supporting members is positioned across said opening from the other, and wherein said platform substantially spans the distance between said supporting members, with a first end of said rectangular platform being pivotally connected to one of said members, and with a second end of said platform being pivotally connected to the other of said members, wherein such connections generally define a pair of points through which a center line axis extends across said pitfall's opening, said center line axis being an axis of symmetry for said platform and said platform being freely pivotally about said center line axis, and wherein

said platform's cross section is curved so that said top surface is concave and said bottom surface is convex, to cause said platform's center of gravity to be slightly offset from said center line axis, and to cause said platform to normally pivot into a position where said center of gravity is positioned below said center line axis, so that said platform is balanced in a manner that said platform's top surface provides said vermin with an appearance of a bridge across said pitfall.

* * * * *

50

55

60

65

United States Patent [19]

Fodor

[11] Patent Number: 4,819,368

[45] Date of Patent: Apr. 11, 1989

[54] DISPOSABLE MOUSETRAP

[76] Inventor: John Fodor, 13 Village Park Cir., Morgantown, W. Va. 26505

[21] Appl. No.: 552,153

[22] Filed: Nov. 14, 1983

[51] Int. Cl.⁴ A01M 23/18; A01M 23/02
[52] U.S. Cl. 43/61
[58] Field of Search 43/61, 60, 62, 67, 70

[56] References Cited

U.S. PATENT DOCUMENTS

2,573,228	10/1951	Slauth	43/61
2,598,007	5/1952	McCormick	43/61
3,729,852	5/1973	Holmes	43/61
3,823,504	7/1974	Dosch	43/61
4,142,320	3/1979	Marcolina	43/61
4,231,180	11/1980	Bare	43/61
4,232,472	11/1980	Muelling	43/61
4,238,902	12/1980	Holl et al.	43/61

Primary Examiner—Kurt Rowan
Attorney, Agent, or Firm—Mason, Fenwick & Lawrence

[57] ABSTRACT

A disposable rodent trap is formed of an aluminum beverage can comprising an internal chamber, a bottom end wall with an opposite end wall including an entry opening therein of sufficient size to permit a rodent to pass into the internal chamber. A door member in the form of a can end is positioned externally of said end wall and movable into a closed position covering and blocking the entry opening by a rubber band. A latch means normally holds the door open by engagement with an edge surface of the entry opening but is movable by rodent contact inside the chamber to unlatched position to permit the rubber band to move the door member to its closed postion to trap the rodent in said internal chamber.

15 Claims, 2 Drawing Sheets

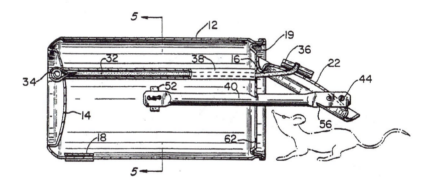

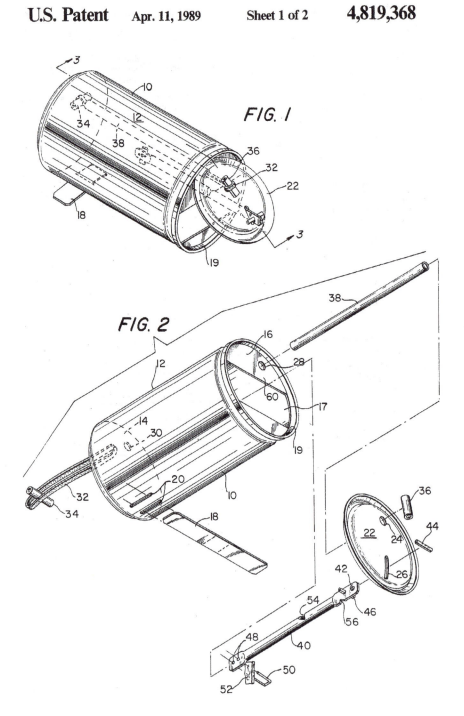

FIG. 1

FIG. 2

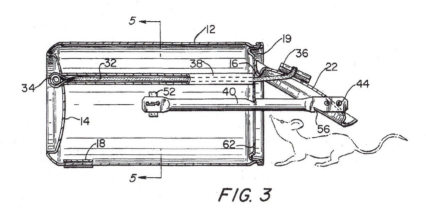

FIG. 3

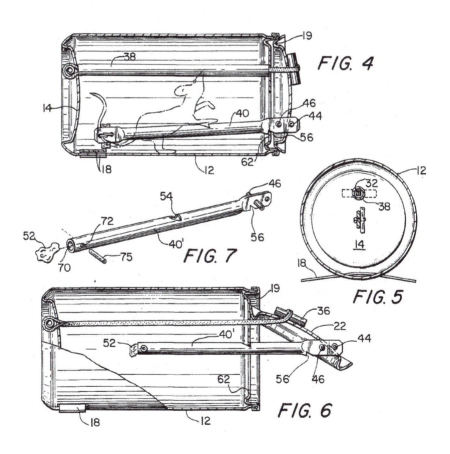

FIG. 4

FIG. 7

FIG. 5

FIG. 6

1

DISPOSABLE MOUSETRAP

BACKGROUND OF THE INVENTION

The present invention is in the field of animal trapping devices and is more specifically directed to a unique disposable rodent trap of particular value for capturing mice.

Numerous devices have evolved over the years for either capturing or killing mice. Many of the known devices have suffered from a number of shortcomings such as failing to operate properly and being overly expensive to fabricate. The most relevant prior known U.S. Patents comprise U.S. Pat. Nos. 100,986; 924,237; 1,261,189; 1,326,662; 1,372,663; 1,415,093; 1,861,478; 2,087,646; 2,434,031; 2,437,020; 2,573,228; 2,608,018; 3,426,470; 3,729,852; 3,733,735; 3,992,802. The present invention overcomes the shortcomings of the foregoing patents in providing a fool-proof functionally operational device that is quick and effective for capturing mice or other rodents and which is economical to fabricate and assemble due to the use of well-known widely available materials many of which are presently thrown away as scrap. It is consequently possible to simply dispose of the subject invention following the capture of a mouse or other rodent.

Therefore, it is the primary object of the present invention to provide a new and improved rodent trap which is functionally more effective than prior known rodent traps and is also economical to fabricate and assemble.

SUMMARY OF THE INVENTION

Achievement of the foregoing objects is enabled by the preferred embodiment of the invention in a remarkably effective manner. More specifically, the preferred embodiment of the invention comprises a container in the form of an aluminum beverage can of the type normally used for beer, soft drinks or the like. Such cans comprise a cylindrical wall member having a bottom end wall and a dispensing end wall with the dispensing end wall of the can used in the present invention including an elongated transverse entry opening of sufficient size to permit the passage of a rodent into the interior of the can.

A movable door is positioned adjacent the dispensing end wall of the can and is connected to an elongated latch member comprising an elongated tubular rod which extends into the interior of the can. Also, a rubber band extends from the bottom wall of the can through the length of the can outwardly through an opening provided in the dispensing end wall and is connected to the movable door member so as to urge the movable door member toward a closed position in which it overlies the entry opening and completely blocks same. The latch member includes a transverse surface engagable with a catch surface adjacent the edge of the entry opening so as to hold the door member in an open position against the urging of the elastic rubber band member. A tubular metal sheath encloses the rubber band member and the span between the dispensing end wall and the bottom end wall of the can so as to prevent any captured rodent from gnawing through the rubber band to permit the door to then open.

The inner end of the tubular latch member is provided with means for retaining bait on the inner end of the latch member for the purpose of attracting mice or

2

other rodents so as to cause them to enter the interior of the can. When such a mouse has entered the can, he will attempt to eat the bait and will dislodge the tubular latch member from engagement with the catch surface so that the elastic rubber band member immediately snaps the door closed and the rodent is consequently entrapped within the confines of the can. Additionally, the latch member is also provided with a lock latch surface which engages a second catch surface along the inside edge of the entry opening upon closure of the door member so as to lock the door member in closed position. Thus, the operation of the elongated elastic rubber band member and the lock surface provides a dual locking function to preclude escape of a captured rodent. In one embodiment of the invention the latch tube receives the bait member in an open-ended recess adjacent the end of the latch member with a transverse bore opening being provided on opposite sides of the opening so as to permit impalement of the bait by a retaining pin extended therethrough. In a second embodiment the bait is retained on the end of the latch member by a wire clip or the like extending through openings provided in a flattened end of the latch member.

BRIEF DESCRIPTION OF THE DRAWING

FIG. 1 is a perspective view of the preferred embodiment of the invention illustrating the door member in open position;

FIG. 2 is an exploded perspective view of the embodiment of FIG. 1;

FIG. 3 is a sectional view taken along lines 3—3 of FIG. 1 and illustrating the door in an opened condition;

FIG. 4 is a sectional view similar to FIG. 3 but illustrating the door in the closed position for imprisoning a rodent;

FIG. 5 is a sectional view taken along lines 5—5 of FIG. 3;

FIG. 6 is a side elevation view of a second embodiment with portions removed for the sake of illustration; and

FIG. 7 is a perspective view of a second embodiment of tubular latch means employed in the invention.

DESCRIPTION OF THE PREFERRED EMBODIMENTS

The preferred embodiment of the invention as illustrated in FIGS. 1 etc. comprises a disposable rodent trap including a container 10 in the form of a disposable aluminum beverage container having a cylindrical body wall 12, a bottom end wall 14 and a dispensing end wall 16. It should be observed that the bottom end wall 14 is normally the "bottom" wall when the beverage can is used for its original purpose whereas the dispensing end wall 16 is the end from which the beverage contained within the container is dispensed. Dispensing end wall 16 includes an opening 17 of sufficient size to permit the passage of a rodent therethrough so as to enter the interior of the container can 10 and also includes a peripheral flange 19. A stabilizer tab 18 extends through slots 20 provided in the cylindrical body wall 12 as best shown in FIG. 2. Stabilizer tab 18 prevents the can from rolling on a supporting surface in an obvious manner.

A floating door 22 comprising an end wall from a similar can is positioned adjacent and in contact with the dispensing end wall 16. Floating door 22 is provided with an upper circular opening 24 and a lower slot 26.

The upper circular opening 24 is in general alignment with an opening 28 in the dispensing end wall 16. The bottom end wall 14 is provided with an opening 30 in alignment with the opening 28 of the dispensing end wall. Biasing means in the form of an elastic rubber band member 32 extends through the openings 28 and 30 with the end of the biasing elastic rubber band member 32 adjacent the bottom wall 14 being anchored by a tubular anchor lug 34 while the opposite end of the rubber band member which extends through openings 28 and 24 is anchored by a similar lug 36. The lug members 34 and 36 can for example be formed of rolled pieces of aluminum scrap or the like. Thus it will be seen that the tension in rubber band 32 tends to move the floating door member 22 toward a closed position. A protective sheath 38 formed of metal in the form of aluminum or the like extends between the bottom wall 14 and the dispensing end wall 16 to fully enclose the rubber band 32 to prevent any rodent on the interior of the can from gnawing or eating through the band so as to cause its failure.

An elongated tubular latch member 40 is provided internally of the container can 10 and includes a flat outer end 42 which extends through the slot 26 and is held in position by an outer keeper pin 44 and an inner keeper pin 46 which are respectively on opposite sides of the floating door member 22. The inner end of the elongated tubular latch member 40 is provided with a pair of openings 48 through which a bait retention loop or wire or the like 50 extends so as to permit the attachment of bait 52 to the end of the latch member. Latch member 40 includes a first transverse latch surface 54 and a second transverse oppositely facing lock surface 56.

When the floating door 22 is in its open position the latch surface 54 is engaged with an upper external catch surface 60 extending along entry opening 17 in the dispensing end wall 16. Thus, the latch member retains the floating door in its open position. A mouse or other rodent can enter the opening 17 and upon attempting to eat the bait 52 will effect dislodging of the latch surface 54 from the catch surface 60 to immediately result in a rapid and quick movement of the door member 22 from the open position of FIG. 3 to the closed position of FIG. 4. The rodent on the interior of the container will consequently be imprisoned. Moreover, movement of the floating door 22 to the closed position immediately results in the lock surface 56 becoming engaged with a lower catch inside surface 62 as shown in FIG. 4. Thus, the floating door member 22 will be held in closed position by operation of the lock surface 56 as well as the elastic urgings of the rubber band 32.

FIG. 6 illustrates a slightly simplified embodiment in which the protective sheath 38 is dispensed with and the bare rubber band extends between the bottom wall 14 and the dispensing wall 16. The advantage of this embodiment is that it is slightly easier to manufacture. Additionally, the embodiment of FIG. 6 is illustrated with a second embodiment latch member 40' which is basically identical to the first latch member with the exception of the manner in which the bait 52 is connected to the inner end of the latch member. More specifically, the inner end of the latch member 40' includes an open end chamber or cavity 70 through which diametric openings 72 extend with the chamber or cavity 70 being of sufficient size to receive the bait 52. A retention pin 75 extends through the opening 72 and the bait 52 to retain the bait 52 in the end of the

latch member in the manner shown in FIG. 6. Otherwise, the second embodiment operates in exactly the same manner as the first embodiment.

It should be understood that, while preferred embodiments of the invention are illustrated herein, numerous modifications of the disclosed embodiments will undoubtedly occur to those of skill in the art. For example, practice of the invention is not limited to the use of beverage cans and other type cans or containers of larger sizes could be employed. In fact, it would even be possible to practice the present invention by the use of such large containers as oil drums or the like for use in capturing larger animals. Consequently, the use of the term "rodent" as discussed herein and as set forth in the claims should be broadly interpreted to include other types of animals. For these reasons, the spirit and scope of the invention should be broadly interpreted.

I claim:

1. A disposable rodent trap comprising a container defining an internal chamber, an end wall having an entry opening therein of sufficient size to permit a rodent to pass therethrough so as to enter said internal chamber, a door member provided externally of said end wall and movable from an open position toward said closed position covering and blocking said entry opening, biasing means comprising a rubber band for urging said door member toward its closed position, latch means having a portion inside said chamber and extending between said door member and a catch surface on, and forming part of, said end wall comprising an edge surface adjacent said entry opening for normally holding said door member in its open position but being movable by rodent contact inside said chamber out of contact with said catch surface to permit said biasing means to move said door member to its closed position to entrap the rodent in said internal chamber and wherein said container is a disposable beverage can having a cylindrical body wall, a bottom end wall and a dispensing end wall with said entry opening being provided in said dispensing end wall which comprises a wall from which beverage would normally be dispensed during usage of said beverage container for its original purpose.

2. The invention of claim 1 wherein said latch member comprises an elongated tube connected at one end to said door member and having a transverse latch surface medially of its length for engaging said catch surface adjacent one edge of said entry opening and further including a lock latch surface extending transversely of said tubular member at a location near the door member for engaging an inner edge surface of said entry opening for latching said door member in said closed position.

3. A rodent trap as recited in claim 2 additionally including a tubular sheath extending between said bottom end wall and said opening in said dispensing end wall for enclosing said rubber band portion inside said internal chamber for preventing any rodent in said chamber from chewing on said rubber band.

4. A disposable rodent trap as recited in claim 3 wherein said door member comprises a can end from a similar can which has one end engaged with said dispensing end wall, said dispensing end wall including a peripheral flange surface which retains said door member in position.

5. A rodent trap as recited in claim 4 wherein said latch member includes means on its end opposite its end connected to said door member for retaining rodent attracting means thereon.

5

6. A rodent trap as recited in claim 5 additionally including transversely extending means connected to said body wall and engagable with a supporting surface for said rodent trap for maintaining said rodent trap in fixed position on said supporting surface.

7. A rodent trap as recited in claim 6 wherein said bottom end wall is provided with an aperture through which one end of said rubber band extends to provide an external loop of said rubber band and wherein said rubber band is connected to said wall by an elongated anchor lug passed through said loop.

8. A rodent trap as recited in claim 7 wherein said door member is provided with an opening through which a loop of said rubber band extends and further includes an anchor lug extending through said loop for retaining said loop externally of said door member.

9. A rodent trap as recited in claim 8 wherein said door member includes a slot through which one end of said latch member extends and said latch member includes keeper pins extending transversely through said latch member on opposite sides of said door member so as to retain said latch member in said slot.

10. A rodent trap as recited in claim 4 wherein said latch member has an open-ended bait receiving cavity on its end opposite its connection to said door member.

11. A disposable rodent trap comprising a container defining an internal chamber, an end wall having an entry opening of sufficient size to permit a rodent to pass therethrough so as to enter said internal chamber, a door member provided externally of said end wall and movable from an open position toward said end wall into a closed position covering and blocking said entry opening, biasing means for urging said door member toward its closed position, latch means having a portion inside said chamber and extending between said door member and a catch surface on, and forming part of, said end wall for normally holding said door member in its open position but being movable by rodent contact inside said chamber out of contact with said catch surface to permit said biasing means to move

6

said door member to its closed position to entrap the rodent in said internal chamber and wherein said container is a disposable beverage can having a cylindrical body wall, a bottom end wall and a dispensing end wall with said entry opening being provided in said dispensing end wall which comprises a wall from which beverage would normally be dispensed during usage of said beverage container for its original purpose and wherein said biasing means comprises an elastic band having one end secured to said bottom end wall, said second end wall includes a small opening spaced from said entry opening and the opposite end of said elastic band extends through said small opening and is secured to said door member by retainer pin means.

12. The invention of claim 11 wherein said latch member comprises an elongated metal tube connected at one end to said door member and having a transverse latch surface medially of its length for engaging said catch surface and further including a lock latch surface extending transversely of said tubular member at a location near the door member for engaging an inner edge surface of said entry opening for latching said door member in said closed position.

13. A rodent trap as recited in claim 12 additionally including a tubular sheath extending between said bottom end wall and said opening in said dispensing end wall for enclosing said elastic band portion inside said internal chamber for preventing any rodent in said chamber from chewing on said rubber band.

14. A disposable rodent trap as recited in claim 13 wherein said door member comprises a can end from a similar can which has one end engaged with said dispensing end wall, said dispensing end wall including a peripheral flange surface which retains said door member in position.

15. A rodent trap as recited in claim 14 wherein said latch member includes attachment means on its end opposite its end connected to said door member for retaining rodent attracting means thereon.

* * * * *

45

50

55

60

65

Sample
Design Patents

(12) **United States Design Patent**   (10) **Patent No.:**   **US D622,178 S**

Kelleghan   (45) **Date of Patent:**   ** **Aug. 24, 2010**

(54) **BELT BUCKLE WITH BOTTLE OPENER**

(75) Inventor: **Brian James Kelleghan**, Longmont, CO (US)

(73) Assignee: **Bison Designs, LLC**, Longmont, CO (US)

(**) Term: **14 Years**

(21) Appl. No.: **29/343,818**

(22) Filed: **Sep. 18, 2009**

(51) **LOC (9) Cl.** **02-07**
(52) **U.S. Cl.** **D11/201**; D11/218; D2/639
(58) **Field of Classification Search** .... D11/200, D11/201, 206, 204, 231; 24/1, 163 K, 196–198; D2/639; D8/34, 40, 43; 7/151–152
See application file for complete search history.

(56) **References Cited**

U.S. PATENT DOCUMENTS

805,486	A		11/1905	Rosenheimer
1,147,955	A	*	7/1915	Langhammer 24/198
1,582,442	A		1/1921	White
2,018,083	A		11/1934	Murdock
D143,233	S	*	12/1945	Moore D8/43
D153,349	S	*	4/1949	Galter D8/40
2,470,606	A	*	5/1949	Dennison 81/3.55
D183,727	S	*	10/1958	Emberton D11/201
3,823,444	A		7/1974	Takahayashi
4,373,234	A		2/1983	Boden
D287,607	S	*	1/1987	Maruyama D21/579
D290,349	S	*	6/1987	Kasai D11/218
D427,547	S		7/2000	Yoshiguchi
6,185,772	B1	*	2/2001	Bates 7/151
D446,162	S		8/2001	Kung
D466,770	S	*	12/2002	Kelleghan D8/40
D470,794	S	*	2/2003	Eddy D11/201

D471,132	S	*	3/2003	Murata D11/218
D475,591	S		6/2003	Luquire
D476,218	S		6/2003	Kelleghan
D484,071	S		12/2003	Kelleghan
D493,386	S		7/2004	Pontaoe
D520,908	S		5/2006	Haymond
D536,280	S	*	2/2007	Wemmer D11/218

(Continued)

OTHER PUBLICATIONS

Black Millenium Scan of Applicant's website showing prior art buckle sold by Applicant.

(Continued)

Primary Examiner—T. Chase Nelson
Assistant Examiner—Kathleen M Sims
(74) *Attorney, Agent, or Firm*—Margaret Polson; Oppedahl Patent Law Firm LLC

(57) **CLAIM**

The ornamental design for a belt buckle with bottle opener, as shown.

DESCRIPTION

FIG. **1** is a top plan view of my new design for a belt buckle with bottle opener.

FIG. **2** is a bottom plan view of FIG. **1**.

FIG. **3** is a front side elevation view of FIG. **1**.

FIG. **4** is a rear side elevation view of FIG. **1**.

FIG. **5** is a right side elevation view of FIG. **1**.

FIG. **6** a left side elevation view of FIG. **1**; and,

FIG. **7** is a top perspective view of FIG. **1**.

1 Claim, 1 Drawing Sheet

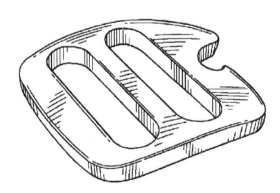

U.S. PATENT DOCUMENTS

D544,768	S	*	6/2007	Book	.... D8/40
D545,243	S		6/2007	Gracer et al.	
D579,819	S	*	11/2008	Brown	.... D11/231
D579,820	S	*	11/2008	Brown	.... D11/231
D586,259	S		2/2009	Kelleghan	

OTHER PUBLICATIONS

Ellipse Scan of Applicant's website showing prior art buckle sold by Applicant.

GunMetal Millenium Scan of Applicant's website showing prior art buckle sold by Applicant.

Kamalok Scan of Applicant's website showing prior art buckle sold by Applicant.

Kids Slider Scan of Applicant's website showing prior art buckle sold by Applicant.

Last Chance Light Duty Scan of Applicant's website showing prior art buckle sold by Applicant.

Last Chance Light Duty Black Oxide Buckle Scan of Applicant's website showing prior art buckle sold by Applicant.

Ribbon Ellipse Scan of Applicant's website showing prior art buckle sold by Applicant.

Ribbon GunMetal Millenium Scan of Applicant's website showing prior art buckle sold by Applicant.

Slider Scan of Applicant's website showing prior art buckle sold by Applicant.

Viper V-Ring Buckle Scan of Applicant's website showing prior art buckle sold by Applicant.

Web Buckle Watchband Scan of Applicant's website showing prior art buckle sold by Applicant.

Wildlife Millenium Scan of Applicant's website showing prior art buckle sold by Applicant.

Top plan view, front side elevation view and rear side elevation view of prior art buckle sold by Applicant.

U.S. Appl. No. 29/303,178, filed February 1, 2008; Inventor: Brian James Kelleghan.

* cited by examiner

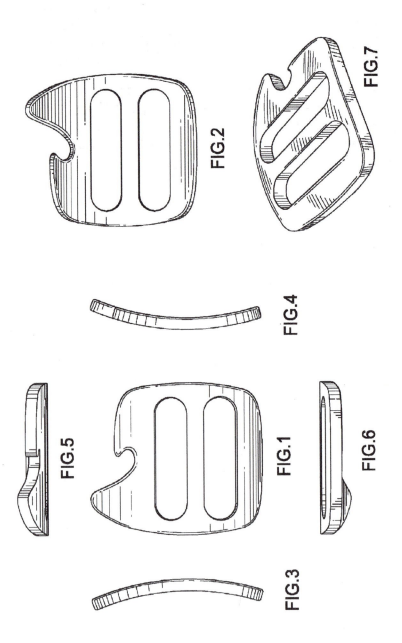

FIG.2

FIG.7

FIG.4

FIG.5

FIG.1

FIG.6

FIG.3

(12) **United States Design Patent**   (10) **Patent No.:**   **US D579,816 S**
     Lambert et al.   (45) **Date of Patent:**   ** **Nov. 4, 2008**

(54) **FLOWER POT**

(75) Inventors: **Fabrice Lambert**, Vaux En Bugey (FR);
                Francois Naimo, Cailloux sur Fontaines
                (FR); **Eric Zuner**, Viry (FR)

(73) Assignee: **Grosfillex SAS**, Arbent, Oyonnax (FR)

(**) Term: **14 Years**

(21) Appl. No.: **29/274,829**

(22) Filed: **May 30, 2007**

(30)   **Foreign Application Priority Data**

   Nov. 30, 2006   (EM)   000630546-0003

(51) **LOC (8) Cl.** **11-02**
(52) **U.S. Cl.** **D11/152**
(58) **Field of Classification Search** D6/403,
        D6/556; D11/143 148, 152 156; D19/77,
        D19/81, 84; D26/9; D34/1–11; D99/5,
        D99/19; 47/32.7, 39, 41.01, 41.1, 41.12–41.15,
        47/44–47, 65.5, 66.1, 66.6, 66.7, 67–71
     See application file for complete search history.

(56)   **References Cited**

              U.S. PATENT DOCUMENTS

   D213,971 S * 4/1969 Black D11/150

D223,464	S	*	4/1972	Tisseet D11/143
D319,606	S	*	9/1991	Etro D11/153
D322,946	S	*	1/1992	Claridge D11/153
D363,897	S	*	11/1995	Carlson D11/152
D431,496	S	*	10/2000	Grosfillex D11/151
D455,099	S	*	4/2002	Chung D11/151
D456,306	S	*	4/2002	Master D11/151
D515,970	S	*	2/2006	Hensen D11/153
D543,327	S	*	5/2007	Snell D34/1

* cited by examiner

Primary Examiner—Caron D. Veynar
Assistant Examiner—Garth Rademaker
(74) *Attorney, Agent, or Firm*—Dowell & Dowell, PC

(57)   **CLAIM**

The ornamental design for a flower pot, as shown and
described.

              DESCRIPTION

The sole FIGURE is a front perspective view of a flower pot
showing our new design, the left side, right side, and rear
perspective views being identical thereto.

              1 Claim, 1 Drawing Sheet

(12) **United States Design Patent** (10) Patent No.: **US D549,427 S**

Gambino et al. (45) **Date of Patent:** ** Aug. 28, 2007

(54) **WAFFLE**

(75) Inventors: **Charles Gambino**, Portage, MI (US); **John B. Edwards**, Battle Creek, MI (US); **David K. Tebow**, Battle Creek, MI (US); **Karla K. Norstrom**, Battle Creek, MI (US)

(73) Assignee: **Kellogg Company**, Battle Creek, MI (US)

(**) Term: **14 Years**

(21) Appl. No.: **29/259,455**

(22) Filed: **May 9, 2006**

(51) LOC (8) Cl. **01-01**
(52) U.S. Cl. **D1/125**; D1/129; D1/130
(58) Field of Classification Search D1/120–2, D1/124–5, 127–30, 199; 426/92, 94, 101, 426/138, 283, 297, 391, 496, 552
See application file for complete search history.

(56) **References Cited**

U.S. PATENT DOCUMENTS

277,422 A		5/1883	Harker et al.
D21,337 S	*	2/1892	Johnson D1/120
D59,285 S	*	10/1921	Richardson D1/127
1,612,747 A		12/1926	Shaffer
D88,675 S	*	12/1932	Schoenleber D1/127
1,899,511 A	*	2/1933	Leaf 426/95
1,947,124 A		2/1934	Clauss
1,950,734 A	*	3/1934	Leaf 426/95
D111,971 S	*	11/1938	Huse D1/101
2,358,452 A		9/1944	Garstang
D141,977 S		8/1945	Forte
D153,537 S		4/1949	Milano
D179,087 S		10/1956	Kelso
D229,642 S		12/1973	Dorsa
3,879,564 A	*	4/1975	Cocozzella 426/283
D254,516 S	*	3/1980	Meibaum D1/127

D277,044 S	*	1/1985	Kuhlman D1/130
4,820,533 A	*	4/1989	Seaborne et al. 426/76
D301,795 S		6/1989	Vitacco
D303,160 S	*	8/1989	Tovey D24/101
D303,312 S		9/1989	Vitacco
D395,535 S		6/1998	Reichkitzer et al.
D418,964 S	*	1/2000	Biton D1/120
2006/0286244 A1	*	12/2006	Fu et al. 426/549

OTHER PUBLICATIONS

Woman's Day, Oct. 1951, Inner Back Cover, McCalls, Mar. 1954, p. 87, Restaurants and Institutions, Jul. 22, 1987, p. 267, Mod Pack, Sep. 1962, p. 31.*
Country Living, May 1985, p. 112, Restaurants and Institutions, Spring 1988, front cover.*
All-Time Favorite Cookie Recipes For America's Tastiest Treats, by Jean Wickstrom Liles, Oxmoor House, AL, © 1995, p. 39.*
Good Housekeeping Illustrated Cookbook: Revised and Expanded Edition, by Hearst Books, NY, © 1989, p. 84.*

* cited by examiner

Primary Examiner—Robin Webster
Assistant Examiner—Karen E Kearney
(74) *Attorney, Agent, or Firm*—Dickinson Wright PLLC

(57) **CLAIM**

We claim the ornamental design for a waffle, as shown and described.

DESCRIPTION

FIG. **1** is a perspective view of the waffle;

FIG. **2** is a rear view of the waffle;

FIG. **3** is a front view of the waffle; and,

FIG. **4** is a cross-sectional view of the waffle taken along section lines **4**—**4** in FIG. **3**.

The waffle includes a substantially flat center surface that is useful for receiving images such as text or graphics.

1 Claim, 1 Drawing Sheet

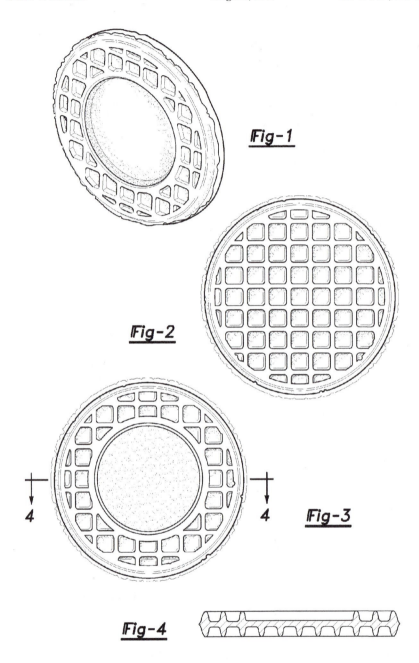

Fig-1

Fig-2

Fig-3

4

4

Fig-4

Index

Abandonment, 116–18, 136 n.249
Abstract ideas, 29–30, 34
All elements rule, 23, 180, 192–94
America Invents Act, 39, 43, 103–4,
    110–11, 116, 118, 136–39
    Advice of counsel, 229–30
    Derivation proceedings, 157
    Elimination of best mode defense,
      103–4
    Post-grant procedures, 46
    Prior art, 110–11, 136–39
    Prior commercial use defense, 209–10
    Priority, 43, 116, 118
Analogous arts, 147–48
Anticipation, 110, 140–43
Application for patent, 14, 19, 37
    Drawings, 20
    Preferred embodiments, 21, 69–70
    Provisional applications, 39–40
    Specification, 20–22, 68–70
Assignments, 54–55, 211
Assignor estoppel, 88
Attorneys' fees, 230–31

Bargain model of patent law, 2–3, 103
Best mode, 21, 103–5
Bifurcation, 220

Burdens of proof, 86–87, 124–26, 217
Business methods, 30–31

Claims, 14, 22–24, 63–84
    Amendments, 38, 106
    Dependent claims, 22, 24
    Doctrine of claim differentiation,
      74–75
    Independent claims, 22, 24
    Interpretation, 63–84, 140
    Jepson claims, 79
    Markush claims, 80
    Means-plus-function claims, 81–83,
      96–97, 203–6
    Ordinary meaning, 66–68
    Preambles, 22, 76–79
    Product-by-process claims, 80–81
    Step-plus-function claims, 83–84
Classification of inventions, 19
Combination of prior art references, 146,
    148–51
Commercial success, 153–54
Computer programs, 10–11, 32–35
Conception, 52, 118–19, 120–26
Constitutional source of patent law, 1–2
Constructive reduction to practice, 121
Continuations, 40–41

Continuations-in-part, 41–42
Contributory infringement, 59, 177–79
Copyrights, 9–11
Critical date, 128

Damages, 224–28
Date of invention, 106, 118–24
Declaratory judgment, 215–17
Definiteness, 92–97
Dependent claims, 22, 24
Derivation, 156–57
Derivation proceedings, 43, 139, 157
Design patents, 14, 239–42
Diligence, 122–24
Direct infringement, 175
Divisional applications, 42–43
Doctrine of claim differentiation, 74–75
Doctrine of equivalents, 97, 182–203
    All elements rule, 192–94
    Improvements, 189–92
    Limited by prior art, 194–96
    Prosecution history estoppel, 196–201
    Reverse doctrine of equivalents,
        206–7
    Unclaimed embodiments, 201–3
Double patenting, 157–60
Drawings, 20
Duty of candor in prosecution, 39

Enablement, 21, 40, 97–102, 109–10
Entire market value rule, 225–26
Equitable estoppel, 236–37
Examination. *See* Prosecution
Exhaustion, 58–59
Experimental use exception to
    infringement, 207–9

Federal Circuit Court of Appeals, 7, 38
File wrapper. *See* Prosecution history
First sale doctrine, 57–59

History of patents, 1–2

Implied licenses, 57–62
Incentive theory of patent law, 2
Independent claims, 22, 24
Indirect infringement, 175–79
Inducement to infringe, 176–77

Industry standards, 61–62
Inequitable conduct, 46, 161–66
Infringement, 15, 171–210
    All elements rule, 23, 180, 192–94
    Burden of proof, 217
    Claim interpretation. *See* Claims
    Contributory infringement, 59,
        177–79
    Direct infringement, 175
    Doctrine of equivalents, 97, 182–203
    Experimental use exception, 207–9
    Geographic limitations, 173–75
    Indirect infringement, 175–79
    Inducement, 176–77
    Literal infringement, 179–82
    Means-plus-function claims, 81–83,
        96–97, 203–6
    Notice of infringement, 231–33
    Provisional rights, 172–73
    Remedies. *See* Remedies for
        infringement
    Repair and reconstruction, 59–61
    Reverse doctrine of equivalents,
        206–7
    State of mind, 175, 228–31
    Willful infringement, 228–31
Injunctions, 56–57, 223–24
Interferences, 43, 138
International Trade Commission
    (ITC), 237
Inter partes review, 49
Interpretation of claims. *See* Claims,
    interpretation
Intervening rights, 45–46
Inventorship, 51–54

Jepson claims, 79
Jurisdiction, 213–14

Laches, 233–25
Legal estoppel, 61
Licenses, 55–62, 211–12
Literal infringement, 179–82
Litigation, 211–37
    Attorneys' fees, 230–31
    Bifurcation, 220
    Burdens of proof, 124–26, 217
    Damages, 224–28

Declaratory judgment, 215–17
Federal Circuit Court of Appeals, 7, 38
Injunctions, 56–57, 223–24
International Trade Commission
    (ITC), 237
Jurisdiction, 213–14
Laches, 233–36
Markman hearing, 220
Notice and marking, 231–33
Preliminary injunctions, 220–22
Presumption of validity, 86–87
Remedies. *See* Remedies for
    infringement
Role of judge and jury, 217–19
Statute of limitations, 231
Summary judgment, 222–23
Venue, 214
Living organisms, 28–29
Lost profits measure of damages, 224–26

Marking of patented goods, 231–33
Markman hearing, 220
Markush claims, 80
Means-plus-function claims, 81–83,
    96–97, 203–6
Mental processes, 32
Misuse, 166–69

Natural laws and phenomena, 26–29
Natural rights theory of patent law, 2
Near-simultaneous invention, 156
New matter, 41, 44, 49
Nexus, 154
Notice and marking, 231–33
Novelty, 110–43

Obviousness, 110, 143–56
Analogous arts, 147–48
Combination of references, 146,
    148–51
Commercial success, 153–54
Near-simultaneous invention, 156
Nexus, 154
Ordinary skill in the art, 144–45
Secondary considerations, 152–56
Teaching away, 148
On-sale bar, 129–33
Ordinary skill in the art, 144–45

Patent Act, 7
Patent and Trademark Office (PTO), 2,
    14, 19, 37, 85–86
Patentable subject matter, 25–36
Abstract ideas, 29–30, 34
Business methods, 30–31
Computer programs, 10–11, 32–35
Living organisms, 28–29
Mental processes, 32
Natural laws and phenomena, 26–29
Printed matter, 35–36
Useful arts, 14, 25, 30, 88
Patent Trial and Appeal Board, 38
Pioneer patents, 195–96
Plant patents, 242–44
Post-grant review, 48–49
Preambles, 22, 76–79
Preferred embodiments, 21, 69–70
Preliminary injunctions, 220–22
Presumption of validity, 86–87
Printed matter, 35–36
Printed publications, 111–15, 137
Prior art, 19, 37, 110–139
Printed publications, 111–12
Prior inventions, 116–18
Prior knowledge, 111–12
Prior patents and patent applications,
    111–12, 115, 136–39
Prior use, 111–12, 137
Prior commercial use defense, 209–10
Priority of invention, 106–7, 116–18
Conception, 52, 118–19, 120–26
Constructive reduction
    to practice, 121
Date of invention, 106, 118–24
Diligence, 122–24
Interferences, 43, 138
Reduction to practice, 118–26
Product-by-process claims, 80–81
Prosecution, 19, 37–40, 85–86
Amendments to claims, 38, 106
Application for patent, 14, 19, 37
Classification of inventions, 19
Continuations, 40–41
Continuations-in-part, 41–42
Divisional applications, 42–43
Double patenting, 157–60
Duty of candor, 39

Inequitable conduct, 46, 161–66
Interferences, 43, 138
Inter partes review, 49
New matter, 41, 44, 49
Patent examiners, 20, 37–39
Patent and Trademark Office (PTO),
    2, 14, 19, 37, 85–86
Post-grant review, 48–49
Prosecution history, 40, 73–74
Prosecution history estoppel, 196–201
Prosecution laches, 233–34
Publication of patent applications, 39,
    172–73
Reexamination, 47–48
Reissue, 44–46
Restriction requirements, 42–43, 160
Supplemental examination, 46–47
Terminal disclaimers, 159–60
Prosecution history, 40, 73–74
Prosecution history estoppel, 196–201
Prosecution laches, 233–34
Provisional applications, 39–40
Provisional rights, 172–73
Publication of patent applications, 39,
    172–73
Public use bar, 133–35

Reasonable royalty measure of damages,
    226–28
Reduction to practice, 118–26
Reexamination, 47–48
Reissue, 44–46
Remedies for infringement, 233–37
    Attorneys' fees, 230–31
    Damages, 224–28
    Entire market value rule, 225–26
    Injunctions, 56–57, 223–24
    Lost profits, 224–26
    Preliminary injunctions, 220–22
    Reasonable royalty, 226–28
    Willful infringement, 228–31
Repair and reconstruction, 59–61
Restriction requirements, 42–43, 160
Reverse doctrine of equivalents, 206–7

Secondary considerations, 152–56
Simultaneous conception and reduction
    to practice, 120–21

Sources of law, 7, 245–46
Specification, 20–22, 68–72
    Preferred embodiments, 21, 69–70
    Use in interpreting claims, 68–72
Statute of limitations, 231
Statutory bars, 127–36
    Critical date, 128
    On-sale bar, 129–33
    Public use bar, 133–35
Step-plus-function claims, 83–84
Summary judgment, 222–23
Supplemental examination, 46–47

Teaching away, 148
Term of patents, 15, 171–73
Terminal disclaimers, 159–60
Trademarks, 11
Trade secrets, 12–14

Unclaimed embodiments, 201–3
Unenforceability, 161–69
    Inequitable conduct, 46, 161–66
    Misuse, 166–69
Useful arts, 14, 25, 30, 88
Utility, 88–92

Validity, 75–76, 237
    Anticipation, 110, 140–43
    Assignor estoppel, 88
    Best mode, 21, 103–5
    Burden of proof, 86–87, 124–26
    Definiteness, 92–97
    Derivation, 156–57
    Double patenting, 157–60
    Enablement, 21, 40, 97–102, 109–10
    Novelty, 110–43
    Obviousness, 110, 143–56
    On-sale bar, 129–33
    Patentable subject matter, 25–36
    Presumption of validity, 86–87
    Public use bar, 133–35
    Statutory bars, 127–36
    Utility, 88–92
    Written description, 40, 105–10
Venue, 214

Willful infringement, 228–31
Written description, 40, 105–10

About the Author

ALAN L. DURHAM is the Judge Robert S. Vance Professor of Law at the University of Alabama School of Law, where he teaches courses in patent law, copyright law, and trademark law. Professor Durham is the author of numerous law review articles, many concerning the scope of patented inventions and the limits of patentable subject matter. These include "Patent Symmetry," published in the *Boston University Law Review*, "Natural Laws and Inevitable Infringement," published in the *Minnesota Law Review*, and "The Fractal Geometry of Invention," published in the *Boston College Law Review*. In other writings, he has explored the role of indeterminacy and information theory in the law of copyright. Before he began his academic career in 1998, Professor Durham practiced law with the Palo Alto offices of Brown & Bain and Morrison & Foerster, representing Silicon Valley businesses in complex patent litigation. He received his law degree from the University of California at Berkeley, where he was selected for the Order of the Coif.